AGGRESSION

AND ITS CAUSES

A Biopsychosocial Approach

JOHN W. RENFREW, PH.D.

Northern Michigan University

New York   Oxford

OXFORD UNIVERSITY PRESS

1997

Oxford University Press

Oxford   New York
Athens   Auckland   Bangkok   Bogotá   Bombay
Buenos Aires   Calcutta   Cape Town   Dar es Salaam   Delhi
Florence   Hong Kong   Istanbul   Karachi
Kuala Lumpur   Madras   Madrid   Melbourne
Mexico City   Nairobi   Paris   Singapore
Taipei   Tokyo   Toronto

and associated companies in
Berlin   Ibadan

Published by Oxford University Press, Inc.
198 Madison Avenue, New York, New York 10016

Oxford is a registered trademark of Oxford University Press

Library of Congress Cataloging-in-Publication Data
Renfrew, John W.
Aggression and its causes : a biopsychosocial approach /
John W. Renfrew.
p.   cm.   Includes bibliographical references and index.
ISBN 0-19-508229-X (alk. paper).—ISBN 0-19-508230-3 (pbk. : alk. paper)
1. Aggressiveness (Psychology)
I. Title.
BF575.A3R46   1996 302.5′4—dc20   95-31920

1 2 3 4 5 6 7 8 9

Printed in the United States of America
on acid-free paper

To Ileana

Contents

Preface

The impetus for writing this book was to satisfy a professional need. I have been teaching an undergraduate course on aggression for several years and have been frustrated in my search for a comprehensive, current textbook. Many texts are available, but they address a relatively limited area of the study of aggression and/or summarize work done only through the 1970s. Although some of them may be useful for an advanced, specialized audience, they are not satisfactory for my needs.

The present work is intended as an introduction to what has been learned about the causes and control of aggressive behaviors. It is written at a level that should be understandable to undergraduate students, but it also includes material that should be of interest to those working in applied areas who wish to further their understanding of the causes of aggression and increase their ability to control it. My undergraduate students come from various disciplines, primarily those of criminal justice, nursing, psychology, special education, and social work, as well as from a smattering of other fields. I also have lectured in Latin America on this topic. There, my audiences have included not only professionals from these fields but also many from other legal and medical specialties, such as lawyers, judges, psychiatrists, and pediatricians. Thus, my preliminary work on this book began in lectures to widely varied groups. This book is an attempt to clearly present what is known about aggressive behaviors without alienating the beginner or insulting the professional.

In my teaching efforts I have assumed that my students have no extensive knowledge of the materials, especially those dealing with more technical matters. Therefore, I have provided fundamental background information where necessary. I have included a review of methodology and basic background material for the biological and environmental approaches to the study of aggression as an integral part of the text instead of including them, as is often done, in a separate appendix. I believe that this tactic will result in more effective communication. Readers with previous knowledge in these areas should feel free to pass more rapidly through these sections.

In preparing this book, I have reviewed the empirical literature, concentrating on studies that investigate the causes of aggression in an objective way. In so doing, I have eliminated consideration of most of the more subjective or speculative material on the causes of aggression in favor of using information that is based on scientific evidence, with the hope of guiding the reader to an understanding of empirically confirmed information. Within this framework, my coverage has been somewhat selective. For example, I have included only limited material on ethological or anthropological studies of aggression. Even within the areas I have selected, my treatment has been tempered by my desire to avoid making the text too unwieldy. Thus, from the extensive research findings for each area, I have chosen illustrative examples that I hope will inform readers about the essential nature of the phenomena being considered. I describe much of the work done between the 1960s and early 1980s, when especially intensive study of aggression occurred. These studies provided the fundamental bases for our present understanding of aggression. I also describe the critical subsequent studies that elaborated on these basic findings. When appropriate, I offer references for more extensive treatments of the topics.

The text begins with an introduction to some difficulties encountered in the study of aggression, including those associated with defining and measuring this behavior. The resulting methodological problems are illustrated later during the analysis of various studies. I have divided the rest of the book into three main parts. The first considers the contribution of biological factors to aggression, the second presents the role of environmental and social factors, and the third discusses several contemporary societal problems where aggression is a major element. In the societal problem section, I describe the application of some factors from the first two sections ("biopsychosocial" factors) that contribute to aggression and also indicate how knowledge of these contributions has or might be applied to controlling the behavior.

During the preparation of this work, I have received suggestions and advice from several sources. These contributions have been very valuable in helping me to organize and clarify my efforts. I thank my friend and colleague, Ron Hutchinson, not only for his advice but also for his invaluable contributions to my professional career. I also value the enormous effort made by my friend, Sue Dreghorn, who helped me communicate more effectively with the educated layperson. Finally, I thank my students for their suggestions as well as for their patience with earlier drafts, and my department for its generous support.

I hope that this book will provide readers with a helpful introduction to the study of aggression; that it will result in an enhanced basic understanding of the aggressive behaviors that readers will encounter in various professional and personal settings; that it will furnish the background for further study in the area of aggression; and that it will foster an appreciation of the importance of continued efforts to determine the causes and controls of aggression. I welcome your comments and suggestions concerning my work. They should be addressed to me by mail at: Department of Psychology, Northern Michigan University, Marquette, MI 49855, USA, by FAX: (906) 227-2954, or by e-mail: jrenfrew@nmu.edu.

Marquette, MI   J.W.R.
October 1995

AGGRESSION AND ITS CAUSES

CHAPTER 1
Introduction

Essentially all people are in some way affected by aggression, whether they are targets of it, engage in it themselves, or are charged with observing and controlling it in others. Thus aggression is of concern to victims, perpetrators, and those professionals charged with its treatment because of personal safety, well-being, or obligation.

Serious problems with aggression occur at a number of levels, from societal to personal, affecting situations not usually associated with extreme violence. For example, in some large urban schools, the high rate of assaults among youths results in mandatory weapons checks at school entrances and police patrols in the corridors. Young school children are taught how to duck under their desks when they hear gun shots. Counselors are once again summoned to help classmates of a child who has been killed on the streets.

In office buildings, aftermaths of attacks by co-workers armed with assault rifles include the provision of psychological services and self-protection instruction for survivors. Supervisors are taught to recognize the signs of extreme stress and how to handle dangerous situations.

In homes, family violence directed at children or spouses leads to public service classes in anger management and conflict resolution. Rapes and robberies by intruders are followed by purchases of alarm systems and the formation of neighborhood protection groups.

Even outside these extreme cases, individuals are involved with preventing and controlling aggression when they refuse to enter parks at night or certain other areas at any time, purchase various implements or learn techniques for self-defense, and avoid interacting with people from particular subgroups of the population.

While problems with aggression are relatively obvious, resolution of those problems is not. People can protest about aggression, the media can describe it, and politicians can legislate against it. However, effective resolution depends on understanding it.

A most effective means of understanding a problem is to study it systematically, utilizing scientific techniques. This text will address the problem of aggression by discussing what has been learned from scientific research about its causes and possible means of controlling it.

In this chapter we will see how the scientific method is applied to the study of aggression. We will identify the general problem of aggression and discuss the importance of precisely defining it. We will then realize that various problems occur that are related to the definition and classification of aggression. We will describe experimental and correlative approaches to the study of aggression, along with their advantages and limitations. Basically, aggression is a behavior affected by multiple influences. For us to discover those influences, we need an appropriate measure of aggression. I will explore the problems in obtaining this measure.

THE MAGNITUDE OF THE PROBLEM

One indication of the extent of problems with aggression can be found from police reports of criminal acts. In the United States, the crime rate is alarmingly high. According to the *Uniform Crime Reports* (FBI, 1990), in 1990 there was an average of one violent crime every 17 seconds. Such crimes include murder, forcible rape of females, robbery, and aggravated assault. Rates for individual crimes ranged from one every 30 seconds for assault to one every 22 minutes for murder, in a population of about 250 million. Also in 1990, the rates of such violence were increasing. They had risen by about one-third since 1981, and by more than 20 percent in the four years since 1986. Even the rates for 1990 were up about 10 percent from just the previous year.

In the mid-1990s, FBI statistics indicate that crime rates are continuing to rise. Although the annual increases in arrest rates are lower for the whole population, the rates still are rising at about 9 percent annually. Further, rates for youths under 18 have been increasing by about 13 percent, and murder rates by youths have been growing by about 33 percent annually.

We should note that official statistics do not include private, non-reported aggression which, while not necessarily criminal, is important to the individuals concerned. Considering all these types of aggression, an individual potentially could be involved in aggression with other family members, such as spouses, parents, and children. Outside the family, one might be in aggressive interactions with acquaintances or strangers. Professionals may encounter aggression directed by their charges toward themselves or others. The psychologist and social worker are concerned with aggression by their clients, the medical practitioner with aggression by patients, the teacher with aggression by students, and the criminal justice worker with aggressive crimes. Even if individuals are not in direct contact with aggressive behaviors, they often can be indirectly affected. For example, those living in an idealistic lay or religious community, even if not directly threatened by internal or external aggressors, may be concerned for the general effects of aggression on the maintenance and well-being of a society. The pervasiveness of aggression and its status as a problematic behavior indicate that it is most important to understand it and so be in a better situation to predict when it might occur, control it when it does occur, or prevent it from occurring. This concern recently has been formally expressed by at least two major professional organizations. Violence in the United States was cited by the American Psychological Society (1992) as one of six broad human behavior problem areas that must be addressed. In 1991, the American Medical Association made the diagnosis and treatment of family violence a top public health priority. Also, the June 14, 1995, issue of their *Journal* was devoted to the problem of interpersonal violence.

DEFINING AGGRESSION

Prior to understanding something, whether aggression or any other topic, it is essential for us to define it. A definition is a prerequisite to efficient communication. Readers who think this is obvious might consider their own assumptions regarding the definition of aggression. A survey of such assumptions can be obtained in your classroom by asking students, on the first day of class, to define aggression. The range of definitions is impressive in terms of the characteristics encompassed. Aggression is regarded as positive (as in assertion) or negative (as in harming others). It is defined by some as being directed or intentional and by others as uncontrolled and undirected. To some it is an intent or feeling, while others view it as an overt behavior. At times prior events or states such as anger or frustration are referred to or even equated with aggression. When students note objects of aggression, they sometimes include other individuals, themselves, animals, and inanimate objects. Obviously, there are a great many possibilities for a definition of aggression. Perhaps this wide variety simply reflects students' lack of sophistication about this topic. To an extent this is true, but unfortunately such variability is not confined simply to the layperson—no clear definition of aggression exists that is commonly accepted by professionals in this area. A review of the literature reveals that some writers do not even bother to define the term. Others consider a definition but find the task an impossible one. Johnson (1972), for example, in his early text on aggression, concluded (perhaps wisely) that aggression was too complex to define, given the many types of aggressive behavior and complexities of its causes. Entire chapters have been devoted to the problem of defining aggression, with varying results concerning specificity (Brain & Benton, 1981b; Siann, 1985).

Part of the problem in defining aggression may be related to the breadth of the professions involved in its study. These include anthropologists, biologists, criminal justice workers, psychologists, sociologists, and social workers. Each area is concerned with its own particular perspective, which in reality encompasses only a small part of the total field of aggression, and these areas are further subdivided. For example, in psychology behaviorists, biopsychologists, clinicians, and social psychologists are involved. Within these areas, we again face problems of arriving at a common definition. Consider the NATO Advanced Study Institute on the Biology of Aggression held in 1980. Such institutes are attended by a select group of leading researchers from NATO countries and have been very helpful in facilitating communication of recent research findings. This institute was no exception, as can be seen from the compilation of published papers (Brain & Benton, 1981a). However, an unpublished attempt of the attendees to arrive at a mutually acceptable definition of aggression was, to put it diplomatically, unsuccessful. There were simply too many different aspects of aggression and too many conflicting orientations about relevant ways of studying it to allow for a definition that everyone could agree on.

Despite this universal failure to achieve a common definition of aggression, it is important for us to have some point from which to start. If a definition is not conclusively established, it sometimes is referred to as provisional or "working." Therefore, as a starting point and to be able to further illustrate the difficulties of defining aggression and the importance of doing so, we propose the following working definition of aggression. *Aggression is a behavior that is directed by an organism toward a target, resulting in damage.*

Note that aggression is classified as a **behavior.** A behavior is an **objective** piece of information: it can be observed by others and, with appropriate definition, two or more observers can agree as to whether it did or did not occur. By restricting aggression to observable behaviors, internal conditions such as aggressive feelings, attitudes, or thoughts are excluded from consideration. We are not suggesting that they do not exist or that they may not be important in determining whether aggressive acts occur. However, since they are internal, they are **subjective:** the question of their existence is determined by individuals' interpretations and personal biases, and they typically are not accessible to objective measurement. Lacking such measurement possibilities, it is difficult for us to make any progress in determining their causes. We prefer to restrict considerations to a limited number of events that we can verify than try to include all potential aggressive states and increase the probability of erring in establishing their determinants.

Note also that in the definition of aggression, we purposely refer to it as **directed.** This is to differentiate aggressive behaviors from others that may cause damage but are not intended to do so. These behaviors are commonly labeled "accidents." The determination of intent is not always simple, and might imply internal subjective processes such as those excluded in our definition of aggression. However, it is possible for us to determine directionality in many cases by observing the events surrounding the behavior or making repeated observations. In a rural situation, for example, consider someone who is driving an old pickup truck that runs into a neighbor's mailbox. If the incident occurred just after some altercation between the neighbors, it might be likely to constitute an aggressive act. If the act is repeated (and no extenuating circumstances such as slippery roads are present and such factors as illness or alcohol are not primary), it might again be considered as being directed. While it is not always easy to determine directionality, it is important to establish it. Its relevance is recognized in legal proceedings, for example, when determining if and to what degree one person caused another's death.

Our definition of aggression includes the terms **organism** and **target.** These are intentionally broad terms that were chosen to allow for a range of aggressive situations. **Organism** refers to both human and non-human animals that have been studied to determine the causes of aggression. We will elaborate on the place of the animal model in the study of aggression later in this chapter. **Target** may signify another individual of the same species, such as when one person strikes another. This is probably our most common concern in the study of aggression. However, aggression may also be directed toward oneself, as in suicide or other self-injurious behaviors. Aggression also occurs interspecifically, as when a dog bites a man (or vice versa). Finally, aggression may be directed against the inanimate environment, such as when a soldier or terrorist blows up the empty home of an adversary or, more simply, when a person gets out of bed in a dark room, stubs a toe against a piece of furniture, and kicks the furniture.

The inclusion of the term **damage** in the definition of aggression indicates some negative effect on the target. This would exclude unsuccessful attempts, such as a bullet that misses its target, since it would have to be determined whether it was directed. In such cases, unfortunately, it may be possible to consider evidence from repeated acts. Also excluded would be acts that do not have a final negative effect, even though they might involve inflicting some destruction or discomfort. The work of a surgeon or a dentist would fall under this category, since these individuals may cut through healthy tissue in order to treat a disease. Although some workers in the broad field of aggression might postulate a role for supposed internal aggressive drives in determining the career choice of, say, a surgeon, this approach involves subjective factors that are minimized in our present approach. Another potential problem with the use of the term damage is that it might not always be easily evident, such as the minimal change in the piece of furniture kicked by the person in the above example. However, regardless of its limitations, inclusion of the term is helpful in our study of aggression.

Readers might already be thinking of some inconsistencies in our working definition. For example, is the act of lawn mowing an aggressive one? Probably not, since the final result is not damage—the grass grows back. However, if someone were to repeatedly drive over a lawn and damage it, this would be considered aggressive. Other destructive behaviors, such as harvesting wheat or eating food, are more of a problem for the definition, although we will explore the relation of eating and aggression later. Regardless of residual weaknesses in our definition, it is useful as an orientation for research and in the analysis of aggression. As we've stated, it is a working definition and subject to modifications. Indeed, it has been modified several times since it first appeared in print (Renfrew, 1979) and surely will be altered in the future.

Some problems arise in determining whether aggression is occurring when individuals or groups with different personal or cultural backgrounds are involved. Consider such situations as when children engage in "king of the hill," grabbing and pushing others off a pile of snow or dirt. Is this aggressive behavior? What about the parent spanking a child? What of the person who indicates to someone that a third person is incompetent? The decision concerning whether aggression occurs in each case will differ if we do not use a common, precise definition of aggression. In the first example, a parent's complaint to a school administrator about the aggression in the school yard may perplex the administrator. What was aggression to one was merely ordinary play to the other. With a common definition of aggression, such as the one we propose, we could determine whether behaviors are directed toward targets, resulting in damage, and decide on this basis if aggression is involved or not. Then we could decide if this school-yard aggression is acceptable or not. We could take a similar approach with such sports activities as football and apply our definition of aggression to the behaviors involved. In both cases, we probably would determine that aggression occurred. However, we might not so easily agree on the acceptability of such aggression.

Considering the aggressiveness in the second example involving spanking again brings up disagreement. One individual might completely fail to see any element of aggression in spanking a child. A second might readily label the spanking as aggressive. A third might note that, while damage apparently is being done, the case is parallel to the actions of the surgeon or dentist; that is, the act is carried out to benefit the child. In this case, having the last two individuals use our working definition did not resolve the issue. They both saw the behavior as directed and inflicting damage but still disagreed about its appropriateness. However, our definition at least clarified what was involved.

The final example, of one person's questioning the competency of another, involves verbal criticism and presents more of a problem. Cultural differences seem to determine how we label verbal behavior. Further, the issue of damage by verbal behavior is not clear. Regarding cultural differences, the act of speaking poorly (or frankly?) about other absent individuals is considered normal by some people and aggressive by others. Even if we eliminate this disparity, however, the question of damage inflicted by verbal behavior remains. Is there damage to another's reputation here and, if so, does this constitute aggression? Even if a comment is made directly to an individual, would we consider this aggression? If the person is offended, do we determine this psychological damage to be aggression? What if the individual is not offended? Alternatively, does intent by the speaker to hurt constitute aggression? It should be evident that even with a relatively precise definition, the situation is still unclear. Because of the problems involved with verbal behavior and psychological damage, we have minimized inclusion of data based on these areas in this text. We should also note, however, that reference to a definition such as ours at least provides a starting point for considering whether aggression is involved in such cases.

Another factor related to defining aggression is justification of certain behaviors by not using the term. Thus, the parent who spanks a child may, without being concerned with the question of damage, not consider this behavior aggressive because the parent sees it as normal, acceptable parental discipline, necessary for raising a good child. Similarly, politicians are loath to label their own country's armed actions toward another as aggressive, yet the politicians of the target country, of course, readily term them aggressive. One's own military rarely "aggresses"; instead it carries out a "preemptive strike," a "police action," or is called into another country to help defend it from its enemies. An interesting example of this is the renaming, following World War II, of the U.S. Department of War to the Department of Defense. A similar semantic ploy is used in attempts to justify aggressive behaviors of individuals. Someone who shoots another may be labeled a "vigilante," who is somehow helping to keep law and order while breaking the law. The question of self-defense is also raised to relieve individuals of responsibility for their aggressive acts. In the cases described here, aggression is considered a pejorative term, and efforts are made to re-label behaviors. However, all these situations (with perhaps a disputable case in the spanking example) fall under the definition of aggression. Perhaps it would be more fruitful for us to first establish that aggression has occurred and then justify the behaviors. All aggression is not necessarily bad; some, as in self-defense, may be quite necessary and adaptive. Concern with aggression arises when it occurs in excess of adaptive amounts or when it replaces non-aggressive alternative behavior. We will focus on these concerns in this text.

CLASSIFICATIONS OF AGGRESSION

Aggression occurs under various conditions and takes various forms. For this reason, some investigators have proposed various classes of aggression and attempted to describe the specific behaviors involved in each as well as delineate the variables controlling each class. While these efforts have been fruitful, they have also resulted in some verbal (aggressive?) interchanges between the investigators when the classification scheme of one was not accepted by another and each would vigorously defend his or her position. Further, the labels applied to the types of aggression sometimes have surplus meanings, extra nuances that are not based on scientific data but interpretations of the terms. As we saw in the example given earlier, the behaviors associated with the term "defensive" are subject to different interpretations. Instead of getting into sometimes irrational discussions over labels, let us concentrate on measuring the specific stimuli and response patterns involved in aggression. One older classification of aggression is useful because it is still cited relatively frequently and serves as a comparison point for other works. In 1968, Moyer (Moyer, 1968) proposed seven different kinds of aggression, most differentiated by their physiological bases and the stimuli that produce them. Moyer's work was based primarily on non-human animal data but is seen by him and others as useful in helping to understand the bases of human aggression. Since we will refer to some of these categories later as we study different causes of aggression, we'll list and briefly discuss them here.

Predatory Aggression. Attack behavior directed by an animal against a natural prey is classified as predatory. At times this behavior is termed interspecific, although several other types of aggression can also occur between species. The eliciting stimulus for this aggression is a prey object, preferably moving. This behavior does not need a specific setting to occur, in contrast to some other types of aggression (e.g., such as maternal aggression, discussed below). Although predatory behavior corresponds to our working definition of aggression, some investigators disregard it as merely a food-getting response, without the strong emotional components of other aggressive behaviors.

Intermale Aggression. This type of aggression occurs intraspecifically, prior to establishing a hierarchy of dominance among the males of a group, who provide the necessary stimulus. Moyer indicated that relatively little such fighting was found among females. As with predatory aggression, a special environmental setting is not needed for this aggression to occur.

Fear-induced Aggression.   This occurs when an organism is confined and cannot escape another threatening organism. It is always preceded by escape attempts.

Irritable Aggression.   This aggression is sometimes labeled "anger" or "rage" or "affective" aggression, and is elicited by a wide range of animate and inanimate objects. According to Moyer, various stressors, such as frustration, pain, deprivation of food, fatigue, and lack of sleep often precede it.

Maternal Aggression.   This refers to the aggression exhibited by a mother to the stimulus of a threat to her young, implying this specific environmental setting for its occurrence.

Sex-related Aggression.   This is produced by the same stimuli that cause sexual responses. As with intermale aggression, this class of aggression was thought to occur primarily, but not exclusively, in males. It was added almost as an afterthought by Moyer as "probably" a class of aggression and was later considered more prominently (e.g., Moyer, 1976).

Moyer's seventh type of aggression was **territorial defense,** which occurs intraspecifically (or conspecifically, between individuals of the same species) or interspecifically, on intrusion into the established territory of an organism. However, Moyer later concluded (1976) that it probably did not have a separate physiological basis, was not well based on objective data, and was too poorly defined to be useful. Further, what some categorize as territorial aggression often involves one of the other classifications we previously listed. Moyer also discussed **instrumental aggression,** which exists only because it has been strengthened by its consequences (this assumedly would not include the effects of success on the types of aggression discussed here). Since this also was not seen to have a separate physiological basis, Moyer did not treat it extensively. Instrumental aggression is involved when the behavior is reinforced by success and therefore increases. Like predatory aggression, it may not have strong emotional components. It is, nevertheless, a very important type of aggression.

THE ANIMAL MODEL IN RESEARCH ON AGGRESSION

The types of aggression defined by Moyer were derived primarily from research with lower animals. A question often asked in such cases is whether information gathered from studies of non-human animals is relevant for our understanding of human behavior. Are the mechanisms for producing aggression the same? Are the controlling factors for aggression equivalent? Despite differences between lower animals and humans, many people investigating aggression agree that the mechanisms and controlling factors are close enough so that much information derived from the study of lower organisms can be beneficially applied to humans. These applications have already occurred. For example, genetic studies with mice have indicated how aggression can be increased in humans by decreasing sensitivity to a brain chemical; brain studies with rats have led to the discovery of the systems that malfunction in schizophrenia; and drug studies with monkeys have shown how addictive behavioral patterns are produced. We will include details of these and many other of the large number of lower animal studies whose results have been used to understand human aggression. We will then be able to see how the animal model for the study of aggression has been invaluable, just has it has been for medicine and several areas of psychology.

Much of the rationale for using animal models derives from the findings supporting Darwin's (1859) theory of evolution. Extensive research has shown that humans and lower animals have common origins and share many characteristics in, for example, brain structures and functions and biochemical mechanisms that affect aggression. A given part of the brain, whether found in rats, cats, monkeys, or humans, has certain connections with other parts, involves particular brain chemical systems, and helps increase or decrease aggression in the same way. The study of one group of animals can quite definitely aid in understanding functions in another.

Despite the valuable contributions made through work on aggression with lower animals, objections to such work, based on ethical and religious grounds, have been raised. People concerned with animal "rights" complain that investigators are abusing those rights when they employ animal subjects, and demand a stop to all lower animal research. Their orientation is that any benefit to humans does not justify depriving lower animals of their rights. These protesters often support their stance with claims that animal research has not resulted in general benefits for humans. Contrary to the polemics that have appeared recently in the United States and some other countries where animal research is carried out, investigators who employ animals are neither masochists who enjoy engaging in fruitless or repetitious experiments nor avaricious individuals who perform research to gain additional grant funds. They continue to work with lower animals because they have been successful in progressing toward a better understanding of human aggression.

In the area of religious objections to research, fundamentalist Christians have been very vigorous in their attempts to have their Creationist beliefs substituted for the overwhelming scientific evidence in support of Darwin's theory. Acceptance of the Creationist viewpoint would mean rejection of the existence of a common link between humans and lower animals and, by implication, there would be no reason to study animals to understand humans. Rejection of evolutionary theory by the general public would result in pressure to deny governmental support for animal research as well as resistance to the application of any results to help understand aggression. It would be very detrimental to progress in the study of aggression if the acceptance of such beliefs resulted in the abandonment of work with lower animals.

THE EXPERIMENTAL APPROACH

Like any model, the animal model for the study of aggression involves both benefits and limitations. Some benefits become clear by considering the common **ex-**

perimental approach to studying aggression. This approach involves manipulating causal factors and measuring their effects. Here, aggression is seen as an effect or dependent variable *(DV)* affected by a number of causes or independent variables *(IV)*. The relationship is expressed simply in the following form:

$$DV(\text{aggression}) = f(IVs: a,b,c \ldots x,y,z)$$

This says that the dependent variable (aggression) is caused by— a function of *(f)*— a large number of independent variables. These might include: biological variables such as brain function, genetic mechanisms, hormonal types and levels; environmental variables such as past experiences, reinforcement, and punishment; and social variables such as living conditions.

For us to determine the existence and relative contributions of the independent variables that affect aggression, we use the experimental approach to manipulate one while holding the others constant via control procedures. Thus, any change in the dependent variable of aggression is seen to be produced by a manipulation of the independent variable. Manipulation and control of the independent variables involved is difficult, if not impossible, in humans. Consider the variety of genetic factors or past experiences or even present experiences that exist. If we tried to study the effect of a certain drug on human aggressive behavior, how could we be sure that any effects are due to the drug's being manipulated as opposed to some uncontrolled or unmeasured change in another variable? Although problems with the control of independent variables must be addressed in clinical tests of drugs or any other independent variable, preliminary investigations are best carried out in conditions where more control is possible. By employing lower animals that come from a line bred for laboratory work, we can control variables such as genetic mechanisms, as well as historical variables such as rearing experiences, diet, and exposure to pathogens, and present variables such as housing conditions, aggressive interactions, and learning experiences. Again, as with humans, we cannot control all variables. Indeed, sometimes new, unpredicted variables affect the results in a study while we are trying to determine the specific influence of a known variable. However, using the experimental technique with lower animals allows more easy and accurate determination of the roles of independent variables.

The results of experimental work with lower animals have been extremely valuable in determining how various independent variables affect aggression. However, there are limits to the usefulness of such information. In a non-laboratory setting, many variables might be operating to produce an aggressive episode. Therefore, it is necessary for us to explore the effects of manipulating multiple variables and determine if the results from a restricted laboratory setting can be generalized to a more natural one. Indeed, the natural setting typically is the starting point for ethologists or animal behaviorists who conduct their studies in the field or at least in a laboratory setting designed to include many variables of a natural setting, such as having the animals establish and live in a large colony instead of individual cages.

We must, of course, establish generalizability of lower animal results to humans. Although the general public, along with many politicians and administrators, often either feels that this in not being pursued or expects it to be accomplished much more rapidly, the need for testing the generality of laboratory findings is acknowledged by essentially all laboratory investigators. They might not, for various reasons, such as lack of access to a human testing facility or lack of support, pursue such testing themselves, but they certainly welcome it. We will see later how laboratory work has been applied to practical problems with human aggression.

THE CORRELATIVE APPROACH

A second major approach to the study of aggression is to determine how aggression varies in relation to a second or even third dependent variable. In such studies of **correlations,** we can express the relationship as follows:

$$DV_1 = f(DV_2)$$

where DV_1 is aggression and DV_2 the other variable. The results of the measure of correlation are expressed either as a positive number up to 1 or as a negative number. The numerical value indicates how closely the two variables are related. A high positive correlation might mean that the two dependent variables are influenced more strongly by the same independent variables, while a high negative correlation may mean that some independent variables affect each dependent variable in opposite ways. Correlations can be valuable for helping to determine if and to what extent common independent variables are operating and may aid in predicting whether aggression is likely to occur, if we have determined the value of the second dependent variable.

We can see an example of the correlative approach in the attempts to understand the relation between watching violent television shows and being aggressive. These attempts are treated in detail later and so we will not now consider them extensively. However, we should emphasize an important feature of these and essentially all correlative studies. These studies are involved in the measurement of two dependent variables, each with its own influential independent variables affecting it. Correlations are a statement of how the two variables occur in the same individual, **not** how one of the variables affects the other. In other words, **correlation is not equivalent to causation.** Even if a relatively high (significant) correlation is found between watching violence on television and being aggressive, this does not show that watching the violence causes the individual to be aggressive. Alternatively, it does not show that watching violent television does not cause aggression. It simply states how the two variables co-vary. We stress this point because many laypersons, including the press, tend to assume causation from correlation. Although the correlative technique is helpful, we must recognize its limitations.

ETHICAL CONSIDERATIONS

A limitation shared by both experimental and correlative studies of aggression involves ethics. Whether an investigator is manipulating an independent variable to increase aggression, or simply observes aggression without trying to interfere, questions arise concerning the acceptability of the manipulation. These questions occur with both human and non-human subjects, but are especially sensitive when humans are involved. Since it is not considered acceptable to encourage or allow humans to aggress against one another, some investigators have used subterfuges to try to fool participants into thinking they are aggressing. For example, subjects are told that their actions will deliver electric shocks to others. Other investigators have employed questionnaires to query participants about how they might have acted. However, the ethical acceptability of even the deceit involved in some of these studies has been questioned. Since no aggression actually occurs, scientists also have challenged the **validity** (whether a method measures what it purports to measure) of this type of study. Lower animal studies have been employed as alternatives to human studies so that we can observe actual aggression.

Producing aggression in lower animals must be undertaken with reasoned concern for the welfare of the subjects, and is governed by codes of ethics such as that of the American Psychological Association and various governmental regulations. The investigators involved strongly support these controls. However, there is also a recognition that such research is essential to help advance the study of aggression and that this advancement for the sake of human well-being takes precedence over the well-being of lower animals.

Steps are indeed taken to minimize the discomfort to animal subjects. For example, some investigators employ anesthetized target animals and others use inanimate targets attached to electronic sensors. These procedures also provide for greater experimental control, since the targets are not moving or responding in unpredictable ways. Discomfort is also minimized by limiting trials and the number of subjects involved to those needed for producing reliable results. Computer models may be developed to substitute for animals, but this process has two major limitations. First, we need observations of actual aggression to provide the data base for developing a computer model and, second, the results from any model would have to be tested for validity in a real-life situation. It seems that animal research is necessary in any case, and while it should be carried out with responsible regard for ethical questions, its contributions to the understanding of aggression make its continuance vitally important.

THE MEASUREMENT OF AGGRESSION

The core of this book will deal with the independent variables affecting aggression. Before we consider its causes, we must examine how to measure it. Previously, we have stressed the importance of defining aggression and have proposed a working definition. However, the most precise definition of aggression is worth little if it is not accompanied by precision in measuring behavior. Appropriate measurement procedures are essential for us to determine whether an independent variable affects aggression and, if so, to discover the exact relationship between the independent variable and aggression.

As with defining aggression, measuring aggression is more reliably done when we employ objective rather than subjective variables. That is, **reliability**—the consistency of the results of a measurement—is aided when we use external behaviors. Further, *direct* observation and assessment are preferred to *indirect* assessment. Using objective, directly observed data helps avoid the two fundamental types of measurement errors, commonly known as Type I and Type II. A Type I error, or False Alarm, involves judging that an event, such as aggression, occurred when in reality it did not. A Type II error, or Miss, involves failure to detect that an event occurred.

Attempts to Measure Human Aggression

Unfortunately, in studies of human aggression, the ethical concerns we previously discussed regarding producing aggression or allowing it to occur in humans limit the measurement possibilities. Thus, we often use subjective, indirect evaluations. An example of this type of evaluation is having a person, such as a parent, teacher, or peer, rate a child's aggressive behavior. The rating scales employed may ask for an apparently objective numerical estimate, such as judging on a scale of 0 to 10, but, even then, the reliability of individual estimates is questionable. Educational preparation and specific and general cultural differences would affect such ratings. The parent with a high school education might rate very differently than one with a college education that included studying the nature of aggression in psychology or sociology classes. A teacher with a background in inner city schools might use different criteria than one who had always worked in a suburban setting. A peer who came from a household where much violence occurred would use different ratings than one from a more peaceful home.

Sometimes we can help make ratings more reliable, but that reliability will still often be suspect. For example, a rating of 7 or "often fights" might be defined as once a day, but a "fight" may be interpreted by one person to include only physical contact, by another to include threats, and by another to involve all verbal challenges. Here again, the necessity of having a specific definition of aggression is obvious. Further, these evaluations may be indirect, since evaluators may rely on others' reports for judging fighting when the evaluators themselves are not present. Even self-monitoring can be unreliable, since it usually involves depending on an individual who is unschooled in objective, systematic observation and recording. Although the observations may be direct, they are not necessarily reliable.

Police reports are an example of information that often is subjective and indirectly assessed. When trying to determine the aggression that was the impetus for a police call, officers must frequently rely on information from bystanders untrained in observation techniques or participants who were emotionally involved. Even when the officers have been well trained in interview techniques, many problems still occur. An entertaining example of the variety of reports that may result from a group of observer-participants is found in the classic 1950 Kurosawa film, *Rashomon,* which shows four very disparate versions of the encounters of two people with a bandit in the forest. The audience, knowing that each individual was describing the same event, can appreciate the exaggeration and selective perception involved in each tale. In a film, this is humorous. Unfortunately, similar versions of such erroneous perceptions occur regularly in police reports. Loftus and her colleagues have determined some ways in which eyewitness reports can be biased and have supported a role of such research in aiding courtroom decisions (Goodman & Loftus, 1992).

Human aggression is sometimes measured in a way that apparently is objective and direct by having participants in an experiment depress a lever and/or adjust the level of shock to be delivered to another human. This method involves deception because the other person is typically a confederate of the experimenter and the shock is usually not delivered. The apparatus employed is sometimes referred to as the Buss aggression machine, after the researcher who popularized its use, and the situation sometimes called the "teacher-learner" paradigm, since the aggressor-"teachers" often are told that they must use the shock to help determine how this affects the "learners" in acquiring some task. The "teacher" can see the level of shock chosen on a numerical scale. The shock level selected, the number of shocks given, and, at times, the lever-pressing duration, can be used as measures of aggression.

Unfortunately, the validity of this teacher-learner method has been questioned. Is aggression really occurring in these studies? The individuals do not necessarily appear to be angry, although sometimes they are physiologically aroused. However, this arousal might simply activate the only available response of aggression, as opposed to specifically producing it. That arousal could just as easily trigger a non-aggressive response if it were available. Further, since the experiment takes place in the artificial environment of a laboratory and shocks are not actually given, questions arise about whether such a methodology provides the appropriate model for aggression that might occur in real life. Some critics suggest that the laboratory setting may lead participants to believe the aggression is sanctioned by the experiment's sponsor and therefore is acceptable. Alternatively, participants may not believe they really are aggressing against another.

Several critiques of the teacher-learner method have been published and make many of the points we've just discussed. For example, Kaplan (1984) indicates that the validity of the technique as a measure of aggression has some support but has not been conclusively established. He found that little recent effort had been devoted to establishing validity or discussing how the results could be generalized beyond the laboratory. He suggests that the "teachers" may be seen more as retaliating than being aggressive. On the other hand, as we might expect, individuals who have employed this method strongly defend its validity (e.g., Berkowitz, 1993). Regardless of its limitations, this technique has provided important support for our understanding of aggression. Its use has pervaded much of the experimentation on human aggression, and we will discuss many of its results in the section on environmental and social factors in aggression.

Measurement of Aggression in Lower Animals

Research on aggression carried out with lower animals has offered opportunities for direct assessment of aggressive behaviors, although the quality of these measurements has varied as experimenters balance various concerns for reliability and validity. Some investigators, for example, feel that the testing situation must approach what happens naturally as much as possible in an attempt to achieve an "ethological validity" (Benton, 1981). Data collected in such situations are often descriptive, and depend on a well-trained observer to identify the initiators and receivers of aggression, the postures assumed, and sometimes the wounds inflicted.

While some investigators typically reject artificial testing situations, others, including this author and his colleagues (Renfrew & Hutchinson, 1983), have used them as a means of allowing for more precise and reliable measurement of the behaviors involved. Readers are referred to the above publication for details, but here let us state that in these studies of aggression, we determined that the behavior would also be directed against an inanimate target. This finding allowed the development of automatic sensors that enabled measurement not only of whether attack occurred but also its frequency, intensity, and temporal patterns. Further, eliminating a target animal had both ethical and control benefits. Ethically, this procedure is preferred because no other animal is being harmed by the aggressor. In terms of control, we avoided the unpredictable movements and counterattack of the target. Thus, by employing the inanimate target method, we could obtain highly sensitive and objective measures of the behavior and minimize Type II errors. The method also allows for improvements in determining the relationships between aggression and the independent variables affecting it. Typically, in the inanimate target method, the behavior measured has been biting behavior, an ubiquitous component of all the various types of aggression listed by writers such as Moyer (1968) in the work previously cited. Thus, we can see that a common component of aggression is being measured. Usually the term "attack" was used instead of the less universally understood "aggression" and, since the research involved more limited situations, we used the terms "biting attack" or simply "biting." Since biting also occurs in other situations, such as eating or gnawing, this was a necessary practice when only biting was measured. However, series of validating studies were also performed to demonstrate that the same variables producing biting typically also produced what others would recognize as aggression. These studies help ensure that the methodology has not resulted in the commission of Type I errors. The biting behavior measured is a legitimate index of aggression, not a behavior that has nothing to do with it. We will review some results of this work in the sections on both biological and environmental factors in aggression. Those sections will also discuss the development of a measure of biting, jaw clenching in humans (Hutchinson, Pierce, Emley, Proni, & Sauer, 1977), which has provided a potentially important means for studying the variables affecting human aggression.

SUMMARY

Problems with aggression range from the sensational violence reported in the media to everyday episodes that affect us all. Official statistics show continued increases in violent crimes, especially those committed by youths.

In order to study aggression, we must establish a clear definition of it. No universally accepted definition exists; however, we provide a provisional one to help guide our discussion. Moyer's popular classification scheme is also useful.

Aggression is the outcome of a variety of causes. We will describe some of these biological, psychological, and social causes later. To determine the contributions of these causes, the experimental approach usually first involves manipulation of one cause while controlling others. This is easiest to do by employing lower animals. Much progress in understanding aggression has been made by our study of lower animals, although we must always establish that the results apply to humans.

The correlative approach to the study of aggression has been useful in establishing how aggression varies along with another behavior or situation. This may help in understanding and predicting aggression. However, correlations do not indicate causal relations between variables.

Problems in the study of aggression in both humans and lower animals include ethical questions related to producing aggression or allowing it to occur. Resolution of these questions is important and sometimes affects the scientific (and societal) value of the work.

PART I

Biological Factors in Aggression

We will now consider how various functions of the body are involved in aggressive behavior. We will thus see how natural, inherited mechanisms contribute to the control of aggression as well as how alterations of these mechanisms can result in alterations in aggression levels.

Chapter 3 will discuss how genetic elements direct the inheritance of aggression, what specific contributions to aggression are inherited, and how genetic abnormalities can affect aggression. We will also examine of the question of sex differences in aggression, as well as the contributions of sex hormones to aggression. We will address methodological problems in each area, along with the controversies concerning these topics.

Chapters 4 and 5 will describe the neural bases of aggression and how they affect human functioning. Chapter 4 will review what has been discovered chiefly from lower animal research on the effects of brain stimulation and lesioning. We will also describe some of the bodily changes that occur as the brain functions operate to increase or decrease aggression. Chapter 5 will study the nature of human brain dysfunctions and how they contribute to changes in aggressive behavior. Again, we will see how the information from lower animal studies helps inform the analysis of the human problems and treatment of the problems.

Chapter 6 will investigate the neurochemical systems in the brain and how some of them are involved in the causes and control of aggression. We will review both experimental work and clinical applications. We will discuss drug effects on these and other systems, both as drugs are employed in therapy and everyday use and abuse.

As we review each area, we should remember that we are not assuming a strict dichotomy in the control of aggression. That is, aggression is not exclusively controlled by one mechanism or another. Neither is the question one of nature *versus* nurture. We do not assume that either biology **or** the environment controls aggression. These two classes of variables are considered to interact in controlling aggression. Indeed, they may have causal effects on each other, as when experience produces a change in brain structure. Nevertheless, this section will examine how the study of each mechanism contributes to understanding the aggression exhibited by an individual and how those mechanisms fit into the equation given in the Introduction—that is, how aggression is a dependent variable influenced by many independent variables. At our present state of research, we cannot state with any great degree of confidence if and how the independent variables interact, but at least the research suggests the potential contributions of each variable to aggressive behavior.

CHAPTER 2

Genetic, Sexual, and Hormonal Factors

Biological factors that contribute to a behavior such as aggression may work by preparing the individual for the behavior or influencing when that behavior will occur. Much of the material in this chapter will examine these preparatory factors.

We will see how the study of genetic factors in aggression involves determination of what inherited elements can affect aggression. We will also address the problem of differentiating the relative contributions of heredity and environment. We will show how these questions are answered using selective breeding studies with lower animals as well as studies of human inheritance factors. In addition, we will describe several genetic abnormalities found in humans to illustrate both how such abnormalities might affect aggression and how their study is problematic.

We will examine sex factors in aggression, including determining if sex differences exist and whether they are biologically or culturally based. Naturally, disagreements abound in this area. We will also investigate the relations between sexual and aggressive behaviors.

In the last section, we will see how the male sexual hormone, testosterone, contributes to increased aggressive behavior as well as to the development of body mechanisms that support aggression. The various female hormones have been less well studied, but we will see how one, progesterone, seems to be involved in decreasing aggression. Finally, we will review work with the premenstrual syndrome and the possible biological events linking it to increased aggression.

THE EVIDENCE FOR CONTRIBUTIONS OF GENETIC MECHANISMS

Genetic factors affecting aggression are those that exist from the expression of some information located in the genes of each cell's chromosomes. This expression of genetic information is in the form of construction of particular structural components or chemical activities of the body. It may occur as a selection from the extensive information normally found encoded in the genes or it may follow some abnormal genetic condition resulting from illness, radiation, drugs, or other chemicals, as when a carcinogen produces cancer. Such a condition can alter the genetic code to create abnormal structures or chemical activities in the body. Conversely, a genetic effect on aggression may result from the lack of expression of information. We will now describe some of the various ways in which these expression mechanisms are thought to affect aggression.

Some Basic Genetic Mechanisms and Their Role in Aggression

First, let's review some fundamentals of genetics. (As we indicated in the Preface, those readers with previous expertise in certain areas are welcome to skip over such sections; they are included for readers with different backgrounds so as to ensure some common knowledge base.) The chromosomes that are found in each cell of the body except the sex cells (the male sperm and the female egg) consist of paired structures, half of which come from each parent. The human cell has 23 pairs of chromosomes, including one pair of sex chromosomes. Microscopic examination of these chromosomes allows us to determine their shapes and sizes in a process called **karyotyping.** The first 22 (autosomal) pairs are numbered according to decreasing size, and the sex chromosomes according to shape, including the large X and the smaller Y. Females typically have double X chromosomes and males an XY pair.

Chromosomes are composed of long strings of the double helix structure, deoxyribonucleic acid or DNA. In humans there are thousands of functional subunits of these strings—genes. Each gene contains a code for the production of a certain protein, which may form part of the cellular structure, have an enzymatic function to facilitate a certain chemical activity in the cell, or be secreted to communicate with another cell. The expression of a gene is initiated when the DNA strands are temporarily separated at that point, allowing for its code to be read. The contents of the cellular environment are thought to determine whether this expression will occur. Thus, genetic mechanisms involve both a relatively static structural element—the gene—as well as an environmental influence, interacting in an ongoing process to produce their effects. An effect might be of an essentially chronic nature, as when a cell develops into a muscle or bone cell, or it might be semi-chronic, as when the cells associated with the secondary sex characteristics, such as body hair, develop when sex hormones are present. Finally, an effect may be relatively short-lived, as when nervous system activity results in an alteration of genetic expression in a nerve cell.

Several observations and studies have found a relationship between aggression and the genetic mechanisms briefly described above. Let us examine how an undisturbed genetic factor can produce effects and how alterations of the operating factors can result in changes in aggression. When functioning, these mechanisms do not directly produce aggression but instead influence biological elements that contribute to it. These effects are considered polygenic—they involve more than one gene. Some effects may be structural, involving elements necessary for aggression, such as bone and muscle development. Others may be functional, affecting levels of activity or sensitivity of specific brain structures, hormonal systems, or sensory mechanisms. Together, these effects contribute to an individual's level of aggression.

We can suspect genetic influences over aggression in several basic uncontrolled observation conditions: (1) When an individual from a normal family is observed to be highly aggressive. The rationale is that since the rest of the family is not especially aggressive, the familial environment must be normal. Therefore, it is possible that the aggression derives from a genetically based biological abnormality; (2) When many members of a family are highly aggressive. Here, while we cannot eliminate common environmental factors, the common genetic factors involved in a family are also suspected contributors to the aggressions; (3) When a particular strain of lower animals, such as dogs, are especially aggressive. Since these animals by definition constitute a unique genetic subpopulation, the differences in their aggression levels are seen to be genetically based. Similarly, strains that exhibit especially low levels of aggression may provide support for a genetic role in determining aggression. Given one of these three conditions of suspected genetic involvement, how do we conduct studies to determine just what role, if any, genetic mechanisms play in determining aggressive behavior?

Information from Studies of Lower Animals

Studies done with lower animals provide useful information on the possibilities for and the specific biological factors involved in genetic effects on aggression. Scientists have tested different strains of species such as dogs and mice for relative amounts of aggression. Various studies indicate that some strains are more aggressive than others, suggesting a genetic basis. However, difficulties have arisen in making aggressive rankings within species such as mice, for example, because of inconsistencies in the methods of testing used. Because of the large number of strains, comparisons of aggressive levels have had to be done across studies. Thiessen (1976) reviewed studies published over a period of 33 years and found differences in aggression between several strains. However, some investigators observed paired mice, some observed groups, some employed intra-strain tests, and some inter-strain tests. They all used many different definitions of aggression. Therefore, we should not find it surprising that no one strain was consistently most aggressive. A strain called C57BL/10 often came out as most aggressive, but not always. For example, on two out of nine comparisons with a strain known as BALB/c, the latter was rated as more aggressive. This inconsistency supports the points we made in Chapter 1. Before determining the causes (here, genetic) of aggression, we must establish a clear definition and an adequate system of measurement.

Selective breeding studies have been useful for examining the role of genetic mechanisms in aggression. In such investigations scientists test several individuals of a particular strain of a species for their aggressiveness. Then, those who are scored as especially aggressive (or, often, especially docile) are bred with others of their particular behavioral subgroup. The offspring are later tested for aggressiveness and similar selective breeding is carried out. This procedure can be repeated for as many generations as desired. Thus, we can determine whether it is possible to breed for changes in aggression and also how many crosses we need before changes are consistently manifested. Further, once we have produced the aggressive differences, we can examine individuals of the subspecies for physical and physiological differences that may underlie those differences.

Selective breeding for various purposes has been carried out for many years (centuries in some cases), since breeders have chosen animals with certain desirable characteristics to try and improve the breed. Aggression has sometimes been of concern to livestock breeders who may wish to produce cattle with low aggression levels to help ensure fewer damaging fights, easier handling, and perhaps more desirable products for consumption. However, efforts to breed primarily for high aggression levels are what we are especially interested in here. Development of such subspecies as Spanish fighting bulls, fighting cocks, Siamese fighting fish, and fighting dogs like the currently infamous English pit bull terrier has frequently been informally carried out by unschooled owners who breed animals they wish to use for fighting, usually to profit from betting on the outcomes. Since the betting and game-fighting of animals also is often illegal, scientific information on the whole breeding procedure and its results is not easily available.

We might suppose that a major element in this breeding selection was that the more aggressive survivors of matches were the ones bred and that physical characteristics aiding the survivor in fights were passed on to their offspring. This might be seen if we carefully examine a fighting cock. Compared to a common rooster, it has thick, well-developed claws and great size, with powerful leg and wing muscles. Its skin is very tough, and its skull extremely hard and thick. Apparently, the many generations of breeding to produce the fighting cock have resulted in individuals with strong appendages and claws to help them deliver forceful blows to opponents along with an especially thick skull that can resist blows from those opponents.

Selective breeding studies carried out in laboratory settings have contributed to our increased understanding of the genetic mechanisms for aggression, beyond what we have obtained from less scientific breeding efforts. Hall and Klein (1942) conducted an early study of the effects of breeding on aggression. They found that rats selectively bred over eight to nine generations for "emotionality" were less aggressive than "non-emotional" rats. An interesting supplemental lesson here, for those who might equate "emotion" with aggression, was that "emotionality" rats really were bred for "fear" or timidity, while "non-emotional" rats were selected for "fearlessness." The study really demonstrated that more fearful rats were less likely to attack than less fearful ones. Similar problems based on imprecisely understood terms are not unprecedented in selective breeding work. The classic series of studies initiated by Tryon in 1930, characterized by many as an attempt to breed for intelligence in rats, actually involved breeding for better performance in his test mazes. While Tryon discussed the inheritance of abilities related to superior maze performance and suggested that these characteristics might be applied to other situations and species, he was more cautious in his generalizations than most modern critics indicate. Indeed, this caution was justified since tests of such rats' performances in other learning situations showed that they did not necessarily perform any better than other, unselected rats (Searle, 1949). Thus, we must exercise care in generalizing from one test situation to others.

Some of the most well-known research on selective breeding for aggression has been carried out in Turku, Finland, by Lagerspetz (1979). In her work, mice were isolated in their cages from the time of weaning and then exposed to non-aggressive mice. Typically, isolation produces aggression in mice, and so this technique allowed Lagerspetz to observe the aggression and to rate it on a seven-point scale. She included observations of attacking, biting, latency to respond, and tail rattling (considered a component of aggression). On the bases of the scale, she then classified her subjects as Turku aggressive (TA) and Turku non-aggressive (TNA). The interbred TNA mice reached significantly lower aggression scores by the second generation, while aggression scores of the TA mice continued to increase up to the tenth generation. By the nineteenth generation, the aggression of the interbred TA mice had risen to a 52 percent biting level, while only 5 percent of the TNA mice bit their non- aggressive opponents. Interestingly, the differences in aggression were later able to be reversed in one generation by further selective breeding between the TA and TNA strains (Lagerspetz & Lagerspetz, 1983). Prior to that crossbreeding, the TA mice were also tested in other situations, and they were determined to be faster at maze learning and less fearful. Biological characteristics of the TA mice also were studied and they were found to have heavier testes and a heavier forebrain. Measurements of brain neurotransmitters revealed that, in comparison to TNA mice, they had more norepinephrine in their brainstems and less serotonin in their forebrains. The significance of these findings will be evident in Chapters 3 and 5 when we discuss the roles of these structures and neurotransmitters in aggression. For now, let us note that specific physical and chemical changes do occur when animals are selectively bred for aggression. These observations can provide suggestions for new biological factors involved in aggression or offer further support for previously suspected biological factors.

We should reiterate that aggression is a product of both biological and environmental factors. While evidence exists for genetic factors in aggression, this does not mean that they are all-determining. Environmental factors, such as learning, also contribute, especially as we ascend the phylogenetic scale. Even with lower animals, these environmental factors have an effect. For example, Lagerspetz (1981) indicates that individuals from each of her strains can be conditioned to change their characteristic aggression levels. Thus, despite popular beliefs, sometimes aided by media hyperbole, we should realize that many species can be tamed. Wolves that have been raised by humans since they were pups, for example, may not be any more aggressive than their dog cousins. Monkeys have often been raised as pets, and "ferocious" circus lions may be more like pussy cats than their owners would have the public believe. However, this is not to say that these animals cannot be aggressive in response to appropriate conditions. One condition that arises as the animals mature is an increase in sex hormones, and sexual maturation is often accompanied by rises in aggression. We will discuss the effects of these hormones later in this chapter.

Genetic Factors in Human Aggression

Earlier, we mentioned that two reasons for suspecting genetic influences in aggression are when an individual from a normal family is especially aggressive and when many members of a family are aggressive. Unfortunately, it is not always easy to determine the actual functioning of genetic influences because of difficulties in controlling other variables. Early studies of possible genetic contributions to behavioral dysfunctions, including aggression, in members of a family were carried out on the "Jukes" family (Dugdale, 1877) and on the "Kallikaks" (Goddard, 1912). The Jukes were found to have a long history of mental, social, and economic inadequacies, while many Kallikaks were involved in crime and degeneracy. Interestingly, the Kallikaks had a normal or superior branch, descended from a formal marriage, and a troubled branch, descended from a liaison with a woman of subnormal intelligence and questionable morals. The problems of this second branch were thought to derive from the contamination of a "good" gene pool by the "bad blood" of the mentally inferior woman. Similarly, genetic factors were blamed for the high level of problems in the Jukes family. However, while these conclusions may have fit the preconceptions of the era in which the studies were done, it is not clear that the families' problems were not caused by the environment they were raised in. Unfortunately, similar preconceptions still exist today, as racial biases lead some to attribute the high crime levels of a societal underclass to genetic origins.

It is not easy to solve the problem of discriminating between genetic and environmental influences over aggression. Certainly, selective breeding and raising of children in highly controlled environments is neither ethically acceptable nor practical. Therefore, researchers have turned to an available approximation of a controlled study, in which they hold the genetic factor constant while changing environmental variables. Identical or monozygotic twins have the same genetic components. Thus, any differences in their behaviors might be attributed to differences in their environments. Alternatively, similarities in their behaviors might be traced to genetic communalities. If their environments have been different, as in adoption and separation at an early age, an even stronger argument may be made for genetic contributions to similar behavioral patterns. To control for possible influences of age differences, researchers often compare the similarities in aggression in identical twins to those in fraternal or dizygotic twins, who are not any more closely related genetically than two siblings of different ages.

Using twins in studies of aggression is not without its difficulties. At times, the determination of monozygosity has been based only on similarities of physical appearance instead of more certain measures such as fingerprints or blood antigens. Therefore, some studies may include fraternal as well as identical twins. Also, the dual problems of the low (less than one in 200) birth incidence of monozygotic twins and lack of accessibility to study them limits the numbers of individuals available and thus the generalizability of the results. This lack of potential subjects affords less opportunity for eliminating some in order to exclude other potential sources of bias in the population. For example, individuals may be included despite the lack of corroborating medical records from their youth, while such inclusion is less likely to occur in a well-conducted study of a more numerous population. A further difficulty in twin studies is that experimenter bias in the evaluation of results is not always controlled. Ideally, measuring aggression in one twin should be done without knowing anything about the results of studying the other to avoid influencing the outcome in the direction expected—that the aggression scores will or will not be similar. A further difficulty lies in the possibility of prenatal environmental influences that may be mistaken for genetic influences. Maternal illness or use of drugs, for example, might commonly affect the aggression levels of twins. Alternatively, differential effects on aggression might result from differences in intrauterine position or umbilical cord function. An experimental observation of the effect of intrauterine position in multiple births was made by Gandelman, vom Saal, and Reinisch (1977), who found that the sex of adjacent embryos affected the later aggression levels of female mice. Those who were attached between two males were more aggressive than those attached between two females. Vom Saal has done extensive work to elaborate on these initial findings. Although the generality and strength of this specific effect have been questioned (Simon & Cologer-Clifford, 1991), the basic concept of behavioral effects of intrauterine events is accepted. This suggests the possibility that male monozygotic twins may behave differently than female twins partly because of intrauterine influences or that dizygotic twins may also be influenced by the combination of sexes involved (whether both are of the same sex or different sexes). We will consider other limitations of twin studies and those that attempt to discriminate genetic from environmental variables during our review of their results in the following section and later in this book.

A useful review of studies of twins and aggression was done by Mednick (1981). He indicated that a simple summary of eight studies of identical twins around the world suggests a 60 percent rate of concordance (sharing by both twins) for problems produced by their aggression, while a 30 percent concordance rate was found for fraternal twins. However, these studies pose many problems, including mismeasurement from a sampling bias. There seemed to be more monozygotic twins studied than would be expected to exist, and several studies came from Nazi Germany. The implication is that at least some studies were biased to fit a political agenda. Mednick's late associate K. O. Christiansen had carried out his own study, utilizing the population of Denmark. Because of the limited migration of its population, its homogeneity, and the extensive records kept for each person, Denmark is a most attractive country in which to study the relative influence of environment and heredity on behavior.

Christiansen first studied all twins in one region. He found that for males, there was a 35 percent concordance rate for aggression problems in monozygotic twins and a 13 percent rate for dizygotic twins. For females, the differences were similar, although the overall level of problems was lower. Rates of concordance for the monozygotic twins were more than two and one-half times greater than for dizygotic twins. This increased concordance for a group with identical genetic makeups implies that genetic factors contributed to the level of aggression. Also, obviously, the fact that the rate was far below 100 percent implies that other factors contributed to those levels. Since this study involved twins raised together, and since we can assume that identical twins often share the same experiences, we cannot dismiss an important environmental contribution to their aggression levels.

To further assess the relative effects of environment and genetics on behavior, Mednick and his associates (1981) studied non-twin population samples. They took psychopathology and criminal behavior as indices of aggressive behaviors and employed a traditional procedure of studying individuals who were adopted at an early age and measuring the relative correspondence of their behaviors to those of their biological and adoptive parents. Greater similarities in one direction or another lend support to a greater influence of either biological or environmental factors.

Hutchings and Mednick (1974) obtained the criminal records of biological and adoptive fathers of 143 criminals and found evidence of criminal convictions for more than twice as many biological fathers as adoptive ones (70 versus 33). This indicated that biological influences on criminality are stronger than environmental ones. The study also found that genetic and environmental factors worked in combination because rates of criminality in a large mixed (for criminality) group of adopted individuals were even higher (36 percent) if both biological and adoptive fathers were criminals than if just the biological father (21 percent) or just the adoptive father (10 to 11 percent) were criminals. A study done in Iowa by Crowe (1975) suggests that a similar relation exists between biological mothers and offspring regarding criminality. Those studies indicate a correspondence between criminality in biological parents and their offspring; it implies genetic transference, but does not demonstrate genetic causality. Data are of the correlative type—they compare observations of the rates of a dependent variable (criminality) in parents and their grown children. Further, we cannot eliminate the contribution of uncontrolled environmental variables. For example, in Denmark adoption agencies make an attempt to fully inform adoptive parents of any known deviancies of biological parents. Thus, the possibility cannot be ruled out that adoptive parents of children of criminals acted in some way to increase the criminality of these children. For example, perhaps they had lowered expectations of them or did not try to change deviant behavior because they considered it biologically determined and therefore unalterable. Nevertheless, the data suggest that a genetic factor is involved in criminality. Wilson and Herrnstein (1985) indicated that other studies done up to 1984 supported the idea of genetic contributions. It will be interesting to examine the results of subsequent studies on correspondences of criminality in parents and offspring; the inherited contributions to criminality might be seen in many ways, at different levels of biological function. A more general effect, for example, might lie in the emotional reactivity of individuals. Mednick indicates that it is more difficult to condition criminals with punishment. Wilson and Herrnstein cite supporting work showing that psychopathic criminals are less likely than others to respond emotionally to impending aversive or other emotionally arousing stimuli. Further, some evidence suggests that psychopathic criminals may have deficiencies in learning. These individuals supposedly would not respond well to attempts to punish their inappropriate behaviors and also might have problems with more positive-based learning. Evidence for a genetic base for psychopathology also exists, so it will be important to determine if and how we can link this general emotional sensitivity problem to genetic processes.

Relatively specific genetic influences on criminal aggression have been suggested from the study of particular gene or chromosomal abnormalities. These abnormalities may result in critical changes in the levels of chemicals that produce aggression or in those needed to suppress it. We will discuss three findings here to illustrate both the promise and the problems involved.

Studies of Human Genetic Defects and Aggression

The Lesch-Nyhan syndrome is a relatively rare (1 in 10,000 male births) but striking condition that offers a straightforward example of how a genetic dysfunction may cause an increase in aggression. It is produced in males by an inherited enzymatic deficiency resulting in an excess of the class of chemical molecules called purines. The behavioral effect includes a high degree of self-mutilation, especially severe biting of lips, fingers, and arms. Also reported are some biting, hitting, and yelling at others, although not necessarily always with expressions of anger, but rather in a compulsive manner. Individuals are also usually retarded and display spastic movements. Some success in controlling the aggression has resulted from a drug treatment that increases a brain chemical called serotonin (which we will discuss in Chapter 5) and by behavior modification (Libby, Polloway, & Smith, 1983).

A second example of studies of genetic effects on aggression illustrates the promise of these studies. Recently, researchers have discovered a mutation in a specific gene found in aggressive men in a Dutch family. Utilizing an increasingly common way to determine genetic influences on behavior, the investigation concerned studying the genetic components in a limited population that shared the behavior. If researchers notice a particular characteristic in the genes of this population and not in control populations, then this genetic characteristic may be important for the behavior. Brunner and his colleagues (Brunner, Nelen, Breakefield, Ropers, & van Oost, 1993) studied the apparent inheritance of several aggression problems over several generations. They determined that something was passed on to the problem men from the X chromosome of their mothers. Most important, they were able to determine the precise gene that was dysfunctional. This gene is important for the breakdown of brain chemicals involved in producing aggression. Thus, if something affects the breakdown of these chemicals, increased aggression would result.

The findings of Brunner and his co-workers are characterized as "promising" because they seem to be consistent within the family and fit with other observations on the roles of brain chemicals in aggression. However, the dysfunctional gene has been discovered in only several members of one family. It is not known if it will be found more generally or, if it is, whether it will have important effects on aggression in all cases. Similar recent findings concerning the genetic bases of schizophrenia and the depressive disorders have not proven consistent or general after more individuals were studied. A further problem with interpreting the study by Brunner et al. is that the men also were mildly retarded. We do not know whether this factor or some environmental element contributed to their aggressiveness. Additional studies should help us delineate the critical variables in these cases.

An example of a problematic effort to determine the genetic bases of aggression comes from the study of the XYY syndrome, in which individuals have an extra Y (male) sex chromosome. Since males are thought to be more aggressive than females, the presence of this extra chromosome suggested to some investigators that these men might be more aggressive. The XYY syndrome is not considered at present by most professionals to result in increased aggression. However, it was once proposed to have such an effect, and the history of work on this syndrome serves as a good example of the types of rationales and research done in this area. Furthermore, some laypeople and even some professionals still link it to aggression.

Much of the work with XYY has consisted of karyotyping (see p. 22) the cells from a population and determining if any relation exists between the presence of the XYY mosaic and aggressive or other deviant behavior. The original work suggesting a relationship was done by Jacobs and her colleagues (Jacobs, Brunton, Melville,

Brittain, & McClemont, 1965). They examined cells from a hospital population for the criminally insane and found that the incidence of XYY individuals was about 3 percent, whereas it was estimated to be about one-tenth of a percent in a normal population. This increased incidence suggested that the syndrome had some causal role in the patients' criminality. Subsequent studies to characterize the XYY men reported that they generally were taller, had higher plasma testosterone (the male sex hormone), larger genitalia, and lower intelligence than non-XYYs and yet came from normal families. The implications were that the extra chromosome resulted in specific physical and behavioral abnormalities that served as the bases for increased aggression. This thesis gained such wide acceptance that criminal defenses were based on it in France and Australia, and a famous mass murderer in the United States was thought (incorrectly) to be an example of how the XYY mosaic produced aggressive men. Apparently, the combination of the murderer's horrible deeds and his physical appearance led to unfounded speculation that he was an XYY man.

Following the original publications supporting a link between the XYY syndrome and aggression, other reports began to question this early research. Some challenged the determination of two basic variables involved: the incidence of the XYY mosaic and the appropriateness of the control groups. Researchers questioned the reliability of the estimates of XYY men in prisons and normal populations. They cited the limited sample sizes employed and the possible errors in karyotyping. They also pointed out that comparing XYY incidence in adult criminals to a control population of newborn babies was inappropriate. Environmental factors at birth, such as radiation, chemical pollutants, common maternal drug use, or consumption of foods with certain additives can all have genetic effects. To the extent that some factors may have been more prevalent during gestation of the XYY men and not during that of the newborns, estimates of the normal incidence of XYY from the control group of newborns would be erroneous. The appropriate control group would be men who were of the same age and came from the same environment as the XYY men. Further criticisms were based on other studies at odds with the original work of Jacobs et al. Some found, for example, decreased plasma testosterone levels in XYYs, and various measures of intelligence showed that they had normal or even exceptionally high test scores.

A widely cited, extensive study of the XYY syndrome was done by Witken, Mednick, Schulsinger, Bakkestrom, Christiansen, Goodenough, Hirschorn, Lundsteen, Owen, Philip, Rubin, and Stocking (1976) in Denmark. As we've mentioned previously, the extensive record system of that country facilitates such a study. Witken et al. did not discover any link between the XYY mosaic and increased aggressiveness. They did find, however, as had others, that these men had lower than average intelligence scores. They concluded that to the extent that XYYs are found in the convicted criminal group, it is probably the result of a lower IQ; they are simply more likely to be caught and convicted of their crimes.

We can conclude that the effect of the XYY mosaic on aggression is at the least uncertain, and, if any effect is present, its mechanism is unclear. Many XYY men appear to be normal and of good intelligence, so the XYY effect does not dominate in all cases. If, however, some XYY males are of larger stature or have lower intelligence, we cannot dismiss possible effects of differential social treatment of them.

That is, although these characteristics do not by themselves necessarily produce higher levels of aggression, society's reactions to a big, unintelligent man might do so.

Interest in the XYY syndrome, while dramatically reduced from that shown earlier, continues because we cannot discount the possibility of its role in aggression. Further, some of the discoveries about body and brain biochemical activities in XYYs fit with others' findings on the causes of aggression. For example, Bioulac, Benezech, Renaud, and Noel (1978) found decreases in the activity of the neurotransmitter serotonin in XYY men. (As we'll see, serotonin is thought to be related to decreases in aggression.) Probably, as long as correlations between the XYY mosaic and increased aggression are reported, suggestions of a causal link will continue. One example is found in a paper presented by Meyer-Bahlberg (1981) that discussed and reviewed studies related to the possibilities that abnormalities in either X or Y chromosomes affect aggression. The principal conclusion was that no evidence proved that aggression is either decreased or increased in such cases. However, the report also included descriptions of selected, striking case studies of the explosive, temper-tantrum characteristics of some XYYs and how they engage in criminal or violent acts at an early age. It appears that it is difficult to definitively reject the possibility of a link between the XYY mosaic and aggression.

SEX AND AGGRESSION

Although the study of behavioral differences between the sexes is currently an especially sensitive field and not many findings are universally accepted, the predominance of evidence seems to be that males are more aggressive than females. For example, Maccoby and Jacklin (1974) extensively analyzed the literature on sex differences and dismissed most purported differences. However, they did conclude that aggression was one of only four basic ways in which males and females differed.

Sex differences in criminal aggression in the United States are very clear. In one assessment, the number of homicides committed by males was five times that of females, and the robbery rate for males was 20 times that for females. In 1990, arrests of males for murder occurred at a rate exceeding that for females by more than eight times (FBI, 1990).

Sex differences in aggression probably do not depend on socialization or acculturation because they are found from early ages and in many different societies. The universality of these differences implies a biologically based phenomenon. However, we must remember that no one aggressive factor is all-determining, or that factors work in a dichotomous or either-or fashion. Sex alone does not determine aggression, and great variety occurs in the levels of aggression both within and between sexes.

Feminist authors have been especially concerned with the implications of the acceptance of biological influences over human behavior (e.g., Fausto-Sterling, 1986). If females are categorized as being less aggressive, this could be a basis for denial of equal opportunities and could be used, for example, as one reason to deny females in the armed forces opportunities for fighting roles. Success in such roles can be a major factor in achieving promotions. In addition, categorization of females as less aggressive might affect their selection for management or leadership roles in business or political life. Thus, there is the possibility for a great potential impact from any conclusions drawn about the amount of and bases for sexual differences in aggression. Such conclusions must be based on scientific evidence, not political orientations. Relatively recently, research on female aggression in both lower animals and humans has been attended to more extensively (e.g., see Björkvist & Niemelä, 1992). Important questions are being raised about past biases in the research on sex differences in aggression. Thus, in the near future a sufficient base of information should allow further refinement of our understanding of sex differences beyond what we have presented here.

Observations of sex differences in aggression have been made at both the lower animal and the human level. In Lagerspetz's work with mice, for example, males were used in the isolation-induced aggression tests because the female mice did not display much aggression in that situation. We earlier described some of the physical and physiological differences between the aggressive and non-aggressive male mice. Similar differences also have been found between male and female rats. Apart from overall body size, male-female differences have been observed in the size, composition, and activity of specific areas of the brain. We will discuss the contribution of brain function to the determination of aggressive behavior in the following chapters.

The generality of differences in aggression between males and females has been well established via extensive study of many species, including rats, dogs, and most primates. Although in some species the female is more aggressive (and usually larger), they are relatively few. Two commonly noted examples are the hamster and the gibbon. Floody (1983) cites these, as well as other cases, to argue for the lack of differences in the relative aggressiveness of the sexes. Also, in selective breeding studies like those of Lagerspetz (see p. 25), Cairns and Hood initially found effects similar to those of Lagerspetz in their males and no aggression in females. However, in further study, Cairns and Hood discovered that measurement of maternal aggression, as well as repeated isolation tests, showed that aggressive behaviors in the females did increase following selective breeding. Thus, evidence exists that breeding can affect aggression in both males and females. Nevertheless, females still were less aggressive than males in isolation tests (Hood & Cairns, 1988).

Most discussions of high levels of aggression in females have mentioned them either as exceptions or, as in White (1983), as examples to counter assumptions that males are always biologically determined to be more aggressive than females. However, there is some concern that inappropriate methodology may have been employed in comparisons of male and female aggressiveness. Lagerspetz, Björkqvist, and Peltonen (1988), among others, have investigated the gender differences in human aggression from the standpoint of provoking situations and outcomes. They found that while 11- and 12-year-old boys were more physically aggressive, girls were indirectly aggressive more often. That is, when angered, the girls were more liable than boys to tell lies about someone, ignore or ostracize them, or sulk. Thus, the type of aggression studied might determine which gender is more aggressive or mask the existence of other types of aggression. The authors indicate that since investigators usually concentrate on more reliably assessed direct measures of aggression, they may be overlooking substantial female aggression.

Sex differences related to aggression in humans include both commonly observed behaviors as well as psychopathological states. Aggressive behaviors that occur more often in boys include physical fighting, counteraggression, imitation of the aggression of others, rough-and-tumble play, and reports of aggressive fantasies (Meyer-Bahlburg, 1981).

Cantwell (1981) notes that Antisocial Personality Disorder is diagnosed more often and at an earlier age for boys than girls, and has been found to follow prior diagnoses of Attention Deficit Disorder with Hyperactivity (ADDH, now known as Attention Deficit/Hyperactivity Disorder or, often, ADHD). Also, via adoption studies, some investigators have genetically linked ADHD to male relatives. In turn, the Antisocial Disorder in girls is more likely to be related to a diagnosis of Hysteria.

As we noted, some objections have arisen about the attribution of sex differences in aggression to biological mechanisms. There also have been questions about the very existence of such differences. Researchers have argued that the definition or measure of aggression in some studies has sometimes been inappropriate and that differences between men and women in perceptions of the acceptableness of aggression may bias the results (Frodi, Macaulay, & Thome, 1977). Some investigators have suggested that female aggression in the United States may have increased as social stereotypes for sex roles have changed. Baron (1977) noted this in his explanation of results of his work in the 1970s. He also reanalyzed some of his earlier work that had indicated males were more aggressive than females. He suggested that those studies involved lower provocations for aggression, and that males, who may have had lower thresholds, were more likely to react, in comparison to females. However, despite this suggestion of an increased readiness to aggress in males, Baron emphasized the similarities in responding by both sexes to increased provocations.

In considering the implications of Baron's work, we should note that he was employing the teacher-learner paradigm previously discussed that involves the subterfuge of the "teacher" being told that he will use electrical shock to help an experimenter learn something about the effects of shock on behavior. Research has suggested that this situation does not involve aggression because no aggressive arousal is noted and that it might better be considered an example of subjects' susceptibility to follow commands given by others, as in Milgram's celebrated studies (Milgram, 1963). Milgram developed a teacher-learner method and found in his first study that two-thirds of his subjects would continue to deliver increasingly strong shocks, even when the shock levels were labeled dangerous. He concluded that the subjects did so because of their tendency to obey an experimenter as a person with authority, which overcame the subjects' reluctance to inflict harm on others. Thus, perhaps the modification of the sex differences found by Baron is a reflection of changes in social roles in areas apart from aggression. Therefore, since investigators are caught in the ethical dilemma of wanting to study aggression in the laboratory but are not willing to allow actual aggression to occur, we cannot answer the question definitively. Given the current increased interest in the topic, however, there certainly will be further attempts to explore it.

Apart from trying to determine whether the sexes differ in their levels of aggression, another approach involves studying the relationship between sexual and aggressive behaviors and between the environmental and biological controls over these behaviors. Informal observations indicate that sexual and aggressive behaviors are intermixed in some species, including cats, horses, and sometimes humans, as, for example, when biting occurs between partners. Further, in human homicides, sexually related attacks provide one of the two primary conditions (the other is child abuse) where the victim is bitten (Levine, 1972). Finally, more formal linking of the behaviors takes place in categorizations of types of aggression, such as in work by Moyer (1968). This author linked several of his types of aggression, including inter-male, sex-related and maternal, to sexual mechanisms. Valzelli (1981) also proposed a typology of aggression, somewhat related to that of Moyer. Valzelli indicated that all aggressive behaviors included in his own list of classes of aggression, except for predation, were affected by sexual hormones.

Some environmental stimuli have overlapping effects on sex and aggression. Painful foot shock produces aggression between male rats (Ulrich & Azrin, 1962) and painful flank shock results in copulation between male and female rats (Barfield & Sachs, 1970). Similarly, tail shock may produce either behavior, varying with environmental conditions (Caggiula, 1972). In addition, tail pinch also can produce aggression and copulation, as well as eating, gnawing, and other behaviors (e.g., see Antelman, Rowland, & Fisher, 1976). Consequently, some have suggested that the link between sex and aggression might not be so exclusive, but rather a part of a series of behaviors that might be elicited by arousing stimuli. (See also Valenstein, Cox, & Kakolewski, 1970), for an early parallel observation of brain stimulation effects, and Falk, 1966, for early work on the effects of food reinforcement schedules.) In humans, some indications are of both sexual and aggressive behaviors being produced in situations such as those involving rape and sadomasochistic sex, but empirical support for these findings has tended to be, understandably, limited to analyses of subjective states. We will describe some studies of the effect of erotic materials on aggression as well as on sexual behavior later in this text.

Work with brain mechanisms for sex and aggression has indicated how various brain structures are involved in both behaviors. MacLean and Ploog (1962) reported many sites where they could apply brain stimulation to elicit either aggression or penile erections in squirrel monkeys. Investigators have also indicated that penile display by primates such as squirrel monkeys is an aggressive response (Candland, Bryan, Nazar, Kopf, & Sendor, 1970). Anthropologists have observed phallocrypt (penis sheath) clicking in dangerous situations and penis-shaking aggressive displays in primitive humans (Eibl-Eibesfeldt, Schiefenhövel, & Heeschen, 1989). In works with cerebral structures, stimulation of the preoptic area, at the base of the brain, has been reported to produce aggression (Hutchinson & Renfrew, 1966; Inselman & Flynn, 1972) and sexual behavior (e.g., Malsbury, 1971). Further, the preoptic area is one structure, although not the only, where sex hormone implants can restore aggression in castrated animals (Barfield, 1984). In humans, hypersexuality as well as hyperaggressive behavior has been reported for women with seizures originating in the temporal lobe (Mark & Ervin, 1970). Finally, the well-known work of Klüver and Bucy (1939) reported an inverse relation between aggression and sexual behavior. They indicated that the temporal lobe lesions they created in rhesus monkeys produced a taming effect while dramatically increasing sexual behavior. We will discuss this and other studies involving the brain in more detail in later chapters.

SEX HORMONES AND AGGRESSION

Earlier we saw how genetic mechanisms can influence aggression, and how one outcome of a genetic mechanism—the sex of the individual—is related to aggression. We will now explore the way in which sex-related factors—the sexual hormones—affect aggression.

Testosterone

Testosterone, often referred to as the male sexual hormone, is a major hormone produced in the testes. It is one of a class of hormones called androgens, which are involved in producing sperm and regulating secondary sexual characteristics. These hormones also have an effect on behaviors, including sex and aggression. Although most of the research we will review here has focused on testosterone, some also implies effects of all the androgens, and we will use the adjective "androgenic" to indicate these latter studies.

Early indications of a role of testosterone in aggression came from correlative studies. Increased aggression in various species was noted to occur during puberty or a mating season, when testosterone production increases. Beach (1948) made some of the first laboratory observations and reported how aggression increases with puberty in several species. Another, later example of such a correlation was given by Hutchinson, Ulrich, and Azrin (1965), who found that pain-elicited aggression in rats increased with puberty. Also, the work of Lagerspetz cited above included a finding of larger testes in her aggressive strain of mice.

The relatively few studies of the relation between testosterone levels and aggression in humans have not yielded consistent results, possibly because of methodological difficulties. Persky, Smith, and Basu (1971) found a positive correlation between self-rated aggression and testosterone production in younger (22 years old) but not in older (45 years old) men. Later, Persky, Zuckerman, and Curtis, (1978) reported a positive correlation between androgen levels and aggression in a psychiatric population. On the other hand, Kreutz and Rose (1972) found no significant correlation between testosterone levels and the results of aggression tests or the number of recent aggressive acts in a prison population, although they did observe that the levels were related to individual criminal histories. Ehrenkranz, Bliss, and Sheard (1974) reported a positive correlation between testosterone levels and past and present violence of prison inmates and also between testosterone and the dominance of non-violent inmates who were leaders in the prison. Therefore, while some studies indicate a positive correlation between testosterone levels and aggression, it has not been found for all ages and populations. Further, other behaviors such as dominance (without violence) are positively correlated with aggression.

These inconsistent findings have been interpreted by some writers as further support for the idea that humans are relatively independent of biological controls. However, although it seems well established that humans are less strongly controlled by biological factors than lower animals, we should not necessarily eliminate such factors from consideration as important contributors to human behaviors. Olweus (1983), for example, studied the blood testosterone levels in normal boys about age 16 and found significant correlations in the three-tenths to four-tenths range between testosterone level and provoked aggressive behavior as measured indirectly on one personality inventory. These results were seen as indicating that increased testosterone made the boys more ready to respond aggressively. However, we should note that the correlations were not significant for all measures of aggression, including other personality inventories, self-reports, and peer ratings. A later study by Olweus and his colleagues again found a significant relation between testosterone level and provoked aggression (i.e., reaction to actions by peers or adults) and also a somewhat smaller relation between the hormone and irritability/intolerance and frustration. By controlling for the contribution to aggression by parental treatment and the boys' personalities, Olweus's group concluded that they have found evidence that testosterone had a causal effect on aggression in the boys (Olweus, Mattsson, Schalling, & Low, 1988). Again, however, peer ratings of unprovoked aggression were not significantly related to testosterone levels. Therefore, while we might conclude that testosterone may affect aggression, its effect is not all-determining.

A question arises when comparing the findings of Olweus et al. to those of Christiansen and Knussmann (1987). These investigators also administered personality tests, which included self-reports of provoked aggression, unprovoked aggression, and irritability (including frustration tolerance), to 117 normal young (average 24 years) men and took several measures of androgen levels. The only significant correlations found were for unprovoked aggression and androgen levels—just the opposite of the findings of Olweus et al. Although the population age and specific measures of aggression were different for these two studies, it would not seem unreasonable to expect similar findings. As Christiansen and Knussmann indicate in their introduction, studies involving self-report measures of aggression have been much less successful in obtaining consistent, significant results compared to those that involve behavioral measures of past or present aggressive acts. This, of course, is a point we made in Chapter 1; direct measures are preferable to indirect ones. It is possible that the results of the two studies differed in part because Olweus et al. employed a more direct measure (ratings by peers) for unprovoked aggression.

Barfield (1984) points to some problems of interpretation in studies of the relations between hormones and aggression, and warns against generalizing too readily from limited studies. Benton (1981b) criticized earlier studies for the way in which they determined testosterone levels. It now is known that testosterone levels follow a circadian pattern—that is, they vary in a repeated pattern each day. Levels of what is called "free" testosterone are believed to be more critical than those of testosterone bound to other molecules. However, many tests of the testosterone-aggression relationship involve taking only one sample, thus perhaps missing important fluctuations, and they often measure just bound testosterone. New studies that consider these relatively recent findings should help us to determine more precisely the correlation between aggression and testosterone levels.

One experimental way of studying the effects of testosterone on aggression has been to measure the changes in aggression when we reduce testosterone levels. Castration has long been used in farm and domestic animals, not only to limit reproduction but also to make animals more tractable. Experimentally, castration of male mice (Beeman, 1947) has reduced their aggressiveness. Also, in the study cited earlier, Hutchinson (1965) showed that castration made their rats less responsive to the pain stimulus for aggression. Human aggression has also been reported to diminish after castration, especially when that aggression was related to sex, as in rape (Bremer, 1959). However, scientists have questioned the extent to which castration reduces human aggression (Benton, 1981b; Mazur, 1983).

Chemical castration, which employs anti-androgenic drugs has been used experimentally and clinically for decreasing aggression. Some drug treatments involve female hormones, such as estrogen and progesterone, whose effects we will consider more extensively. Erpino and Chappelle (1971), for example, used progesterone to reduce testosterone-mediated aggression by mice. In men, estrogen is usually not given because of inconsistent results as well as the resulting feminization of the body and other physiological complications. More commonly, studies use drugs that increase progesterone levels. Even then, it is recommended that these drugs be employed as a last resort and should be accompanied by psychotherapy (Blumer & Migeon, 1973; Maletzky, 1991). Clinical tests of Provera, a drug that is very similar to natural progesterone, have resulted in a reduction in sexual offenses in mature men (Money, 1970) and a decrease of sexual and aggressive activity in boys (Lloyd, 1964). Feminization and other side effects may occur, but they are not severe. The side effect of a significant reduction in aggression, apart from affecting sexual behavior, has made Provera an attractive substance for controlling these problem behaviors (Maletzky, 1991). Tetrahydrocannabinol (THC), the critical active substance in marijuana, also has an antiandrogenic effect that may be responsible for its pacifying effect (Thiessen, 1976). We will discuss some empirical tests of the effects of THC on aggression in Chapter 5.

The facilitating effect of testosterone on aggression has been demonstrated in studies where the hormone has been injected, resulting in increased aggression. Thus, Beeman (1947), in the classic study on castration effects, found that she could re-establish aggression in mice with testosterone injections. Researchers have also found that pre-pubertal injections of testosterone result in an early onset of fighting in non-castrated male mice (Bronson & Desjardins, 1968). One limitation of the Beeman technique was that castration does not block aggression if done after the age when aggression commences in an individual. In other words, the study implied an organizational role of testosterone on aggressive mechanisms as did studies on the effects of pre-pubertal testosterone. Testosterone apparently is responsible for the development of permanent biological contributions to aggression, such as the areas of the brain that control aggression. This effect can be seen even in females. In an early study, Levy and King (1953) showed that early postnatal injections of testosterone in female mice produce male-type fighting levels in the females as adults.

Researchers have observed the general effects of testosterone on the organization and differentiation of sexual characteristics in experiments done in rhesus monkeys (Goy, 1968) and from clinical treatment errors in humans (Money & Ehrhardt, 1968). In these cases, drugs that increased testosterone early in development resulted in female pseudohermaphrodites—genetic females with male-like genitalia and behaviors. The male behaviors in the monkeys included some associated with aggression, such as elevated (compared to normal females) levels of rough play, chasing, and threats. Similarly, in the humans, behaviors included a tendency toward higher aggression, although the amount is uncertain. Money indicated only that the girls were more likely to engage in more boy-like rough play and activities (like tomboys). More recently, Ehrhardt and Baker studied girls who had an endocrine dysfunction that resulted in prenatal exposure to high androgen levels (see Meyer-Bahlburg & Ehrhardt, 1982). Ehrhardt and Baker found slight increases in actual aggression (the initiation of fighting) in the girls. However, they could not rule out other factors, such as the possibility that this resulted from imitating the aggressiveness of the girls' male playmates.

The organizational effects of testosterone on aggressive mechanisms are clear in lower animals, as shown in the Bronson and Desjardins (1968) study, cited above, where aggression in male mice was increased by early testosterone injections. Shortly thereafter, Conner and Levine (1969) found that castration of male rats neonatally or at weaning would result in a decrease in their aggression as adults. They also discovered that testosterone therapy could restore aggressive levels, but only in rats castrated at weaning. Apparently, the mechanisms for sensitivity to testosterone were not developed in rats castrated at birth. This implies a second important element in the effects of testosterone on aggression—that is, some sort of receptive capacity is established early in development. This capacity is the device by which subsequent testosterone activity can work to enhance aggressive behaviors.

These studies indicate via several types of observations and manipulations that testosterone facilitates aggressive behaviors. Aggression levels are positively correlated with testosterone levels and reductions in testosterone result in reductions in aggression. Augmentation of testosterone results in increased aggression. Testosterone seems to be critical for the development of aggressive mechanisms. Its role in aggression is more clear in lower animals, but there is some strong evidence for its relevance to aggression in humans as well. In considering the role of testosterone, the male hormone, in increasing aggression, we have seen that female hormones that counter it may have a role in decreasing aggression. We will consider this role in the following section, along with information on hormonal effects that may increase aggression in females.

The Female Hormones and Aggression

We will now examine some major efforts to understand the roles of hormones in female aggression. However, as Floody (1983) among others points out, this area of study has not been pursued sufficiently to allow us to make definitive statements. Further, the studies that have been conducted were affected by biases about the relative lack of female aggression and disregarded differences between species and between different measures of aggression. These factors have impeded the development of a clear understanding of the roles of hormones in female aggression. Therefore, the studies we discuss should be taken as illustrative of possible approaches to studying hormonal influences.

The three hormones we will primarily consider are progesterone, prolactin, and estradiol. Progesterone, as the name implies, is important in preparing for and maintening pregnancy. It is one of a class of hormones called progestogens that are produced by the ovaries. Prolactin's function is also implied by its name; it promotes lactation. Prolactin is secreted from the anterior pituitary. Estradiol is responsible for the development and maintenance of the female sexual characteristics and for sexual receptivity, among other functions. It is one of a class of hormones called estrogens also produced by the ovaries.

The roles in aggression played by the female hormones are suggested by their functions. We would not expect a female preparing for or in the midst of pregnancy to be well served by being aggressive, so we might deduce that progesterone would have an effect of reducing aggression. Some evidence for this already has been analyzed. Similarly, the lactating female would do well to defend against any threat to her offspring, but not be engaged easily in other aggressive encounters that could result in direct or incidental injury to her offspring. Studies with mice demonstrate that maternal aggression is high during the initial stages of lactation, as the mother will defend against intruders (Svare & Gandelman, 1973). There also is an inhibition of other aggressive mechanisms, such as the response to injections of testosterone (Svare, 1980). In humans, Carroll and Steiner (1978) report that high prolactin levels, combined with low progesterone, may cause anxiety or irritable aggression.

Given the lowered aggression associated with females, we would expect that estrogen, the hormone associated with female sexual characteristics, would promote lower levels of aggression. The Bronson and Desjardins (1968) study cited earlier also included injections of estradiol into male rat pups, resulting in reduced adult aggression. However, we should also note that there is increasing evidence, provided by Brain and others, that testosterone has its effect on aggression via aromatization (conversion) to estrogen in the hypothalamus (e.g., see Brain, 1983). Some evidence points to a relation between different rates of aromatization and differences in aggression (Schlinger & Callard, 1989). Further, anti-estrogens have been shown to have anti-aggression effects in rats and mice (Brain, Simon, Hasan, Martínez, & Castano, 1988). Conflicting results concerning the role of estrogens in aggression probably reflect differences in such factors as methodology, species, and type of aggression studied.

Studies of the effects of injecting female hormones in humans have suggested that they can affect aggression. (We use the term "suggested" instead of "demonstrated" deliberately, given the limits of definition and measurement of aggression in humans.) For example, Herrmann and Beach (1978) reported that injections of a progesterone reduce irritability. This effect has been utilized successfully to decrease problems associated with Pre-Menstrual Syndrome discussed below. Further, Meyer-Bahlburg (1981) reports on some effects on fetuses from hormones given to help sustain a pregnancy. Excesses in prenatal progesterone result in lower levels of subsequent aggression in both males and females. Similarly, Yalom, Green, and Fisk (1973) tested aggression levels in 10-year-old-boys who received prenatal progesterone and indicated that the effect is even greater in males if estrogens were also given.

The Pre-Menstrual Syndrome

Investigations of the effects on aggression of changing levels of female hormones associated with estrus in lower animals and menstruation in humans have suggested a cyclicity of aggression in females. Although mice (Hyde & Sawyer, 1977) and hamsters (Floody & Pfaff, 1977) exhibit lower levels of aggression during estrus, less consistent changes in aggression have been measured during estrus cycles in rats and in other studies of hamsters (Floody, 1983). In rhesus monkeys, increased aggression has been observed during estrus as well as just prior to menstruation (Sassenrath, Rowell, & Hendrickx, 1973). Similar elevations in menstruation-related aggression have been reported for humans and are labeled as Pre-Menstrual Syndrome or PMS.

The work of Dalton (1964) was a major impetus for the study of PMS. She reported serious emotional and behavioral problems just before and during menses, with an incidence of about one in 1000. Later, Floody (1983) reviewed studies that found severe PMS irritability in 6 to 13 percent of women. In Dalton's correlative studies of female truants, she reported that 49 percent of her subjects committed their crimes during this time. Similarly, while incarcerated, 62 percent of infractions of prison rules occurred just prior to or during menstruation. On the basis of this and much subsequent work, PMS clinics and information-activist groups have been established in the United States over the last decade.

A category, Late Luteal Phase Dysphoric Disorder, based on PMS, was proposed for the American Psychiatric Association's DSM-III-R (APA, 1987), but was only included in an appendix of diagnoses needing further study to establish their validity. (*The Diagnostic and Statistical Manual of Mental Disorders* is considered the definitive compilation of psychiatric illnesses in the United States. Inclusion in the *Manual* occurs only after extensive study to determine if sufficient good evidence is present for the existence of a psychiatric problem.) The newer DSM-IV (APA, 1994) also lists what now is called Premenstrual Dysphoria Disorder in an appendix of proposed diagnoses. However, it treats it much more extensively than DSM-III-R did, and differentiates it from PMS in the greater severity of its symptoms and impairment produced. Thus, much of the past work with serious PMS aggression probably would be currently referred to as related to Premenstrual Dysphoric Disorder. However, we should note that this recent review of information concluded that there still was not enough evidence to include this disorder as a valid psychiatric classification.

Scientists have not been able to establish a physiological basis of PMS. Many chemical changes occur during a woman's menstrual cycle, involving several non-sexual hormones and neurotransmitters and related substances. Reid and Yen (1981) provide a good review of the chemical events that might possibly be responsible for PMS. A combination of hormonal and neurotransmitter (brain chemical messenger) mechanisms have received support as possible bases. Eriksson, Sundblad, Lisjö, Modigh, and Andersch (1992) found in a preliminary study that free testosterone and some other androgen levels were higher in women who reported severe premenstrual irritability compared to a matched control group of women without such premenstrual complaints. They suggested that the increased levels of free testosterone, in combination with falling progesterone levels just prior to menstruation, may cause the increased irritability, as the antagonistic effects of the progesterone on testosterone-induced aggression are overcome by increased testosterone.

Eriksson et al. note how the change in hormone ratios may affect serotonergic activity. (As we indicated previously, serotonin is a neurotransmitter often found to inhibit aggression.) Some evidence indicates that decreased serotonergic functions are found in some, although not all, women who have PMS (Halbreich & Tworek, 1993). One line of supporting evidence is that drugs that increase the effectiveness of serotonin, such as fluoxetine (Prozac), help to relieve PMS complaints. For example, Menkes, Taghavi, Mason, and Howard (1993) observed that 15 of 16 women who were tested had good improvement in several measures of PMS problems, including hostility and irritability, compared to when they did not take any drug or took a placebo.

Some success in treating PMS has been reported by supplementing falling progesterone levels. Dalton and others have indicated that administration of a progesterone is effective. Some beneficial effects of birth control pills have also been claimed. However, success has not been consistent, and in controlled studies progesterone has not always been any more effective than placebos (Eriksson et al., 1992). Indeed, placebos, which are non-drug pills or injections used in control tests, often seem to produce an effect themselves (e.g., in Menkes et al., 1993). The results of this and other work have led some authors, including Reid and Yen, to suggest that psychological (read non-biological) factors are the bases of PMS, if it indeed exists.

Critics of research on PMS point out methodological problems (Parlee, 1973; Frodi, Macaulay, & Thome, 1977; Caplan, McCurdy-Myers, & Gans, 1992). They indicate that many reports of increased irritability are subjective and/or self-reports and are unreliable. Therefore, some question whether the irritability really exists and, if so, at what level. Also, blind evaluations are not always used, so a person previously labeled as having PMS is more likely to be judged as having problems with aggression. Further, few control groups are employed. The scales devised to measure effects have biased questions (also evident in the title of at least one: Moos' "Menstrual *Distress* Questionnaire") that assume or lead the subject to focus on any problems involved with menstruation instead of simply asking about it. Similarly, a cultural bias concerning menstruation, at least in the United States, creates an expectancy of problems. Young women have been taught that menstruation is a disagreeable, uncomfortable burden they must bear. Finally, some researchers have pointed out that if there is an effect of menstruation on aggression, it might be secondary to the increased discomfort involved and not caused by body chemical changes directly affecting aggression mechanisms.

It seems that even though researchers have indicated that PMS occurs only in a small number of women, there is a concern that some (especially men) will generalize this problem to all women thereby threatening women's opportunities for advancement in contemporary society. Thus, feminist critics, such as Caplan et al., may acknowledge that important menstruation-related mood changes occur but argue that this should be addressed as a medical problem, not a psychiatric disorder. Their position is that the inclusion of the problem in the DSM reflects a prejudicial attitude of the psychiatric community toward women, and that this attitude contributes to the demeaning of women by society in general. This is a legitimate concern, given the general sexual biases in the United States and past failures to attend to scientific over illogical emotional bases for societal decision making. The recent hysteria over the communicability of AIDS is a good example. On the other hand, it is hoped that these lateral concerns do not result in decreased research on PMS necessary for a clearer understanding of its nature.

A promising example of a new research direction is that of Bancroft and his colleagues (Bancroft, Williamson, Warner, Rennie, & Smith, 1993), who share others' dismay with the inconsistent findings associated with PMS research, as well as with the lack of progress in treating it. They suggest that the previous orientation of arbitrarily defining PMS does not adequately encompass the range of problems women experience both before and during menstruation. They propose an alternate approach to investigation, based on the assumption that some combination of three factors contributes to PMS and that considering all of them will lead to a more useful model, while also defusing some of the political implications of PMS. As Bancroft (1993) indicates, identifying PMS as an extreme of cyclic variations experienced by all women implies that all women share some elements of this disturbance. Treating PMS as involving factors that not all women share removes most women from such categorization.

Bancroft's factors include timing, associated with hormonal variations in the menstrual cycle, a menstrual factor that is related to the buildup and shedding of the uterine lining, and a more general and constant vulnerability factor, such as neuroticism or a tendency toward depression. While the timing factor by itself may produce PMS, this is thought to be rare. Instead, we can understand a wide range of problems associated with menstruation by addressing the relative contributions of these three factors in individual cases. For example, women who complain of excessive menstrual bleeding or pain, along with premenstrual problems, would be seen as having a high contribution from the menstrual factor. Perhaps a change in orientation such as Bancroft's will help achieve further progress in research in this area, as it reduces political opposition.

There is resistance to accepting the influence of biological mechanisms over human behaviors, because some people feel that it implies their behaviors are determined by factors outside their control. They seem to fear that this will denigrate humans, reducing them to the status of animals. However, the question should not revolve around the existence of biological mechanisms but the extent to which they influence human behaviors. As we indicated previously, the evidence for the existence of phenomena such as the XYY syndrome and PMS is not unequivocal, but information concerning biological influences needs to be examined if we are to understand the causes of aggression to the greatest extent possible. By denying the existence of these influences, we preclude further investigation of these possible causes. This question will arise again as we discuss the neural and biochemical bases of aggression in subsequent chapters.

SUMMARY

Some biological factors help prepare individuals for the expression of aggressive behaviors, while others more directly aid in determining when aggression will occur. Genetic factors have more of a preparatory role when they contribute to the development of sensory capacities, body size, and motor functions needed for effective aggression. They also can affect neural structures and body chemistry that control aggression.

Breeding studies with lower animals have helped show genetic bases for aggression. Genetic studies with humans are much more difficult to analyze since it is difficult to control the variables contributing to aggression. Separating environmental from genetic influences is especially difficult, although both adoption and twin studies have been helpful and support a genetic contribution to aggression. Studies of chromosomal abnormalities suggest how genetic mechanisms could affect levels of critical body chemicals. However, genetic studies also have resulted in controversy and possible misinterpretations, such as in the XYY syndrome.

Males usually have been found to be more aggressive than females for both lower animal species as well as for humans. While most investigators accept these findings and interpret them to reflect a biological factor, cases are made that female aggression has been inadequately and inappropriately studied, and any differences may be culturally based.

There is evidence for a relation between sexual and aggressive behaviors, in part from the simultaneous occurrence of both behaviors. Environmental stimuli can also produce both behaviors as can brain structures involved in both.

Testosterone has been linked in a number of ways to increased aggression as well as to the development of biological contributions to aggression, although this relation is not as strong in humans as in lower animals. Some inconsistencies in human studies might be related to the difficulties of measuring human aggression. Various studies also show how lowered levels of testosterone are associated with lowered aggression, and this has led to the development of some treatments for increased aggression.

The role of two female hormones, prolactin and estrogen, in aggression seems to vary with testing conditions. Progesterone has been more consistently associated with lowered aggression.

The premenstrual syndrome, involving increased irritability and aggression, has been the focus of much controversy because of its implications for the status of women. Some writers question its existence or posit a cultural rather than a biological basis, while others suggest that it be considered a medical, not a psychopathological condition. Other investigators have found evidence linking PMS to increased testosterone and a series of related chemical events that help explain the success of some drug therapy. Again, however, human studies involve inconsistent results that have led some investigators to propose new approaches to studying this syndrome.

Suggested Readings

Simmel, E. C. (Ed.) (1988). *Aggressive behavior: Genetic and neural approaches.* Hillsdale, NJ: Lawrence Erlbaum Associates.

Svare, B. B. (Ed.) (1983). *Hormones and aggressive behavior.* New York: Plenum Press.

CHAPTER 3

Neural Bases

The basic questions we will consider in this chapter involve whether there are aggression "centers" in the brain and, if so, how they control aggression. Do they increase it, inhibit it, or somehow modulate it? How do they produce their results? What specific mechanisms controlled by them affect aggression? What other factors, such as hormones, external stimuli, motivation mechanisms, and so on, are involved? Note that the word "centers" has quotation marks around it because, although this term is used by many, its meaning is not always well understood. There are no brain areas that simply control aggression by themselves. Instead, these areas work in conjunction with other brain areas and interact with non-neural factors to influence aggression. In other words, instead of being "centers" for aggression, they constitute part of a *system* that governs aggressive behavior.

For us to answer questions involving the neural bases of aggression, we will first examine the objective, controlled experimental work done with lower animals. We will then apply this knowledge to the understanding and treatment of human clinical cases.

METHODOLOGICAL CONSIDERATIONS

Studies of aggression in both lower animals and humans have used three major methodological approaches in determining brain function. Two are called **lesioning** and **stimulation** techniques. They are experimental techniques because they involve manipulation of an independent variable—brain function—to affect a dependent variable—aggression. (Although their use in humans would be primarily for therapeutic ends.) The third approach, **electrical recording**, is a correlative technique that involves simultaneous measurement of the two dependent variables of brain activity and aggression. We will briefly describe this technique here; however, its most common applications have been in work with humans, so we will study it more closely in Chapter 4.

The lesioning technique permanently or, in some cases, temporarily terminates the function of some area of the brain. A common way of doing this is to insert an electrode, usually a thin wire that is insulated except at its tip, into the brain, pass a destructive electrical signal through it, and damage the brain area around the tip. Lesions do not always have an effect on aggression and thus scientists assume that the structures involved are not related to aggression. When the lesions do affect aggression, it may be to decrease or increase it. If a lesion decreases aggression, we might conclude that the damaged structure was involved in producing aggression. If a lesion results in an increase in aggression, we assume the structure had an inhibitory role that was eliminated (disinhibition occurs). Although more subtle concerns are involved with interpreting the results of lesions, they usually will not be important here.

Stimulation involves activating the brain, usually temporarily. An electrode is inserted into the structure to be studied so that an electrical signal can be applied to it. The characteristics of that signal are selected so that the area immediately around the electrode tip will be excited but not injured. Although the electrical signal normally does not resemble the brain's natural electrical activity, the behaviors produced often closely approximate natural aggressive acts. If an aggressive behavior is increased during brain stimulation, we can assume that the structure is involved in the production of aggression. If aggression is terminated or blocked, we conclude that this structure has an inhibitory role. As with lesions, some problems of interpretation of the results arise.

Electrical recording involves the registration of the activity of some area of the brain. This may be done at different levels: from the scalp surface, as with electroencephalograms or EEGs that are records of a large area of the brain; from macroelectrodes about the size of a sewing needle that are placed within the brain near some specific structure of interest; or from microelectrodes that are so small they can record from individual nerve cells (neurons). Scientists can take records of the individual structure while measuring aggressive behaviors to determine if the structure is especially active or inactive during the aggression, implying some role in the behavior.

The Challenge of Working Deep within the Brain

The determination of brain functions is impeded by the brain's relative inaccessibility. Encased as it is within the cranium, it is not easily approached for us to manipulate it or even measure its activities. One approach to direct access is a craniotomy, or cutting away of part of the skull. This permits direct recording, sampling, or manipulation, but only of the brain's outer structures, called the cortex or neocortex. While these structures are vitally involved in the most complex neural functions and have various effects on aggression, most of the more critical structures for our purposes are located below the cortex in the brain's subcortical regions. Access to the subcortical structures implies passing through the cortex, with attendant destruction of it, possibly radically altering the brain's function and thus impeding our understanding how the intact brain functions.

In the early scientific studies of brain function carried out in the latter part of the nineteenth century, gross lesions were made in anesthetized animals, and scientists noted the subsequent effects on their behavior after they recovered from the operation. These lesions involved either cortical or cortical-subcortical targets, but could not be restricted just to subcortical areas because refined surgical techniques had not been developed. Rudimentary information on brain functions was obtained. For example, Goltz (1892) found that removing the neocortex from a dog had a disinhibitory effect on aggression. However, progress was limited by the inability to make precisely controlled lesions and locate them exclusively in subcortical areas.

The development of the **stereotaxic** technique by Horsley and Clarke (1908) provided a means for accurate access to subcortical brain structures. This technique relies on the fact that the brains of most members of a species are essentially of the same size and structure. Further, a consistent spatial relationship exists between cranial landmarks and structures in the underlying brain. On the basis of these observations, Horsley and Clarke and their followers developed stereotaxic atlases, or three-dimensional maps of different species, by which each point in the brain could be located as corresponding to certain values on stereotaxic axes.

This system is similar to the method we use to locate points on earth. Longitude is specified in terms of direction and degrees from the reference Greenwich meridian and latitude in terms of direction and degrees from the equator. With a final specification that the point lies on the earth's surface, its location can be communicated very precisely to someone else. Similarly, with the stereotaxic system, we can specify cranial reference points such as a vertical plane that passes through the ear canals, a horizontal plane that goes through the lowest point of the eye socket, and a third through the midline of the skull. We can then measure a typical brain of the species on axes passing perpendicular from each of these three planes to specify where a particular structure is located. Instead of specifying degree latitude or longitude as on earth, we can locate structures by their distance from the reference planes in the skull. To implement this technique, Horsley and Clarke also developed the stereotaxic instrument. This allows researchers to hold the head of an anesthetized animal firmly, usually by attaching the instrument to the skull at the reference points. It also permits the precise movement of an electrode in each of the stereotaxic axes. With this instrument, we can insert the electrode, with minimal damage to the overlying brain structures, into any subcortical structure.

The original stereotaxic technique allowed scientists to place subcortical lesions, and, following recovery from the operation, they could then assess their effects on the animal's aggression. However, stimulation and recording were limited to the period when the animal was still anesthetized and in the stereotaxic instrument, since electrodes could be placed only acutely, or during the operation. This severely restricted the possibilities for studying aggression, given the limits of technology at that time. However, in the 1930s, W. R. Hess, working in Switzerland, developed a method for the chronic or permanent attachment of electrodes (described in Hess, 1957). It then was possible to measure activity or stimulate structures in a conscious animal after recovery from the implantation operation. Indeed, Hess was the first to report the elicitation of aggression from brain stimulation. He carried out a series of studies on brain function, and was awarded the Nobel prize for these studies. This chapter will show how Hess' technique has helped others determine the aggressive functions of many subcortical structures.

NEUROANATOMICAL CONSIDERATIONS

To facilitate communication, we must review some basic terminology and other information related to neuroanatomy, the structure of the brain. Again, readers who have been exposed to this material should feel free to skim through it.

Terminology

The neural elements of the brain are divided into two basic types of structure: (1) groupings of neurons that interconnect with each other called **nuclei** or, at times, **areas**; and (2) groups of the parts of neurons (axons) involved in carrying messages from one part of the nervous system to another called **tracts** or **bundles** or **lemnisci**. These two types of structure in turn constitute larger structures of the brain, which are arranged into larger subdivisions. While the nuclei and other structures are identified because they are physically distinct, they are also usually functionally distinct. All the component neurons in one nucleus may be related to the same role in aggression, and the components of a given structure may be related to the same general type of behavior. The names given to the various structures unfortunately do not follow a single pattern. Although some are named for their function (e.g., olfactory tract), others are named for their location (e.g., forebrain), relative location (e.g., hypothalamus), shape or appearance (e.g., aqueduct), or in honor of someone (e.g., Sylvian aqueduct). Unfortunately, for those whose Greek and/or Latin is not what it should be, the names of the structures are often Anglicized versions of the two ancient languages.

Basic Nervous System Organization

The brain communicates with the rest of the body via the autonomic nervous system (ANS) and the somatic nervous system. The ANS consists of subdivisions that control the storage and conservation of energy (parasympathetic) and the expenditure of energy, including fight-or-flight reactions (sympathetic). The somatic system involves control of skeletal muscles and the receipt of somatosensory information from the body. As we consider the roles of various brain functions in aggression, we will see how various parts of these bodily systems are involved.

The function and structure of the brain become more complex going from posterior to anterior. What follows is a rough introductory description of the progression as it relates to aggression. Also, essentially all the major brain structures involved in aggression are illustrated in the first three figures. The reader may then consult these figures as necessary when we present more specific descriptions of brain-aggression relations.

Figure 3.1 is a general view of the human skull and brain, as seen from the middle and looking to the right. The most posterior parts (lowest in this view) communicate most directly with the spinal cord and have basic survival roles that help control breathing, digestion, and sleep. Several structures critical for aggression are found in the subdivisions and structures of the **brain stem**. Moving upward (anterior) in this figure, we see that the structural complexity increases to handle more complex functions such as those involved in motivation and emotions. A major group of interrelated structures concerned with these functions is called the **limbic system**. Papez (1937) is usually credited with linking these and related structures to the control of emotions. For them to carry out their complex functions, these elements are connected with the body through the brain stem as well as to higher brain areas. Naturally, many of the neural components that we will discuss are included in this system.

Figure 3.2 shows how the major components of the limbic system lie deep within the brain. It also illustrates how they are connected to one another for communication. In some cases, activity in one area will help increase the aggressive behaviors associated with activity of a second area. In other cases, activity in one area helps limit that of a second area. Together, the structures of the limbic system can interact to provide the complex integration of factors involved in aggression. For example, the organism must receive and analyze information on its general situation, the nature of its opponent, and the specific sensory stimuli it is receiving. It must decide

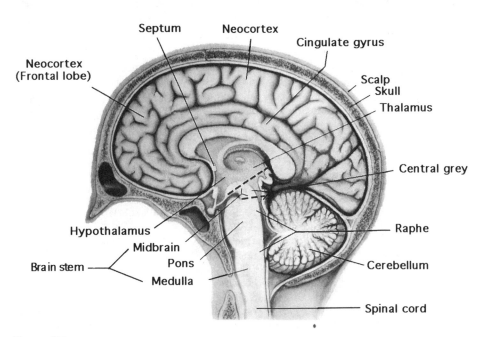

Figure 3.1   A midline view of the right half of the brain, encased in the skull. Some of the principal structures and areas relevant to aggression are labeled. (Modified from Noback, C. R. & Demarest, R. J., *The Human Nervous System.* Copyright © 1975, McGraw-Hill Publishing Company. Reprinted by permission.)

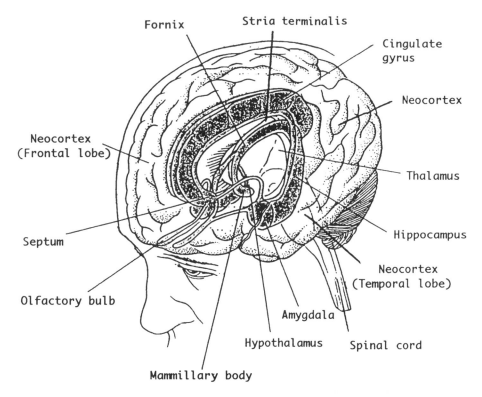

Fornix

Stria terminalis

Cingulate gyrus

Neocortex

Neocortex (Frontal lobe)

Thalamus

Hippocampus

Septum

Neocortex (Temporal lobe)

Olfactory bulb

Amygdala

Hypothalamus   Spinal cord

Mammillary body

Figure 3.2   The brain, with shading indicating some of the principal limbic system components and interconnections. (Modified from Galluscio, Eugene H., *Biological Psychology.* Copyright © 1990, Macmillan Publishing Company. Reprinted by permission.)

whether to attack and how, based on part on past experiences and must execute the attack while continuing to analyze the situation. Thus a number of elements of the limbic system are needed for managing various aspects of the situation, and they communicate with each other to determine the aggressive outcome.

In addition to the simpler structures of the brain, Figures 3.1 and 3.2 show the most complex structures, constituting the **neocortex**. The neocortex is divided into different lobes as well as subdivisions of various sizes. It is so named because of its relatively recent evolutionary development and to distinguish it from the older cortex of the limbic system. The work of Goltz has indicated how the neocortex can have an inhibitory role in aggression. Lower on the phylogenetic scale, the neocortex is less developed and orders below mammals usually are considered to have only a more primitive cortex and no neocortex. However, despite the regression in cortical development and general size, the subcortical structures of the various mammalian species are markedly similar in their detail.

The cross-species similarities in brain structures are very evident when we compare sections of the brain of a human, a monkey, a cat, and a rat in Figure 3.3. Although the absolute size of the brains is different, detailed examination of these cross

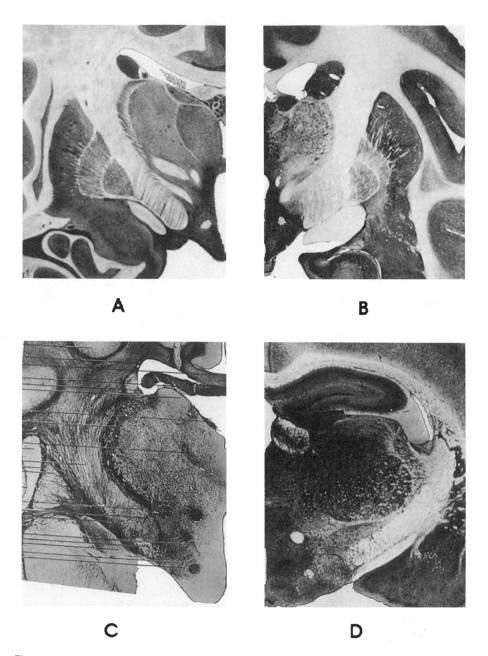

Figure 3.3 Subcortical brain cross sections taken through the thalamus and hypothalamus. Sizes were adjusted for comparability. (A) human—left half; (B) squirrel monkey—right half; (C) cat—left half; (D) rat—right half. The white horizontal structure at the upper middle of A, B, and D is the corpus callosum, and the large grey area halfway below is the thalamus. The two white dots at the lower middle of each section are limbic system tracts that pass through the hypothalamus. The large diagonal white band connects the neocortex with the brain stem. In C, different staining techniques made the corpus callosum, limbic, tracts and other white matter appear dark. (A—Modified from Smith, Carlton G., *Serial dissections of the human brain*. Copyright © 1981, Williams and Wilkins Publishers. Reprinted by permission; B—Mod-

sections—presented as two sets of mirror images—reveals impressive similarities. In each case we see the same basic pattern of white fiber tracts and gray nuclei. For example, two circumscribed white dots (black in C), one above the other, are located in the lower middle of each brain section. The lower of these two dots is a cross section of the fornix, one of the limbic system structures shown in Figure 3.2. The darker area around the fornix is the cross section of the hypothalamus, which contains other parts of the limbic system. The hypothalamus has many nuclei and areas that unfortunately we cannot easily see at this magnification. They are named for their positions, such as lateral (side), ventral (below), dorsal (above), and medial (middle). The upper white dot is the cross section of another limbic structure, the mammillothalamic tract, which connects the hypothalamus and thalamus. The thalamus is the relatively large gray mass dorsal and lateral to this tract. Many of the thalamic nuclei are also named for their position in the structure.

Fortunately for experimental studies of the brain, the structural comparability we see in Figure 3.3 is accompanied by a functional comparability. For example, in all four species, the hypothalamus has an important role in controlling aggression. This has facilitated generalization from lower animal studies to work with humans.

Since there will be extensive discussion of research done with the components of the limbic system, we will offer a brief preliminary description of its components here. It may be helpful for readers to refer to Figure 3.2 as we discuss the different structures. These structures are all interrelated—they are linked together both physically and functionally. Activity related to aggression that occurs in one structure may result in information being transmitted to another, producing an effect on the aggression. Much of the work with aggression we will examine has involved the limbic structures called the hippocampus and amygdala, located in the temporal (lower lateral) lobe of the brain. The amygdala has phylogenetically older corticomedial and newer basolateral subdivisions and important connections to the rest of the brain that have all been investigated especially thoroughly. Two other structures located in the middle of the base of the brain are the hypothalamus and thalamus. Both have numerous nuclei and several of them have been linked to aggression. Other limbic structures, such as the cingulate gyrus and septum (or septal area), also have been found to affect aggression.

ELECTRICAL BRAIN STIMULATION STUDIES

Neural Controls for Initiating Aggression

The early work employing electrical brain stimulation to produce aggression involved more or less general, somewhat subjective definitions of aggression. Typi-

---

ified from Gergen, J. A. & MacLean, P. D., *A stereotaxic atlas of the squirrel monkey's brain.* Published 1962, U.S. Government Printing Office. Reprinted by permission; C—Modified from Snider, R. S. & Niemer, W. T., *A stereotaxic atlas of cat brain.* Copyright © 1961, University of Chicago Press. Reprinted by permission; D—Modified from König, J. F. R. and Klippel, R. A., *The Rat Brain.* Copyright © 1963, Robert E. Krieger Publishing Co. Reprinted by permission.)

cally, an investigator stimulated the animal while it was alone in a cage or restraining chair. Cats were often used in early studies because of their availability, cranium uniformity, and richness of their emotional displays. If the animal appeared to be angry—that is, if it snarled or vocalized and perhaps manifested some autonomic reactions associated with emotions, such as pupillary dilation, piloerection, voiding, or salivating—the stimulation was considered to be evoking an aggressive reaction. Specific definitions of aggression varied between laboratories, which were located in different European countries and the United States. Despite these inconsistencies, early studies provided an important contribution to our understanding of the neural bases of aggression and an invaluable impetus to later work.

Hess was the first to elicit aggression. He reported that cats stimulated in the perifornical (around the fornix) and posterior areas of the hypothalamus would hiss, spit, and growl, lash out with unsheathed claws, and emit various autonomic responses such as hyperventilation, salivation, piloerection, and urination and defecation (Hess & Brügger, 1943). As demonstrated in later studies, this response typically builds with time, starting with an alerting reaction, continuing with increased piloerection and breathing, followed by increased hissing, standing in an arched-back posture, and then explosively striking out. Hess's findings were extended several years later by Kaada (1951), working in Norway. He produced an aggressive response in cats by stimulating the amygdala in the lateral and posterior regions of the basolateral area. He could not define particular nuclei where the stimulation was effective, but reported that zones were involved in the response. Investigations in the United States began with the study by MacLean and Delgado (1953), who stimulated the amygdala and hippocampus in cats. They also demonstrated the generality of the effect across species by showing that stimulation in squirrel monkeys produced directed attack and autonomic responses. Soon after in Italy, Zanchetti and Zoccolini (1954) reported that medial cerebellar stimulation in cats produced an aggressive response. Although the cerebellum is usually associated with sensorimotor coordination, recent work has led some to relate it to the limbic system. Other, non-limbic structures were involved in another United States study with cats and rhesus monkeys by Delgado (1955). Delgado was able to produce aggression by stimulating the ventroposterolateral (mercifully shortened to VPL) nucleus of the thalamus and the tectum (a brain stem structure) and its connections. Next, Hunsperger (1956), working in Germany, stimulated the central gray, in the brain stem of cats, to produce a response very much like what Hess and Brügger reported. Returning to the limbic system, workers showed some of the connecting fiber tracts could also be stimulated to produce aggression. Fernandez de Molina and Hunsperger (1959) stimulated the stria terminalis, which primarily connects the corticomedial region of the amygdala with the hypothalamus and septum, among other structures. Later, in England Hilton and Źbrozyna (1963) found increases in aggression from stimulation of the ventral amygdalofugal ("fleeing from the amygdala") pathway, which is thought to take information from the anterior amygdala to the lateral area of the hypothalamus.

A major advance in the methodology of studying aggression produced by brain stimulation occurred with the work by Wasman and Flynn (1962) in the United States. Instead of stimulating their cats in an isolated situation, they provided a target for them. This enabled investigators to determine whether the behavior would be directed.

As Wasman and Flynn and others have observed, brain stimulation, even in the presence of a target, will sometimes produce the various components of aggressive behavior without actual attack. Therefore, testing in the absence of a target could lead to incorrectly labeling a response as aggression. Although some early investigators utilized a target such as their gloved hand or a stick, they did not do this in a consistent, systematic way. For this reason, we must view the results of the early work cited above with caution. In Wasman and Flynn's work, the principal target was a live rat, although in brief tests, some aggression was also directed at other animals, including another cat, and at inanimate objects. We will consider the implications of these latter findings below. Wasman and Flynn selected cats that did not attack rats spontaneously and found that they could discriminate between two types of attack. **Affective attack**, apparently similar to that reported by Hess, occurred during stimulation of points more medial in the hypothalamus. In addition to the striking behaviors and autonomic activities Hess observed, the cats would direct first claw and then biting attacks against the rats, often injuring or killing them. During stimulation located more lateral in the hypothalamus, they observed **stalking attack,** when the cats typically displayed little autonomic activity or vocalization, but instead moved quietly around the cage, pinned the rat down, and killed it via bites to the back of its neck.

Several studies carried out in Flynn's laboratory extended his technique, although anesthetized rats were used, which spared the targets from pain and also controlled for the target's position and responses. Affective and stalking attack could be elicited from other areas of the brain such as from two sites in the brain-stem reticular formation (Sheard & Flynn, 1967) and in various other brain-stem areas. Also, Mac-Donnell and Flynn (1968) showed that stimulation of the medial thalamus of cats would produce attack against rats.

In the late 1960s, work with aggression elicited by brain stimulation was extended to rats. Thus, King and Hoebel (1968) demonstrated that rats would kill mice (muricide) during hypothalamic stimulation, and DeSisto and Huston (1971) reported that rats would kill frogs (ranacide) during brain stimulation. Both mice and frogs are natural predatory targets of rats (i.e., they are killed and consumed by wild rats), so these studies probably involve the same phenomenon as the stalking attack by cats found by Wasman and Flynn. Other stimulation work with rats produced behavior that by its description seems parallel to Wasman and Flynn's affective attack. This was reported as a response to hypothalamic stimulation (Panksepp, 1971; Woodworth, 1971) and both investigators used unanesthetized live rats as targets. Somewhat later, Kruk, Van der Poel and De Vos-Frerichs (1979) described an attack jumping response by rats against a frozen-rat model target.

Motivational Components of Aggression Produced by Brain Stimulation

Research with aggression elicited by brain stimulation showed that various motivational factors were involved in the types of aggression produced. In an early study, MacLean and Delgado (1953) reported that stimulation can produce aggression associated with fear. That is, the first response of their subjects was to escape the situation. When the subjects were restrained from flight, they would attack the person restraining them. Similar observations are common in both cats and rats. In other aggression work (Hutchinson & Renfrew, 1966), hunger motivation was implicated, as both eating and stalking attacks were produced. At various sites in the hypothalamus where relatively high-intensity stimulation elicited stalking attack, weaker stimulation produced eating. The cats, who were not hungry and otherwise would not eat, would approach and eat a dish of horse meat during the weaker stimulation, while stronger stimulation produced attack against a rat. A similar effect was found for stimulation of the cerebellum (Reis, Doba, & Nathan, 1973).

Relationships between aggression and motivational systems other than eating are suggested by comparisons across studies. Valzelli (1981) points out that common hypothalamic and hippocampal stimulation sites have been used to elicit aggression and maternal behavior as well as aggression and sexual behavior. Still other investigations have helped differentiate further between motivational characteristics of various types of aggression. They found that stimulation of brain loci that produced an aggressive response in squirrel monkeys was reinforcing and/or aversive, depending on the locus of stimulation (Renfrew, 1969). Later, Panksepp (1971) demonstrated this relationship for rats and also showed differential effects of the administration of a psychostimulant (an amphetamine). Affective attack was increased by the drug, while stalking attack was decreased. We will discuss the implications of this result for the chemical systems involved in Chapter 5.

Brain Structures and Types of Aggression

The facts that stimulation of different points in the brain produce apparently distinct types of aggression and that motivational and other characteristics associated with different points seem to differ have helped lead to the classification systems for types of aggression. Referring to Moyer's (1968) classification discussed in Chapter 1, for example, we see support for a neurological basis for his predatory aggression in the stalking attack reported by Wasman and Flynn. Valzelli pointed out possible neural bases for Moyer's maternal aggression and for sex-related aggression. MacLean and Delgado found a neural basis for fear-induced aggression. Bases for irritable and intermale aggression are not so clear, in that the affective attack elicited by brain stimulation might correspond to either one. Moyer (1976) categorized this affective attack as irritable aggression. Alternatively, what was labeled as affective attack might have been an example of fear-induced or sex-related aggression.

Unfortunately, published descriptions of the behaviors elicited by brain stimulation have not always been very precise, so it is difficult to determine what type of aggression is involved. Behaviors with one animal attacking another sometimes are simply labeled as aggression and no attempt is made to tie that aggression to one type or another. Part of this lack of precision is related to the difficulty of making observations of a rapidly moving pair of animals. At times researchers have made films, and they have helped to specify the behaviors involved more accurately. However, films are not always used, in part because of the expense of high-speed photography. Even when they are, it is not always possible to capture the subjects at just the right angle needed for a precise description of the interactions. Also, the intensity of these interactions cannot be recorded on film.

One result of this limited precision in measuring attack produced by brain stimulation is that it still is unclear whether there are separate neural bases for the different types of attack and to what extent these neural bases are distinct. While it would seem to make sense that if there are different types of aggression, different neural bases should exist for each, but this is not necessarily the case. Possibly a relatively small number of neural systems for attack are involved when any of a subset of conditions for attack occur or perhaps just one major system. The answer to the questions concerning these possibilities may have important ramifications for our understanding and treatment of human aggression. While all the questions have not yet been answered, many investigators have successfully attempted to pursue them.

Progress in Measuring Behaviors Involved in Aggression

A series of findings from studies of the environmental stimuli that elicit attack resulted in development of the methodology for more accurate measurement of attack produced by brain stimulation. First, investigators discovered that painful stimuli not only produce fighting between squirrel monkeys but also cause grabbing and biting of an inanimate target (Azrin, Hutchinson, & Sallery, 1964). This finding is incorporated in the definition of aggression in Chapter 1. Recall that the targets of aggression may include a variety of living and non-living things. The finding of inanimate target attack allowed scientists to develop an inanimate target that would provide automatic recording of aggressive responding. They used a hose attached to a pressure transducer so that they could record bites on the hose. This now allowed not only just dichotomous measurements of whether attack occurred, but also sensitive measurements of biting frequency and intensity patterns. That development facilitated the search for the existence and nature of differences in the way that distinct brain areas control such aggressive behavior. Instead of trying to detect and interpret aggressive behaviors via observation, the automatic method offered a detailed record of biting behaviors. In addition, as we pointed out earlier, this technique had other methodological and ethical advantages in that it involved elimination of a target animal whose position and reactions could not be controlled and was liable to be injured or killed. Although other investigators of the aggressive effects of brain stimulation either had utilized inanimate targets only briefly or without much success, it is possible to elicit consistent hose biting with brain stimulation in squirrel monkeys (Renfrew, 1969). However, progress in establishing brain stimulation-biting relationships was slow. Researchers could explore only a limited number of sites when fixed electrodes were used because of the space restraints in a small animal cranium. Further, misplaced electrodes resulted in further delays while another animal was prepared.

Many years ago, Bremer (1936) developed a neural preparation called *encéphale isolé*, involving a brain that was isolated from the rest of the nervous system by a spinal cord cut. This provided a functioning brain, easily accessible for electrode studies, that could be maintained in a highly controlled environment. Thus, the effects of brain stimulation could be determined while eliminating variability from inputs from the body and the animal's major movements. More recently, when it was observed that these animal preparations would bite a finger carelessly placed in their mouths, researchers decided to try applying the brain stimulation-biting technique to them. In an extensive series of studies, the Bremer technique was developed for squirrel monkeys and rats, norms for caring for them and controlling painful stimulation were established, and the relative normalcy of their responsivity and learning were demonstrated (Hutchinson & Renfrew, 1978). The effects of brain stimulation on hose biting were then measured. The animals were maintained, under local anesthesia, in a stereotaxic instrument (see p. 46). Therefore, investigators could place brain electrodes, assess the reactions to stimulation, and then move the electrodes. This moveable electrode procedure allowed for the study of dozens of neural sites in each animal, instead of the few possible with traditional fixed electrodes. A similar technique for intact (non-lesioned) cats has been developed by Flynn and his students (e.g., see Bandler, 1975) in order to find effective stimulation sites prior to fixing electrode positions for later, more traditional testing cage observations. However, no extensive measures of biting are made and typically researchers test only one effective neural site.

Two Principal Neural Systems for Aggression

Brain stimulation in *encéphale isolé* rats and monkeys produces several basic patterns of biting. One, which was expected, is that biting occurs during the onset of stimulation (ON). This corresponds to most of the older published observations of attack taking place during brain stimulation of intact animals in a testing chamber. The parallel findings also help validate this newer technique. It also was found that for some areas, biting occurs only after the offset of stimulation (OFF). While there had been a few reports of attack or irritability associated with stimulation of these areas, the exact stimulation-attack relationship was not always clear because of the imprecision of the observation technique used. The automatic bite recording system enabled investigators to observe the relationship easily. A third pattern that was found involves a combination of ON and OFF biting.

For us to more fully understand the nature of stimulation of the multitude of areas involved, we searched the literature for other effects. In areas where ON biting was produced, some investigators had reported aversive effects during stimulation. That is, such stimulation would be escaped or avoided if possible. (Individuals will increase behaviors that terminate or postpone it.) The neural sites include many areas of the brain, but are primarily in the limbic system and/or pain mediation structures, where body pain sensations are received and processed. Some pain mediation structures are part of the limbic system (see Figure 3.2), while others are interconnected with limbic structures. Included are the components in what has been called the Brain Aversive System, identified as those areas where various aversive effects of brain stimulation occur (see Melo, Cardoso, & Brandão, 1992). This system includes parts of the hypothalamus and central gray (see Figure 3.1) as well as parts of the amygdala (see Figure 3.2).

The literature search also revealed that at neural sites where OFF biting was found, many other studies have reported rewarding effects during stimulation. After the discovery by Olds and Milner (1954) that rats would learn a behavior that turns on brain stimulation, extensive work by Olds and others established that a system of interrelated structures mediated these "pleasurable" effects. The system involves components that run parallel to the aversive system (also described by Olds) in the brain stem and hypothalamus and includes the limbic system structures. While the offset of activity in this system can produce aggression, we will see later that onset of activity in the system can help limit aggression.

The stimulation work with the *encéphale isolé*, along with the analysis of other brain stimulation literature, suggests one answer to the questions raised earlier (see p. 44) about the neural bases of aggression. There are two principal systems involved when aggression occurs, and these may function separately or jointly. Activation of elements in a basic system that mediates aversive states (**Onset Aggression System**) produces aggressive behaviors during such activation. Termination of the activation of the system that mediates pleasurable states (**Offset Aggression System**) produces subsequent aggression. Combining activation of the two systems produces aggression both during and following the activation. As we will see in Chapter 6, the effects of activating the two systems probably correspond to two major environmental factors that produce aggression. The onset of aversive environmental stimuli, such as painful stimuli, can produce aggression. Also, the offset of reinforcing environmental stimuli, by removing or blocking access to them, which happens in frustration, is a common cause of aggression.

Neural Subsystems for Attack Types

Although the Onset and Offset Aggression Systems constitute the two principal neural systems that underlie aggression, the observations by Flynn and others that different types of attack can be elicited by brain stimulation suggests the existence of subsystems that may supplement the principal systems. The recordings of biting by the *encéphale isolé* animals also support the existence of subsystems. In the original studies of biting, researchers realized that replicable specific biting patterns occur during stimulation of a site. For example, ON biting might occur with a high frequency for some sites and a lower one for others. Some bites are very intense, others more weak. Further studies were designed to explore these specific patterns. They found that certain patterns would occur, specific to the site being stimulated, in any animal that was tested. That is, the patterns are characteristic of the neural areas, not the individual animals. These patterns can be characterized by the frequency, intensity, latency, and regularity of the biting as well as by whether they occurred at the onset or offset of stimulation. It is possible for us to distinguish distinct biting patterns related to different areas of the hypothalamus (Renfrew, 1981).

Figure 3.4 illustrates several distinct biting patterns for three hypothalamic structures as well as for the central gray in the midbrain. This finding expanded on the earlier, more broad statements about the two general types of biting patterns: ON, which occurs with the onset of aversive stimulation; and OFF, which occurs with the offset of reinforcing stimulation. It also gave support to the idea that different types of aggression may be characterized in part by different biting patterns, which might supplement other work differentiating types of aggression. For example, the neural systems involved in stalking and affective attack were described some time ago by Chi and Flynn (1971). They lesioned hypothalamic structures where stimulation could produce aggression and traced the resulting degeneration of the neural structures connected to these areas.

The stalking attack system of the cat brain includes particular hypothalamic, thalamic, and brain-stem structures, while the affective system contains different hypo-

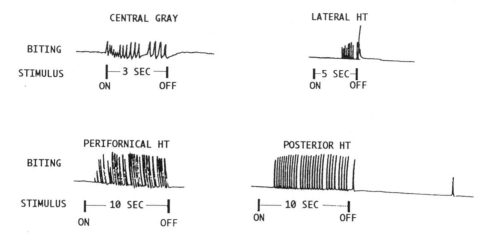

Figure 3.4   Biting patterns produced during onset and after offset of electrical stimulation of four brain areas associated with aggression. These patterns are distinct in terms of latency, increases and decreases or consistency in intensity, and existence and relative intensity of offset biting.

thalamic and midbrain structures. Studies have shown that stimulation of the connected structures of each system produces the respective type of aggression. It would be interesting to determine whether consistent patterns of biting are also produced. If they are, this would be evidence for the maintained integrity of the aggression-controlling circuits. However, some subtle change in the patterns might also be found that may have been missed by traditional observation techniques. This would not be entirely unexpected, considering that the different parts of the systems have distinct connections with other neural areas. The result of such a study would aid our understanding of the way in which neural circuits help control aggression. Such an approach also could be carried out for neural areas involved in other types of aggression. The discovery of similar biting patterns elicited by stimulation of different areas would lend support to these areas being part of the same aggression system. Such a finding would then be supported by testing the aggressive behaviors elicited in intact animals when stimulated in these areas as well as by neural degeneration studies, such as those done by Chi and Flynn.

Changes in Body Mechanisms for Aggression Produced by Brain Stimulation

The specific nature of the way in which brain structures control aggression has not been completely determined, but some progress has been made. As indicated earlier in our discussion of genetic mechanisms, there is no inheritance of increased aggression *per se*, but of some mechanisms that facilitate aggression. In the case of brain structures, genetic studies such as those of Lagerspetz (1979) have found differences in neural structures between aggressive and nonaggressive strains, but what does this imply? One possible answer is that the more well-developed structures might augment emotional reactions. For example, we know that the hypothalamus helps to control the autonomic nervous system, so the autonomic emotional effects that accompany aggression would be increased via different development of these areas in aggressive strains. Genetic influences also might aid aggression-linked sensorimotor mechanisms such as those found to be enhanced during aggression elicited by brain stimulation. MacDonnell and Flynn (1966) found that tactile sensitivity around the mouth of cats was increased during stimulation. Thresholds decreased (it was easier) for the elicitation of head turning toward the side of a touch and for mouth opening to a contact on the lips. Bandler and Flynn (1972) showed how stimulation increases the number of cat foreleg areas where paw striking can be elicited in response to touch. Bandler and Abeyewardene (1981) demonstrated that visual stimuli were more critical than auditory or olfactory ones for a stimulated cat to find its prey and suggested that brain stimulation of some areas enhances the visual mechanisms used to locate an attack object. The sensorimotor changes produced by brain stimulation make sense when we consider the necessary components for a cat to be successful in predation. By "priming" the response mechanisms, the cat will be able to respond more readily—for example, to turn its head toward the side where a mouse is and open its mouth when it is in contact with the mouse. If these movements had to be carried out only after the cat "recognized" the mouse and then "decided" that it should try to catch the mouse, the neural processing time for these perceptive and cognitive activities might be so long that it would allow a prudent mouse ample time to escape. While the same specific considerations might not seem to apply to humans, the activation of the sympathetic branch of the autonomic nervous system that often occurs during both lower animal and human aggression helps enhance sensory functions and carry out more rapid or forceful responding by supplying more oxygen and energy to critical areas. There are also indications of radical drops in sensory thresholds during aggression associated with brain seizures, as we will discuss in the following chapter.

Neural Controls for the Limitation of Aggression

We must also understand how aggression is not ubiquitous—that it may occur rarely or never in some situations—and how it is terminated once it occurs. Some brain stimulation studies have helped explain how neural mechanisms aid in limiting aggression. In many, if not all, cases, stimulation occurs in the brain structures of the Offset Aggression System. Here the predominant effect is related to the pleasurable state produced by the onset of such stimulation. Any aggression occurring at the offset of the stimulation may not have been noted.

Most investigations have used brain stimulation to inhibit or terminate aggression produced by external factors, while some have demonstrated how stimulation in one area can inhibit aggression produced by stimulation in another. These studies sometimes help illustrate how the two areas are neurally linked. An early example of this approach was the study by Egger and Flynn (1963), who demonstrated that hypothalamically elicited attack could be decreased by basolateral amygdaloid stimulation. Later, Siegel and Flynn (1968) reported that stimulation in the dorsal (top) hippocampus could inhibit aggression. Stimulation of other limbic system structures, such as the septum (Siegel & Skog, 1970; Potegal, Blau, & Glusman, 1981) and the cingulate (Siegel & Chabora, 1971), has been found to decrease aggression, although cingulate stimulation also may increase it, depending on the subsection involved. Some areas of the hypothalamus have also been linked to the inhibition of aggression. Adamec (1976), for example, reported that predatory attack was inhibited by stimulation of the ventromedial area of the hypothalamus (VMH) and the mammillary bodies, an adjacent limbic system structure. Food deprivation, which increased predation, decreased activity in these inhibitory areas. (Inhibition of an inhibitor may increase a response, just as double negatives in English cancel each other, or two minuses multiplied create a positive in mathematics.)

Stimulation of two brain-stem structures has been reported to inhibit aggression, assumedly because of the neurochemical effects produced. Sheard (1974) found that rats were less aggressive toward mice during raphe nucleus stimulation. The raphe system (see Figure 3.1) is the primary source of serotonin in the brain. We will discuss serotonin's function in aggression more fully later, but for now let us note that Sheard's work suggests an inhibitory function. Renfrew and LeRoy (1983) stimulated an area in the posterior midbrain central gray that has been identified as a source of endogenous opiates (opiate-like substances originating from within the body). This stimulation resulted in the suppression of an aggressive response elicited by pain. Thus, we can see that these chemicals can also help inhibit aggression. Knowledge of the various neural areas associated with the inhibition of aggression may be useful not only for understanding why aggression is sometimes uncontrolled but also for developing means of controlling it, possibly with techniques that increase the activity of these inhibitory centers.

BRAIN LESION STUDIES

The work with brain stimulation has shown how the activities of particular structures of the brain are involved in producing and limiting aggression. Lesion studies have often provided complementary information on the roles of these structures. As we noted earlier, researchers have discovered the functions of some neural structures by how stimulation increases those functions or how lesions result in a loss of those functions. Lesion studies are also used to study the functions of larger parts of the brain that cannot be stimulated effectively because of their size. Lesions may result in either an increase or a decrease in aggression and we will discuss them according to their different effects.

Evidence for Structures That Inhibit Aggression

Many problems associated with human aggression appear after brain lesions occur. The present section will describe what lower animal lesion studies have revealed about neural factors in aggression. For example, several brain areas have been assigned an inhibitory role in aggression, primarily because lower animal studies demonstrated the disinhibitory effects of lesions in them. Goltz's study (1892), in which neocortical lesions in dogs were shown to increase aggression, was followed by a series of studies with cats by Cannon, Bard, and their colleagues that involved lesions of the neocortex as well as other structures (Bard, 1928; Bard & Mountcastle, 1948; Bard & Rioch, 1937; Cannon & Britton, 1925). (These and other structures can be identified from the human brain illustrations, Figures 3.1 and 3.2.) Not only neocortical lesions but also lesions of components of the Offset Aggression system, including the limbic cortex, the thalamus, and the anterior hypothalamus, resulted in increased rage behavior in which cats would viciously attack individuals who came near them. This impressive display of aggression was sometimes referred to as "sham rage" because it seemed to involve disorganized, explosive behaviors that occurred in response to otherwise innocuous stimuli such as stroking the cat's back. However, careful observations show that this rage is organized because it is directed toward contact with a target. Only when the lesions encompassed the posterior hypothalamus (part of the Onset Aggression System) as well as all structures anterior to it were the attack behaviors fragmented and disorganized (Bard, 1928).

Rage reactions have been reported to follow lesions of two small components of the Offset Aggression System, the septal area in rats (Brady & Nauta, 1953) and the VMH, or the ventromedial nucleus of the hypothalamus, in cats (Wheatley, 1944). Both lesions also result in increases in consummatory behaviors, with septal lesions followed by increased drinking and VMH area lesions by increased eating. As with Bard's cats, the animals become hypersensitive to stimuli. Some researchers have suggested that the rage is false, but tests show that while the behavior is wild, it does result in regular target contact. More recently, Vergnes and Karli (1963) reported increases in aggression by rats following olfactory bulb lesions. They attributed this to removal of inhibition over the corticomedial amygdala, which facilitates hypothalamic mechanisms for attack. Vergnes and her associates (Vergnes, Penot, Kempf, & Mack, 1977) also found increased muricide (mouse killing) by their rats following raphe system lesions, which lowered brain serotonin levels. This result, as well as those of several studies cited here, complement other work involving inhibitory effects of stimulation of other brain structures in the Offset Aggression System. However, since whole cortical areas cannot be stimulated simultaneously, there are no extensive complementary studies for the neo- and limbic cortex, although some evidence exists for pleasurable effects of brain stimulation at points in these structures.

Evidence for Structures Important in Producing Aggression

Support for the role of several structures in the Onset Aggression System as facilitators of aggression comes from lesion studies in which aggression is decreased. Hunsperger (1956) studied the relative importance of the hypothalamus and the central gray of the midbrain by lesioning one or the other in cats and assessing the effect on aggression elicited by brain stimulation of the other structure or by the presence of a dog. He found that the central gray was more critical; without it, hypothalamic stimulation did not elicit aggression. But without a hypothalamus, central gray stimulation still elicited aggression. Supporting Hunsperger were Ellison and Flynn's results (1968); they found that even when the hypothalamus was isolated from the rest of the brain via knife cuts, it was still possible to elicit predatory and affective aggression by brain stimulation in other areas. Also, the cats still reacted to external stimuli such as a tail pinch, and would visually follow a mouse.

The studies of Hunsperger and Ellison and Flynn do not show that the hypothalamus has no role in aggression, only that it is not the only structure involved. Indeed,

Karli and Vergnes (1964) reported that muricidal behavior was suppressed by lateral hypothalamic lesions. Eating was also lost, but was recovered later, followed by aggression. Adams (1971) reported loss of an aggressive behavior, specifically territorial aggression, following lateral hypothalamic lesions. These two results may seem contradictory, since they found that the same lesions affect different types of aggression. However, the testing conditions involved different target species. The muricidal behavior, which Karli and Vergnes also refer to as neophobia, occurs when a strange mouse is introduced into the rat's area. This may be functionally parallel to Adam's test of putting a strange rat into the territory of his rat subject.

Lesion studies have provided evidence that structures of the Onset Aggression System outside the hypothalamus and central gray have roles in aggression. Kanki and Adams (1978) showed that visually based irritable aggression elicited by foot shock is reduced in rats with ventrobasal thalamic lesions. Earlier, Sprague, Chambers, and Stellar (1961) had shown that lesions of an input to the thalamus—the medial lemniscus—reduced aggression of cats toward dogs and mice; that is, both affective and predatory aggressive responses were eliminated. These examples are just a few that demonstrate via lesion techniques how various structures are involved in controlling different types of aggression.

A Study with Major Impact on the Treatment of Humans

A report of decreased aggression following brain lesions may be one of the most important brain experiments ever done because of the ramifications of its results in treating human aggression. Klüver and Bucy (1939) performed temporal lobectomies (removal of the temporal lobe; see Figure 3.2) in rhesus monkeys and reported a series of behavioral changes known as the Klüver-Bucy syndrome. These changes include hypersexuality, hyperactivity, increased oral testing of objects, loss of fear to previously avoided stimuli, and, most significant, a marked taming effect. Laboratory monkeys, unless trained, are usually very aggressive toward their handlers. The Klüver-Bucy subjects became quite docile after the brain surgery. Later, Schreiner and Kling (1953) showed that the critical lesion area for producing the Klüver-Bucy effects, including taming, was the amygdala. Others have reported similar effects from amygdala lesions in several species. However, other studies raised some questions about the universality of the effect and its nature. Rosvold, Mirsky, and Pribram (1954), for example, reported increased aggression in a food competition test and found that different results depended on whether testing was done in pairs or groups of animals. Kling (1972) discovered that lesioned animals released into a natural, free-ranging situation were socially inept (they did not adhere to the hierarchical norms of their group), and usually died of hunger. Essentially, their behaviors were more deficient in social communication than simply being less aggressive. Despite the discrepancies in the findings associated with amygdala lesions, the work of Klüver and Bucy has been used to support attempts to decrease human aggression via brain lesions or psychosurgery. We will discuss the results of such attempts in the following chapter, along with critical analyses of these studies.

SUMMARY

For us to better understand how various brain areas are involved in aggression, experimental techniques are used to change brain functions. The activity of an area is increased by stimulation or terminated by lesions, and researchers study the resulting changes in aggressive behavior to determine if the area is involved in the production or the inhibitory control of aggression. Since these areas are usually deep within the brain, scientists use the stereotaxic technique to place electrodes or other devices for stimulation or lesioning.

Important neural influences on aggression are found in the brain stem and limbic system. Because these components are very similar in lower animals and humans, use of lower animals in studies of brain function is widespread.

Stimulation studies have shown that various types of aggressive behaviors can be produced in several species. Primary areas are in components of the hypothalamus, amygdala, and the central gray of the midbrain. Effects have been linked in some cases to other motivational mechanisms such as for fear and eating. These effects involve changes in sensory and motor functions that facilitate aggression.

Methodological developments have made it possible to objectively study the patterns of biting, a common component of aggression, and compare the patterns produced by stimulation of many brain areas. Parallels have been found between two major types of environmental events that produce aggression and the ways in which brain stimulation contributes to aggression; either by the onset of aversive events or the offset of pleasurable states. The two principal neural systems for aggression, which correspond to these environmental effects, are called the Onset Aggression System and the Offset Aggression System. In addition, at least two subsystems supplement the principal systems when different types of aggression occur.

Some neural areas, usually from the Offset Aggression System, where the onset of stimulation produces a pleasurable state, have been found to contribute to decreases in aggression by direct inhibitory influences over parts of the Onset Aggression System. Other areas are involved with neurochemicals that decrease aggression.

Brain lesion studies have shown how the neocortex and other higher structures help inhibit the Onset Aggression System, since aggression increases after lesions of these areas. Studies of lesions of the Offset Aggression System structures complement stimulation studies that suggest their inhibitory role in aggression during their activation. Lesion studies that result in decreased aggression support important roles of the central gray and parts of the hypothalamus in the systems for producing aggression.

Klüver and Bucy's finding of reduced aggression following lesions involving the amygdala resulted in attempts to control human aggression, despite some inconsistencies in subsequent studies. We will describe the application to problems of human aggression of the results of these and other studies in the next chapter.

Suggested Readings

Netter, F. H. (1983). *Nervous system: Part I. Anatomy and physiology*. West Caldwell, NJ: CIBA Pharmaceutical Co.

Valzelli, L. (1981). *Psychobiology of aggression and violence*. New York: Raven.

CHAPTER 4
Neuropsychology and Human Aggression

The previous chapter described how two basic neural systems—the Onset Aggression System, involving aversive states, and the Offset Aggression system, involving pleasurable ones—are implicated in producing and limiting aggression. The work forming the bases of the discussion used lower animals. This chapter will examine studies done with humans in order to (1) assess the generalizability of the results from lower animal studies to humans, and (2) describe attempts to apply what has been learned from lower animal experiments to understanding and controlling human aggression. The term "neuropsychology" in this chapter's title refers to the body of work that primarily concerns the relationships of human brain dysfunctions to human behavioral problems. An even more explicit term would be **clinical neuropsychology,** to distinguish it from the work in **experimental neuropsychology**, which is what we discussed in the last chapter.

Human brain dysfunctions often involve effects parallel to those of the stimulation or lesion studies done with lower animals. We will describe some sources of these dysfunctions, along with their relations to aggressive behaviors. We will also examine several unusual electrical brain wave patterns found in aggressive individuals.

Once scientists discover a brain dysfunction, various treatments are suggested from the nature of the dysfunction. While the treatments we describe here are biologically based, some nonbiological therapies are also used. The biological treatments include neurosurgery to remove damaged tissue, and psychosurgery, which may involve removal of healthy tissue that helps produce aggression. We will explore various psychosurgical studies, along with critical assessments of their procedures.

Brain stimulation has been practiced on humans for many therapeutic ends. We will review several studies of stimulation increasing or decreasing aggression since they contribute to our understanding of how the brain controls aggression.

GENERALIZING FROM LOWER ANIMAL STUDIES TO HUMANS

The brain stimulation and lesion studies done with lower animals have provided information on which brain structures are involved in the Onset and Offset Aggression Systems, as well as how structures of the Offset System serve in limiting aggression. The question then arises: can this information be applied to understanding how the human brain works in the control of aggression? The answer would indicate if the human neural controls function in a way parallel to those for lower animals and if the same brain areas are involved. As Chapter 3 indicated, there are close structural similarities between the brains of humans and lower animals, especially in subcortical regions. Although the human brain is bigger than that of most other animals and has a very highly developed neocortex, it still shares most of the fundamental **structural** elements that have been implicated in aggression in other animals. Further, many studies have illustrated parallels in the **functions** of these elements. Consequently, it is very probable that aggressive functions will turn out to be similar in both humans and lower animals. If so, we still are not saying that aggression is controlled in exactly the same way with humans as with lower animals. After all, we must still consider the important influence of the development of the neocortex and other structural differences. However, it is most important for us to be aware of the potential contributions of subcortical mechanisms since they can be critical determining factors in human aggression. This occurs in two different ways: (1) in the abnormal, dysfunctional brain, aggression-inhibiting structures may not be functioning or aggressive centers may be directly excited; or (2) in the normal brain, the influence of subcortical aggression centers might predominate at times, for various reasons. Some investigators (e.g., Valzelli, 1981) view the second case as one in which the individual brain "regresses." Aggression is elevated as a result of dominance by the more primitive subcortical structures that humans share with the lower animals.

Apart from the desirability of determining if and how the two basic neural systems for aggression function in the human brain, it would be valuable for us to determine if a human parallel exists to the subsystems for types of aggression found in lower animals. If various types of human aggression exist, as they do in animal aggression, it might be expected that they would function in a similar way. That is, different neural structures would control each type, and different variables would affect each type. For example, sexual hormones would have more effect on some types of aggression, as would environmental variables such as pain or the sex of the other person present. Prior to determining the influence of these independent variables, however, we must be able to identify the dependent variables—the various types of aggression. Unfortunately, very few innate behaviors can be examined in humans in order to determine links with biological brain functions. Some possibilities are the activities associated with the autonomic nervous system, body gestures, facial expressions, and, perhaps, jaw clenching. Little definitive work has been done with any of these activities. For example, general autonomic activation is associated with human rage, and Netter (1983, pp. 216-217) provides a dramatic illustration of this in his medical book on the nervous system. He shows an image of a furious man, with numerous participating organs and body parts, along with the brain structures controlling the rage reaction. However, researchers have not established specific subcategories of autonomic patterns related to different types of aggression. Hutchinson et al. (Hutchinson, Pierce, Emley, Proni, & Sauer, 1977) studied jaw clenching and measured different electromyographic (EMG) patterns associated with two clenching patterns. However, these patterns have not been linked to different types of aggression. As Moyer (1976) points out, detection of the different types of aggression in humans is complicated by the extensive learning influences that modify not only aggressive behaviors but also the relations between these behaviors and their associated stimuli and targets. Because of these complications, differentiating types of aggression in humans remains to be accomplished, and their very existence has yet to be demonstrated definitively. However, evidence suggests that some types do seem to occur, and that may help us comprehend the control of human aggression.

SOURCES OF NEUROPSYCHOLOGICAL PROBLEMS

Brain dysfunctions that may produce problems with aggression have many sources, some operating alone and some in conjunction with others. A convenient way to consider these sources is chronologically, starting with a brief treatment of genetic sources and then progressing to prenatal, birth, and postnatal sources.

We discussed genetic sources of dysfunction at length in Chapter 2. Recall that these sources may include effects that damage the brain or impair its normal function. The Lesch-Nyhan syndrome is one example of such an effect, which in this case is **hereditary** or genetically passed by a parent along to the offspring. Further genetic dysfunctions may result from chromosomal mutations in the sex cells of the parents that are produced by events during the development of those cells. These **congenital** genetic abnormalities may be caused by such factors as irradiation, environmental pollutants, or legal or illegal drug use.

Prenatal sources of brain dysfunction may occur because of some of these same environmental factors, except now the damage occurs directly to the fetus and alters the brain's normal developmental course. Even drugs that have been prescribed by a physician to help maintain a pregnancy have had disastrous side effects on the fetus. Maternal illness or accidents, stress, and inappropriate nutrition may also be important sources of fetal brain dysfunction. In addition, disturbances in the placental system or umbilical cord may contribute to neurological problems.

During the birth process, the brain may be damaged in several ways. During a long labor or because of an abnormal fetus position, anoxia might occur as the umbilical oxygen supply is impeded. Drugs used to aid the birth process, such as excessive anesthesia, might also cause neural damage. Finally, physical trauma might result from conflict between pelvic size and fetal head size or because of the use of forceps to aid delivery. Although many procedural improvements now reduce such sources of damage, they have not been completely eliminated, even where more advanced medicine is practiced, and they still are important factors in less well-developed countries or regions.

Postnatal factors resulting in brain dysfunction include some that affect brain development, such as poor nutrition, and others that may directly damage it. In the latter category are illnesses, such as encephalitis, and the concomitants of illness, such as febrile convulsions. Brain damage may also occur from trauma or tumors. Even if tumors are not directly involved in neural damage, they may produce damage by exerting pressure on other neural structures or interrupting the circulation of cerebrospinal fluid. Cysts may have a similar effect. Cerebrovascular accidents (strokes) may occur when the blood supply to a region of the brain is lost because of hypertension, arteriosclerosis, or aneurysm, with resulting damage to that brain region.

SEIZURE DISORDERS AND AGGRESSION

Seizure disorders, commonly known as epilepsy, which involve excessive, disorganized electrical brain activity, may follow brain damage from a number of sources (symptomatic), although a specific cause usually is not found (idiopathic). Continued seizure activity itself may produce brain damage. Epileptic seizures sometimes cause bizarre motor effects such as rhythmic contractions of parts or all of the body and may involve alterations of consciousness. Further, seizure disorders are found in some brain- damaged individuals who also have intellectual deficits. Thus, the common term "epilepsy" has negative connotations for many, and suggestions that epileptics can be dangerously aggressive are easily accepted. However, little evidence supports such suggestions, especially in the non-institutionalized population. Because of the stigma accompanying the label of epilepsy, professionals now more frequently employ the term "seizure disorder."

One type of seizure disorder, temporal lobe or psychomotor, is of special interest in studying aggression because of claims that it is occasionally associated with increased levels of violence. Although seizure disorders are found in only 2 percent of the population and only 18 percent of this population experience psychomotor attacks (Berkow, 1987), this still constitutes almost one million people in the United States alone. This great number of potential aggressors represented by even a fraction of such a population merits examination. We should make clear, however, that the existence of psychomotor aggression has been disputed for some time (e.g., see Siann, (1985), and that even those investigators who support the link of this seizure disorder to such aggression do not state that all temporal lobe patients—and certainly not all the total population of people with seizure disorders—are likely to be aggressive.

The temporal lobe contains the amygdala and the hippocampus, two limbic structures linked to the control of aggression from extensive research. Thus, there is support for the association of temporal lobe dysfunction with aggression, if we assume that excessive activation of these structures occurs during the seizures or that some structural abnormalities exist in these structures that may affect their function. For example, a history of seizure activity may result in a lowered threshold of excitability for the limbic structures (Devinsky & Bear, 1984). During a temporal lobe seizure, a person typically does not exhibit the convulsive behaviors and loss of consciousness often associated with seizure disorders. Instead, he or she remains conscious and is able to move around. However, the person may be confused and not maintain normal interactions with the environment as well as exhibit automatisms (repetitive motor behaviors) such as lipsmacking and purposeless motor movements. The individual may also experience emotions such as fear, anxiety, and, at times, anger. More important, when not having seizures, the person acts in a more natural way and is alert and attentive but may be easily provoked to commit aggression, either in a relatively brief outburst or over a long period of time.

Problems with aggression are more likely to occur in children and youth with temporal lobe disorders. Many reported cases also involve aggressive adults, but they are more likely to suffer from depression (Serafetinides, 1970). Indeed, a relatively high incidence of depressive and schizophrenic psychoses is associated with temporal lobe disorders in adults (Berkow, 1987). As we will see in Chapter 13, these psychoses are in themselves involved with aggressive problems, resulting in confusion concerning whether any aggression is related to the seizure disorder or the psychosis. In temporal lobe patients who are aggressive, researchers have observed aggression during the ictus, or seizure (see Monroe & Lion, 1978). After the seizure, the patient may exhibit amnesia for what occurred during it. However, such ictal aggression is generally considered rare. More reports of aggression have been made for the interictal (between seizure) period. For example, Falconer, Hill, Meyer, and Wilson (1958) reported that 38 of the 50 temporal lobe patients they studied were persistently aggressive. Change in sexual orientation or activity has been reported to accompany it, along with hyperreligiosity, hypergraphia (extensive writing), and various neurotic and psychotic problems (Rossi, Marino, & Yazigi, 1979). Pontius (1984) described eight patients who were extremely violent and whose rage would occur as an explosive reaction to some event and suggested that a neural imbalance was responsible for their failure to control limbic system impulses to violence. Fenwick (1989) deplores the negative attitudes that the populace has concerning epilepsy and indicates how uncontrolled seizure behaviors can be misinterpreted as aggression. However, he also discusses how aggression can occur prior to, during, or following a seizure, although he questions the relationship between interictal aggression and epilepsy.

Drug treatments may partially or fully control the seizures involved in psychomotor disorders. Phenytoin (Dilantin) is an anticonvulsant that historically has been extensively employed, and carbamazepine (Tegretol) has been found especially useful for temporal lobe disorders. Many other drugs are available, and new ones being developed. Thus, if a patient is insensitive to a drug or disturbed by such side effects as nausea and memory loss, another can be tried. However, in 15 percent of cases, no reduction in seizures can be obtained with drug treatment. Sometimes the drug treatment decreases the seizures but does not affect the behavioral problem (Devinsky & Bear, 1984). Neurosurgery will occasionally be performed on people experiencing symptomatic seizure disorders in an attempt to remove the lesion producing the seizures. We discuss this procedure later in this chapter.

EEG ACTIVITY ASSOCIATED WITH AGGRESSION

Scientists have measured the brain's electrical activity in their attempts to diagnose seizure disorders as well as search for EEG correlates of aggression. Typically, the procedure involves placing a large number of electrodes on the patient's scalp at standardized positions. Recording is done simultaneously between selected pairs of electrodes and registered on a multi-pen electroencephalograph or magnetic tape. The record from each pair represents the activity of perhaps millions of neurons, primarily cortical, that underlie the electrode pair. In rare instances, depth electrodes, placed with the stereotaxic technique, have also been used to record from subcortical structures.

Various problems are involved in studying the EEG. In temporal lobe disorder, for example, the EEG is expected to show abnormally high, sharp "spike" waves or abnormal slowing in recordings from electrodes over the temporal lobes. However, a certain proportion, perhaps 10 to 15 percent, of the EEGs of temporal lobe patients will not reveal such abnormalities. This would constitute a Type II error or a miss, as defined in the first chapter. Type I or false alarm errors also occur with EEGs, at about the same rate, as apparently abnormal activities are registered from normal brains. If doctors take only one EEG which is common because of the time and expense involved, the error rate might be higher. Ajmone-Marsan and Ziven (1970) studied more than 300 known cases of seizure disorder and could identify only 55 percent by means of one EEG recording session. Repeated recording sessions yielded a detection rate of 92 percent. To facilitate such detection, researchers sometimes use various neural activation techniques to help identify neural supersensitivity associated with seizure disorders. For example, they may use photic or auditory stimuli such as flashing lights or a recording, or the patient may be asked to hyperventilate. Drugs may be used to remove neural inhibitory influences or directly facilitate seizures. However, these activation techniques are not universally employed.

Despite the limitations of EEG studies, some interesting correlations have been found between particular EEG activities and problems with aggression. These correlations may prove helpful in identifying future problem cases and increasing our understanding of the neural involvement with aggression. A general finding that supports this hope is that while only 5 to 15 percent of normal children have abnormal EEGs, 50 to 60 percent with behavioral problems have such abnormalities (Monroe, 1970).

A principal way of characterizing brain activity is by its frequency. This is expressed in peaks of electrical activity that occur each second, or **hertz (Hz)**. Different frequency ranges are given Greek letter labels within the usual 1 to 30 Hz frequency spectrum. Typically, particular frequency ranges are predominant in particular neural regions and under particular conditions of arousal, waking, or sleeping. Deviations from the norms may represent deviations in the activities of the source structures. One such deviation was found in theta (6–8 Hz) waves from the temporal lobe. Monroe, Balis, and McCulloch (1978) and Williams, (1969) observed higher incidences of theta waves in aggressive youths and in murderers with a history of unmotivated, habitual aggression. Aggression was more likely to occur interictally in these cases.

In an early study of EEG and crime, Monroe (1970) discussed the 6- and 14-Hz positive (upward on recording) spikes—possibly from the hypothalamus—that have been found in people with various problems, including impulsive behaviors (reckless, inconsiderate of others, sometimes harming them) rage, theft, arson, sexual crimes, and unprovoked murders. In a population of children and young adolescents whose EEGs contained the spikes, 72 percent were classified as impulsive, 58 percent had school conduct problems, and only 1 to 3 percent were normal. Monroe implies that for some reason an increased amount of activity occurs in the hypothalamic structures associated with aggression. However, we should note that some unanswered questions concern the normal incidence of such spikes and whether the EEG samples taken were representative. Further, this is a correlative study, so it does not demonstrate causation, but supports the involvement of the hypothalamic structures in aggression.

Lorimer (1972) found evidence for the function of the frontal lobes in aggression. He recorded 30- to 40- Hz brief frontal-lobe bursts of neuronal activity that occurred especially during the early stages of sleep. Also, contrary to seizure disorder patients, these individuals had high thresholds for seizures. Their aggressive behaviors, which included senseless, animalistic acts, were associated with sensory disturbances, gastro-intestinal upset, blackouts, fight-flight reactions, and states of "furor."

Instead of focusing on the specific EEG activities we previously discussed, many studies have taken a broader approach in examining the relationship between abnormal EEGs and aggression or between other signs of brain dysfunction and aggression. Results of such studies are helpful because they determine the association between brain dysfunction and aggression; however, they are limited since they are correlational and often not very specific concerning the structures involved. For example, Nelson (1974) obtained EEGs from a population of 194 prisoners, including 100 non-psychotics, 56 aggressive psychotics, and 38 non-aggressive psychotics, and found 40 abnormal EEGs, with the highest number from the aggressive psychotics. Other studies of highly aggressive mental patients have found increased incidences of variables associated with brain dysfunction, such as familial seizure disorder, brain trauma from various sources, neurological impairment, and hyperactivity.

The neurological impairment in some aggressive mental patients is measured by abnormalities found during neurological tests. These abnormalities may involve sensory functions, such as extreme sensitivity to touch or light, motor difficulties, such as problems in following commands to move a limb, or lack of strength in specific muscles, or reflexes, such as pupillary response to light or skeletal muscle reactions to stretch. In cases where a seizure disorder is suspected but not supported by an EEG, a combination of these may be taken as a "soft" sign of the disorder.

The hyperactivity manifested by some aggressive mental patients refers to Attention-Deficit/Hyperactivity Disorder (ADHD), the psychiatric classification thought by some to involve a subnormal level of central nervous system arousal, characterized in part by higher thresholds for reactions to stimulation, accompanied by problems in attending to environmental events. The biological involvement in many cases is supported by the success of psychostimulants, such as methylphenidate (Ritalin) and dextroamphetamine in controlling hyperactivity. However, we should recognize that much controversy surrounds this condition concerning its causes and the advisability and efficacy of using drugs to treat it. For example, it is possible that its origins are environmental factors that produce a physiological effect and treatment of that physiological aspect would not address the basic causal factor. Nevertheless, some investigators have noted the aggressiveness associated with hyperactivity and how it may be reduced by psychostimulants. Alpert, Cohen, Shaywitz, and Piccirillo (1981) point to similar aggression problems in some antisocial delinquents and adults that also have been reduced with psychostimulants. This reduction suggests that similar neurological bases may underlie all of these cases.

Lewis, Shanak, Pincus, and Glaser (1981) explored the possible links of aggression to neurological dysfunction, such as those found in psychomotor disorders or other, less specific types of dysfunction. They studied almost 300 court-referred clinical cases for symptoms of seizure disorder and discovered an incidence that was about 20 times that of a normal population. They performed EEGs on some of the 18 individuals suspected of having a seizure disorder; 11 showed definite or possible abnormalities, with three abnormalities involving the temporal lobe. Of the 18 suspected individuals, 78 percent had either a current or past charge of assault or murder, while only 10 percent of the rest of the cases involved such charges.

Lewis's group also studied approximately 100 boys who resided in a correctional school. The investigators obtained ratings for their subjects' levels of violence and for neurological signs—the soft signs discussed above—of psychomotor dysfunction; they also obtained EEGs for about three-quarters of them. Perhaps the study's strongest finding was that 98.6 percent of the 78 most violent boys had more than one sign of neurological dysfunction, and 30 percent of those who were tested had abnormal EEGs. Two-thirds of the 19 least violent boys had more than one neurological sign, and none of those tested had abnormal EEGs. However, there are some difficulties with the methodology of Lewis's group. Their categorizations of neurological dysfunction are not precise—they did not obtain EEGs for all subjects, and employed very weak criteria for determining neurological dysfunction. Further, their methods did not discriminate between violent and non-violent cases as distinctly as we might expect. For example, if two-thirds of the boys with low violence had more than one sign of neurological dysfunction, how could investigators use these signs to identify the more violent ones? Certainly biological mechanisms are only one of many that affect aggression and neurological dysfunction does not necessarily imply problems with aggression. The authors recognize this in their work when they refer to the **biopsychosocial** determinants of aggression. Nevertheless, their main thesis is still useful. It concerns a biological basis for delinquency, and their work lends some support to that thesis, despite these methodological questions.

BRAIN DAMAGE AND AGGRESSION

As indicated in Chapter 3, the destruction of a brain structure may result in increased aggression if there is a loss of some inhibitory mechanism for the basic Onset Aggression System. Brain damage might also provoke an increase in the activity of the system structures by initiation of epileptiform activity or direct physical stimulation, as from a growing tumor. However, the effects of damage may be more subtle than those involving a frank increase in aggression. For example, an impairment of mechanisms necessary for dealing effectively with social functions or an impairment of tolerance to frustrations may result. In any case, when an uncharacteristic increase of aggression occurs over a relatively short period of months or even a few years and no other apparent factor, such as hormonal or environmental causes, is evident, observers may suspect a brain lesion. This aggression may be characterized by sudden brief periods of intense rage, out of proportion to the initiating stimulus, or by general increases in hostility, restlessness, or social interaction problems.

Several case studies have been published that detail aggression problems accompanied by damage in various areas of the limbic system and frontal lobes of the brain (Silver & Yudofsky, 1987). One study (Reeves & Plum, 1969) involved an accountant who over several years became increasingly irritable and also gained a considerable amount of weight. She sought help and, during examination by her physician, she suddenly became uncooperative and hostile. She hit, scratched, and tried to bite the examiner. At times, following such episodes, she would be distressed with what she had done and express her regrets. The source of her problem was a tumor that involved the ventromedial region of the hypothalamus (VMH). As we saw in Chapter 3, this area has been found to have inhibitory properties related to aggression as well as eating. Unfortunately, it was not possible to remove the tumor, and the patient died within three years after her problems had started. Other cases, reported by Zeman and King (1958), involved apparently normal people who became hypersensitive and irritable, made threats, committed assaults, and even attempted murder. They were found to have tumors in the septal region, another limbic system structure that helps inhibit aggression.

Brain damage caused by an illness may result in an increase in aggression, as we can see in the examples below. Rabies is usually transmitted to humans via a bite from an infected animal. The infecting virus is found in the animal's saliva and enters the human's body via the wound. The infection may involve damage to the medial hippocampus and irritation of it. The illness has occasionally been reported to result in dramatic increases of aggression, as well as sexual behavior, in addition to excessive salivation and pain while swallowing (producing hydrophobia). Another illness is encephalitis, produced by a virus that causes nervous system damage. It may be accompanied by personality changes, loss of inhibitions, and aggression directed at both oneself and others. Sex offenses may be involved in the aggression toward others. Brain damage, especially in young children, has been found in the hypothalamus, brain stem central gray, and the temporal lobes.

In one case that I studied with a colleague (first reported by Krawchik, 1986), a young man of 18 was brought to a hospital in a state of almost constant aggression. He had to be physically restrained to prevent him from harming the staff. He was a large person who used his physical size to intimidate others to avoid punishment or obtain what he desired. He had encephalitis when he was seven months old, which left him with some motor problems as well as generalized epileptic seizures. While his vocabulary seemed to develop normally, he had scholastic difficulties starting in the first grade. His aggression appeared as a problem when he was about 10, after which it became increasingly worse. Neuropsychological testing indicated that much of his brain was damaged, with the greatest damage in the left temporal lobe. We will discuss the treatment of this case later.

TREATMENT OF AGGRESSION RELATED TO NEURAL DYSFUNCTION

The approach taken to control aggression related to neural dysfunction naturally varies according to the perceived source of the problem and the methodology we have for dealing with it. In cases of aggression associated with seizure disorders, the first choice for treatment is an anticonvulsant. Such a drug is sometimes sufficient for controlling the problem. In some cases, when other factors are contributing to an individual's behavioral problems, professionals can administer various psychological treatments. In addition, they may employ other drug therapy in an attempt to directly control the biochemical contributions to aggression. We will examine some of these treatments in the next chapter.

Neurosurgical Treatment.   In situations where drug therapy or psychological approaches are not successful, physicians have used neurosurgical techniques. In many cases, the most direct path is taken to control the neural dysfunction. For example, if a tumor or cyst is interfering with the function of healthy neural tissue or threatens to further damage the tissue at or near its locus, often the only recourse is to remove the source of the problem. Further, if surgeons can identify an epileptogenic focus that is caused by a lesion in the brain, they can remove the focus. If the target is located in the subcortical areas, the procedure is more dangerous and difficult, but the stereotaxic method, as previously discussed, can be applied successfully in many cases. In other cases, where a brain lesion has destroyed an inhibitory control over aggression, there is at present little that neurosurgery can accomplish. Perhaps in the near future we will develop methods to help restore the functions of such areas, just as brain implants have been used (with limited success so far) to treat Parkinson's disease (see Lindvall, Brundin, Widner, Rehncrona, Gustavii, Frackowiak, Leenders, Sawle, Rothwell, Marsden, & Björklund, 1990). In such an attempt, healthy neural tissue or some other substance might be used to maximize the function of the remaining parts of the lesioned structure, help generate regrowth of its components, or provide supplements to its function by producing the neurochemicals healthy tissue normally secretes. Fetal tissue has been one source for implants. The finding by Reynolds and Weiss (1992) that adult mouse brain cells could be induced to replicate has suggested the possibility that application of the technique to humans might provide a way to grow substitute neural tissue. Progress continues in this area—January 1995 saw four reports of promising work with rodents, as researchers improved the survival rate of transplanted tissue, found a way to provoke the development of replacement cells that might be used for implantation, and tested a substance that could prevent cell death and alleviate Parkinson's-like symptoms (Barinaga, 1995).

At times, when a therapeutic team has decided that no other treatment has been or promises to be successful, neurosurgeons have intentionally lesioned brain structures that control increases in aggression. Such treatment is usually called **psy-**

chosurgery because it is a brain operation intended to change an individual's behavior. They use this treatment in cases where the effects of seizure disorders or brain lesions have not been able to be controlled, but it does not necessarily directly involve the dysfunctional structures. Instead, the surgical target may be other structures related to controlling the problem behaviors. In some cases, psychosurgery has been applied where no known neural dysfunction is evident, but where aggression is an overwhelming, uncontrolled problem. Naturally, such a radical means of treatment, involving the destruction of apparently healthy neural tissue in an apparently irreversible way, is very controversial.

The targets of psychosurgical techniques have included many areas of the brain, with the frontal lobes the most widely employed. Other targets have included structures found in the Onset Aggression System. Probably the most common psychosurgical target for controlling aggression has been the amygdala or, at times, the whole temporal lobe encompassing it. Usually the reported effect is that aggression is decreased, at least to some extent, but in some cases no change results or aggression may even increase. When neurosurgeons perform amygdaloid operations, they lesion the structures by inserting a probe to heat, freeze, or chemically destroy them. Some early practitioners of such techniques reported high rates of success. In Japan, Narabayashi (Narabayashi, Nagao, Saito, Yoshida, & Nagahata, 1963; Narabayashi, 1972) indicated that 85 percent of 51 patients showed improvement in that they were less excitable and displayed more normal social behavior. In work with 37 children, a small 3- to 4-millimeter lesion in the medial lateral amygdala was made, to produce what have been characterized as "dramatic" results in the children, who had been severely incapacitated. Heimburger, Whitlock, and Kalsbeck (1966) reported that 23 of 25 of their institutionalized mental patients were improved enough, after psychosurgery, to either be released or at least allowed more freedom in their activities. In a later report, Heimburger, Small, Small, Milstein, and Moore (1978) operated on 58 patients, 40 of whom were aggressive, while the others had some sort of conduct disorder. The authors indicated that over 80 percent of their patients improved in some way.

Hitchcock (1979), in an ambitious project carried out in Scotland, treated 18 patients, 16 of whom were classified as epileptics with behavioral problems, including much aggression. He obtained measures of the problems prior to surgery as well as after, and continued to study the patients for up to six years post-surgery. He also took urine and cerebrospinal fluid (CSF) samples to study hormone and brain chemical changes, although no striking effects were found in this part of his study. Hitchcock reports detailed results for 13 of his patients. Following surgery, 3 were either employed or participating in vocational training, 9 showed improvement in their aggression, and 10 had improvement in their psychiatric problems. None of the patients suffered any cognitive function deterioration following surgery. Mark and Ervin (1970) also reported success in several cases that were studied at Massachusetts General Hospital in Boston. We will discuss some of the results later in this chapter when we review work with human brain stimulation.

A combined surgical-behavioral approach to treating aggression may be useful. In Krawchik's case of encephalitis-related aggression, traditional psychotherapy and behavioral therapy were not initially successful in controlling the aggression. However, neurosurgeons then made bilateral amygdaloid lesions, which resulted in a great reduction of the "neurally based" aggression. After that, a behavioral approach was successful in reducing the "environmentally based" aggression. There are promising possibilities for such behavioral neuropsychological approaches. Essentially, psychologists perform neuropsychological evaluations to determine what neural areas are dysfunctional and thus suggest appropriate modes of treatment, such as psychosurgery or drug therapy, or indicate strengths and weaknesses to consider. Based on these findings, they then design an appropriate behavioral program. We will discuss several examples of specific behavioral techniques later.

Even though the temporal lobes have been the most common site for psychosurgery, several other structures have also been targeted. Again, these targets have been elements of the Onset Aggression system. After receiving lesions in different parts of the cingulate lobe of the limbic system, patients' aggression and other problems have been reported to be reduced either satisfactorily, only partially, or only temporarily (O'Callaghan & Carroll, 1982). Starting in the early 1960s, Sano practiced what he called "sedative" surgery, involving removal of the posterior hypothalamus in male and female children and adults who exhibited violent aggressive behaviors. Sano indicated that he did this to restore the balance between the calming anterior hypothalamus and the excitatory posterior region and so control the aggression. The same surgery has also been found to provide relief from intractable pain. Sano and Mayanagi (1988) reported good or excellent success with about 80 percent of 37 patients at from 10 to 25 years after surgery. Similarly, Schvarcz (1977) operated on the medial posterior hypothalamus and reported that 70 percent of his 35 patients had reduced aggressive levels. In further work, Rubio, Arjona, and Rodríguez-Burgos (1977) reported "excellent" results in 17 of 24 cases, and "good" in three others. Most of their patients with seizure disorders improved in this area as well.

In some studies, the thalamus has been a target of psychosurgical interventions. Spiegel, Wycis, Freed, and Orchnik (1953) lesioned the dorsomedial nucleus and found decreases in their patients' anxiety and aggression. Andy and Jurko (1972) reported that when they lesioned the centromedial or nearby intralaminar (between layers) regions of the thalamus in 30 patients, 20 percent showed good improvement and about two-thirds of the patients improved at least somewhat. Finally, researchers have also lesioned the frontal lobes, although with varying results. The prefrontal lobotomy procedure has been practiced on thousands of psychiatric patients in an attempt to relieve various psychiatric problems, especially those involving extreme anxiety and obsessions and compulsions. Many prefrontal patients exhibited increased aggression, and one of the expected results of this surgery was to make them less aggressive and more tractable. However, even when this tractability resulted, the broader serious intellectual deficits, lack of behavioral initiative, and personality changes that accompanied the tractability produced great opposition to the continued practice of prefrontal lobotomies. (See Valenstein, 1973, for an historical sketch of the procedure's use). More promising results have come from lesions restricted to the more ventromedial regions of the frontal lobe where researchers have reported good aggression-reducing effects without the intellectual deficits (e.g., Hirose, 1977).

Psychosurgical approaches to the treatment of aggression have been the subject of much debate, raising both ethical and methodological questions. While it is beyond the scope of this book to consider all the points in detail, we will briefly discuss the major ones here. Readers may also wish to refer to other sources, such as the work edited by Valenstein (1980) for further details. Also, Kleinig (1985) presents a very well-reasoned ethical analysis of the questions raised by psychosurgery.

Ethical Questions about Psychosurgery.   The ethical questions related to psychosurgery derive in part from the technique's irreversibility as well as questions about its efficacy. While usually there is little question of the ethics of removing diseased bodily tissue, such as an infected appendix, or even of excising damaged brain structures, as with tumors or epileptogenic foci, the removal of apparently healthy brain tissue in order to effect a behavioral change has provoked much debate. Questions have been raised whether all less drastic approaches have been thoroughly tested. After all, testing of alternative approaches is very tedious and time consuming compared to neurosurgery.

Concerns have also been voiced about whether psychosurgical procedures have been carried out primarily for the benefit of the patient or those affected by the patient. Caretakers may have great difficulty in controlling the patient, and their task is often much easier following an operation. Alternatively, more radical critics have suggested that the neurosurgeons are crassly experimenting on humans without any concern for them. Still further ethical problems arise when we consider the uncertainty of the outcome and the nature of the clients. The procedure of informed consent consists of telling patients what will be done to them and informing them of possible outcomes, both positive and negative. Given the inconsistency of the results of psychosurgery, it would be very difficult to adequately inform a prospective patient. Problems arise because many patients are psychotic, with impaired cognitive functions and diminished contact with reality, and they therefore may not readily understand the implications. In extreme cases, decisions have been left to legal guardians, who may or may not be acting in the patient's best interests. Another aspect of informed consent is that it be given without coercion. However, many patients have been psychiatric hospital residents or incarcerated individuals whose prison term may be affected by their decisions, and they cannot be considered free of coercive influences.

Methodological Questions about Psychosurgery.   The methodological questions about psychosurgery are related to whether the studies of its effects have been appropriately designed and executed for providing adequate information for evaluation. Carroll and O'Callaghan (1981; O'Callaghan & Carroll, 1982) point to many characteristics of the studies that lack the scientific rigor needed for clear conclusions. The precise location and size of the surgical lesions are not always known, since it has been difficult or impossible to do adequate exams of living patients—therefore, a major independent variable is inadequately specified. Also, they indicate that studies of the effects of psychosurgery have typically been done with few subjects, raising questions about the generalizability of results. Further, few control groups (of psychotic individuals not operated on) have been employed. When such controls were used, some suggestive evidence indicates that the rates of improvement in the operated (about 40 percent) are no better than those in the control groups. It is also possible that the operation may have done no good whatsoever. The improvement of problems with aggression may have occurred because of other influences, even if the operation has not been done. Carroll and O'Callaghan state that measurement of the dependent variable—the aggressive behavior—has been poor in psychosurgical studies. Few pretests of aggression are made for comparison with post-test levels, and post-test follow-up studies have been limited in duration. This makes it difficult to be sure that a reduction in aggression has indeed taken place and whether any effect is a lasting one. The actual measurements taken are usually subjective and often done by the surgeons or others who are aware of the study's goals. Therefore, bias in interpreting the results may occur as the informed observer sees the expected effects. A final, related area of concern is that effects are often not very specific and may not involve aggression **per se.** They may produce vague change in social adaptability as opposed to reductions in aggression itself, making the results more difficult to interpret. In addition, other important unmeasured results of the surgery may occur, such as the intellectual deficits produced by prefrontal lobotomies.

Because of these ethical and methodological concerns about psychosurgery, much of it was curtailed during the late 1970s and early 1980s. Contributing to this decline was the development of more effective antiepileptics and behavior-controlling drugs. However, psychosurgery continues to be practiced, with reports of rates of 70 to 80 percent improvement, including especially good effects from cingulate lesions (Valenstein, 1986). However, the development of alternative treatments should further reduce the amount of psychosurgery deemed necessary. Considering the current rapid development of techniques in the field of neurosciences, new, less questionable methodologies may be developed that will result in a resurgence of attempts to treat directly brain dysfunctions associated with aggression.

ELECTRICAL BRAIN STIMULATION STUDIES

Brain stimulation in humans has been carried out as part of the treatment of mental patients or others who have problems with aggression. At times it has been employed in an attempt to produce beneficial effects or facilitate interactions with patients. In other cases, it is used in conjunction with a psychosurgical approach. Human brain stimulation has been reported to produce a wide range of effects, including confusion and the recall of memories, positive states such as relaxation and euphoria, and negative states such as sadness, fear, anxiety, and aggression. Although interpretation of some of these effects is subject to the same limitations as for those of brain lesions, they have a certain face validity. In addition, the results typically correspond to what we have learned about brain functions from research with lower animals. That is, stimulation of the elements of the Onset Aggression System produces aggression or a related subjective report, such as feelings of anger and pain. Onset of stimulation of the Offset Aggression System elicits positive feelings of various sorts, in support of associating activity in this system with pleasurable states. Thus, these results are interesting for what they seem to add to understanding the neural bases of human aggression.

PRODUCTION OF AGGRESSION BY STIMULATION

Heath (1955) performed one of the early studies involving the production of aggression during the onset of brain stimulation in humans. He stimulated the anterior midbrain to produce pain, tension, and rage in his patients. In a subsequent demonstration, King (1961) stimulated the amygdala of a mental patient, eliciting a rage response. His patient reported feelings of anger at the onset of stimulation and of wanting to hit the investigator and begged him to stop the stimulation. Somewhat more recently, Mark and Ervin (1970) discussed their work with a man who had a history of attacking his family, associated with seizures and severe abdominal or facial pain. During stimulation of the medial amygdala, they produced a report of the same feeling of pain and loss of control that usually preceded the man's seizures and aggression. However, they terminated the stimulation before an aggressive outburst occurred.

Mark and Ervin found that testing conditions were important for eliciting aggression. In a young female patient, they were unable to produce any aggressive response initially, when she was alone in her room. On the other hand, when a radio transmitter was used for delivering the stimulation, through a small receiver attached to the patient, two instances of aggression were produced at the onset of stimulation of the hippocampus and the amygdala. In one instance, the patient was alone in a room. She became quiet at the onset of the stimulation, then gradually grew more agitated and exhibited some facial grimacing. Finally, she flung herself against the wall and struck it with her fists. A film clip of this behavior was included as part of the *Mind* series presented in 1988 on public television (PBS). The series of reactions to brain stimulation in the patient are remarkably similar to those observed during stimulation in a cat.

In the second instance of aggression by Mark and Ervin's patient, she was playing her guitar in the presence of her psychiatrist. Upon stimulation, she interrupted her playing and became quiet. As the stimulation continued, she took the guitar and threw it across the room, narrowly missing the psychiatrist and smashing it against the wall. The effects of stimulation were described as being very similar to those that accompanied her usual seizures, following the sequence of an interruption of attention, quieting, and then lashing out. During previous unprovoked seizures, the patient had attacked two people with a knife and a pair of scissors. After she had undergone psychosurgery, her aggressive problems were reported to diminish. In a recent interview done for the *Mind* series, she described her past experiences as a participant in the Mark and Ervin study and indicated that her problems with aggression were solved.

Reports of aggression produced by brain stimulation in humans have involved various sites in the Onset Aggression System: the medial hypothalamus, centromedial thalamus, cingulate, and brain stem, including the central gray (see Valzelli, 1981). Hitchcock (1979), in the psychosurgical work previously discussed, also stimulated five patients in the medial amygdala just prior to lesioning this area. These patients can be operated on under local anesthesia, since no pain sensations occur simply from passing the electrode wire through the brain. During stimulation, a range of behaviors associated with aggression were observed, including swearing and cries of anger, a threat, and destructive behavior.

INHIBITION OF AGGRESSION BY STIMULATION

Aggression may be reduced via excitation of inhibitory centers in the brain in a way similar to its control during stimulation of the Offset Aggression System in lower animals. Mark and Ervin (1970) discussed some of several reports of such inhibition of aggression via brain stimulation. During stimulation of the lateral amygdala, one patient reported a pleasant effect, similar to that found after an injection of Demerol (a potent analgesic) and said that he was peaceful and satisfied. (In all reports, the effects of such stimulation were expressed by the patients in terms of their individual experiences.) Stimulation in this case produced a sense of relaxation for 4 to 18 hours. With daily stimulations, the patient's aggressive problems were alleviated for two months. Later, medial amygdala lesions were made, resulting in a reduction in his aggression, although his psychiatric problems continued. After a period of time, his aggressiveness returned, but it was controllable with a drug treatment. In a second patient of Mark and Ervin, brain stimulation had an even longer effect. The patient remained free of aggressive episodes for a year afterwards. Sem-Jacobsen and Torkildsen (1960) also reported calming effects that outlasted the stimulation. They stimulated several areas of the frontal lobe, and reported that 15 minutes of stimulation in a psychotic patient would result in a day of calm behavior, accompanied by improved verbal communication.

Short-term calming effects were reported by Heath (1963), who found that septal stimulation, delivered either by the patient through a self-contained unit, or by the therapist, could produce reduction of anger, increases in good feelings, and increased sexual excitement in his patients. Other short-term inhibitory effects on aggression have been reported from stimulation in the hippocampus, corticomedial amygdala, and the cerebellum. Long-term periodic stimulation of the cerebellum has been reported to successfully control aggression over a multi-year span (Heath, Llewellyn, & Rouchell, 1979).

THE SCIENTIFIC VALUE OF STIMULATION STUDIES AND FUTURE RESEARCH POSSIBILITIES

The various reports of effects of brain stimulation on human aggressive behavior seem to support what has been learned from lower animal studies about the role of brain structures in aggression. Although work done with humans is limited by lack of adequate histological information on electrode sites and somewhat crude methodology, it helps to corroborate previous findings that the Onset Aggression System has a central role in producing aggressive behavior and supports the existence of the pleasure effects involved with onset of stimulation in the Offset Aggression System. However, involvement of the latter system has focused on using positive effects to reduce aggression, rather than offsetting these effects to increase it.

As further advances are made in brain research techniques, we hope there will be an increase in our understanding of the role of various brain structures in aggression. Perhaps scientists will use relatively non-invasive techniques, such as the Positron

Emission Tomography (PET) scan. The PET scan involves an imaging technique that provides pictures of brain slices, along with the relative amount of activity of each structure in the slices. Thus, this technique could help reveal just how the brain structures are active during aggressive episodes in both normal and dysfunctional brains. While this technique may not have been applied to study aggression, it has started to be employed in studying related matters. For example, Gottschalk, Buchsbaum, Gillin, Wu, Reynolds, and Herrera (1991) have done exploratory work in which PET scans were made during sleep in normal male adults. Although the measures of emotions were subjectively based (e.g., judged by analysis of verbal reports of dreams), the study illustrated how the PET scan can reveal changes in activity patterns during different emotional states. Other work suggests a neural basis for sex differences in aggression. Gur, Mozley, Mozley, Resnick, Karp, Alavi, Arnold, and Gur (1995) found that PET scans taken during a quiet, relaxed state usually showed higher levels of activity in male's temporal cortex, hippocampus, amygdala, cerebellum, and orbital frontal cortex, with lower cingulate gyrus activities, compared to women. Differences in activity in these components of the neural aggression systems may provide a base for differences in aggression.

Computerized tomography (CT) scans and Magnetic Resonance Imaging (MRI) are two relatively new techniques that have been used to provide images of brain slices in living individuals. These techniques offer much more accurate and detailed pictures than those available with old radiographic techniques and possibly will be employed more extensively to detect brain lesions that are correlated with aggression problems.

SUMMARY

Brain mechanisms are similar for lower animals and humans, especially at the subcortical level. This suggests that the information from lower animal studies on the production and limitation of aggression may be useful for understanding how the human brain is involved in aggression. Studies of human brain dysfunctions indicate some such generalizations are appropriate.

Human brain dysfunctions can be produced in a number of ways and at different developmental stages. They may result in excessive stimulation of the brain, as in seizure disorders, or in lesioning of the brain, as in traumatic injuries.

Seizure disorders are usually not associated with increased aggression. Indeed, many workers deny any consistent link of a seizure disorder with aggression. However, in some cases, people with temporal lobe seizures have been found to exhibit increased levels of aggression, typically in the intervals between seizures. Other studies have suggested a connection between more general seizure disorders and violent criminal acts in boys. Still another area of study has found that one of several unusual brain wave activities is present in individuals who have a history of violent crimes. While these studies are correlational and thus do not demonstrate causes of aggression, they may be useful in identifying individuals with a high potential for violence and may also lead to the discovery of neural causes of aggression.

Brain lesions caused by tumors or illness may result in increased aggression, seen as a relatively short-term unexplained growth in an individual's aggressiveness. Although clinical lesions are typically not as circumscribed as experimental lesions, some cases have involved effects remarkably similar to those from experimental work.

The treatment of neural dysfunctions sometimes involves surgery to remove a tumor or cyst damaging the brain, or scar tissue or other damage that is producing seizures. In other cases, psychosurgery is performed to decrease aggression. Neural targets have included structures in the Onset Aggression system, such as the amygdala, the posterior hypothalamus, and the medial thalamus, as well as prefrontal areas.

The psychosurgical technique is controversial because it may involve permanently damaging healthy neural tissue to control aggression. Both ethical and methodological criticisms have been made about psychosurgical procedures. The methodological criticisms question whether it has been demonstrated scientifically that psychosurgery does control aggression. For various reasons, psychosurgery is not practiced as extensively as it has been.

Electrical brain stimulation has been reported to affect aggression. Studies that involve the increase of aggression help confirm the role of neural structures of the Onset Aggression System. Such stimulation often has been done to determine a target for psychosurgery. Studies involving the decrease of aggression by onset of stimulation of the Offset Aggression System have been concerned with therapeutic attempts to control the aggression.

Suggested Readings

Kalinowsky, L. B., Hippius, H., and Klein, H. E. (1982). *Biological treatments in psychiatry*. New York: Grune and Stratton.

Kleinig, J. (1985). *Ethical issues in psychosurgery*. Boston: George Allen and Unwin.

CHAPTER 5

Neurotransmitters and Drugs

In previous chapters, we have seen how brain structures contribute to the control of aggression in both lower animals and humans. One important way they carry out these control functions is through chemicals that transfer information from one neuron to another. These chemicals are called **neurotransmitters** or, at times, neurohumors. Many types of known neurotransmitters are thought to function in the brain; others are still being discovered. After a brief introduction to neurotransmitters and drug effects, we will discuss the suspected role of four of the more well-known neurotransmitters that contribute to aggression. As we might expect, these neurotransmitters are involved in activities of the structures of the two basic neural aggression systems. They are found in relatively discrete systems that form parts of one or both of the neural systems. Thus, they can help integrate activity in the systems or bring in moderating influences. In addition, since drugs also are thought to affect aggression, usually by interacting in some way with neurotransmitter systems, we will discuss the role of both therapeutic and recreational drugs here.

Three specific goals motivate the study of the neurotransmitter systems. First, we must determine the role of the systems in controlling aggression in the normal brain. It is important for us to see which system or systems are involved in the production of aggression, what neural structures they are operating in, and if they are related to any particular type of aggression. Similar determinations must be made for the systems involved in the inhibition of aggression. As we will see, the information related to all these points is incomplete, but some important progress has been made. The second goal for studying these systems is to assess their function in the abnormal brain. At times we can detect an excess or deficit in a particular system or systems, which may suggest corrective action that can be taken or at least may help increase our understanding of the brain's normal functioning. The third goal for neurotransmitter study is to determine how drugs interact with these systems. This type of study operates in two directions. The effects of some drugs to increase or decrease aggression might be understood via determination of what systems are being affected. Alternatively, anti-aggression drugs might be developed on the basis of which systems they affect.

AN INTRODUCTION TO NEUROTRANSMITTERS AND DRUG EFFECTS ON THEM

Before discussing specific neurotransmitter systems, we should explain some basic facts. As in earlier chapters, the informed reader is welcome to skim quickly over familiar materials.

Chemical neurotransmission is a complex process that involves a number of steps to prepare the chemicals, position them, release them, and terminate their activities, besides the transmission itself. As shown in Figure 5.1, these activities take place in and around the communication space between two neurons called the **synapse.** The

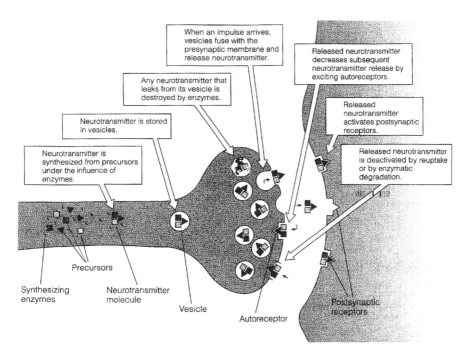

Figure 5.1   A neuronal synapse and the basic neurochemical activities involved in synaptic transmission. (Modified from Pinel, John P. J., *Biopsychology, 2nd ed.* Copyright © 1993, Allyn and Bacon. Reprinted by permission.)

process varies in detail from one system to another, but basically contains the following steps. The neurotransmitter first has to be manufactured or synthesized from components. This often is a multi-step process that includes taking **precursor** molecules and modifying them with the aid of proteins called **enzymes** into other forms, until they produce the appropriate molecule. The availability of the precursors and enzymes can affect whether and how much of a neurotransmitter is produced. Once synthesized, the chemicals are placed in containers called **synaptic vesicles** that hold large numbers of them and protect them from other degradation enzymes that otherwise would break them down again. Once an electrical transmission is sent down a neuron to the synaptic area, the vesicles migrate to the **presynaptic membrane** and release their contents into the synapse, where, among other things, they diffuse over to the **postsynaptic membrane**. They then affix themselves to specific **receptor** sites and produce an excitatory or inhibitory chemo-electric effect in the target neuron. Other **autoreceptor** sites are located in the membrane of the presynaptic neuron to further regulate its activity. To maintain the coding of information that was represented by pulses of information in the presynaptic neuron, the effect on the target neuron must also be controlled. Therefore, the neurotransmitters are either broken down or taken back up into the presynaptic neuron soon after they are released. Thus, new pulses of information can produce their own, relatively separate effects.

Drugs can affect the neurotransmitter system at any or several of the steps outlined above. For example, they may provide precursors so that more of a neurotransmitter can be synthesized. They may supply more of the enzymes needed for synthesis or perhaps more of the degradation enzymes. They may affect the storage or release of the neurotransmitters from the vesicles. They may act on the receptor sites or the termination of the transmission process. Some drugs facilitate the working of certain neurotransmitter systems and are referred to as **agonists**. Other drugs interfere with systems and are called **antagonists**. Drugs often have multiple effects and may function as agonists for some systems and antagonists for others.

In addition to drugs, other factors may affect the neurotransmitter systems. These include environmental toxins or trauma that may directly damage a system, diet that may modify precursor and enzyme supplies, and stress and autoimmune influences that may affect the operating level of systems. In addition, genetic factors may influence several variables, including the availability and structure of precursors and enzymes, the storage and release of neurotransmitters, and the receptor site structures. Such effects might be the mechanism by which certain neural structures are more or are less active in producing inherited differences in aggression.

Methodological Concerns in Drug Research

The experimental study of the neurotransmitter systems often has been pursued in a way that leads to misleading or incomplete results. While the methodological problems we discuss here will be in the context of our study of aggression, there are apparent similarities to the results of tests for other drugs, such as those thought to treat cancer. Drugs have been found to control "aggression" and touted as major discoveries. However, subsequent investigations reveal that the drugs affect aggression only in a limited situation: perhaps only with one species of animal, or in one specific stimulus situation, or with only one type of aggression. In other words, the initial tests were insufficiently broad. Another problem is related to drug doses. At times, massive doses are used that alter neurotransmitter systems far beyond what would occur naturally. While there are good justifications for such doses, based on statistical and practical considerations, individuals have occasionally been misled into believing that abnormal dose results demonstrate a normal function in aggression for the neurotransmitter.

A difficulty in studies aimed toward understanding neurotransmitter functions arises at times when scientists use single drug administrations. Single drug injections may affect aggression differently than multiple doses. For example, one type of antidepressant drug decreases aggression following a single administration, but increases it after being given for six days. If data were collected only for the first day, conclusions about the effect of that drug on aggression would be the opposite from those from a multiple administration study. Further, longer term administration of drugs has often been found to result in decreases or increases in the number of receptor sites, as the neural system compensates for prolonged over or understimulation by regulating receptivity to a drug.

Another problem in drug studies occurs when scientists use the effects of only one dose amount of a drug. Although prudent investigators clearly state that their work pertains only to what actually was studied, the results of such limited studies are sometimes taken as an indication of the drug's general effect on aggression. It is preferable to determine effects of a whole range of doses and obtain what is called a **dose-response function**. When this was done in the past, some drugs have produced linear increases or decreases in aggression as the dose was increased, but others have produced reversals. Aggression sometimes rises with increased doses to a peak, then decreases with further increases in dose. In a single-dose study, the conclusions about the drug's effect on aggression might be that it increases it, decreases it, or perhaps does not affect it, depending on the dose tested. Some drug studies involve problems with discriminating between primary versus secondary effects on aggression. While a final effect of a drug might be to change aggression levels, this might not occur through a specific effect on the neural systems directly involved with aggression— instead that effect may be secondary. For example, the drug may produce confusion and thus perhaps result in frustration of the individual, which in this case would be the primary cause of aggression. Alternatively, a drug may cause incapacitating seizures or heavy sedation of an individual, thus effectively preventing aggressive acts from occurring. Concluding that either one of these drugs had a direct effect on aggression could result in erroneous assumptions about the neurotransmitter systems underlying aggression. While the results with sedating drugs may indicate a possible way of controlling aggression in a patient, they are misleading in our search for the bases of aggression.

Some factors that affect the results of drug tests are beyond the scope of this discussion. Students wishing further information are referred to a text dedicated to psychopharmacology (e.g., Julien, 1995). For now, we should recognize the methodological limits to much of what we will discuss concerning the role of neurotransmitter systems in aggression. However, a good start has been made in implicating several systems in controlling aggression and understanding how certain drugs work via these systems.

Neurotransmitters Involved in Aggression

Acetylcholine (ACh) is a neurotransmitter that has been linked in several ways to increased aggression. It is found in many areas of the brain, including the neocortex and the limbic system, as well as in many areas of the body. (*Note:* You may want to refer to Figures 3.1 and 3.2 as we mention neural structures here.) Rather recently, the popular press has mentioned ACh because of associations of cortical deficits in ACh with memory losses that are characteristic of Alzheimer's disease. However, linking it to aggression usually relates to its function in the Onset Aggression System. For example, ACh is found in parts of the hypothalamus, thalamus, hippocampus, amygdala, and cingulate area.

Several early studies demonstrated that cholinergic (the adjective for acetylcholine or a drug that acts in the same way) stimulation could produce increased aggression in cats. MacLean and Delgado (1953) worked with neural structures such as the hippocampus, where electrical stimulation produced aggression and showed that cholinergic substances injected there would increase aggression and components of affective behaviors in cats. Grossman (1963) injected a cholinergic agonist into the amygdala of cats and produced a chronic increase in affective aggression. The cats previously had been rather tame, but, after only one injection, they were extremely vicious, biting and scratching anyone who attempted to handle them.

Cholinergic stimulation has been found to increase aggression in rats. Smith, King, and Hoebel (1970) injected a cholinergic agonist into the lateral hypothalamus of rats and reported that those who previously would not kill mice became muricidal. Bandler chemically stimulated still other parts of the brain, including the thalamus (Bandler, 1971a) and midbrain area of the brain stem (Bandler, 1971b), in rats. He reported facilitation of predatory aggression. Together, these studies demonstrate a role of ACh in different types of aggression, controlled by several structures in two different species.

Critics have suggested that some studies may have produced aggression as an artifact of uncontrolled extreme excitation resulting from high doses of the drug directly injected into the brain. However, this work is supported by other types of manipulations. For example, a dose-response study involving injections into brain ventricles resulted in hierarchical increases in vocalization, fighting, and biting. Then, only at the highest doses, more uncontrolled responses occurred, including fighting but also precipitating convulsions (Beleslin & Stefanović-Denić, 1986). Further support comes from studies showing that the pesticide carbaryl has a strong agonistic effect on cholinergic systems throughout the body (Fernández, Falzon, Cambon-Gros, & Mitjavila, 1982). Exposure to this substance has resulted in increased aggression in humans (Gershon & Shaw, 1961). In at least one recent instance, this possibility was cited by the defense in a murder case. A lawn care worker went into a rage and killed a woman who yelled at him for urinating on her lawn. The man had no past history of violence; however, he had been exposed to high doses of a pesticide while mixing chemicals for spraying. The defense contended that the pesticide produced a lowered threshold for violent reactions to stimuli. Increased acetylcholine activity also affects the autonomic nervous system control over urination, which would explain the man's reported increased urge to urinate. Unfortunately, the defense argument was rejected.

Smith, King, and Hoebel (1970) utilized spontaneously muricidal rats to confirm ACh's role in aggression. The authors showed that they could suppress the muricidal behavior by injecting a central nervous system cholinergic antagonist into the lateral hypothalamus. Bandler (1971a) similarly demonstrated that an anticholinergic, especially when injected into the medial thalamus, would decrease aggression.

Some correlational studies have found a positive relation between acetylcholine and aggression in both rats and humans. Spontaneously aggressive rats have higher amounts of central ACh activity, as measured in the amygdala (Ebel, Mack, Stefanović, & Mandel, 1973). Also, one of the neurotransmitter changes occurring in women in their premenstrual period associated with aggression in some is an increase in ACh. In addition, some drugs that help to decrease aggression, such as lithium, and some antipsychotics may produce decreases in central ACh. In general, several types of research support the thesis that acetylcholine contributes to the production of aggressive behaviors.

Norepinephrine (NE), also called noradrenalin, has been observed to be positively related to aggression in various methods of study. This neurotransmitter is found in two major pathways that are widely distributed in the brain and include numerous structures in both the Onset and Offset Aggression Systems. The pathways pass from the brain stem to the cerebellum and hypothalamus, and connect to structures such as the thalamus, amygdala, hippocampus, septal region, and the cingulate, as well as to the neocortex. Norepinephrine is one of a group of neurotransmitters called **monoamines** because they each have one of the nitrogen-hydrogen components called amines. Two other group members are dopamine and serotonin. Dopamine is the immediate precursor of NE and thus very closely related to it structurally; both belong to the subgroup called **catecholamines.** This relationship has lead to some difficulty in interpreting drug studies, since many drugs affect both dopamine and norepinephrine. Further, some drugs affect all monoamines.

One way NE has been linked to aggression is by studies that have produced increases in its levels, accompanied by increased aggression. In an early study, Randrup and Munkvad (1969) used drugs to increase catecholamine levels in their cats and found that aggression increased. Further manipulations demonstrated that the increased aggression was produced by elevations in norepinephrine, not dopamine. Bandler (1971b) found that when he induced increased NE levels in the midbrain, his rats became more aggressive. Other studies have shown that enhancing the utilization of NE increases pain shock-elicited aggression in rats. For example, Eichelman and Barchas (1975) demonstrated two such effects. Monoamine oxidase inhibitor (MAOI), which increases NE (and the other monoamines) by inhibiting its degradation enzyme (MAO) was shown to increase aggression. Again, as in English or mathematics and as we saw earlier for brain functions, two negatives make a positive. Antidepressant drugs, which facilitate NE by prolonging its presence in the synapse, were also found to augment aggression. The withdrawal of morphine from addicted rats provokes an increase in NE, accompanied by increased aggression (Boshka, Weisman, & Thor, 1966). Finally, administration of amphetamines and apomorphine facilitates attack (Gianutsos & Lal, 1976). Both types of drugs increase NE, although apomorphine has a greater effect on dopamine.

Drugs that are antagonists to NE have been demonstrated to decrease aggression in two ways. First, depletion of NE stored in synaptic vesicles results in lowered aggression (e.g., Reis, 1972). Second, drugs that block synaptic transmission of NE also block aggressive behaviors of various types (e.g., Gianutsos & Lal, 1976). An example in further support involves propranolol, a drug that decreases NE in the brain (while temporarily increasing dopamine) (King, Turkson, Liddle, & Kinney, 1980). Propranolol has been used to decrease aggression in brain-damaged patients and has been of some use in controlling emotional states that contribute to aggression (Johnson, 1984).

The utilization of NE in the brain has been correlated with increased aggression. Reis and Gunne (1965) detected a depletion of NE when attack episodes occurred in cats. Also, rats who engage in fighting elicited by electrical shock have increased turnover (utilization and replacement) rates of NE (Stolk, Conner, Levine, & Barchas, 1974). Such stressful situations as sleep deprivation and immobilization, which sometimes produce increased levels of aggression, provoke increased use of NE (e.g., Lamprecht, Eichelman, Thoa, Williams, & Kopin, 1972).

The manic stage of Bipolar Mood Disorder (commonly referred to as bipolar affective disorder, or, less recently, as manic-depressive illness) at times involves increased levels of aggression, as well as elevated levels of NE. An example of the relation between mania and NE was given in a study by Bunney, Goodwin, and Murphy (1972), who made behavioral ratings of institutionalized men every eight hours and also obtained urine samples from them each day. Urine contains metabolites or breakdown products of the neurotransmitters used by the brain and body and can be analyzed to determine relative amounts of neurotransmitters use. Bunney et al. found that NE levels increased just one day before the manic behaviors began, thus suggesting the possibility of their involvement in producing the manic stage.

It is possible to produce a manic-like episode with injections of amphetamines, which elevate NE levels in the brain. These can result in increased agitation, anxiety, impaired judgment, and physical distress, accompanied by aggression (APA, 1994). Similarly, antidepressant medication given to some individuals has been found to produce manic-aggression, probably because it increases central NE levels (Rambling, 1978). Also, a decrease in NE activity, provoked by drugs such as reserpine that deplete catecholamines, can convert a person from an aggressive manic stage into a depressed one (Kalinowsky, Hippius, & Klein, 1982). Woodman and Hinton (1978) provided further support for this relationship between NE and aggression while measuring the relative amounts of biochemicals released during stress. They found unusually high ratios of urinary norepinephrine versus epinephrine in violent maximum security hospital patients who anticipated stressful situations, compared to ratios found in nonviolent mental hospital patients and normal control groups. (These closely related substances are both produced by the core, or medulla, of the adrenal gland during stress.) The more violent security hospital patients had much greater increases in their production of NE.

All the various findings discussed above on the relation between aggression and NE support the idea that this neurotransmitter has a facilitating role in aggression. As with ACh, increases or decreases in its activity produce or accompany a corresponding increase or decrease in aggression. With this knowledge, we can better understand the effects of various drugs on aggression—drugs that affect aggression may do so because they affect NE or ACh. This information may also be used as a guide for developing new drugs. This is not a simple task, however. Both ACh and NE are involved in other important roles, such as regulation of the autonomic nervous system, and it is necessary to maintain those roles at an appropriate level. Further, not all evidence is consistent with the findings of a positive correlation between NE and aggression. Some work with predation in lower animals has reported a negative correlation between NE function and this aggression. That is, increased NE levels were associated with lower predatory aggression.

Another body of work does not support the role of NE in aggression, but emphasizes the role of one of the other catecholamines, **dopamine** (DA). Like NE, DA has several pathways that pass from the brain stem through the hypothalamus and into limbic structures such as the septal region, hippocampus, and amygdala. One pathway, called the mesolimbic, has special relevance to the Offset Aggression System, since it is a principal part of the brain's pleasure system. Thus, it is involved in limiting aggression during activation, as well as in generating aggression following its termination. However, DA also has been reported in onset aggression, assumedly via another pathway. For example, Datla, Sen, and Bhattacharya (1992) showed that pain-elicited fighting in rats was increased by DA agonists and decreased by DA antagonists. A more detailed discussion of research in this area can be found in reviews such as that of Alpert, Cohen, Shaywitz, and Piccirillo (1981). An illustrative example of earlier conflicting views of the relative roles of the two catecholamines is contained in successive presentations by Everett and then Eichelman at a neuropsychopharmacology conference (Eichelman, 1977; Everett, 1977). More recently, while Nikulina, Avgustinovich, and Popova (1992) provide an argument for the important role of decreased DA in reducing the aggression of domesticated rats against men, they also note that domestication affects NE, as well as serotonin, levels. Thus, they could not discount the role of domestication-induced changes in these neurotransmitters in reducing aggression. Attempts to develop a drug that specifically affects only aggression have been frustrating. We will discuss some of these attempts below, after examining one last neurotransmitter, serotonin, which may have an inhibitory effect on aggression.

Serotonin (5-HT, for the abbreviation of its molecular name) levels have been manipulated in several ways, with results indicating that it has an inhibitory effect on aggression. It may function by reducing activity of elements of the Onset Aggression System. The source of central 5-HT is the raphe system in the brain stem. From there, neuronal fibers go to a wide range of structures, including the thalamus, hypothalamus, other limbic structures, such as the amygdala, hippocampus and septal area, and the cerebellum. Serotonin is synthesized, via an intermediate process, from the amino acid tryptophan, which must be supplied from the individual's diet (and thus is an "essential" amino acid). Tryptophan is converted to 5-HTP, which is then converted to 5-HT. As we noted above, 5-HT, with norepinephrine and dopamine, is a monoamine.

If 5-HT levels are decreased or increased experimentally, there is a corresponding inverse effect on several types of aggressive behavior. That is, as 5-HT decreases, aggression increases, while aggression decreases following increases in 5-HT. The drug parachlorophenylalanine (PCPA) blocks 5-HT synthesis and results in increased aggression as well as increased sexual behavior, along with a disturbance in sleep. These effects are reversed when 5-HTP injections are given to increase 5-HT levels (Sheard, 1969). Surgical interventions also have been employed to decrease 5-HT levels. Vergnes, Penot, Kempf, and Mack (1977) showed that raphe lesions in rats result in increased muricidal behavior. In addition, dietary manipulations that decrease tryptophan result in increased fighting by rats (Kantak, Hegstrand, Whitman, & Eichelman, 1980). In turn, increases in 5-HT produced by injections of its immediate precursor, 5-HTP, result in decreased muricidal behavior by rats (Kulkarni, 1968). Also, direct electrical stimulation of the raphe causes decreases in attack elicited by brain stimulation (Sheard, 1974). Some evidence also indicates that both drug and dietary manipulations directed toward increasing brain serotonin can control self-injurious behavior in the mentally handicapped (Gedye, 1990).

Changes in levels of 5-HT have been found to correlate with aggression levels. In one experiment scientists administered PCA, an amphetamine, which resulted in first an increase and then a decrease in 5-HT levels. These changes were accompanied by first a decrease and then an increase in aggression (Sheard & Davis, 1976). For humans, Brown, Goodwin, and Bunney (1982) reviewed work showing that as suicide risk increased, levels of a metabolite of 5-HT decreased. The implication is that this self-directed aggression increased as a function of the decreases in 5-HT, although these were only correlative studies. The authors also list many other correlations between elevated aggression and lowered 5-HT. For example, in general males have lower 5-HT levels than females, suggesting a further biochemical factor in the increased aggression of males.

Åsberg, Bertilsson, and Mårtensson (1984) reported that not only people with suicidal behaviors but also murderers of lovers or sexual rivals have low serotonin levels. They also made a methodological comment supporting the observations in Chapter 1 on the desirability of using objective measures of aggression instead of indirect measures. They and others, such as Brown's group, found that self-report measures of suicidal thoughts or aggression are not related to serotonin levels in a way parallel to suicide **acts.** Thus, in such studies, dependence on an individual's revelations of his or her aggressive thoughts or activities probably would not have resulted in the discovery of the apparent co-relationship between suicide and serotonin levels.

In some cases of increased aggression in lower animals, researchers have found an interaction of low 5-HT and high NE levels. For example, as we mentioned in Chapter 2, Lagerspetz (see Lagerspetz, Tirri, & Lagerspetz, 1968) found that the aggressive (TA) inbred mice had an 11 percent higher level of NE and a 19 percent lower level of 5-HT than non-aggressive (TNA) mice. In another case, preliminary evidence (all the planned studies have not yet been done) indicates that oral administration of modest amounts of the sugar substitute aspartame (NutraSweet) increases shock-elicited fighting in rats (Toner, Woodfill, & Renfrew, 1990). The experiment was devised because among the purported effects of aspartame is an increase in brain NE levels and a decrease in 5-HT levels. Aspartame has been reported to produce a number of adverse reactions, including extreme irritability in humans (Roberts, 1988). However, consistent effects of aspartame on human behavior have not been found.

A relation parallel to that found by Lagerspetz et al. in mice has been reported for male humans institutionalized with personality disorders. Brown, Ballanger,

Minichiello, and Goodwin (1979) measured the neurotransmitter metabolites in the CSF (cerebrospinal fluid) of their patients and correlated them with ratings on an aggression scale and with attempted suicides. They found that both aggression scale ratings and suicide attempts were positively correlated with NE metabolite levels and negatively correlated with 5-HT metabolite levels. In a situation inverse to these studies, the lowered aggression in castrated rats is correlated with increased 5-HT and decreased NE levels (Bernard & Paolino, 1974).

The materials we have reviewed thus far indicate important roles for acetylcholine, norepinephrine, and serotonin in controlling aggression. The first two typically have been involved in increased aggression, probably as they operate to increase the functions of neural elements in the Onset Aggression System. In turn, serotonin may have its effect by decreasing functioning in the Onset system. A fourth neurotransmitter, dopamine, has been linked to the pleasurable effects occurring during onset of activity of the Offset system, although some investigators also attribute a role to dopamine in what apparently would be the Onset system. The concentration on these neurotransmitters reflects the large number of investigations involving them. Other neurotransmitters, however, have also been associated with the control of aggression, in part through reports of the effects of various drugs on aggression by interactions with these other neurotransmitters.

THERAPEUTIC DRUGS AND THE CONTROL OF AGGRESSION

Various classes of drugs have been used to control aggression. Typically, these drugs were not developed to affect aggression *per se*, but have been found to decrease aggression while treating other problems. Thereafter, some of the drugs are used with aggression as their primary target.

The **major tranquilizers,** also called **antipsychotics** or **neuroleptics,** include classes of drugs called phenothiazines, butryophenones, and thioxenthines. They block dopamine circuits and cholinergic activity. As their general names indicate, they have a quieting (but not necessarily sedating) effect on psychotic patients (primarily those classified as schizophrenics) by acting on the nervous system. They also have pacifying effects on nonpsychotics and have been used in hostile, irritable, depressed elderly patients with organic brain syndromes. Children with brain damage or primary behavior disorders also have been treated with these tranquilizers to reduce their aggressive and hyperactive behaviors. The phenothiazines (e.g., chlorpromazine) have been reported as being especially effective, with a distinct anti-aggressive result, although they also have side effects on electrical brain activity and motor control. Also very potent are the butryophenones (e.g., haloperidol), which are effective blockers of dopamine. This class of neuroleptics has been reported to be effective on a wide range of patients, including acute psychotics, schizophrenics, the emotionally disturbed, and the developmentally disabled. The specific reason for the effectiveness of these drugs is not clear, since they have multiple effects. For example, the psychotic may simply be less frustrated or confused after being placed on an antipsychotic drug, and this in itself may eliminate causes of aggression. Alternatively, the elimination of disturbing or provocative hallucinations and delusions can remove their contributions to aggression. However, the successful use of antipsychotics in controlling aggression in non-psychotics implies a more direct, albeit undetermined, effect on aggression mechanisms, purportedly apart from any sedative action. Future research is still needed to clarify just how an anti-aggressive effect is executed.

The **minor tranquilizers** include a class of drugs called benzodiazepines, among which Librium (chlordiazepoxide) and Valium (diazepam) are the most well known. While it has been suggested that they have an effect on serotonergic (5-HT) systems, they more likely affect another transmitter called GABA (gamma-aminobutyric acid), which has an inhibitory effect on excitatory mechanisms. The minor tranquilizers are usually thought to reduce aggression, although results have either have been inconsistent or open to interpretation. For example, aggressive animals have been tamed by tranquilizers, but rats have been reported to increase their mouse-killing behavior following injections (Leaf, Wnek, Gay, Corcia, & Lamon, 1975). Further, when taming occurs, it is not clear if this is because of an anti-aggressive action of the drug or simply from a sedative effect that reduces behaviors in general. In humans, the minor tranquilizers have been used to reduce aggression in psychotics and are effective in controlling the aggression of psychotic criminals. For example, Tupin (1988) recommends it as a first step for controlling episodes of extreme aggression in emergency situations. However, there also are instances (3 to 4 percent) of tranquilizers producing paradoxical increases in aggression in psychotic individuals. In the laboratory, students made hostile by frustrating them were found to have their levels of hostility increased rather than decreased when given tranquilizers (Salzman, Kochansky, Shader, Porrino, Hormatz, & Sweet, 1974). Again, however, the effect was not consistent across individuals. Therefore, while the general effect of minor tranquilizers seems to be a reduction in aggression, the reason for this is not clear, and the results are not consistent across cases.

Psychostimulants include several drugs, such as the amphetamines, Ritalin (methylphenidate), and pemoline. They produce increased activity in the catecholaminergic (norepinephrine and dopamine) systems. The amphetamines have an anorectic or eating-suppression effect and have therefore been a component in diet pills. As mentioned previously, Ritalin has been used with Attention-Deficit/Hyperactive Disorder children to decrease their hyperactivity. Since psychostimulants are usually believed to have an excitatory effect in other humans, their calming effect in hyperactive children is considered paradoxical. Supposedly it results from the enhanced activity of the attention mechanisms in the brains of these children. There also are indications that in some cases the hyperactive syndrome continues into adulthood (labeled Attention-Deficit Disorder, Residual Type or ADD, RT) and administration of Ritalin or other psychostimulants to these adults may help reduce their aggressive behaviors (Wender, 1988). Finally, effective control of aggression by giving psychostimulants to delinquents not classified as hyperactive (e.g., Conners, Kramer, Rothschild, Schwartz, & Stone, 1971) has been reported. This may result from the drug's calming influence as well as the enhanced attention and intellectual functions produced (as reported by Rapoport, Bushbaum, Zahn, Weingartner, Ludlow, & Mikkelsen, (1978). Thus, the response of hyperactive children to the drugs may not be paradoxical, and perhaps psychostimulants can be of more general use in controlling aggression. Such attempts must progress cautiously, however, as psychostimulants can also produce increased aggression, as we will see later.

Lithium salts have been used rather successfully to control aggressive behaviors in clinical cases. Scientists have not established lithium's effect on biochemicals, but have suggested that it includes multiple influences on the neurotransmitters implicated in controlling aggressive behaviors. Lithium apparently decreases both the catecholamines, affects acetylcholine activity, and stabilizes serotonin activity (Hollister & Csernansky, 1990).

Lithium has been shown to have an anti-aggression effect on rats as well as on a variety of aggressive human populations. For example, Sheard (1971) found that lithium was effective in reducing the aggression of a group of 12 prisoners who were aggressive both prior to and during incarceration. These individuals were relatively normal in that they were not brain damaged, psychotic, or retarded. Their reduced aggression was noted in self-evaluations as well as in decreased rule infractions and lowered verbal aggression. A second example by Sheard, Marini, Bridges, and Wagner (1976) was especially convincing because it involved a double-blind method, in which neither evaluator nor subject knew if lithium or some control substance was being administered. Such a procedure helps to control bias on the part of an evaluator who perhaps expects a particular effect; it also takes into account a placebo effect on a subject who expects the treatment to work and therefore acts accordingly. This method has helped make a strong case for the efficacy of lithium in controlling aggression. Another double-blind study was done by Craft, Ismail, Krishnamurti, Mathews, Regan, Seth, and North (1987). They found a significant reduction, over a period of 12 weeks, in aggression ratings for institutionalized retarded adults.

Tupin (1977) has demonstrated the effects of lithium on psychotic children as well as prisoners and found general reductions in aggression in each population. In early work, for example, 8 of 10 prisoners were free of disciplinary problems during three months of treatment. Coffey (1988) also reports extensive use of lithium for controlling aggression in children and adults from a number of diagnostic categories.

Anticonvulsants, as we saw in Chapter 4, are thought to control the aggression that accompanies some seizure disorders. In addition, they have been reported to reduce aggression in patients with no certain EEG indications of seizure disorders (e.g., Luchins, 1984). There have been informal reports that drugs developed as anticonvulsants have apparently specific effects in reducing aggression in laboratory animals. It will be interesting to follow future developments in this area to see if researchers can confirm specific antiaggressive properties of the anticonvulsants and determine just how they produce their effect. One possibility is that they change levels of critical neurotransmitters. Carbamazepine, for example, is especially effective in controlling aggression, and it increases a precursor of serotonin. Carbamazepine has been reported to be useful for several psychiatric classifications, whether or not patients show signs of seizure disorders (Post, 1989).

COMMON DRUGS AND AGGRESSION

Several types of drugs, both legal and illegal, that are rather frequently used or abused in the United States and elsewhere have been studied in relation to their effects on aggressive behavior. Because of the common, uncontrolled use of alcohol, cocaine, or even caffeine, for example, some misunderstandings have arisen concerning their relationships with aggression. Since usually no control exists over who takes the drugs or the type or amount that is consumed, it is difficult to assess their effects. For example, individuals who are more aggressive initially may tend to consume a particular drug more often, and thus studies of the drug's supposed effect on aggression are biased by a second individual factor, the initial hyperaggressivity. Or an unrecognized component in a drug being consumed may either mask or enhance the real effect of the basic drug component. Even scientific studies of the effects of drugs have not always resulted in clarifications of their roles. Different investigators may employ different definitions and measures of aggression or different doses of the drug. With these caveats in mind, we will review some of the work on aggression and some common drugs not previously discussed.

Alcohol has been cited as a contributing factor to increased aggression in various types of studies, but not all investigations find that it consistently increases aggression. Further, there does not seem to be complete agreement concerning alcohol's biological effects. Most general references about its effects suggest that it results in a loss of inhibitions. Monroe and Lion (1978) indicate more specifically that it has an activating effect on the EEG, producing abnormally lower frequencies and sometimes episodes of behavioral dyscontrol. On the other hand, Berry and Brain (1986) point out that alcohol has a nonspecific behavioral effect because it dissolves the outer layer of nerve cells, and in doing so may result in an increase or decrease in many neurotransmitter processes, producing simultaneously both inhibitory and excitatory effects. Others indicate that it results in altered levels of the neurotransmitters linked to aggression (see Badawy, 1986).

Some of the data linking alcohol to increased aggression is of the correlative type. Therefore, such findings as those showing that about two-thirds of the homicides and about half the rapes in a city involved drinking by the perpetrator or victim are taken to indicate some causative contribution of alcohol to aggression. Similarly, involvement of alcohol consumption in family altercations and juvenile delinquency seems to support the thesis of alcohol's facilitating role in aggression. However, while these data are suggestive, we must remember that causation is not demonstrated by correlation. Consider that many non-aggressive acts, such as those involved in automobile, industrial, and domestic accidents, are also correlated with alcohol use. This suggests that alcohol has effects not specific just to aggression, but are more general. These effects include decreased sensory function, impaired motor skills, and increased reaction time, along with impaired judgment. All of these may contribute to accidents, while the last, impaired judgment, probably is a factor in both accidents and aggressive behaviors. However, regardless of this nonspecificity of alcohol's effects, we can find experimental demonstrations of an alcohol-aggression relationship.

MacDonnell and his colleagues studied the interactions of alcohol with aggression produced by brain stimulation in cats. They found that low alcohol doses produced shorter latencies of hissing associated with the affective attack produced by medial hypothalamic stimulation, but that medium doses resulted in a series of alternating increases and decreases in the potentiation of aggression (MacDonnell, Fessock, & Brown, 1971). The effect of alcohol on stalking attack produced by brain stimulation was mixed, in that increasing doses of alcohol produced delays in attack, while biting force increased (MacDonnell & Ehmer, 1969). These studies indicate that dose and time elapsed since administration are important variables in alcohol's effect on aggression. Berry and Smoothy (1986) reviewed the work of MacDonnell and his colleagues as well as some studies of other species in social conflict situations. These studies also indicated that low doses of alcohol facilitate fighting while high doses suppress it. Berry and Smoothy pointed out how such results depend on the testing situation as well as individual differences in such factors as social status and aggressive experiences. They concluded that alcohol-related increases in aggression are due more to disinhibitory effects than to direct aggression-producing effects. Thus, while there is experimental evidence for lower animals that alcohol can increase aggression, it does not always do so.

Experimental work with humans has been limited by ethical considerations to subjective studies or tests of mock aggression. Researchers have suggested, for example, that aggressive imagery in projective tests increases with increasing amounts of alcohol. Alcohol also seems to increase aggression in the competitive reaction time test of Taylor. Higher doses of alcohol resulted in competitors selecting higher amounts of shock to be delivered to losing opponents (Taylor & Gammon, 1975). However, again results are not uniform. All individuals do not act more aggressively after alcohol consumption, and even those who do, do not do so at the same dosage levels. The effects of alcohol in humans seem to be affected by expectations, "personality" factors, and perceptions of responsibility for one's acts. The drug's physiological effects do not appear to be sufficient in themselves to determine any effect on aggression (Berry & Brain, 1986). Similarly, Bushman and Cooper (1990) indicate from their analysis of 30 human experiments that alcohol may facilitate aggression, but only when combined with physiological and psychological factors. Further, they note that larger effects of alcohol have been reported in studies that failed to control for experimenter or subject biases and allowed no non-aggressive response alternatives.

Amphetamines and cocaine are two psychostimulants reported to increase aggressive behavior in both lower animal and human studies. These drugs increase the activity of the catecholaminergic neurotransmitters. Given the link of norepinephrine to aggression that we previously discussed, their effects are probably mediated via this catecholamine. However, we cannot discount the role of dopamine definitively. The aggression-enhancing effects of psychostimulants would seem to be contradictory to the aggression-lowering effects of amphetamines discussed earlier. However, this apparent contradiction is really a reflection of how dose and administration regime can affect a drug's observed relation to aggression. For example, Emley and Hutchinson (1983) found, like others, that several doses of both amphetamines and cocaine can produce increased aggression in their experimental animals. They also observed that higher doses resulted in decreased aggression. In earlier work with cocaine in their laboratory, they noted that the effects differed, depending on several variables, including acute versus chronic administration and the means of evoking the aggression (Hutchinson, Emley, & Krasnegor, 1977).

Caffeine, found in coffee, tea, and chocolate, as well as some soft drinks and medicines, is a psychostimulant that has different effects on aggression, depending on various factors. It may increase post-synaptic neuronal activity in the catecholaminergic systems (Waldeck, 1973), and thus should be an agonist for these neurotransmitter systems, although it also has been reported to have varying effects on norepinephrine and dopamine. Researchers have reported that chronic administration of caffeine increases self-aggression in rats (Peters, 1967), while acute administration produces decreased isolation-induced aggression in mice (Valzelli & Bernasconi, 1973). Extended use of caffeine by humans is said to cause caffeinism, which includes hyperirritability as one of several symptoms. However, dysphoria, usually including irritability, nervousness, and restlessness, occurs on withdrawal from caffeine, and is relieved by resumption of consumption (see Valzelli, 1981). The effects of caffeine may occur via direct action on the catecholaminergic and serotonergic systems or production of long-term changes in their receptor populations.

Nicotine, as found in tobacco, may have an inhibitory effect on aggression. Among other effects, it stimulates one class of cholinergic receptors in the brain and body and may also increase dopaminergic activity in related brain systems. Waldbillig (1980) reported that nicotine injections in rats reduced attack against mice and other rats. Emley and Hutchinson (1983) noted that injections of low and intermediate doses of nicotine into squirrel monkeys reduced their biting attack behavior in response to tail shock. Further, humans emit less aggressive jaw-clenching behavior in response to stressful stimuli when given nicotine. The withdrawal of nicotine from an addicted individual has an opposite effect on aggression. Humans who recently have quit smoking emit higher levels of jaw-clenching behaviors during the first several days afterwards (Hutchinson et al., 1977). Similarly, smokers who were temporarily deprived of cigarettes and also provoked by having money taken away from them exhibited this same "aggressive" behavior, and in turn took money from the supposed culprit. Decreased aggression occurred as the subjects smoked cigarettes with increased nicotine content (Cherek, 1984).

Marijuana or its critical component, delta-9-tetrahydro-cannabinol (THC), has popularly been associated with both increased and decreased aggression, although the preponderance of research indicates that it reduces aggression. Abel (1977) reviewed how a popular myth from the time of Marco Polo and the similarity of the words "assassin" and "hashish" (a variety of marijuana) contributed to its association with violence. This association was further supported by more contemporary correlative studies of criminals who use marijuana. However, Abel found no consistent causative link.

It seems that only under special conditions is marijuana associated with increased aggression. For example, Carlini and his associates reported increased aggression in rats given the drug when under stress, such as that produced by sleep deprivation (Alves, Goyos, & Carlini, 1973) or food deprivation (Carlini & Masur, 1970). In further work, Carlini referred to human cases involving the loss of inhibition, psychotic states, and some temporal lobe dysrhythmias that follow marijuana use, and he indicated that aggressive effects in humans may be enhanced, as in rats, by stressful situations.

As we saw earlier with other drugs, the effects of marijuana on aggression may change with variations in testing situations. For example, Carder and Olson (1972) first found that marijuana increased shock-elicited fighting in rats. However, they then observed that higher doses and/or repeated testing resulted in decreases in aggression. A parallel finding for humans was reported by Myerscough (see Taylor & Leonard, 1983), who employed the Taylor competitive reaction time test described earlier in our discussion of alcohol's effects. Low doses of THC resulted in subjects selecting increased levels of shocks for losers, while higher doses were followed by selecting lower shock levels to be delivered to the opponent.

In animal work with various species and types of aggression, marijuana extracts have been found to decrease aggression (e.g., McDonough, Manning, & Elsmore, 1972; Miczek, 1978; Santos, Sampaio, Fernández, & Carlini, 1966). When THC does lower aggression, the reason is not clear. The discovery of a brain receptor and, more recently, a possible endogenous (natural internal substance) neurochemical that acts on the receptor (Devane, Hanus, Breuer, Pertwee, Stevenson, Griffin, Gibson, Mandelbaum, Etinger, & Mechoulam, 1992) promises to help explain how THC functions and may lead to the development of a drug to help reduce aggression.

Anabolic steroids, taken to increase muscle bulk by athletes and others, have been associated with elevated levels of aggression and manic-like psychotic episodes (Pope & Katz, 1990). Accounts of their ability to produce excessive violence in athletes are, regrettably, legion, and the problems seem to be increasing (see Brower, Blow, Eliopulos, & Beresford, 1989). Anabolic steroids also produce many other undesirable side effects. For example, while they can be derived from testosterone, their extensive use may create a negative feedback effect that results in lowered body testosterone and testicular atrophy. Further, they may be converted to estrogen and produce breast growth in men. In women, they may disrupt reproductive functions and cause masculinization. Taylor (1991) presents an extensive description of problems involving their abuse.

Lysergic acid diethylamide (LSD) is a hallucinogen that seems to have dose-related effects on aggression. As a potent seratonergic antagonist at low doses, LSD facilitates aggression in lower animals. At higher doses, however, it inhibits the usual target cells for serotonin, mimicking the action of serotonin and reducing aggression (Sheard, Astrachan, & Davis, 1977). Its effect on human aggression is hard to predict and probably also depends on dose levels as well as expectations, individual differences, and the particular types of hallucinations this drug produces. Following extensive abuse, a long-term psychiatric problem, resembling bipolar affective disorder, can occur.

OTHER DRUGS ASSOCIATED WITH INCREASED AGGRESSION

The abuse of a number of drugs results in various severe psychiatric problems with enough consistency that they are listed in compendia of disorders such as the DSM-IV (APA, 1994). (See p. 40). Guides for professionals treating violent patients also describe the aggressive effects of drugs. For example, Tardiff (1989) indicates that several of the following drugs or drug types have been associated with increased aggression. Causation has not necessarily been established, and variations in dose and other factors might be expected to produce differing results. However, these drugs have been consumed by many violent patients. Julien (1995) provides further details on the functions and effects of these and other drugs affecting aggression.

Phencyclidine (PCP) is a psychoactive drug with a wide range of effects on the central nervous system since it is an antagonist to part of the glutamate neurotransmitter system. (Glutamate is the major excitatory neurotransmitter found throughout the brain.) While it is sometimes grouped with LSD as an hallucinogen, it is more likely to produce delusions and mood disorder. It has a dissociative and disinhibitory effect that can be accompanied by extremely high levels of indiscriminate aggression, along with impulsivity and severely impaired judgment. Even with limited use, long-term psychotic effects can occur.

Inhalants, such as the fumes from gasoline, glue, paint thinners, and other substances, may result in intoxication and initial behavioral effects much like those of PCP. Inhalant intoxication is considered more likely to produce aggression than alcohol intoxication.

Sedatives and anxiolytics, taken in excessive doses, may cause increases of aggression attributed by some to disinhibition and impaired judgment, although aggression from sedatives and anxiolytics is less likely than that associated with the use of inhalants and alcohol. We discussed the paradoxical aggression produced by tranquilizers during therapy earlier. Withdrawal may also produce increased aggression.

SUMMARY

Neurotransmitters are involved in the communication between the nerve cells concerned with aggression. Their study is important in understanding the way in which the Onset and Offset Aggression Systems affect behavior. A number of steps occur in neurotransmitter preparation, release, receptor effects, and effect termination. Drugs can facilitate or interfere with neurotransmission at each step. Unfortunately, our knowledge of neurotransmitter roles in aggression and the effects of drugs has been impeded by methodological problems.

Acetylcholine has been found to increase aggression when administered to temporal lobe, hypothalamic, and other neural areas in several species. General, accidental exposure to cholinergic agonists can also increase human aggression. Still other observations and manipulations support acetylcholine's facilitatory effect on aggression.

Norepinephrine has been associated with increased aggression in drug experiments where aggression is elevated or reduced in parallel with norepinephrine levels. Also, increased utilization of norepinephrine occurs during aggression. In humans, manic states follow spontaneous rises in norepinephrine or can be produced by agonists and reduced by antagonists.

Dopamine is a fundamental neurotransmitter involved in the pleasurable effects related to the aggression-limiting function during activity of the Offset Aggression System. It also has been associated with increased aggression in experiments involving its manipulation. Disagreement arises over the relative roles of dopamine and norepinephrine. Part of this disagreement stems from the fact that dopamine is a precursor to norepinephrine, and drugs that affect aggression often affect both neurotransmitters.

Serotonin has been consistently associated with decreased aggression in lower animal experiments involving both augmentation and reduction of serotonergic activity. Decreased levels of activity have been found in suicidal individuals and sex-related murderers.

Various classes of drugs have been effectively used to control aggression. Many affect the neurotransmitters that influence aggression. Some that are known from their administration to psychotics, such as the major tranquilizers and lithium, are also used to control aggression in non-psychotics. Similarly, the psychostimulants used for hyperactive disorder and the anticonvulsants for seizure disorders have been reported to help control aggression in individuals in the absence of clear evidence of these disorders.

Common drugs affecting aggression include legal, relatively unrestricted substances such as alcohol, nicotine, and caffeine, and restricted substances, including the amphetamines, marijuana, and anabolic steroids. Their effects have been studied experimentally, with some conflicting results, and they have been linked to effects on various neurotransmitters. Some of these drugs can decrease aggression; however, most abuse of the drugs has been associated with increased aggression.

Suggested Readings

Julien, R. M. (1995). *A primer of drug action*. New York: W. H. Freeman.
Tupin, J. P., Shader, R. I., and Harnett, D. S. (Eds.) (1988). *Handbook of clinical psychopharmacology*. Northvale, NJ: Jason Aronson.

PART II

Environmental and Social Factors in Aggression

Now that we have examined some of the contributions of biological factors to aggression, we can explore the influences of variables originating externally and deriving from an individual's experiences. Again, we should keep in mind that while we discuss biological and environmental/social factors separately, they do function interdependently. Many environmental and social factors depend directly on biological mechanisms for their effects, and relatively separable influences from either biology or the environmental/social setting typically interact in some way to determine levels of aggression.

The present section will proceed from simple to more complex ways in which aggression is affected by the environment. Thus, we will first examine the stimuli that more or less naturally produce aggression.

Chapter 7 will describe how conditioning can expand the number of stimuli that produce aggression and how the learning process involving antecedents and consequences of aggression can increase its occurrence in the future. We will see how conditioning and one type of learning process have adaptive functions that help individuals to reduce aversive stimulation. Also, we will learn how aggression can be increased by a history of obtaining rewards for it. We will also discuss applications of conditioning and learning principles for reducing aggression.

Chapter 8 covers the learning of aggression via social contributions. This will include how aggressive acts are acquired and maintained by observation and social interactions and how cognitive functions may contribute.

The last chapter in this part will expand on Chapter 8 to examine how observational learning may occur via the media, especially by watching television. We will review the bases for conclusions that watching violence in the media can produce violence and discuss how any such effect might be reduced. We will also present criticisms of the conclusions.

From the materials in this part, readers should have a good understanding of the major ways in which an individual's experiences can affect aggression. By combining these materials with those from Part I, we can understand the fundamental biological, psychological, and social causes of aggression, as well as appreciate the possibilities for controlling it.

CHAPTER 6
Eliciting Stimuli

This chapter examines various types and examples of environmental conditions that may result in aggression. Usually, attempts to understand environment-aggression relationships do not consider involvement of biological mechanisms. However, we must remember that biological and environmental factors are not necessarily independent, and in the case of aggression, scientists have found an important functional parallel. As indicated earlier, the production of aggression by stimulation of the Onset and Offset Aggression Systems in the brain follows the same relationship as production of aggression by two classes of environmental events—presentation of aversive stimuli or removal of pleasurable stimuli. In addition to this neural-environmental parallel, environmental effects on aggression are determined in part by inherited biological mechanisms that help assure the survival of individuals. Biologically based functions determine both sensitivity to stimuli and behaviors elicited by them. That is, aggression produced by the environment may have a self-protective function developed during the evolution of a species. This aggression either serves to help the individual react effectively to minimize damage inflicted by others or may help maintain resources important to the individual's well-being. In this chapter, however, we will de-emphasize biological influences in favor of descriptions of how external stimuli affect aggression.

In discussing the stimuli that produce aggression, we again emphasize that in this text aggression is considered as always being determined by some variable, never without cause. There is no such thing as an "unprovoked first attack," as some people define aggression. It may not be easily discovered, but an initiating condition for aggression always exists. We will detail some of those conditions here.

THE PRESENTATION OF NOXIOUS STIMULI AND AGGRESSION

Noxious stimuli are those whose onset is unpleasant in some way to the individual, and possibly harmful to it. The potential of these stimuli for harming the organism is a threat to its integrity, and various biologically programmed reactions have developed to limit such stimuli. Indeed, since noxiousness can be a rather subjectively defined condition, stimuli suspected of being noxious preferably are judged by the organism's response to them. A common way of objectively defining noxious stimuli is to determine whether the individual will do something to terminate (**escape**) them or prevent (**avoid**) their occurrence, or whether a behavior followed by them will be suppressed (**punished**). Aggression is a frequent reaction that terminates noxious stimuli. Thus, aggressive responses to noxious stimuli may also be used for evaluating the character of the stimuli. When a stimulus affects behavior in one or more (preferably all) of the ways previously described, it is considered an **aversive** stimulus. This section presents descriptions of studies about the unlearned effects of various aversive stimuli on aggression. Chapter 7 will include discussion of how learning affects aggressive responding to aversive stimuli.

Pain is one type of noxious stimulus that has been extensively employed in studies of aggression. Pain is also a subjective condition, since different individuals may give different estimates of pain for apparently identical stimuli. However, the pain perceived by an individual for any given stimulus can still be defined objectively by measuring its effect on behavior. Unfortunately, such definition exercises sometimes involve circular reasoning, but if several behavioral effects are measured, we can make a stronger case. Thus, instead of defining pain as a stimulus that will be escaped and then turning around to define escape as occurring when a painful stimulus is present, the painful stimulus can be defined by (1) its effect on escape as well as (2) its effectiveness as a punisher and as (3) an elicitor of aggression. Despite its subjective components, the term "pain" has been used frequently in scientific literature to connote a stimulus whose characteristics have been established by such multiple tests.

Progress in our understanding of the relation between pain and aggression has been greatly facilitated by extensive laboratory studies involving delivery of electric shocks to lower animals. We discussed the ethical concerns of aggression research in Chapter 1 and remind readers that each experiment must follow the ethical guidelines of the profession. Electric shock has been used because its values can be highly specified and controlled and it can be adjusted to produce an effect that is brief and does not involve tissue damage. This has allowed a more precise determination of the effects of painful stimuli than would, for example, the use of physically damaging blows or lacerations, and at the same time has limited actual damage to the subjects.

Investigators with naturalistic or ethological orientations have stated, correctly, that essentially no animals fight in nature because of electrical shocks, and they therefore have attempted to dismiss research done with shocks. However, many others have seen that shocks are simply a useful substitute for natural aversive stimuli and have employed shock to produce what are considered valid research results. Support for the validity of a finding includes evidence that the finding is not a limited artifact of the testing conditions and can be applied (generalized) to other settings and subjects. We will include several examples of validation later in this chapter and support other findings not discussed here. For example, many results of shock studies are reinforced by parallel findings from studies that involved other, more natural, stimuli for aggression. Further, the behaviors produced by shock are like those behaviors occurring in relation to pain in more natural situations. As we noted in Chapter 1, while some investigators have debated specific labels used for these behaviors and situations, the behaviors produced by shock correspond to general definitions of aggression, such as that given on p. 6—that is, they are directed toward a target and result in damage.

The use of shock to produce aggression became widespread following the report by Ulrich and Azrin (1962). In their study, foot shock applied to two rats in a small cage caused them to rear up and strike and bite at each other, in much the same way as wild rats fight. Although several earlier investigations had pointed out the relation of foot shock to aggression in mice and in rats, the results of the earlier studies were not widely known, in part perhaps because of the modesty of the authors' efforts. Azrin and his colleagues engaged in a major series of exhaustive studies to specify the nature of the shock/aggression phenomenon. It was not sufficient for them simply to note that shock could produce fighting in rats. Rather, they had to establish the specific nature of the relationships in order to understand them more fully and appreciate their implications.

Azrin and his colleagues continued to explore the effects of the different parameters or characteristics of shock on fighting, including measuring the effects of different shock durations, frequencies, and intensities. One interesting finding, shown in Figure 6.1 (solid line), was that fighting increased with shock intensity to a point, but further increases resulted in decreased fighting (Ulrich & Azrin, 1962). This nonlinear or parabolic relationship between eliciting stimulus and aggression also occurs in human studies. In other work with rats, researchers found that a first and preferred response to shock was to escape it. However, if escape was not possible, fighting occurred (Ulrich & Craine, 1964). Also, more crowded conditions tended to potentiate fighting (Ulrich & Azrin, 1962). The exploration of the crowding variable in humans also produces similar results, as we will discuss later.

The validity and relevance of any experimental finding are increased as its generality is established. If the fighting elicited by shock occurred only under very limited conditions and only with rats, then it would not be of great general interest. However, various studies demonstrated the effect's generality. Ulrich and Azrin (1962) and others showed that stimuli other than shock, such as heat or a pinch, will result in fighting. Thus, the fighting is not just an effect of unnatural shocks. (To encompass these various stimuli as well as other results, this relationship is often referred to as **pain-elicited fighting** instead of shock- or pain shock-elicited fighting.) A further indication of generality is that shock applied to the flanks via implanted wires or to the tail produces upright fighting like that produced by foot shock. Thus, the upright fighting posture is not just an artifact of rats reacting to minimize the shock

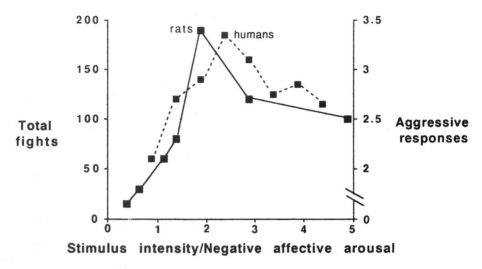

Figure 6.1   The effect of increasing eliciting stimulus intensity on aggressive responding. The data for rats were taken from Ulrich and Azrin (1962). Stimulus intensity was measured in milliamperes of electrical foot shock, and numbers of fights were recorded by observers. The data for humans were taken from Bell and Baron (1976). Degree of affective arousal was estimated from a combination of tone of evaluations, temperature of testing environment, and similarity of attitudes between evaluator and subject. Aggressive responding was measured from a combination of shock intensity and durations selected in button pressing by the subjects in the teacher-learner situation.

applied to their feet. Indeed, rats who have been made hyperemotional by septal lesions display the upright fighting activity in the absence of shock, following contact of one by the other.

Various studies have demonstrated the generalization of the shock-fighting relationship to other species. Hutchinson (1973) summarized much of this work, which includes more than 30 species, over a wide phylogenetic range, from insects through primates. In humans, some of the neuropsychological studies discussed in Chapter 4 reflect a relationship between pain and aggression. Brain lesions that reduce aggression may also alleviate pain, while stimulation that produces aggression also may induce pain. Other work done with different stimuli has found similar stimulus-aggression relationships in humans.

Shock-aggression relationships occurred between species as well as within species, as Hutchinson also found (1973). Thus, "natural" enemies, such as cats and rats (who, it should be recalled, do not always fight without special provocation), will fight on receiving foot shock. Also, less natural pairings between animals such as rats and squirrel monkeys produce fighting.

The results of these studies indicate that the shock-fighting relationship first found for rats receiving foot shock has great potential as a model for studying the determinants of aggression. Although a complete description of this model's applications is beyond our scope here, an impressive range of studies has been carried out throughout the scientific world employing this model to study various factors, including neural, pharmaceutical, and environmental, that affect aggression. Viken and Knutson (1992) summarize some of this research, along with work cited above, that demonstrates the parallels in control of shock-elicited aggression and other types of aggression, and they review some advances in the general understanding of aggression resulting from using this technique. They indicate how shock-elicited fighting is affected by several variables—the sex of the subjects, castration of males, and conditions in living cages—in the same way that these variables affect aggression studied under more "natural" conditions, such as in interactions in the territories where the animals live. Further, differences in experiences with "natural" fighting affect the amount of shock-elicited fighting that can be produced. Thus, they argue that the shock-elicited fighting method is a valid and valuable way of studying aggression. Its validity is supported by the parallel effects of various independent variables on it and more natural aggression, as well as its interaction with more natural aggressive experiences. Its value is shown in how it helps to study the effects of the independent variables under sensitive, highly controlled conditions.

As we have noted before, one common component of the adaptive attack behaviors of the various species studied is that the attacking individual usually will bite its opponent. This often results in severe wounding of the other animal. Not only is this of ethical concern, but it also creates a chaotic fighting situation difficult to control and measure. Therefore, researchers pursued the study of biting itself. After they observed that squirrel monkeys would grab and bite an inanimate object (a terry-cloth-covered tennis ball) in response to shock (Azrin, Hutchinson, & McLaughlin, 1965), they developed attack targets that allowed for accurate, sensitive measures of biting responses. Thus, instead of simply having a dichotomous (yes–no) measure of fighting, they could record the latency, frequency, intensity, and patterns of biting responses. This "victimless" method of studying aggression has been extended to other species, including normal human volunteers of various ages (Hutchinson, Pierce, Emley, Proni, & Sauer, 1977). Naturally, it should be remembered that biting (or jaw clenching) behavior is not the only response involved in aggression. Further, biting, as included in, say, eating or gnawing, and jaw clenching, as when preparing to lift a heavy object, occur in situations other than those apparently associated with aggression. Therefore, using biting or jaw-clenching behaviors to study aggression has necessitated systematic comparison with the results of studies involving other more complex displays of aggression. Nevertheless, the results parallel those involving live opponents and less controlled interactions, and so these studies of biting have been demonstrated as valid ways of studying aggression. More important, they have provided valuable new information about the causes and control of aggression.

These studies indicate that the pain-aggression relationship is consistently found in a wide range of conditions and species. Further, aggression is a common behavior in humans who are suffering from painful injuries or conditions (e.g., burns, severe back problems). Uncontrolled observations of everyday life, however, might point out that it does not occur with the same consistency in all cases. One individual might react aggressively to pain very readily while another does not. Apart from variability in sensitivity to pain, other explanations for these individual differences are possible. For example, past consequences for an aggressive response may operate to enhance it. A probable common cause for this is that aggression has been followed by the cessation of pain or escape from it; the inflictor of the pain was defeated or ran away. Alternatively, aggressive behaviors might be at a high level because the individual has learned through past experience that aggression will be followed by something desirable, such as approval from friends. Consequences for an individual's aggression may also produce decreased responding to pain if the aggression was punished or otherwise discouraged. For example, the typical child in many societies is taught by parents or other caretakers at a very early age that it is not appropriate to be highly aggressive. Biting, the ubiquitous component of aggression measured in the laboratory, is often chastised, perhaps accompanied by the admonition that "Only babies bite." (Despite this, the details of assault records show that it remains as a common element in altercations between adults. Forensic odontology includes the study of bite wounds on victims and suspects. For example, see Levine, 1972; Sperber, 1990.) Similarly, adults are discouraged by most others to refrain from aggressive reactions to pain. The nature and effects of these and other learning processes on aggression have been studied extensively and we will discuss them in the next chapter.

In addition to the effects of learning processes on the consistency of the pain-aggression relationship, another experiential variable can affect it. Hutchinson, Renfrew, and Young (1971) showed that long-term administration of shock to squirrel monkeys resulted in extremely large increases in the animals' aggression. Following a one- to two-month period when shock was given daily in sessions lasting about an hour or less, the biting would occur not only just after shock delivery but also during the approximately four minutes between shocks. This elevated aggression level would start in the latter part of a session and continue until the session ended, and the cycle would repeat itself in subsequent sessions, although beginning earlier and earlier in the sessions. Apparently, the procedures produced a "chronic" state of aggression. We will analyze why in the next chapter, but for now should note that the situation can be taken as a possible model for how high levels of aggression may be produced in humans under long-lasting stressful conditions.

SOCIAL PSYCHOLOGICAL STUDIES OF STIMULI THAT PRODUCE AGGRESSION

Social psychological studies are those done to examine aggressive interactions between two or more individuals. Obviously, there are many ways to approach such study. For our purpose, we use the label of **social psychologists** to indicate a subgroup of investigators who share a general theoretical orientation and employ similar methodologies to study aggression in humans. For example, in considering stimuli that produce aggression, social psychologists usually recognize the role of stressful environmental events as contributors to aggression. Such events are not typically seen as sufficient in themselves to cause aggression, but they may contribute to some cognitively mediated subjective state that may in turn lead to aggression. An example of such a model is found in Mueller (1983). In his schema, environmental stressors are capable of producing an emotional effect or contributing to a change of state in the individual. These conditions in turn may be affected by ongoing anger or may produce a cognitive state that finally leads to some type of aggression. The orientation of Baron (1977), a major contributor to this area of research, is similar in that he emphasizes the importance of the cognitive mediation of a stressful stimulus to explain why aggression occurs. As one part of his analysis, he describes the relation between an emotional state called "negative affect" (as in discomfort associated with anger or an aversive environment) and the amount of aggression a person displays. He finds a non-monotonic or parabolic function, in which as negative affect increases, aggression increases to a point and then decreases. This relationship is, of course, essentially the same as we saw for the relationship between shock level and aggression in rats. Figure 6.1 illustrated both relationships, and we can see that they follow a very similar pattern. The basic difference is that shock level is an objectively defined external variable, while negative affect is a subjectively defined internal state.

Because of the difficulty of determining internal conditions, such as negative affect, many investigators who do not follow the approach of the social psychologists have preferred simply to focus on objective variables, as we do in this book. They assume that better progress in understanding aggression will occur if attention is given to the measurement of observable events as opposed to the postulation of internal states for explaining external behaviors. However, many other investigators follow Mueller and Baron's orientation. Some have taken a parallel approach when they refer to internal factors as mediators for determining whether aggression will occur. For example, Mawson (1987), like the social psychologists, emphasizes the role of stressors, such as unemployment or interpersonal problems, on the production of uncharacteristic aggression or other criminal acts ("Transient Criminality") when the stressors result in some incongruity with the individual's "cognitive map" (expectations and sense of order) of his or her environment.

Social psychologists have produced much of the research on aggression and probably have been responsible for the majority of the experimental psychology work done with human aggression. Further, the results of part of their work complement those of the work with lower animals we previously described. Indeed, Berkowitz (1993) has emphasized the parallels between lower animals and humans in how aversive stimulation can produce aggression. He also notes how cognitive processes in humans affect the aggressive response. Despite the methodological difficulties of the social psychological approach, the correspondence of its results to those from other methodologies lends support to their validity. Therefore, we will describe some of the more relevant studies here.

The Effect of Noise

Noise is an auditory stimulus that is considered aversive at high intensities. It is also an arousing stimulus that can generate various adaptive emergency reactions, including fighting. Fighting might be seen as an adaptive response to noise if it results in the noise's termination. Apart from whether this adaptive function is fulfilled, organisms have developed so that noise itself can elicit aggression. This relationship has been demonstrated in rats, where some success has been achieved in eliciting fighting in response to noise (Ulrich & Azrin, 1962). A parallel finding has occurred in studies of humans. Hutchinson, Pierce, Emley, Proni, and Sauer (1977), using jaw clenching as a measure of aggression in four volunteers, presented 110-dB 3000-hz tones for two seconds every three minutes. This noise intensity was below the 120- to 130-dB level considered painful, although just 60 dB—the level associated with a conversation—is thought sufficient to produce arousal. In any event, the 110-dB tone was at a level judged to be aversive. In this study, all the subjects responded with increased jaw-clenching responses after the tones.

Noise, in conjunction with other variables, has been employed by social psychologists to increase aggressive responding. Apart from having lower noise levels and a different aggression measure than Hutchinson, et al., a different orientation is used. As we indicated, the social psychological approach usually considers stressful stimuli as contributors to internal states that determine whether aggression will occur. Therefore, social psychologists also attempt to manipulate internal states. They may, for example, try to anger their subjects, or justify the aggression, or inform them about physiological effects of stimuli. In an early study on noise by Geen and O'Neal (1969), some subjects were exposed to a 60-dB noise, considered arousing but not annoying. To affect their tendencies to aggress, researchers showed the subjects one of two types of sports films. One subgroup saw an aggressive boxing film, while the other watched an exciting, but non-aggressive track film. Aggression was measured by the teacher-learner technique and a Buss-type shock apparatus, as described earlier (p. 16). In this situation, the "teachers" (really the subjects) selected levels of shocks that they thought were delivered to "learners" (really confederates of the experimenters) for errors in essay writing or some learning task. The subjects were told to use the shocks to aid in their "teaching," but researchers took the intensity and number of shocks chosen as measures of aggression. The main effect was that the subjects exposed to the noise and the boxing film selected the greatest number and intensity of shocks. For some reason, the subjects who saw the track film but were not exposed to the noise were somewhat more aggressive than those who saw the boxing film. Also, for subjects watching the track film, those who were exposed to the noise appeared to be less aggressive than the others.

Donnerstein and Wilson (1976) obtained results similar to the main findings of Geen and O'Neal, but with higher noise levels and a different complementary variable. They found that when subjects were exposed to 65- or 95-dB noise levels, the higher levels resulted in increased shock levels on the Buss machine, but only if experimenters had also angered the subjects.

Konečni(1975), explored the effects of different types of noise as well as intensity. Here, he varied both loudness and complexity (number of frequencies involved) of the stimuli. They found that angered subjects delivered more Buss-machine shocks when exposed to loud simple, loud complex, or soft complex sound than those exposed to soft simple sounds or no sounds. Sound stimuli by themselves were found to have no effect on aggression.

One explanation given by some social psychologists for the emotional effects of stressful stimuli is that they produce a physiological arousal that may be attributed to an ongoing emotion. Conversely, if researchers explain the physiological effects to a subject, the individual will not react emotionally to them. An early model for such an approach is that of Schachter and Singer (1962). They reported that subjects injected with adrenalin would react more emotionally than others, unless the drug's effects were explained to them. While this work has been criticized for having minimal effects and being poorly controlled, the paradigm has continued to be used by others. Harris and Huang (1974) applied this technique to subjects being exposed to noise. They found that those who were **informed** about the arousal effects of noise as well as angered would exhibit less oral aggressiveness than those who were **ignorant**. However, a study by Geen (1978) indicated that informing subjects did not eliminate the aggression-producing effects of noise. His informed subjects who were exposed to a 90-dB noise were still more aggressive than non-informed, low-noise subjects. Therefore, it seems that noise itself produces increases in aggression, while ignorance of its arousing effects may raise it still further, but that information about its arousing effects does not completely eliminate the increased aggression that noise produces.

The Effect of Heat

Heat has been a moderately effective stimulus for increasing aggression in rats, when applied to their feet (Ulrich & Azrin, 1962), and works as an environmental stressor in mice (Greenberg, 1972). Also, high environmental temperature has been found to augment the aggression produced by foot shock in rats. Berry and Jack (1971) reported increased fighting as they raised test chamber temperatures from 4° to 21° to 38° Celsius. (40°, 70°, 100° Fahrenheit). On the other hand, increased temperature and humidity may not increase aggression in tropically reared monkeys. A graduate student, whose name and institution are mercifully withheld, displayed great engineering ingenuity but little understanding of nature as he tried to see if placing squirrel monkeys in a high heat and humidity environment would make them more aggressive. A similar approach seemed more effective with some humans, although measurements of aggression were somewhat subjective. Rohles (1967) reported that juveniles (but not graduate students—who perhaps are adapted to "heat" as an integral part of their training) placed in a heated chamber had higher aggression levels in their interactions with others.

Two attempts to study the effects of temperature on human aggression have yielded inconclusive results. Baron (1972) tested male college students in either 23° or 34° Celsius temperatures. He had the students write essays that were arbitrarily either positively or negatively graded. The negative grade was meant to anger the subjects, who then were allowed to select shock levels for others. This first study found that **less** aggression occurred in the higher temperature condition. Further, a second study, by Baron and Bell (1975) showed inconsistent results. In a summary of their work, Bell and Baron (1981) attributed the discrepancies to possible differences in procedures that made the essay evaluations less threatening in some cases. They also suggested that differences in the outside temperatures at the two schools where the studies were done may have resulted in differential effects of the experimental temperatures.

Researchers have examined the relation of heat to political and criminal violence in several correlational studies. Schwartz (1968) studied incidences of political violence in 51 countries. To encompass the wide range of possible temperatures in the different countries, he analyzed them by quartiles—for example, he divided the temperature range for each locus into four equal subranges. Schwartz found a non-linear distribution of violence, with incidences increasing with temperature up to the third temperature quartile and then decreasing during the highest temperature quartile.

Baron and Ransberger (1978) first noted data indicating that, of 18 riots occurring in the United States during 1967, nine took place when the temperature was above 30° Celsius and the rest occurred at temperatures above 26° Celsius. They extended this study to 102 riots between 1967 to 1971, in various seasons, regions, and climatic zones, and found a non-linear relationship. The number of riots increased with temperature to a peak at 27 to 32° Celsius and then decreased at higher temperatures.

The Schwartz and the Baron and Ransberger studies seem to support the thesis that heat results in increased aggression. Furthermore, they appear to suggest that a non-linear relation exists between a stressful stimulus and aggression. However, subsequent studies showed that the non-linearity was an artifact of the methodology employed.

While Baron recognized the limits of correlational studies and initially presented his data only as an interesting apparent support of his other work (Baron, informal communication), further analysis challenged this support. Carlsmith and Anderson (1979) pointed out that the decreased number of violent events at high temperatures may have simply reflected the fact that fewer days had these temperatures. In fact, when they calculated the relationship between temperatures in New York City and the local Mets baseball team playing a home game, they found the same non-linear relationship as Baron and Ransberger reported; for example, the probability of playing at home peaked at 27° to 32° Celsius. Turning to the question of violence, when Carlsmith and Anderson controlled for differences in the probabilities of days with different temperatures, they observed a linear relationship between urban riots and temperature, which contrasts with the non-linear relationship found by Schwartz and by Baron and Ransberger.

It has been suggested that other variables in addition to temperature may have been operating to produce higher rates of summer violence. For example, during the hot summer, juveniles are not in school and unemployment is greater. Also, more transients are in the cities, more alcohol is consumed, and more interpersonal contacts occur outside. Thus, these variables and not just temperature may have contributed to the higher incidences of violence. Nevertheless, a linear relationship between heat and riot, as well as between heat and a number of violent personal crimes, has been discovered in several studies of temperature by Anderson (1989) and others, even when some of these contributing variables are controlled. Thus, general support exists for the contribution of temperature to aggression.

The Effect of Exercise

Exercise as a stimulus for aggression has been examined in studies that suggest that stronger exercise may, because of its arousal effect, increase aggression (Zillman, Johnson, & Day, 1974; Capara, Renzi, D'Augello, D'Imperio, Rielli, & Travaglia, 1986). For example Capara et al. found that subjects who were required to pedal for two minutes on an ergometer and then participate in a modified teacher-learner situation delivered higher levels of shock than those who simply waited, instead of pedaling before participating. Further factors affecting aggression were individual levels of irritability, the sex of the subjects, and whether they were insulted.

Capara et al. felt that this part of their study supported their position that such stimuli as exercise might facilitate any number of subsequent behaviors, including aggression. However, further findings by them and others indicate that a specific instigation to aggress is important in determining whether aggression will occur.

Both the Zillman et al. and Capara et al. studies suggest that physiological arousal from one source, such as exercise, may later contribute to aggression directed at another object. Contrary to these findings, psychodynamic views of aggression would indicate that it is a drive that can be redirected and satisfied via substitute activities, such as exercise. Thus, supporters of these views would encourage vigorous activities, such as football, to help express aggressive tendencies in a more-or-less controlled, acceptable fashion. People sometimes feel that when they are angry, a good, vigorous exercise period helps them to work off their anger. Goldstein (1989), however, discusses how a number of incorrect cultural beliefs have contributed to a "mythology" of sports violence. It is unlikely that football or other exercise aids in reducing aggression. Consider the violence witnessed on the football field and media stories of the aggression of football players off the field. Any reduction of aggression related to exercise probably occurs because the exercise is incompatible with expressing the aggression—for example, aggressive behavior is precluded while exercising. Also, exercise might reduce aggression because it leaves the individual too tired to aggress. Although Zillman's and Capra's studies suggest that exercise may increase aggression in the teacher-learner situation, it is possible that exercise may reduce aggression produced by pain. It has been found that exercise can elevate pain thresholds in rats and humans. Pertovaara, Huopaniemi, Virtanen, and Johansson (1984) showed that strong but submaximal effort on a bicycle ergometer elevates pain thresholds as measured by a reaction to electrical shocks to teeth. The authors suggest that a modest increased stress hormone release during exercise contributes to the reduced pain sensitivity.

Obviously, the relationship between exercise and aggression is not simple. While there is empirical evidence that exercise can facilitate one type of aggression—in the teacher-learner situation—it also would seem able to reduce pain-based aggression. However, this effect was not explored in the Pertovaara et al. study, so we have only the evidence suggesting that exercise may contribute to increased aggression.

The Effect of Erotic Stimuli

Erotic stimuli can, under certain conditions, increase aggression. For example, Donnerstein and Barrett (1978) angered their male subjects and exposed them to nonviolent erotic films. This resulted in increased aggression, especially against males, in the teacher-learner situation compared to that for those not exposed to the erotic films. In a later study (Donnerstein, 1980) male subjects exposed to violent erotic films but not angered were reported to be more aggressive when their targets were female. However, Donnerstein and others (e.g., Baron & Bell, 1977) also found that mildly erotic films may actually lower aggression in angered subjects, possibly because they distracted the subjects from their aggression.

Laboratory studies by Donnerstein and others indicate that pornography can increase aggression, but also can decrease it. Despite these latter findings, interpretations of findings about increased aggression have been made in attempts to outlaw pornographic materials. Donnerstein and his colleagues reviewed these attempts as well as the research on pornography. They were careful to point out that non-violent pornography has been shown to increase aggression only in special laboratory conditions involving other variables, and that even violent pornography, while more likely to produce aggression, has not been demonstrated to have a long-term effect that results in actual aggression outside the laboratory. That is, it has not been demonstrated that pornography is an independent causal agent of violence (Donnerstein, Linz, & Penrod, 1987).

A prohibition of pornography would have important implications for U.S. Constitutional rights. Further, it may deceive the country into thinking that the fundamental cause of sexual crime has been eliminated and thus delay consideration of more important contributors. Donnerstein, Linz, and Penrod support alternative approaches involving education to mitigate effects of pornography on attitudes concerning sexual violence. We will consider this topic further in Chapters 11 and 12, under our discussion of sexual violence against children and women.

The Effect of Territory and Crowding

Stimuli related to **territory** and **crowding** have been found to produce aggression, or at least contribute to it. While these two variables are not identical, we will consider them together because they are probably related. Although territory is the space that an individual may defend as his or her own, the degree of crowding of individuals into a limited space should be expected to affect the establishment of territories and their potential violations. The ethologists, notably characterized by Tinbergen's Nobel prize-winning work with the stickleback fish, have demonstrated how a wide range of species develops territories and vigorously defends them against intruding individuals. Aggression in the form of territorial defense by resident rats who bite in response to the introduction of non-resident rats has been a main focus of study (e.g., Blanchard, Takahashi, & Blanchard, 1977). Ethologists and many others also have shown how crowding of populations results in increased levels of fighting. We already have noted that Ulrich and Azrin (1962) demonstrated that crowding (produced by reduced testing-cage space) resulted in increased shock-elicited fighting by their rats. Although extensive studies have not been done with humans, some indications are that they also are affected by space variables.

Crowding by itself does not seem sufficient to produce aggressive behavior. Simple measures of correlations between density of populations in cities and rates of aggression do not usually yield significant results. Favorable socioeconomic conditions in luxury high-rise apartments, for example, would outweigh any effects of the high population densities found in such neighborhoods. On the other hand, greater amounts of crowding in living conditions found in homes, college dormitories, and prisons might very well be expected to be associated with higher levels of aggression. Again, it is difficult to determine the effects of crowding while holding other important variables constant. In one experiment (Matthews, Paulus, & Baron, 1979), individuals were put into high- or low-density conditions and given either competitive or cooperative tasks. The high-density condition resulted in lower aggression for those who had been in the competitive task. These findings, along with the others indicating that crowding can help increase aggression, might be taken to support the conclusion that a curvilinear relationship holds between the amount of crowding and the amount of aggression. That is, increased crowding is associated with increased aggression up to a point, after which further crowding is accompanied by reduced aggression. This, of course, is the same general relationship Figure 6.1 illustrated (and claimed by some for heat).

Studies of human territoriality have ranged from observations of urban gangs' establishment and defense of their turf to studies of individual's responses to invasion of their personal space. We will discuss gang territorial behavior in Chapter 10, but here will briefly describe some attempts to study personal space.

Evaluations of territoriality and personal space have indicated that individuals are more aggressive when they are in their own areas. Thus, students are more aggressive in defending their positions in discussions that take place in their own dorm rooms than elsewhere (Martindale, 1971). Also, males (but not females) participating in a mock jury situation are said to be more likely to mete out punishment when they are seated in tighter arrangements than in looser ones (Freedman, Levy, Buchanan, & Price, 1972). Other studies of personal space have measured how closely an individual will allow others to approach and still be comfortable. Individuals who are considered more aggressive have larger personal spaces, and angered individuals increase their personal space. Although measurement made in these studies may not be as objective as we would hope and while there may be questions concerning the validity of the aggression in these situations, the results are interesting for their support of a link between human territoriality and aggression. The role of personal space violation in aggression needs to be more thoroughly examined in future research.

We have seen how the presentation of a number of stimuli can produce aggression by themselves or may at least help to potentiate aggression. Some of the effects seem to be directly related to the production of pain in the subjects. Others might better be considered to have their effects via a general physiological arousal. Understanding such effects will help in recognizing possible causes of aggression. With this information, we can prepare for such aggression and minimize its effects, or perhaps eliminate or minimize such stimuli to reduce aggressive behaviors.

THE REMOVAL OF REINFORCING STIMULI AND AGGRESSION

In addition to the aggression that occurs when aversive stimuli are presented, aggression can also be produced by the removal of reinforcing stimuli. If an individual already possesses or has had access to reinforcers—such as food—that are then taken away or kept from further access, aggression may result. Aggression in such a situation will benefit the organism if it results in recapture of the reinforcers. Therefore, the aggressive reaction might be biologically programmed since it aids in the organism's survival. Regardless of whether or not an inherent mechanism exists for the reaction, it is found widely in many species, including humans.

The Effects of Frustration

The seminal work in the study of aggressive responses to the removal of reinforcers was done in the late 1930s by a group at Yale University (Dollard, Doob,

Miller, Mowrer, & Sears, 1939), who formulated what is known as the **frustration-aggression hypothesis.** Their first statement gave prominence to frustration as the cause of aggression and considered aggression the inevitable result of frustration. Later work by them and by others resulted in less extreme positions, granting other sources of aggression and other outcomes for frustration, but the frustration-aggression relationship is still considered, in some form, of major importance.

Frustration is thought by some to produce aggression not only in short-term interactions but also in long-term situations. For example, economic hardship or chronic underemployment may be considered a frustrating condition that results in increased aggression. Aggression may be further increased by observation of a contrast between the level of living conditions for one group and that of another. Revolts and revolutions can be seen to occur in part from the frustration of the oppressed, who are denied those things possessed by the oppressors. A common historic example of the effects of frustration in a society is the purported relationship between lower prices of cotton in the old South and the number of lynchings of blacks. More recently, rising unemployment rates have been linked to increased crime. Such claims, of course, result from observations in uncontrolled conditions and certainly are oversimplifications. Only a small percentage of white Southerners participated in the lynchings and few of the unemployed turn to crime. Other factors such as adverse past experiences with minorities or a history of criminal behavior were more likely contributors. In addition, it is risky for us to generalize to a sociological condition from a principle derived from the psychological study of individuals. However, we can use the principle in predicting aggression in individual, closely observed cases.

Work on frustration in lower animals has supported and helped refine its relationship to aggression. One finding is that frustration may produce a general arousal in an individual that can be detected by increased levels of behaviors. Skinner (1938) noted bursts of responses by rats during extinction (when the response was no longer rewarded). Amsel and Roussel (1952) worked with rats running down alleys for food. They devised a two-alley situation in which the subjects were trained to run to the end of the first alley for a food reinforcement and then, a short while later, to run from there down a second alley for more reinforcement. When the first-alley reinforcement was eliminated, the rats ran faster down the second alley. Although the original theoretical explanation for this, based on increased motivation, was later found to be incorrect, the frustrating experience did seem to produce a physiological effect associated with arousal.

A similar effect may have occurred in a study of lever pressing by rats. They were being reinforced with lateral hypothalamic brain stimulation on a schedule of reinforcement called Fixed Interval, where only responses that occur after a set period of time are reinforced (Renfrew, 1966). Thus, the rats' initial responses after a previous reinforcement are not reinforced. Immediately following reinforcement, an atypical burst of lever-pressing responses occurred. In both the alley-running and lever-pressing situations, frustration-produced aggression may have resulted if the appropriate target had been available. Alternatively, some investigators (e.g., Falk, 1966) have indicated that aggression is just one of several "adjunctive" behaviors that might be aroused after reinforcement. That is, it is part of an excitatory effect produced by the reinforcer itself, not by non-reinforcement. The orientation of the social psychologists is similar in their claim that aggression is not an inevitable consequence of a stimulus event. In their studies of various environmental stimuli that produce aggression, such as noise, they cite the arousing effect of the stimuli and indicate that those effects lead to increased aggression only when certain supporting cognitive or emotional conditions are present.

Whether aggression is a selected response to arousal or only one of several possible responses is not always able to be determined from most studies, where response possibilities are limited. What is important is that a consistent relationship has been found between the environmental condition of the offset of reinforcement (frustration) and the behavior of aggression. Many studies have shown that aggression occurs as a directed response to frustration: the organism orients toward a target, approaches it, and attacks it. In this sense it is not just a simple, uncontrolled reaction to stimuli, but a directed reaction. Moreover, even if aggression were only one of several possible reactions associated with arousal, its inclusion in these possibilities implies that it can occur and must be studied if we are to fully understand the causes of aggression.

Aggression Following Removal or Reduction of Reinforcers in Lower Animals

Azrin, Hutchinson, and Hake (1966) showed that termination of food reinforcement for pigeons who had been trained to peck at a key was followed by attack against other pigeons. Subjects were studied in a cage where the key and food tray were on one side and a target pigeon restrained on the other. During reinforcement, no attacks occurred, but soon after the reinforcement ended, the subject approached and pecked at the target. When stuffed pigeons were substituted for the live targets, attacks also occurred, although at a reduced level.

The effects of stopping reinforcing brain stimulation have been shown to produce aggressive responding. As we noted in Chapter 3, Hutchinson and Renfrew (1978) found that the offset of reinforcing brain stimulation in **encéphale isolé** subjects produced biting. Further, rats who were pressing a lever for brain stimulation reinforcers would bite the hand of an imprudent experimenter who tried to handle them just after stimulation ended (Renfrew & Hutchinson, 1983a).

Researchers have found that aggression will occur when reinforcement occurs only intermittently. Hutchinson, Azrin, and Hunt (1968) reported that squirrel monkeys who were trained to press a lever for food would bite a hose target during a Fixed Ratio schedule, when a high number of responses was required for each reinforcer. Biting occurred at times just after a previous reinforcement, and happened most often following that, as the next long series of responses was starting. Other studies have demonstrated that this non-reinforcement time period in ratio schedules is most aversive to subjects, probably because it is associated with the time when reinforcement will not occur and with the start of the long series of responses needed to obtain the next reinforcer.

The generality of this aggressive effect of non-reinforcement was supported by demonstrations that other schedules of intermittent reinforcement, such as Fixed Interval, will also produce aggression. Richards and Rilling (1972) demonstrated that pigeons will attack when exposed to such schedules. The highest percentage of attacks occurred in the period just after reinforcement, when no further reinforcement was possible.

Aggression can be produced when intermittent reinforcement takes place only on some timed schedule. Just the termination of reinforcers—and not a response requirement—is sufficient to produce aggressive responding; Azrin, Hutchinson, and Hake (1966) observed attack responses by their pigeons that occurred when free access to food was terminated for five minutes. In addition, presenting reinforcers only occasionally will produce target attack. Flory (1969) found that such attack occurred maximally when pigeons were given food automatically every one to two minutes. This is the same type of effect found in **encéphale isolé** subjects after the offset of brain stimulation in reinforcing areas.

Removal or Reduction of Reinforcers in Humans

The effects of reinforcer removal and intermittent reinforcement just discussed have been studied in humans. Hutchinson et al. (1977) measured the jaw clenching of paid volunteers, recorded just before and after quitting smoking. This situation was considered an example of the removal of a powerful reinforcer. Seven of the eight subjects who quit had increases in the frequency and duration of jaw clenching, usually peaking in the initial week after they stopped smoking. In another situation not involving smoking, payment for the sessions was indicated by regular increases on an electronic counter placed in front of the subjects. After several sessions, the counter was stopped after the first few numbers, indicating that no more money was forthcoming. This cessation of reinforcers had no noticeable effect during the first session, since the four subjects probably believed the counter had broken. However, they were paid the reduced amount; during subsequent similar sessions, biting increased after the counter was deactivated. In these sessions, the subjects also became verbally aggressive, with strong threats to quit and complaints about the conditions of the experiment. A bonus promised for completing the whole experiment apparently helped maintain their attendance.

In their extensive study, Hutchinson et al. measured the effects of intermittent reinforcement. They required their subjects to earn money for responding under a Fixed Ratio schedule, just as in the study with squirrel monkeys responding for food. Jaw clenching increased to some extent for most subjects as more work was required, and increased clenching was observed during the time just after reinforcement. These results were similar to those obtained for the squirrel monkeys. In other situations, humans not only clenched their jaws but also, as reported in informal observations, were seen to swear, kick the apparatus, slam books down, and threaten the experimenter when reinforcers were reduced. As noted earlier, the observation of parallels between effects in studies of lower animals and humans, and, for humans, between jaw clenching and other, more common examples of aggression, supports the validity of using jaw clenching as an index of aggression. Further support for the validity of this method is that similar manipulations (e.g., schedules of reinforcement) produce similar aggressive behavior patterns. Finally, the validity of the results is supported by their generality within humans, which occurred for subjects of both sexes and a wide range of ages (17 to 59 years).

In a study demonstrating the outcome of frustration in children, Todd, Morris, and Fenza (1989) measured the effects of extinction on preschoolers' aggression. The children were taught to work for reinforcement by taking a marble from one location to another, passing a punching bag on the way. When extinction periods were programmed, almost all the children punched the bag at an increased level, up to 10 times more frequently. The results of this study and that of Hutchinson et al. show that jaw clenching, as well as other behaviors commonly labeled as aggressive, occur in humans under conditions of reinforcer reduction like those that produce aggression in lower animals.

We noted that reinforcer removal or reduction can produce increased aggression in humans in experimental settings. This aggression production has also been observed in humans in various situations outside the laboratory. Such more generalized findings support the validity of the frustration-aggression hypothesis. One relatively common way used to control inappropriate human behavior is called **timeout**. In timeout, access to reinforcers is withdrawn for a limited time period after misbehavior in order to try to suppress it. Informally, it is done by parents who send children to their rooms or remove privileges of some type following unacceptable behaviors. Teachers may do this by having a student stand in the corner of a room. Such tactics are effective if applied properly (ideally under the guidance of a trained professional), but because they involve reinforcer removal, they also can produce aggressive behaviors.

Lovass and Simmons (1969) reported greatly increased self-hitting by autistic, severely retarded children at the start of reinforcer withdrawal. Others have observed increased aggression in clients given fines or placed in a timeout condition following deviant behaviors. For example, Benjamin, Mazzarins, and Kupfersmid (1983) found that longer timeouts resulted in longer delays in stopping outbursts by children in their psychiatric ward.

The effect of frustration on aggression is seen when procedures are used to deliberately increase aggression so as to study the variables associated with it. Bandura, Ross, and Ross (1961), for example, let children play with toys for a while and then interrupted their play, thereby increasing the probability that they would imitate the aggressive acts of an adult model. We will discuss the main effects of such modeling studies by Bandura and others in detail in Chapter 8. The important point here is that Bandura as well as many other investigators commonly use frustration in adults as well as in children as a device for increasing aggressive responding, indicating their support for a basic frustration-aggression relationship.

STIMULUS DEPRIVATION AND AGGRESSION

Isolation is a condition associated with increased aggression that might have been included in the section on frustration except that it goes beyond the removal of reinforcers to include the reduction in many other stimuli an individual normally experiences. Also, while frustration and isolation both involve removal of stimuli, the way in which isolation produces aggression probably differs from that of frustration. Frustration seems to cause aggression against any appropriate target that is present at the time. Isolation achieves its effect by making the individual hypersensitive to stimuli presented after isolation (such as the introduction of another individual) that did not produce aggression before the isolation. In a way, isolation-produced aggression involves aggression produced by the presentation of stimuli, and could have been included at the beginning of this chapter. However, since isolation-produced aggression is identified by most investigators by its involvement with stimulus removal, we include it here.

The effects of isolation include multiple disturbances, as studies of several species have shown. Male mice who have been isolated for several weeks in individual small cages display an "isolation syndrome" that includes persistent, compulsive aggression directed at other mice introduced into their proximity after isolation. In addition, they exhibit deviant sexual behavior, impaired learning and memory, and various physiological changes. Isolation has been used to test the effects of various drugs on mouse aggression (Valzelli, 1973). In the early 1960s, Harlow (1962) began a famous study that demonstrated the effects of prolonged social isolation on rhesus monkeys, The isolation, especially when it occurred for the first six months of age, resulted in chronic increased aggression directed at the isolates themselves and other monkeys. Isolation can also produce elevated fear and abnormal sexual behaviors in these animals.

Investigators have suggested that in humans, early somatosensory deprivation can produce high amounts of self-mutilation and other pathological behaviors. One of the first observations of deleterious effects of an isolation-like situation was made by Spitz (1945) who employed the term "hospitalism" for the effects on children of being brought up in a foundling home. In such situations, infants were deprived of normal human contact, as they were attended to only as often as necessary to feed and keep them clean. Meanwhile, they were exposed to an almost uniformly white environment; their cribs, bedclothes, room walls and ceiling, even the attendants' uniforms, were white. The children later showed increased hyperreactivity, hostility, violence, and aggression, in addition to moodiness, verbal retardation, and slow physical development. As with many observational studies done in an uncontrolled setting, questions arise concerning the accuracy of the categorizations of these conditions and measurement of the behaviors. Nevertheless, contemporary treatment, in part reflecting the observations of investigators such as Spitz and Harlow, has been modified to include more physical contact with infants as well as more varied, stimulating surroundings.

Short-term sensory isolation or deprivation has been associated with increased aggression. Total sensory deprivation, in which volunteer subjects lay on a bed in a quiet, dark environment, and have restricted visual, auditory, and tactile input, has been reported to produce psychotic symptoms as well as hostile behaviors and unmotivated aggression (Rosenzweig & Gardner, 1966). To a lesser degree, prisoners are often deprived of many stimuli by being kept in a limited, small environment. Drtil (1969) has reported several effects of such deprivation, including increased irritability and aggression directed at themselves as well as others. Favazza (1987) and others suggest that the self-aggression serves to provide stimulation, especially in psychopathic prisoners. Finally, there has been speculation that the effects of socioeconomic deprivation include increased aggression, in addition to anxiety, depression, and sleep disturbances. However, it is not clear whether such increased problems result from deprivation in the sense that we have discussed here or to the effects of frustration or some other factor.

OTHER STIMULI ASSOCIATED WITH AGGRESSION

The various categories of aggressive behavior formulated by Moyer (1968) and described in Chapter 1 included the stimuli necessary to produce them. We have already described the stimuli for some of these, such as irritable, territorial, and sex-related aggression, and, for the sake of completeness, will now note some others. Fear-based aggression occurs in a situation where an individual is surprised or pursued by an attacker and tries to flee. If the individual's escape route is blocked, this is said to produce fear and a counterattack by the trapped individual against the original aggressor. Such a situation seems to produce a distinctive form of attack in lower animals (Leyhausen, 1956), which also is produced by brain stimulation in distinct areas, such as the dorsal hypothalamus. Uncontrolled observation of humans suggests that a fear situation can elicit aggression in them also.

Maternal aggression requires a special situation to occur, usually involving a lactating mother, her offspring, and a threat to them. As with fear-based aggression, maternal aggression has been studied extensively in lower animals (e.g., Svare & Mann, 1983), but human examples of this are usually limited to informal observations.

Intermale aggression occurs in the presence of other males, prior to the establishment of a dominance hierarchy. Some early observations of this phenomenon were made in chickens, related to pecking orders, which actually are established by female as well as male chickens (Guhl, 1956). Intermale aggression also has been commonly observed in humans, often in studies of juvenile gangs and prisoner groups.

Consideration of the various stimuli associated with Moyer's categories of aggression, in addition to those previously discussed, is important when we attempt to predict and/or control aggression. For example, the law officer who realizes that a fugitive trapped with no chance to escape is more likely to attack might effect a peaceful surrender by backing away somewhat to reduce fear-provoking stimuli. Or the social worker who knows that a new group of young males might challenge each other for dominance might provide some non-violent way for them to do so. The teacher who has learned that such stimuli as crowding and high noise levels may increase aggression in students may take measures to limit these effects in the classroom. Even if one cannot eliminate the stimuli that produce aggression, at least knowing about them can help one prepare for the resulting aggression.

SUMMARY

Various environmental stimuli can produce or facilitate aggression. The mechanisms for such actions seem to be acquired during evolution and passed on genetically since the relationships between the stimuli and aggression have typically been found throughout the strains of species studied, including humans. The stimulus classes most extensively studied have been those producing painful responses and those resulting from the withdrawal of or reduction in reinforcing stimuli. These two classes of environmental events produce aggression in ways parallel to those of the two basic neural systems for aggression.

Experimental studies with lower animals have provided detailed information on the many variables affecting the relationship between pain and aggression. They also have demonstrated the generality of the findings and their applicability to humans.

Extensive laboratory studies by social psychologists have resulted in findings similar to those for lower animals—that unpleasant stimuli can help produce increased aggression in humans. The additional role of internal states, such as arousal, and of cognitions, such as justification, is suggested to explain how results vary from one situation to another.

The removal of reinforcing stimuli, or frustration, was once proposed to be the only cause of human aggression. While this proposal was changed later to allow for other sources of aggression, the importance of frustration has been supported and extended in a series of studies with lower animals. The reduction as well as the termination of reinforcement in a number of ways has been shown to produce aggression, as has the simple withdrawal of the reinforcers themselves. Similar findings have been demonstrated experimentally in humans and during behavioral treatment programs.

Isolation and sensory deprivation are other conditions that can produce increased irritability and hypersensitivity to new stimuli, resulting in aggression. Effects have been studied in humans as well as in lower animals and examined to help explain pathological aggressive reactions. Several other contributing stimulus classes, related to Moyer's types of aggression, must be considered for a more complete understanding of the stimuli that produce aggression.

Suggested Reading

Kaplan, R. M., Konečni, V. J., and Novaco, R. W. (1984). *Aggression in children and youth*. Boston: Martinus Nijhoff Publishers.

CHAPTER 7
Conditioning and Learning

In the previous chapter, we considered some of the stimuli that produce aggression. The aggressive reaction to a stimulus probably is governed by genetic mechanisms that aid in the individual's survival. That is, an aggressive response to a damaging stimulus from an assailant may help limit the damage from the stimulus. While this reaction is useful, it is not ideally protective of the individual, who must wait until he or she is already being harmed before reacting. One is, of course, not limited to such a state if one can recognize a dangerous situation before one is harmed and respond in anticipation of the stimulus. This occurs via a conditioning process that allows one to benefit from past experiences by changing one's reactions to stimuli.

In this chapter, we will examine evidence for the conditioning of aggressive responses in both lower animals and human beings. The possibilities for such conditioning in lower animals will be described, and we will see how applying the principles of conditioning helps explain increases in aggression. We will also describe attempts to apply these principles to laboratory studies with humans.

Conditioning is also seen by some investigators as a component of another effect of experience, in which behaviors are learned because their consequences are the removal or prevention of damaging stimuli. Learning from these consequences is further process that allows more flexible responding to a threatening environment, and so we will also discuss the role of this learning in relation to aggressive behavior.

Learning is also involved when aggression is followed by rewarding consequences. Such consequences do not necessarily function to protect the individual from harm, but they do represent another major way in which experience affects aggression. We will review several studies that illustrate the various ways in which this learning can increase aggressive behaviors. In addition, we will examine the rewarding characteristics of aggression itself.

The final areas we address will be how different principles of conditioning and learning are applied to decrease aggressive behaviors. We will also learn how punishing consequences have been used to control aggression.

CONDITIONING OF AGGRESSION

The conditioning process we discuss here is known by several names, including **classical conditioning** (for its traditional status), **respondent conditioning** (for its involvement with responses to the environment), and **Pavlovian conditioning** (for its discoverer). Pavlov (1927) described various inherent reflex mechanisms, in which an unconditioned stimulus elicits an unconditioned response. The classic example occurs when the stimulus of food in the mouth evokes the response of salivation. Such unconditioned reflexes (or unconditional, as originally written, indicating their inherent nature) can serve either to facilitate biological processes, such as saliva for the ingestion and digestion of food, or protect the organism, as when a more viscous saliva is produced in response to an acidic substance's being placed in the mouth.

Conditioning of reflexes takes place as new (conditioned) stimuli are repeatedly paired with the unconditioned stimuli and come to elicit a response essentially like that which occurred to the unconditioned stimulus. Thus, an auditory signal, when paired with food in the mouth, can come to elicit salivation, as in Pavlov's famous example. Such conditioning mechanisms facilitate the organism's interactions with its environment so it can respond more flexibly to it. In the case of salivation, the individual does not have to experience food in the mouth before starting to salivate, but can begin to prepare for receiving food by salivating at the sight of a familiar food. This visual stimulus, having been paired with the stimulus of food in the mouth, becomes conditioned.

In Chapter 6, certain environmental stimuli, essentially painful ones, were shown to produce aggressive responding. The first extensive studies (e.g., Ulrich & Azrin, 1962) have suggested that this relationship is a reflexive one. Such a reflex would have a protective function for the organism, like those we discussed at the start of this chapter. Although the complexity and duration of an aggressive response would seem to be much greater than for those simple responses Pavlov studied, exploring the possibility of conditioning aggression was considered worthwhile by investigators. If such conditioning existed, it might help explain why certain situations—such as being in the presence of an old enemy or in a tavern where fights have occurred previously—are sometimes associated with increased incidences of further aggression. Similarly, an aggressive response to the appearance of a police officer might be because of past aggressive interactions with police. Although many more factors are certainly involved, perhaps classical conditioning contributes to the production of aggression in these situations.

CONDITIONING IN LOWER ANIMALS

Lower animal studies, done under controlled laboratory conditions, indicate that it is possible to condition aggressive behaviors. In early work, Vernon and Ulrich (1966) and Thompson and Sturm (1965) demonstrated that originally ineffective or neutral stimuli, when paired with an unconditioned stimulus for aggression, would come to elicit aggressive behavior. The first investigators demonstrated this by pairing a visual stimulus with painful foot shock in rats. The visual stimulus eventually elicited fighting in the rats. The second pair showed that, in Siamese fighting fish, the process of pairing a visual stimulus with the unconditioned stimulus of the sight of a conspecific (another of the same species) would produce the aggressive fighting display to the originally neutral stimulus.

Hutchinson, Renfrew, and Young (1971) examined the possibilities for conditioning aggressive hose-biting responses by squirrel monkeys. They had observed that the biting, originally elicited only by tail shock, seemed to be coming under the control of other stimuli. When the shocks were first given, hose biting would occur immediately afterwards and then cease until the next shock, in a pattern similar to that observed for two rats who fight in response to foot shock. However, they studied the animals for extended periods, to further assess the shock-biting relationship. After a long history of such tests, the monkeys began to bite not only after each shock but also throughout the inter-shock interval. Since they suspected that the pairing of shock with the testing environment stimuli may have conditioned these stimuli, they conducted several tests to determine this possibility.

Although the pairing of stimuli can produce classical conditioning, that conditioning is lost if the pairing is discontinued. This process is called extinction. Thus, Hutchinson et al. attempted to achieve extinction by placing the monkeys in the testing environment and no longer delivering shock to them. At first, biting occurred in the absence of shock, suggesting that the testing stimuli alone were functioning as conditioned stimuli and eliciting the biting. Then, as expected, when the monkeys were exposed to the testing stimuli in the absence of shock, their biting responses decreased until they no longer occurred. It seems that the extinction process was functioning.

To make sure that classical conditioning of hose biting in response to shock is possible, these investigators tried to produce it deliberately. Therefore, they presented an auditory or visual stimulus just prior to the shocks—an ideal relationship for conditioning. These stimuli came to be conditioned—after pairing they too elicited biting. The conditioning was easier for auditory than for visual stimuli, perhaps due to the particular stimulus characteristics they employed. It also is possible that unknown inherent mechanisms influence when such conditioning occurs. For example, possibly in squirrel monkeys auditory stimuli are naturally more critical than visual stimuli in aggression. Such dependence on auditory over visual stimuli could result from the limited usefulness of visual stimuli in the dense jungle environment in which the monkeys evolved.

Conditioning of hose biting in response to tail shock is difficult to achieve and maintain. This may happen because, as we indicated earlier, aggressive behaviors are more complex and of longer duration than those usually involved in classical conditioning. For example, a common conditioned response is a brief eye blink, which lasts less than a second. On the other hand, an aggressive response by a cat to brain stimulation may take 10 to 20 seconds to occur and involves a series of behaviors. At the onset of stimulation, first the EEG changes. Then the cat becomes alert and attends to the target. It then gets up, approaches the target, and bites it or strikes it. I have had only very limited success in conditioning such responses produced by brain stimulation in cats. It was possible to condition only the EEG, alerting, attending, and partial approach to the target. Similarly, Masserman's early attempts (1942) also failed to achieve such conditioning. Despite such failures, even the conditioning of arousal and preparatory components of the response may contribute to increasing aggression by facilitating the response. Therefore, we may state that these studies indicate that classical conditioning of aggressive responses, or at least components of them, can occur in lower animals.

CONDITIONING OF AGGRESSION IN HUMANS

Studies of classical conditioning of aggression in humans have usually been constrained, because of ethical concerns, to attempts to detect the effects of past conditioning on present behaviors exhibited in a mock aggression situation. Berkowitz, for example, proposed that **aggressive cues**—conditioned stimuli associated with present or previous instigators of anger or with aggression in general—should serve to increase aggression. To test this hypothesis, Berkowitz and LePage (1967) studied the effects of guns on aggression. They arranged for a confederate to anger male college students and then allow the students to aggress against the perpetrator with a Buss-type shocker. A so-called **weapons effect** occurred, in that those who shocked in the presence of a nearby pistol and shotgun were found to deliver greater numbers of shocks.

In addition to Berkowitz and LePage's study, other studies provide further support for the possibilities of conditioning human aggression. In one series by Berkowitz and his associates, subjects were shown a movie about a prize fighter. Some also were subjected to a negative evaluation of their efforts in a problem-solving task. They were then allowed to "shock" their evaluators. Increased shocks were selected by the subjects for those evaluators associated with the violence as, for example, those said to have the same name as the fighter (Berkowitz & Geen, 1966). The authors' interpretation of the results was that this effect occurred because of a classical conditioning process. The association of the person, via their name or major, with the fighting, established them as conditioned stimuli for aggression. Although this might have occurred, no specific conditioning procedure was carried out. We should note that the situation did not correspond to that usually employed for effective conditioning. There were only a few pairings of the fighter with aggression and these were not in the ideal relationship for the formation of a conditioned response (the conditioned stimulus should be presented only just prior to the unconditioned stimulus). Toch (1969) has reported that a longer, more direct pairing of stimuli and aggressive activity can have an effect in real life, one of two in his studies of chronically assaultive individuals. In one example, a man became violent upon any provocation by a larger man. He had been beaten regularly by a larger man when he was a boy, and the sight of someone larger was a conditioned stimulus for aggression.

Questions have been raised about the experimental conditioning of aggression in humans. Although some later studies supported the findings of Berkowitz and LePage, (see Berkowitz, 1993) others did not. Buss, Booker, and Buss (1972) found, for example, that they could not replicate these results. Replicability, of course, is a fundamental requirement for accepting any results of an experiment. Contrary to expectations, Buss et al. also found no effect on the results of actually firing the gun, nor even of having had previous experiences with guns.

Berkowitz and LePage's subjects may have been responding more aggressively as a result of a perceived demand. The subjects interpreted the presence of guns as part of an intent by the investigator to have them act more aggressively and they complied. This would reflect a learned aggressive response that is affected by a reinforcing consequence, as we will discuss in the next section. This unintended effect of subjects' interpretations of the experimental situation seems to constitute a major limit to the laboratory studies of human aggression that employ construed situations. While they may be good models for social interactions in controlled settings, they do not necessarily provide adequate information that helps us to understand real-life situations. However, they do offer various professionals, from social psychology as well as other areas, ample incentives for further studies to help interpret the results. For example, see Turner and Leyens (1992) for a review of further work in this area.

Geen (1983) suggested that unrecognized conditioning factors may have contributed to failures in replicating Berkowitz and LePage's results. He describes a 1977 study by Berkowitz and Frodi in which they put subjects in a situation where they were directed to operate a noise machine that delivered a noxious sound to another person, and thus commit an act considered aggressive. The subjects were then either reinforced, punished, or treated in a neutral way. Later, the old machine was present when the subjects were asked to employ a new machine to deliver the noise. The subjects who had been reinforced for their previous activities delivered more noise when the old machine was present. Those who had been punished and tested with the old machine present displayed the lowest levels of aggression. Geen suggested that the subjects of the replication studies who did not perform as in the Berkowitz and LePage study may have had some punishment associated with guns and thus did not act as aggressively in their presence. Geen offers a further explanation that the subjects in the replication studies may have been affected by "evaluation apprehension." That is, the experiment might have been run in a way that made them fear that they would be judged negatively if they aggressed. Finally, the subjects may not have focused on the aggressive nature of the stimulus. He refers to a study by Leyens and associates in which they directed the subject's attention to the aesthetic aspects of a gun (the beauty of the carved wood stock) rather than its potential use, and indicated that this lowered the amount of aggression they exhibited.

Post hoc explanations, such as those given above, of the failure to replicate laboratory studies of human aggression are helpful and interesting, but it must be distressing to the student of aggressive behavior that so much effort is directed at explaining inconsistent results instead of discovering new information concerning the causes of aggression. Unfortunately, since ethically real aggression between humans cannot deliberately be produced just for the sake of understanding it, work must progress with the best substitutes available. Prudence would dictate, however, that we always keep in mind the limits of the methodologies we employ. This caveat applies, of course, not only to human studies but lower animal studies as well.

LEARNING OF AGGRESSION

In the previous section, we examined aggression as a reflex-like behavior that can be elicited by stimuli; it also can exist as a learned, instrumental behavior that is affected by its consequences. The principles of learning of instrumental or operant behaviors have been well established by researchers who followed up on Skinner's first efforts (1938) by carrying out numerous laboratory investigations with lower organisms and humans. The principles of **operant conditioning** have been applied to many practical situations outside the laboratory, in the field known as behavior modification or applied behavior analysis. These applications have helped behavior therapists understand and manage a wide variety of problems, ranging from self-control (e.g., eating excessively) to community concerns (e.g., conserving resources).

A fundamental characteristic of the principles of operant conditioning is an emphasis on how the outcomes of behaviors affect their development and frequency of occurrence. In contrast to reflexive stimuli and behaviors, relationships of operant behaviors to their outcomes may either be quite arbitrary or occur in natural environmental interactions. This section describes how several principles can affect aggressive behaviors in the natural environment and explains how we can use these principles to control such aggression.

NEGATIVE REINFORCEMENT OF AGGRESSION

One basic principle of operant conditioning is **negative reinforcement**. Behaviors are reinforced or strengthened by removal **(escape)** or prevention of **(avoidance)** some aversive condition. Such a mechanism serves the organism well as an adaptive device to limit its exposure to damaging conditions. Since the conditions involved in aggression, such as painful stimulation, are typically aversive, it should come as no surprise that negative reinforcement sometimes is the basis of learned aggression. An individual's aggression against an attacker may be reinforced by terminating the attack (escaping from the aversive stimuli involved in the attack). The individual may also learn to avoid attacks by attacking first (in what the military might call a preemptive strike) and thus prevent any application of aversive stimuli.

Studies of Negative Reinforcement of Aggression by Lower Animals

Perhaps the first laboratory demonstration of negative reinforcement of aggression was reported by Miller (1948), who trained rats to rear up and strike each other to terminate a painful foot shock. Of course Ulrich and Azrin (1962), when investigating this situation, found that it was not necessary to reinforce the rats; the subjects would attack each other when shocked without training. As we indicated earlier, this fighting is an unlearned reflexive-type response to painful stimulation. Nevertheless, Miller's procedure may have produced an even greater level of aggression. This possibility was suggested in a later study by Azrin, Hutchinson, and Hake (1967). They placed squirrel monkeys in an apparatus developed to measure reflex-like hose biting in response to tail shock. In the absence of shock, the subjects did not consistently bite the hose until they were trained to do so during a warning tone, in order to postpone (avoid) the brief shock for 15 seconds. If biting did not occur, shocks would be delivered every five seconds. The monkeys learned to bite readily when the tone was presented, thus demonstrating negative reinforcement of operant biting behavior. We should note that this biting was a learned response to avoid shock. Any one of several motor responses could have been taught in this way. For example, researchers often use depression of a small lever or bar that protrudes into the testing chamber in operant experiments. They used hose biting because it is the same type of reflex-like unlearned response elicited by painful stimuli in this situation. Indeed here, occasionally, the monkeys did not bite after hearing the tone and therefore received the shock. This would produce further, reflexive, biting that in turn would help them avoid further shocks.

In the Azrin et al. study of squirrel monkeys, an interaction of both operant and reflexive biting took place, probably like that occurring naturally in situations outside the laboratory. People who learn to fight to avoid aversive stimulation most likely experience some pain before they are successful in avoiding it by fighting. This success produces even more fighting, which may contribute to their efforts. Azrin et al. also note, informally, that operant and reflexive biting episodes can differ. They observed that bites during avoidance were hard enough to operate the pressure-sensing switch connected to the hose, but that the monkeys seemed more aroused and bit harder during the shock-elicited biting. This suggests a basic difference in the nature of operant and reflexive fighting. Indeed, in this example, people who fight as an escape response probably will fight more vigorously and emotionally if they are hurt by their opponents. Professional fighters certainly must be aware of the differences between operant and reflexive fighting and be ready to balance and control each type in themselves and their opponents. Reflexive aggression may be more vigorous, but it also may be less well controlled.

Negative Reinforcement of Human Aggression

Negative reinforcement of aggression in humans has been reported formally in clinical treatment as well as observational studies. For example, in Krawchik's case study (1986) that we discussed in Chapter 4, the young man with brain damage from encephalitis exhibited operant aggression as well as that related to his brain dysfunction. Given his large physique, he had learned that he could escape or avoid punishment for some misdeed by attacking or threatening others. Carr, Newsom, and Binkoff (1980) suspected a similar source for the strong aggressive behavior of Bob, a retarded 14-year-old boy. If adults made demands of Bob, such as telling him to sit in a chair, he often responded by scratching, hitting, kicking, and biting the adult and thus aggressively escaped from this aversive demand situation. This analysis was supported when Bob's therapist, clothed in protective gear, was attacked even more strongly when he did not retreat immediately after an attack or when a set number (fixed ratio) of attacks was required before the therapist would retreat. Bob's attack behavior adapted to the requirements or contingencies for reinforcement just as the squirrel monkeys of Azrin et al. adjusted their hose-biting intensity to satisfy the contingencies fixed by the pressure-switch setting.

In a well-known observational study, Patterson, Littman, and Bricker (1967) studied the aggressive behaviors of children in a nursery school over a nine-month period. They noted that when relatively passive children were attacked and could counterattack successfully and escape further attack, their future attack behaviors increased. Patterson and his colleagues have made extensive studies of how such aversive interactions, especially in families, contribute to the development of aggressive deviancy. In the home, for example, they estimated that negative reinforcement occurs for about 20 percent of a child's aversive reactions to social interactions with parents or siblings (Patterson, Dishion, & Bank, 1984). Observations of aggressive interactions between older children and adults have shown that the encounters may have an escalating nature. If the victims strike back to try and terminate the attacks, the aggressors in turn augment their own attacks, which might increase the intensity of the attacks by the victims, etc., in a growing spiral until one of the individuals is defeated. Such an escalation, of course, may include interactions of operant escape responding and reflexive fighting, as we observed previously in squirrel monkeys.

Positive Reinforcement of Aggression

While negative reinforcement increases aggressive behaviors by reducing aversive stimulation, a second principle of instrumental learning may apply to increase aggressive behaviors in the absence of immediate aversive stimulation. **Positive reinforcement** of a behavior occurs when the behavior is followed by the presentation of some rewarding stimulus or event. Thus, if aggression results in the acquisition of some desired object, that aggression is more likely to occur in the future under similar conditions. In lower-animal societies, such aggression might be labeled goal-directed. Animals may aggress to maintain or gain territory, which has advantages of food or water, or being able to engage in mating behavior. Similarly derived processes may occur in humans, although with less obvious goals. By aggressing, the mugger acquires money or something else of value and then can use this to acquire other things. Juvenile gangs fight to establish territories that may give them access to similar reinforcers.

Positively reinforced instrumental or operant aggression happens under the control of **discriminative** stimuli that are associated with probable success. Faced with the image of a dominant animal, a potential aggressor usually does not challenge him for his territory. However, he will more readily attack a smaller animal that is lower in the dominance hierarchy. Faced with someone in a well-lighted area, with others present, or with someone who seems capable of self-defense, the mugger usually will not attack. However, a meek-looking individual isolated in a dark place may be a prime target. Knowledge of such relationships is typically used by consultants to formulate advice for helping people avoid various street crimes. Although the extreme gang violence of recent years may seem out of the control of any discriminative stimuli—such as the presence of potential witnesses or innocent victims—it probably is affected by these stimuli to some extent. For example, violence toward other gangs is probably more likely to occur in the absence of police and other people than in the presence of them, and more likely to be directed at small numbers of opposing gang members instead of large numbers of them.

Lower Animal Studies of Positive Reinforcement

To better understand the way in which positively reinforced aggression is learned and controlled, we can examine the results of laboratory studies. An early example of reinforced animal aggression is found in the work of Scott and Marston (1953). They trained mice to fight by pairing them with smaller mice who did not effectively fight back. They found that the mice allowed to win had increased their levels of aggression. Some classical conditioning of the fighting behavior was also reported. Their trained mice would initiate fighting behaviors when they heard the scratching of another mouse on a door that was later opened to allow fighting. An alternative interpretation is that the scratching was a discriminative stimulus associated with fighting and its reinforcement. As with negative reinforcement, however, it is not always possible to separate reflexive and operant processes.

Stachnik and his colleagues studied operant reinforcement to train behavior like that seen in reflexive fighting (Stachnik, Ulrich, & Mabry, 1966). They employed reinforcing brain stimulation to train rats to rear up and paw at other rats, cats, and monkeys. The rats learned to emit the selected responses, although this behavior lacked the vigor noted when pain is used to elicit aggression. This result is parallel to that of Azrin, Hutchinson, & Hake (1967) when they trained monkeys to bite by using negative reinforcement. That is, both studies showed that an operant attack behavior could be developed by applying reinforcement, although the precise characteristics of operant and reflex-like aggression seem to differ.

If operant attack is like any other operant behavior, such as lever pressing, then it would be possible to understand and control this attack by employing the general principles of operant learning. We may establish the validity of considering operant attack as an operant behavior by showing the generality of this type of attack as well as demonstrating similarities in how operant attack and other operant behaviors are controlled.

Several studies have proven the generality of operantly reinforced attack. First, various types of aggressive responses can be trained. In addition to the several responses discussed above, Keehn (1976) showed that rats could be trained to bite an inanimate object for reinforcement. Second, several species can be trained. In addition to rats and mice, Reynolds, Catania, and Skinner (1963) taught pigeons to attack other pigeons for a food reinforcer.

Operant attack has been shown to be controlled in the same way as other operant behaviors. For example, Reynolds et al., in the previous study, showed that pigeons' attack behaviors were closely controlled by the discriminative stimulus associated with reinforcement conditions. The pigeons attacked only when a particular color of light was present and not when a white light was present, since attack was reinforced only during the colored light. This is similar to the type of control possible for other operants such as lever pressing. Also, Azrin and Hutchinson (1967, as well as Keehn, 1976) demonstrated that the patterns of responding generated by operant reinforcement of aggressive behaviors were essentially like those generated for other operant behaviors. They trained pigeons on a Fixed Interval schedule, so that the first response after a set time period was reinforced. The pigeons' fighting responses directed at another pigeon followed the same basic time pattern that occurs for pigeons who simply peck at a disk on a wall for reinforcement—that is, they attacked very little just after a reinforcement and then attacked with increasing frequency until the next reinforcement. This indicated that operant fighting is controlled by reinforcers in the same way as other operant behaviors.

In further support for many of the findings reviewed above, Renfrew and Hutchinson (1983a) demonstrated positive reinforcement of a response employed in aggression by training *encéphale isolé* rats to bite a hose by reinforcing them with pleasurable brain stimulation in the Offset Aggression System. The rats learned to bite at a high rate when the biting was followed by brain stimulation. Furthermore, they showed, as had Reynolds, Catania, and Skinner (1963), that the behavior could be controlled by discrimininative stimuli. Biting occurred only when a light was on, indicating that reinforcement was available. A control animal (an intact rat pressing a lever for brain stimulation reinforcement) responded in a similar way.

The *encéphale isolé* rats who learned operant biting for brain stimulation reinforcement also offer a further example of how operant and reflexive biting can occur in the same situation. Discrimination training of these animals involved reinforcing them to bite while a light was on, and then turning off the light while terminating reinforcement. On their initial exposure to the non-reinforcement, before learning that the light's being off was a signal that biting would not be reinforced, they exhibited a marked increase in intensity, duration, and frequency of biting. It seems that removal of the reinforcers produced increased, reflexive biting. This effect of removing positive reinforcement is the same as the frustration-produced aggression we discussed in the previous chapter. Such effects occurred, for example, in the Azrin, Hutchinson, and Hake (1966) study of aggression produced by pigeons when food reinforcement was removed. As with the Azrin et al. (1967) study of negative reinforcement of hose biting by squirrel monkeys discussed earlier, the reflexlike biting produced by non-reinforcement was more vigorous than that required for operant reinforcement. After the discrimination was learned, this reflexive biting no longer occurred when the light was turned off.

The nature of operant attack behaviors is similar to that of other operant behaviors. These behaviors can be increased by reinforcement, they can come under the control of discriminative stimuli, and they follow a characteristic pattern under a schedule of reinforcement. In addition, termination of reinforcement for operant attack elicits reflex-like attack, similar to what occurs for termination of reinforcement of other operants. Thus, the extensive research on operant behaviors in general can be applied here.

POSITIVE REINFORCEMENT OF AGGRESSION IN HUMANS

Humans most certainly engage in much aggression that is positively reinforced. Violent assaults of various kinds are reinforced when the perpetrator gains money, property, or territory. When that gain is the sole determinant of behavior, the aggression often may be just strong enough to obtain reinforcement (e.g., the money). Other factors, such as retaliation or the fear of it or the effects of drugs, may produce higher levels of aggression. Somewhat more restrained aggression may occur in children. Fagot (1984) observed toddlers interacting in small play groups and found that

81 percent of aggressive responses by boys were responded to by their peers or teachers. Although negative responses occurred 25 percent of the time, even these responses can be reinforcing to the children. In addition, teachers responded positively 40 percent of the time. These responses probably contributed to the high stability of the aggressive behaviors over the year of observations.

Aggressive behavior by children can be effective in acquiring items possessed by others, as shown in some observations of nursery school children by Patterson, Littman, and Bricker (1967). In this study, positive reinforcement occurred when an attacked child would give up a toy or withdraw from the area following the attack. If unsuccessful, the attacks were increased in intensity. Eighty percent of all such attacks resulted in reinforcement. Similarly, positive reinforcement of children's aggression by parents is considered an important component in developing and maintaining the aggression in home settings (Patterson et al., 1984).

Researchers have reported effective experimental manipulation of positive reinforcement of human aggressive responses. For example, Cowan and Walters (1963) used marbles to reinforce young boys for punching an inflatable plastic "Bobo" doll. They thus were able to increase the punching. Greater persistence in punching occurred when more than one blow was required for each marble. This effect parallels that found typically with such reinforcement requirements for non-aggressive operant behaviors. In a further parallel, when Fixed Ratio (FR) reinforcement was applied (the children had to punch the doll six times for reinforcement—FR 6), this produced even more persistent punching. The FR effect was even more apparent in a study of children institutionalized for behavior disorders. Walters and Brown (1963) found that similar reinforcement, in addition to frustration, produced generalized aggression. After training these children to hit the doll on an FR 6 schedule, some were intentionally frustrated by having a movie shut off or with someone taking and throwing away their candy. These children, in a subsequent free play situation, aggressed more physically than groups of children who were given continuous reinforcement for punching the doll or were simply frustrated. Generalization of the reinforcement of aggression also has been reported for adults (Parke, Ewall, & Slaby, 1972), when reinforcement of hostile remarks was followed by increased physical aggression.

The effect of reinforcement on aggressive responding has been reported in the teacher-learner setting typically employed by social psychologists, as well as in a clinical situation. Geen and Stonner (1971) verbally reinforced adults for pressing the stronger intensity shock buttons on a Buss box apparatus. They reported that subjects chose increased intensities as the study progressed. This study also demonstrated, in a controlled way, how experimenters employing the teacher-learner technique can affect the results. That is, deliberate reinforcement in the form of approval increased the selection of high shock levels. This gives more support to the claims of similar uncontrolled effects involved in the technique, as subjects may select shocks to receive assumed approval by the experimenters. In a clinical setting, Vollmer, Iwata, Zarcone, Smith, and Mazaleski (1993) confirmed previous work indicating that self-injurious behavior (SIB) is increased by reinforcement. In this study, the SIB levels in three retarded women who lived in a residential facility were increased when attention to the SIB, in the form of reprimands or expression of concern following it, was given. We will discuss the therapeutic treatment of these women later in this chapter.

AGGRESSION AS A REINFORCER

Taken together, all these studies provide empirical support for the idea that aggression can be increased by positive reinforcement. A related question concerns whether being aggressive is in itself reinforcing. Some evidence supports an affirmative answer. Occasionally, the presence of a stimulus that causes aggression provides the motivating condition for learning an instrumental response that results in a target for aggression. For example, Azrin, Hutchinson, and McLaughlin (1965) demonstrated that squirrel monkeys who were being given a painful tail shock would learn to pull a chain to produce a biting target (a terry-cloth-covered tennis ball). Roberts and Keiss (1964) showed that cats receiving brain stimulation in a neural area that produced aggression would learn which arm of a maze contained a rat attack target.

In everyday situations, individuals may get some sort of reinforcement for aggressing. The civil service clerk who reverts to some arcane regulation to deny a request for the processing of a document, the public employee who creates inordinate delays at a service window, or the graduate school secretary who terrorizes students with threats of rejecting their theses are sometimes labeled as being aggressive because they are harming others (although the "damage" they inflict constitutes a substantial extension of the definition of aggression given on page 6) and they seem to enjoy it. Perhaps frustrations inherent in these positions provide the antecedent conditions during which aggression is directed toward the nearest target, the client. Or perhaps the reinforcing aspect of being able to control someone else's behavior maintains the aggression. In each laboratory and everyday cases, identifiable antecedent conditions make it reinforcing to aggress. These relationships go beyond the reflexive-like eliciting of aggression discussed earlier by involving additional motivational factors, for which the consequences of the behavior are relevant as well. Renfrew and Hutchinson (1983b) provide a more extensive discussion of these motivational factors involved in aggression.

Some direct internal effects produced by the aggression may make it reinforcing. For example, in a series of studies by Hokanson and his co-workers (1970) the researchers measured cardiovascular activities in students while they were insulted and then given the opportunity to physically or verbally aggress against the insultor. The insults produced elevations in heart rates and blood pressure, which were greatly reduced when they were allowed aggressive responses. The studies did not find such reductions in the cardiovascular activity for aggression directed against innocent individuals, or when the aggressions were simply imagined, as in a fantasy. Interpretation of these results is complicated because the studies also found differences in effects related to learned attitudes toward aggression. Individuals who had been reinforced in the past for being aggressive were more likely to show cardiovascular activity reductions following aggression compared to individuals without this reinforcement history. Also, Hokanson and his colleagues observed similar reductions in blood pressure in women if aggression was punished and the women were reinforced for positively rating their insultors. Further, other investigators have discovered that aggression sustains or possibly **increases** blood pressure (e.g., Kahn, 1966). Therefore, the studies cited here indicate that the expression of aggression may produce a reduction in cardiovascular activity. However, it does not always do so. Also, non-aggressive activities can cause the same reductions.

A popular interpretation of why aggression occurs is related to its apparent reinforcing properties; that it reduces some state of imbalance in the organism. Such an interpretation goes beyond the operation of motivational factors in aggression that we discussed above. Instead, it assumes some regular ongoing system that produces aggression. Various attempts to understand aggression posit some sort of aggressive drive, like a hunger drive, that must be satisfied by exhibiting some sort of aggression. The catharsis hypothesis proposed by psychoanalytic theory incorporates this orientation. This hypothesis suggests that the aggression relieves some pressures, resulting in reduction of the need for further aggression. Even substitute activities may serve this purpose. As discussed in Chapter 6, participation in contact sports, such as football, is thought to allow for the discharge of aggressive tendencies that might otherwise be expressed by less legal means. Similarly, simply watching another person aggress is thought to reduce one's own aggression. However, as Geen (1990) among others has pointed out, no solid evidence supports this hypothesis.

Baron (1983) also criticized the idea of catharsis as a control over aggression and indicated that it functions only in highly specific circumstances. The expression of aggression may help reduce further expression, but only if directed against the instigator of the aggression. Further, this effect was seen to have a short duration. Retaliation against one's nemesis results only in a temporary decrease in aggression. Reports of situations in which the expression of aggression is followed by reductions in the behavior seem to involve either questionable subjective evidence or mechanisms other than catharsis, such as fatigue or some of the learning factors we discuss in the next section.

Bandura's (1973) work with imitative learning, which we will describe extensively in Chapter 8, provides further evidence against the concept of catharsis via observation of aggression. Bandura concluded that observing others' aggression does not reduce the observer's aggression but instead increases it. His conclusions were supported by other early studies of filmed aggression (e.g., Walters, Thomas, & Acker, 1962; Hartmann, 1969). While the catharsis model would predict that watching an aggressive film would help reduce aggression in viewers, these results indicate that it will increase it by offering an instigating model for it.

LEARNING TO DECREASE AGGRESSION

Principles of conditioning and learning not only provide methods for increasing a behavior but also methods of decreasing it. This may be accomplished in two basic manners. First, if a procedure, such as reinforcement, has been applied to increase a behavior, it is often possible to terminate the application of that procedure. The result should be that the behavior will revert to its original strength. Second, if a behavior is occurring at a high level as the result of unknown or uncontrollable factors, procedures developed to reduce such behaviors can be applied. Conditioning and learning principles are applied deliberately by professional therapists to reduce problematic aggression. They are also used in everyday settings as untrained people interact to prevent and control aggression (e.g., parent-child, neighbor-neighbor, supervisor-worker).

Decreasing Aggression by Extinction

Extinction is a technique employed in both classical conditioning and operant learning to reverse the effects of reinforcement. Basically, it simply involves the removal of reinforcement; that is, either terminating the pairing of a conditioned stimulus with an unconditioned stimulus or withdrawing the reinforcing consequences for an operant behavior. While most investigators have been more concerned with demonstrating or discovering the possibilities for increasing aggression through the application of conditioning or learning principles, there have been studies of decreasing aggression via extinction.

In the conditioning study discussed earlier, Hutchinson, Renfrew, and Young (1971) demonstrated the effects of extinction on classically conditioned hose biting by squirrel monkeys. Following the inadvertent conditioning of biting to the stimuli in the test apparatus, exposure to these conditioned stimuli without the unconditioned stimulus of tail shock resulted in the elimination of biting to the apparatus stimuli alone. The planned conditioning procedure, using a light or tone as conditioned stimuli, produced similar results, although it proved more difficult to eliminate biting to a tone-conditioned stimulus than to a light-conditioned stimulus. The study showed that extinction of a classically conditioned aggressive response is possible, and suggests how the procedure could be applied elsewhere.

Extinction may be a means of decreasing conditioned aggression in humans. In a laboratory setting, for example, the subjects of Berkowitz and Geen (1966) were conditioned to be more aggressive toward someone named "Kirk" after seeing Kirk Douglas in a boxing film. Theoretically, these subjects should have reduced their aggressive responses if they had then viewed Douglas in a more peaceful role. In a therapeutic situation, exposing someone to a previously conditioned stimulus, such as fighting in a bar, and preventing fighting while there, should reduce the classically conditioned component of aggression. Perhaps alcohol consumption itself has conditioned stimulus properties that could be reduced by eliminating the association between drinking and fighting.

In cases of operantly reinforced aggression, we should be able to decrease the aggression via extinction. If young children, such as those observed by Patterson, Littman, and Bricker (1967), for example, have been reinforced by obtaining toys they have taken from others, the other children could be trained to be more assertive so that they will not easily give up their toys when confronted by others. Although the initial effect of extinction may be an initial increase in aggression, as we saw in the previous chapter, longer term application of this procedure should produce a loss of the aggressive response.

Extinction of negatively reinforced behavior involves terminating the possibility of using aggression to escape or avoid an aversive situation. For example, if children have learned that they can escape from carrying out some unpleasant chores by yelling or otherwise aggressing against their parents, the appropriate technique would be to insist that the chores be done. A comparable situation occurred in the large young brain-damaged patient treated by Krawchik that we described earlier. Once it was apparent that he was aggressing to escape punishment, researchers applied an extinction procedure. He was no longer reinforced for such aggression (the punishment was given regardless of his aggressive response to it), and this operant escape responding gradually was eliminated. Similarly, Carr, Newsom, and Binkoff (1980), in the study also described earlier, observed that their young retarded boy was aggressing to escape a situation that involved responding to the demands of his caretakers. They showed that once such aggression was no longer successful, it decreased.

While extinction alone should be sufficient for decreasing a previously reinforced behavior, the procedure may take a rather long time to have an effect, especially when the behavior has been reinforced for a long time. Further, extinction may produce a type of behavioral vacuum. The original situation that was being responded to still exists, but the behavioral response to it is eliminated. Also, as we mentioned earlier, an attempt to extinguish aggression may produce an initial increase in this and other undesirable behaviors. Therefore, it is helpful to train an individual to replace the aggressive response with another one.

Carr, Newsom, and Binkoff (1980) chose a neutral behavior of finger tapping as an escape response more appropriate than aggression for a patient when demands were being made on him. This resulted in a rapid increase in finger tapping accompanied by a decrease in aggression. Typically, the substitute behavior is an acceptable one that is incompatible with aggression, such as a helping or cooperative behavior. Wahler and Fox (1980) used the behavioral substitute tactic to decrease the undesirable oppositional and aggressive behaviors of four children. When the children were reinforced for solitary play with toys, the undesirable behaviors decreased over 10 observation sessions. The method used in this study is called differential reinforcement of incompatible behavior (DRI), since it involves selective reinforcement of a behavior (solitary play) that cannot occur simultaneously with the target behavior (aggression).

A method for response reduction that is similar but less selective than DRI is differential reinforcement of other behavior (DRO). Here, any behavior apart from the target behavior is reinforced. Rcdmon (1987) applied this technique to a severely retarded young male who had made violent attacks on others in his group home and workplace. If these attacks did not occur for four hours, this resulted in praise and a mark on a chart. Increasing numbers of sequential marks were needed to receive objects or engage in activities. This procedure resulted in eventual elimination of the attacks. Thus, the provision of reinforcement for any non-aggressive behaviors, along with no reinforcement for aggressive behaviors, was successful in controlling aggression. In the study with retarded women by Vollmer et al. mentioned earlier, they also found that SIB was reduced when a DRO schedule was used. Here, absence of SIB for a set time was followed by reinforcing attention. In addition, a procedure of simply giving attention noncontingently (independently of SIB) was successful, as gradually less attention was provided over time while SIB was held at a low level. This non-contingent procedure was favored by the authors because it did not produce the behavioral increases sometimes associated with non-reinforcement during DRO procedures. That is, if responding is at a high level during DRO, then no reinforcement is given, thus producing an extinction-like situation.

At times, extinction procedures, even coupled with training of incompatible responses, are either impossible—because the reinforcement cannot be controlled by the person attempting to decrease the aggression—or they take too long. If aggressive behavior results in serious danger to the client or others, it must be decreased as rapidly as possible. However, in cases were aggression has been classically conditioned, it may be possible to condition an opposing response. This procedure, counterconditioning, has been used very successfully in cases of incapacitating conditioned fear responses, or phobias. Wolpe (1958) developed the most widely employed technique, called systematic desensitization, which usually includes training a patient to relax while being exposed to the feared stimulus. Thus, while the conditioned stimulus is no longer being paired with a fear-producing stimulus, as in extinction, a new conditioning is occurring to the incompatible relaxation stimuli. In an approximation of the application of systematic desensitization with people in a troubled community situation, past associations of police with violence might be reversed by having police associated with positive activities. For example, if images of non-violent police and their associated stimuli (uniforms, cruisers) were systematically paired with thoughts of non-aggressive humorous images, after many training sessions the sight of a police officer would evoke a positive instead of negative emotion.

Punishment as a Means of Decreasing Aggression

Operantly conditioned behavior can be decreased by the procedure called **punishment**. This involves presenting an aversive stimulus immediately following the behavior. While this procedure can be very effective, it presents a number of problems that limit its usefulness. Two are especially relevant here. First, since punishment involves the application of aversive stimulation, it may in itself produce aggression. For example, Ulrich, Wolfe, and Dulaney (1969) attempted to punish pain-elicited nose biting in squirrel monkeys and initially elicited increased biting. Biting finally was suppressed only by highly increased punishing stimuli. Most applications of punishment employ as mild a punisher as possible, while making sure that it is strong enough to suppress the behavior. Second, the effect is one of suppression, not elimination of a behavior. Therefore, while it may provide a relatively rapid way of controlling aggression, the behavior may return, indeed at an increased level, when the punishment contingency is removed. It is necessary then either to continue to punish or to train an acceptable response that would substitute for the aggression. Another consideration is that punishment may not have equivalent effects on all individuals and thus might not be a good general technique (Wilson & Herrnstein, 1985). On the other hand, a number of successful attempts have used punishment to decrease aggression.

Timeout procedures, in which termination of access to reinforcers is used as a punishment, have been successful in controlling the behavior of individuals. Further, although the withdrawal of reinforcers can produce aggression, this effect may not be as strong as that of the presentation of painful stimuli. Also, it may be ethically more acceptable. For example, while rapid, successful suppression of SIB in children and young adults has occurred via automatic delivery of a painful shock (Linscheid, Iwata, Ricketts, Williams, & Griffin, 1990), the method has provoked much controversy.

Using two-minute timeouts contingent on aggression, Bostow and Bailey (1969) showed that the behaviors of two retarded individuals could be suppressed. Mace,

Page, Ivancic, and O'Brien (1986) demonstrated that a set two-minute timeout interval was as effective in eliminating aggression for three developmentally disabled children as one that was extended based on further aggressive or disruptive behaviors. Wahler and Fox (1980), in the study cited earlier, also used timeout when they found that the original effects of reinforcing individual toy play did not persist. When they combined a timeout punishment contingency for fighting or oppositional behaviors with reinforcement for the incompatible toy play, they successfully controlled the undesirable behaviors.

The roles of conditioning and learning in aggressive human behaviors are very important. Aggressive behavior not only can be increased by conditioning and learning processes but it can also be controlled by them. Socialization involves specific learning processes that most probably play the predominant role in determining aggressive responding in humans. Therefore, it is of paramount importance for us to understand the principles of learning discussed in this chapter. In addition, other learning processes—sociopsychological and media-influenced—have been discovered more specifically from observations of social situations, involving two or more individuals. Because so much research has been dedicated to this area, we will treat it in the following two chapters.

SUMMARY

Conditioning and learning processes can function to help an individual benefit from experiences. In conditioning, the individual who reacts aggressively to other stimuli associated with noxious stimuli can limit exposure to the noxious stimuli. In learning, aggressive responses can help terminate or avoid noxious stimuli or gain rewarding stimuli.

Classical conditioning of aggression to noxious stimuli has been demonstrated in lower animals and used to explain excessive aggressive behaviors in an experimental situation. Conditioning is rather difficult to establish and maintain, possibly because aggression is relatively more complex than the responses usually studied in conditioning, but it can contribute to increased aggression.

Successful attempts to demonstrate conditioning to aggressive cues in humans have been reported. However, there have been failures to replicate, and various interpretations of the results, which illustrate the difficulties in studying human aggression in the laboratory.

The learning process involved in negative reinforcement is adaptive by teaching an individual that noxious stimulation can be terminated or avoided by aggression. Both experiments and observations of spontaneous interactions have shown that aggression is increased by negative reinforcement.

Learning may result in an increase in aggression when an individual is positively reinforced following an aggressive behavior. Thus, this learning is not involved in adaptive protection as in the first two situations. Instead, the learning aids in gaining rewarding outcomes. Positively reinforced aggression follows the same principles as other operant behaviors, and so operant principles can be applied to predict and control it.

Aggression can not only be reinforced but can also serve as a reinforcer. Individuals will learn to exhibit aggressive responses under the appropriate motivating (antecedent and consequent) conditions. However, no convincing evidence supports the existence of an aggressive drive or a cathartic effect of aggression.

The principles of conditioning and learning have been utilized to decrease aggression. Extinction is effective in both areas. Eliminating the association of a conditioned stimulus with a noxious stimulus results in loss of aggressive responding to the first stimulus. Terminating negative or positive reinforcement of learned aggression decreases it. Counterconditioning and learning an incompatible response help to accelerate the decrease of conditioned or learned responses, respectively. Finally, punishment of an aggressive response sometimes can help to decrease it, although increased aggression could also be produced. A mild form of punishment, timeout, has been used effectively to decrease aggression.

Suggested Reading

Goldstein, A. P., and Keller, H. (1987). *Aggressive behavior: Assessment and intervention.* Elmsford, NY: Pergamon Press.

CHAPTER 8

Sociopsychological Factors

This chapter will further consider the role of learning in aggression that we discussed in Chapter 7. We have regarded respondent and operant conditioning as processes by which experience can affect the range of stimuli that produce aggression and by which individuals' aggressive behaviors are increased or decreased by preceding and subsequent events. Another way in which individuals learn by experience is by observation of others. This has been shown to be especially important in acquiring complex behaviors such as aggression. Therefore, this chapter will include an introduction to the basic concepts of **social learning theory**.

The development of contemporary social learning theory was initiated from experiments demonstrating how children can learn aggressive behaviors by observing others. We will describe some key experiments here, along with how the theory accounts for the occurrence of observational learning. Apart from stressing how environmental events produce learning, we will focus on the important role given to internal, cognitive processes. We will also see how this theory has been applied in investigations of how to control aggression.

A principal developer of social learning theory was Albert Bandura. Some writers may include Bandura's work as simply another part of the operant learning area, which constitutes the major basis for behavior modification (and indeed an early text by Bandura (1969) is titled *Principles of Behavior Modification*). However, his approach differs from many behavior modifiers in that he puts less emphasis on the consequences of behaviors and more on the role of antecedent stimuli. He particularly emphasizes the influence of the stimuli presented by other individuals as mod-

els for the observer's behavior. Furthermore, Bandura has emphasized, starting in his early work in the 1960s, the role of cognitive (mental) evaluations of a situation in the determination of behaviors, while behavior modification approaches only more recently have encompassed cognitive procedures in the treatment of behavior and attended to how cognitions affect an individual.

Much of Bandura's work with the role of models in influencing aggressive behaviors has led to many further investigations by other workers, especially in the area of social psychology. We will review the principal components of Bandura's theory here, along with some tests of their application. Then, in the next chapter, we will discuss the role of symbolic modeling, as in television, movies, and other media.

BANDURA'S CONTRIBUTIONS TO SOCIAL LEARNING

Bandura's stress on modeling as a mechanism for learning involves an important extension of operant learning since it suggests a relatively efficient way for complex behaviors such as aggression to be acquired. That is, while applications of basic operant principles encompass the possibility of learning complex behaviors, they involve a relatively slow process of acquisition, as in **shaping** or **chaining,** in which reinforcement occurs for gradual approximations to the final behavior or by a linking of simple behavioral elements. While such processes probably do occur, as illustrated in Chapter 7, the existence of a modeling process helps explain how the acquisition of any specific aggressive behavior may take place more rapidly and how the form of the aggression may be common to several individuals. Modeling mechanisms have been postulated, for example, as an explanation of "copycat crimes," where an unusual form of aggression by one individual serves as a model for another. We will examine the role of the media in such cases in Chapter 9.

Modeling is sometimes also referred to as **imitation** or **vicarious learning**. The term "vicarious" refers to how we may learn something without experiencing it directly. In addition to the primary role of simple observation of a behavior in our acquiring of it, Bandura's theory also indicates how observation of the consequences of another person's behavior, such as reinforcement or extinction, can affect the occurrence of the observer's own imitative behavior. Thus, the theory refers to "vicarious reinforcement" and "vicarious extinction," as well as other vicarious processes in which the observer's behavior is affected.

Bandura maintains that cognitive mechanisms often affect behaviors. These mechanisms function in addition to modeling. For example, cognitions involving the intent of an apparently aggressive act by one person toward another are thought to influence the reaction. If the target person believes the act is accidental, he or she may not retaliate. Here, the victim does not attribute the cause of the pain to the perpetrator of the act and therefore inhibits his or her reflex-like response to the pain.

While tempering of aggressive reactions can be subsumed under a purely operant framework (people are taught by discrimination training that they will not be reinforced by aggressing against a dentist who hurts them, or that it is more appropriate to clench your jaw or yell slightly when a medical worker causes you discomfort, rather than aggress against the worker or anyone else who happens to be present),

Bandura and other social learning theorists have found it helpful to refer to cognitive factors as a way of explaining the variability of responses in situations where we might expect aggression. Thus, in the dental and medical situations, social labeling of intent or responsibility for an apparently aggressive act will determine whether aggression is an appropriate response. Turner, Fenn, and Cole (1981) indicate that while frustration may produce aggression, it will occur only if the frustrating force is perceived as being controllable by the aggression; otherwise, a problem-solving response will occur to eliminate the frustrating situation.

The Bobo Doll Studies

Bandura and his colleagues, including Ross and Walters, started working in the early 1960s (Bandura, Ross, & Ross, 1961) with observations of aggressive behaviors of preschool children toward a popular inflatable plastic toy known as a Bobo doll. The doll is decorated as a clown, with a large bulbous nose, and weighted at the bottom so that it bounces back upright if pushed over. In the original study the children watched while an adult woman "played" with the doll, exhibiting several relatively unusual ways of aggressing against it. Later the children were placed in a play situation and then frustrated by being interrupted in their play. They then were allowed into the room with the Bobo doll and observed as they interacted with it. As expected following the frustration, the children were aggressive. More important to Bandura's theory, the specific aggressive behaviors that they emitted included some close imitations of the teacher's behaviors. The films taken of the teacher and of the children include strikingly similar actions directed toward the Bobo doll. Frames from these films have appeared in many introductory psychology texts. Bandura's work indicated that such a great correspondence between the teacher's and children's aggressive acts was not a coincidence and that such acts were learned by the children via a modeling process.

Further studies by Bandura and his colleagues demonstrated that imitative learning could occur if children watched the model on television. It also was shown that less aggression was displayed when no model was used and that a decrease in aggression occurred when they used a non-aggressive model. Several additional studies explored other influences. A person dressed as a cat familiar to the children from a cartoon was imitated, but was not as effective a model. Cartoons themselves were not as effective in producing imitative aggression, although they may have had a disinhibitory effect in that overall aggressive acts were increased after watching them. Imitative aggression was increased when a higher status model was employed or when the model verbalized while aggressing. Consequences for the model's behavior were also influential. Models who were rewarded were imitated more, while models who were punished were imitated less.

A study related to those of Bandura was carried out by Hicks (1968), who showed children television episodes of an adult male in a playroom aggressing against a Bobo doll in ways similar to those modeled in the first Bandura studies. An adult male observer was in the viewing room and either approved, disapproved, or was silent during the viewing of aggression. The children then were taken to the playroom. When their aggression was measured while the observer was present, his earlier approval was associated with a high level of imitative aggression, his neutral stance with a moderately high level, and his disapproving stance with a very low level. However, if the observer was not present during the test of the children's aggression, his earlier comments were unrelated to their aggressive levels. This last finding has interesting implications for the effectiveness of some parents' attempts to attenuate the effects of their children's viewing of televised aggression. Voicing disapproval of aggressive acts that they mutually observe might result in lower levels of imitation of those acts, but the effect might be limited only to when the parent is present. The lessons learned about aggression may not generalize from the situation when they are present (to perhaps back up their teaching with further disapproval of their own child's aggression) to other situations.

A study by Eisenberg (1980) offers further support for the relatively weak effects of an adult observer's disapproval. Children who had observed an adult approving of filmed violent actions subsequently scored higher on a projective test of verbal aggression (again, stretching the original definition of aggression in Chapter 1) given by another adult. Those who had observed an adult voicing disapproval were less likely to be verbally aggressive later, but were not significantly lower than children who had watched alone or with an adult who did not comment.

Russell and Pigat (1991) summarized several studies of attempts to use adults (parents and others) to affect children's aggressive reactions to television. They found inconsistent effects on subsequent aggression when the adults watched violent television with the children and made either critical or supportive comments. Thus, the comments of adults on what is viewed may not have an effective influence on aggression. We will discuss the more general question of the effects of viewing media violence in Chapter 9.

Questions have arisen concerning the validity of using attacks against the Bobo doll to represent aggressive behavior and the generalizability of the response to settings outside the laboratory (e.g., see Kaplan, 1984). However, a large number of studies have supported and extended the original findings with the Bobo doll to establish the importance of imitative learning as a mechanism for increasing aggression. Although earlier work in psychology (e.g., Freudian, Gestalt) included imitation as a general phenomenon, the work of Bandura was especially important because it involved an extensive examination of the variables affecting imitation and also suggested how the media might be involved in teaching aggression via a **symbolic** modeling process. To better appreciate the way in which Bandura's work was developed to aid our understanding of aggression, we will outline his analysis of this behavior as presented in his early text on aggression (Bandura, 1973).

BANDURA'S SOCIAL LEARNING THEORY AND AGGRESSION

Bandura's definition of aggression is rather similar to our earlier one, in that he treats it as a behavior directed toward personal injury or property destruction. A comparison of what is studied under his definition and the one we employ illustrates some differences between his broader orientation and our strictly objective one. His definition of personal injury includes psychological devaluation and degradation. Also, he would exclude socially sanctioned aggression and include aggression that misses its target. Thus, he uses some instances that we usually do not because of difficulties of interpretation of damage or intent or because of value judgments. As might be expected from the description of social learning given above, he also includes labeling processes in people's determination of whether aggression is occurring toward themselves or others. Thus, he indicates that people's personal and general cultural backgrounds will influence whether they label an act aggressive. He also points out that observers might consider such factors as the degree of emotion exhibited and the energy of the aggressor's behavior, and the reaction of the target, in judging whether aggression has occurred.

In 1973, Bandura (1973) described three major influences—**Origins, Instigators,** and **Maintainers**—that operate on aggression. Although the formulation of these influences happened more than two decades ago, it continues to be useful and is still employed by social psychologists (e.g., Geen, 1990). Further, Bandura has incorporated the formulation into his more recent Social Cognitive Theory (e.g., Bandura, 1994). We will describe each influence separately below.

Origins of Aggression

The Origins of aggression concern the manner of acquiring both specific aggressive acts as well as more general aggressive strategies. For humans, Bandura sees these primarily as deriving from environmental influences, although biological limits may also have effects. Observational learning (**modeling**) is considered very important for the acquisition of aggression, although reinforcement can also contribute. While observation is important, however, its effect is not automatic. Individuals must use memory mechanisms and rehearse the behaviors for them to be retained. Further, they must have the physique or other means to carry out aggressive behaviors.

Given a functioning memory, the possibility for rehearsal of aggression, and the means to execute it, there are three primary ways in which an individual can acquire aggression via modeling. First, familial influences may contribute. Parents who employ punishment, for example, are said to show their child that aggression is the appropriate way to deal with the world. Second, subcultural influences can contribute. If individuals are raised in a neighborhood where aggressive behaviors help them to gain status or are encouraged in other ways, they are likely to acquire aggressive behaviors. Similarly, a military environment may be influential in teaching aggression as an appropriate behavior. However, fortunately, once an individual leaves the military, the excessive aggressive behaviors usually are lost or at least greatly reduced. Stimulus control processes, as outlined earlier, probably function to prevent generalization of aggression from one situation to another; the soldier discriminates between a strange setting, in which the enemy often is of a different race or speaks a different language, and his familiar home setting.

The third way in which aggression is acquired is by symbolic modeling, especially through the presentation of aggressive models in television and movies. Here, the modeling functions on both a personal and cultural level. At the personal level, exposure to a range of violent acts, greater than what would be encountered in real life, helps increase the variety of aggressive acts that are learned and thus generally increase the possibilities of aggression in an individual. Further, specific original acts of violence may be acquired and copied. We see this in cases where a popular television show involves an unusual aggressive act (e.g., murder with a fishing spear) that then occurs in various cities where the program was broadcast because it was imitated by people watching the show. At the cultural level, modeling is seen to contribute to the spread of tactics by protesters, as occurred in the United States when peaceful civil disobedience in response to the Viet Nam War escalated to forcible occupations of "establishment" offices and buildings. Counteraggression also may spread in a similar fashion. Continuing with the Viet Nam era example, the counterattacks by "hardhat" construction workers against young protestors were repeated in several cities after television news reports of it in New York were shown nationally. More recently, the particular aggressive behaviors of delinquent gang members or some radical social protestors such as those involved in organizations involving animal rights, or protesting abortion, or opposing discrimination against minorities may be perpetuated by the press attention given to them.

Bandura does not seem to regard reinforcement as being necessary for modeling to occur, but does acknowledge that it can contribute to the acquisition of aggressive responding. In the absence of any model, aggression followed by a reinforcer should increase, just as any operant behavior. Similarly, punishment for aggression can decrease its occurrence. We presented evidence for such effects of consequences on aggression in lower animals and humans in Chapter 7. Bandura also indicates that modeling and reinforcement may interact. In some cases, imitative learning might be involved in the acquisition of an aggressive response, which then might be strengthened and perfected by reinforcement.

Instigators of Aggression

Bandura views the acquisition of aggressive behaviors as being distinct from their performance. For performance of aggression to occur, there must be an Instigator. Most instigators are acquired through past learning. Insults and status threats, the presence of enemies, and the recognition of occasions when aggression will be reinforced—all are previously learned instigators. Models may be involved in the instigation process. If an individual is angry and sees justification for being aggressive, a model may show how reinforcement can occur for aggressing. Further, the model may function to disinhibit aggression by showing that no retaliation will occur.

Many instigators of aggression are identical or similar to the stimuli for aggression discussed in Chapter 6. Emotional arousal may function as an instigator. This arousal may come from a variety of sources, e.g., sexual arousal or arousal produced by environmental events such as excessive noise. Aversive treatment of an individual, including frustration, might provide an instigation to aggress, because it arouses and motivates the person to cope with the stress of the treatment. Similarly, physical assault can produce aggression. However, in contrast to the orientation of the work cited in Chapter 6, Bandura indicates that the aggressive response will occur only if the individual perceives, based on past experiences, that aggression will be successful or appropriate. Also, while Bandura talks of the classical conditioning of aggression, as described in Chapter 7, his treatment is more cognitively oriented. Verbal threats and insults, especially when paired with a model and its disinhibitory influence, may also instigate aggression.

Bandura indicates that reductions in the level of reinforcement can instigate aggression. Such instigators include general conditions such as economic deprivation, especially when the deprivation is perceived by individuals to be worse for them than for others. For example, youths from 18 to 20 years old who are unemployed and without parents are more likely to commit homicide. Further, the expectation of a reward for the aggression makes it more likely. Studies of American urban riots indicated that those 15 to 20 percent of the population who perceived a payoff for participation (e.g., goods obtained by looting) were more likely to take part.

Instructional control is an instigator for aggression. As seen in Milgram's studies on obedience (1963), employing his "teacher-learner" method (see p. 16), individuals who otherwise would not aggress may do so in response to perceived demands. This is especially true when they have a past history of reinforcement for obedience and also when they cannot see the suffering caused by their acts. Bandura includes obedience as only one of many instigators for aggression in the natural environment.

A final instigator is delusional control. Here, psychopathological conditions, such as those involving hallucinations, paranoia, and delusions of grandeur, may produce aggressive acts.

Maintainers of Aggression

Once aggressive acts are acquired and occur, some conditions must exist to ensure that they will continue to happen. External Maintainers are similar to those reinforcers discussed so far in this and the previous chapter. Indeed, Bandura cites some of the same literature to support his notion of external maintainers. In everyday life, criminals who obtain goods or dictators who amass riches are examples of individuals whose aggression is maintained by external reinforcers. Social status is another functional reinforcer of aggression. Status is reinforcing for gang members whose aggressive acts are praised by their peers and for soldiers, whose acts result in medals.

Negative reinforcement may be involved in maintaining aggression. Escape from harm is an external reinforcer that sustains an aggressor's behavior. Related to this, expression of injury by a target may help to maintain aggression, especially if it is a sign of relief of discomfort by the aggressor. If a victim is being harmed and retaliates, the pain expressed by the aggressor is reinforcing because it indicates that the victim's counteraggression is successful and should result in the termination of the original attack. Also, if the aggression is occurring in competition for some rewarding outcome, an opponent's expression of injury may be reinforcing because it indicates success.

Vicarious and Self-reinforcement Maintainers

Bandura also writes of Vicarious and Self-reinforcement Maintainers of aggression. Vicarious maintainers function when an individual witnesses others being reinforced for aggression. This raises expectations that the observer will be similarly reinforced. Self-reinforcement occurs when someone feels satisfaction for an aggressive act. (Self-criticism, on the other hand, can result in a lowering of aggression.) Such independent, self-mediated processes may result in an excess in aggression if individuals become disengaged from external reactions and rationalize acceptable bases for their aggression. Another self-mediated process cited by social learning theorists is that of **self-efficacy**. If an individual believes that the behavior can be performed, and especially if he or she believes a certain outcome will occur, the aggression is more likely to occur. Thus, such cognitive processes are thought to influence the occurrence of aggression. Individuals who tell themselves that they can beat up others and this will prevent the others from attacking them are more likely to aggress than those who tell themselves that they are ineffective fighters and decide to run away.

Bandura's social learning approach to understanding aggression has many elements in common with the operant learning approach. Both acknowledge aggression as a behavior that may be elicited by the environment and can be affected by its consequences. Both approaches also acknowledge the behaviors of others as influences over the acquisition, expression, and maintenance of aggression, although Bandura describes these influences more extensively. He also emphasizes the role of cognitions more than the operant approach does.

OTHER SOCIAL LEARNING INVESTIGATIONS OF AGGRESSION

Social Control

Social learning has been developed by many social psychologists and has resulted in a substantial number of studies of aggression, including explorations of alternative techniques for controlling aggression. Exposure to a restrained, non-aggressive model is one possible effective strategy. Baron and Kepner (1970) employed a test of this model with the teacher-learner paradigm (see p. 16). They employed two "teachers," one an accomplice of the experimenters who served as a model-teacher for the other, who was the naive subject-teacher. After the subjects were insulted (to help instigate aggression), some were paired with either a high or low aggressive model-teacher, who was the first to select the shock levels for teaching. The high aggressive model-teacher used high shock levels of from 8 to 10 to punish the learners, while the low aggressive model-teacher used shock levels of from 1 to 3. A third condition involved no model-teacher. Instead, the subject-teacher was the first to shock the learner.

Baron and Kepner found that the subject-teachers exposed to the high aggressive models selected the highest intensities of shock and pressed the shock buttons for the longest durations, although the intensities selected were below those employed by the models. The intensities chosen by the subjects who had low-intensity models were the lowest, as were the shock-button durations. The subjects who had no models chose an intermediate level of shock intensities and employed intermediate durations. Therefore, the results were interpreted as showing that a non-aggressive model can help reduce aggressive behaviors. In an extension of this work, it was indicated that a low-aggressive model could cancel out the effect of a high-aggressive model.

Cognitive Strategies

Baron, among others, has proposed that cognitive strategies may help control aggression. The independent variables in some of the studies of cognitive strategies are difficult to control and thus produce inconsistent results. However, we will review these studies here because they suggest possible controls over aggression. For example, if victims are given reason to believe that attacks on them occurred under mitigating circumstances, they may not counterattack or even become angry. Zillmann and Cantor (1976) demonstrated this for male subjects who were told they were participating in a study of the effects of visual stimuli on physiological activities; their blood pressure was taken periodically during the study, purportedly to assess the stimuli's effects. To instigate aggression, the subjects were individually exposed to both a polite and a rude experimenter. The rude one insulted the subject and the other experimenter. For one group, the polite experimenter explained beforehand that the other (rude) experimenter was nervous about his upcoming mid-term exams. For a second group, this mitigating circumstance was offered after the insults occurred. For a third group, no explanation was given for the insults. Following the insult part of the procedure, the subjects were asked to rate the two experimenters for suitability as future graduate assistants. The ratings were used as indices of aggressive responses.

Zillmann and Cantor found that subjects provided prior explanation for insults gave the least negative ratings, followed by those given subsequent explanation. Similarly, the blood pressure readings, taken as an indication of anger (although they actually measure only arousal), showed that the highest levels of response occurred in subjects given no explanation for the insults. The subjects who did not receive a prior explanation originally also showed a high response level, but it was reduced after the explanation. Thus, the results of this study are taken to indicate that people's cognitive interpretation of aggressive acts can function to reduce their aggressive responses to them.

Incompatible Behaviors

Several studies have suggested that the generation of incompatible behaviors may help control human aggression. Aggression cannot occur at the same time as other more positive or distracting behaviors take place, so if these other behaviors are increased, aggression should decrease. This is a strategy employed successfully by behavior modifiers to reduce aggression as well as other undesirable behaviors, and it is an integral part of Wolpe's (1958) systematic inhibition technique for treating phobias. Social learning research has provided some possible extensions of these techniques in studies of the effects of empathy, humor, and mild sexual arousal on aggression. Again, as with work on cognitive strategies, the results of the studies are not always consistent. We discuss them because they pose interesting possibilities for controlling aggression. We will also consider reasons for their inconsistencies and suggest how such studies might be improved.

Empathy

The social learning studies of empathy center on the feedback effect of a target's pain on a subject's aggressive behavior. We saw how Milgram's subjects were more likely to follow orders to aggress when they could not see the suffering they produced. This suggests that observing suffering might help inhibit aggression. Baron (1983) describes his work, involving the teacher-learner paradigm, in which subjects were angered and asked to shock "learners." In these studies, subjects were able to see on a meter the amount of pain supposedly felt by the learners. The pain was labeled "mild," "moderate," or "very strong." The subjects who saw the "very strong" indication employed lower levels of shock on the Buss machine. However, further study, employing a stronger initial provocation of the subjects, did not show this empathy effect. As discussed previously, Bandura lists target pain feedback as a maintaining condition, since it signals success in aggression. Feedback may help reduce aggression only in low arousal conditions, as in Baron's first study.

The inconsistency of the results for the empathy studies serves as a good methodological lesson concerning the dangers of overgeneralizing from limited data. The manipulation of arousal conditions and the measurement of their effects in common social learning approaches are subjective, making them difficult to specify and control. "Anger," for example, probably is not produced and experienced in the same way by all subjects. There is a need to develop more objective paradigms. This was also evident in the earlier work of Baron described in Chapter 2, which dealt with sex differences in aggression. Early conclusions that males were more aggressive than females in the teacher-learner tests had to be reassessed when later tests employed higher levels of anger provocation. The latter tests showed comparable levels of responding for both sexes.

The apparent inconsistencies in the results of the teacher-learner studies may be due in part to the limited number of stimulus values employed. The advantage of parametric studies, where the values of one variable are manipulated systematically, is shown in lower animal studies such as that of Hutchinson, Renfrew, and Young (1971) discussed in the previous chapter. For example, we demonstrated that shocking squirrel monkeys with different intensities produced very different biting trends during sessions. Lower intensities resulted in a gradual lowering or negative acceleration of biting while higher intensities produced a positive acceleration. Introducing a second independent variable therefore would be expected to have different effects, depending on the shock level it was combined with. We found, for example, that only higher intensity shocks, delivered relatively infrequently over a long series of sessions, would produce the initial classical conditioning of the biting (when it came to be elicited by the apparatus stimuli as well as by the tail shocks). It would seem that the social learning approach to the study of aggression would benefit greatly if it had a base of systematic study comparable to that of the lower animal aggression work.

Humor

Humor (barring the sadistic or hostile) was reported to interfere with aggression in studies such as that of Baron and Ball (1974). They angered subjects, who later were given the role of "teachers," in order to study their button-pressing behavior. Meanwhile, subjects were asked to participate in the evaluation of stimuli. The stimuli they would evaluate were either amusing, non-violent cartoons or neutral scenes of landscapes or objects such as furniture.

Baron and Ball's subjects who were not angered exhibited slightly higher durations of button pressing if they had viewed cartoons. Possibly watching the cartoons disinhibited their aggressive behaviors. However, the more dramatic effect was that the subjects who were angered and viewed the neutral scenes pushed the shock buttons for much higher durations than those who viewed the cartoons. The effect of humor on reducing aggression was supposed to result from either distracting the subjects from their anger or from the production of responses incompatible with aggression.

Mild Sexual Arousal

If a subject in the teacher-learner paradigm is exposed to pleasurable, mildly arousing sexual images between being angered and exhibiting aggression, these images may reduce the aggressive responses. In two studies involving Baron (1974; Baron & Bell, 1977), males were shown photographs of explicit sex acts, of nude women from *Playboy* magazine, of clothed, "cheesecake" photos, or of neutral scenes. Both the *Playboy* and cheesecake photos produced comparable reductions in aggressive responding. The other, more explicit materials did not have this inhibiting effect. In part of a later parallel study with females (Baron, 1979), they were shown pictures of either male nudes or "beefcake" photos (or explicit or neutral pictures). Here, only the beefcake pictures were followed by reduced aggressive responding, and the sexual act photos greatly **increased** aggression. Baron suggested that the male nude photographs were highly arousing to the females and thus did not result in a reduction of their anger. Contrary to traditional conceptions, several studies of sexual arousal to erotic materials or hard-core pornography have reported that females are at least as aroused as males to such material (Rosen & Beck, 1988). Donnerstein (see Donnerstein, Linz, & Penrod, 1987, for a summary of his work) has indicated that viewing films of sex acts can arouse males and combine with previous anger to increase aggression. In addition, Baron reported that females reported negative reactions of disgust to the nude photos (and even more so to the sex act photos), so possibly, as in Donnerstein's work, the combination of high arousal and negative emotions precluded a decrease in aggression.

In an experiment conducted after those of Baron and Bell, White (1979) studied the intermixing of sexual arousal and other emotions in males. Photographs were selected that either were highly or mildly arousing sexually and produced either positive (pleasant or entertaining) or negative (disgust, nausea, guilt) affective (emotional) states in his subjects. He employed the teacher-learner method, and the subjects were told to deliver shocks to distract the learner from memorizing a word list. Some subjects had earlier been rated negatively by the learners in an attempt to anger them. As might be expected from the various studies previously discussed, the viewing of highly arousing photos combined with a positive affect resulted in a decrease in aggression, while high sexual arousal combined with a negative affect was followed by somewhat increased aggression. These results supported the interpretation that positive and sexually arousing stimuli may inhibit aggression by producing a state incompatible with it.

Baron (1976) conducted a field experiment that attempted to address several factors that might reduce aggressive responding. His measure of aggression was the honking of a car horn by drivers who were held up at a green light by "pedestrian" doing one of the following: hobbling along in a cast (to provoke sympathy), dressing and acting as a clown (to provoke humor), being provocatively dressed (to evoke sexual arousal), or merely distracting the driver. The first three manipulations produced less aggression, as measured by decreased proportions and longer latencies of honking, while the distraction condition produced no differences compared to a control condition. While we might question the index of aggression and control over the conditions employed here, the study suggests the possibility that using empathy, humor, or sex might be explored in attempts to control aggression. Individuals might be trained to defuse a potentially violent situation with humor. A strategy for prevention of rape, discussed in Chapter 12, involves eliciting sympathy from the attacker. Also, individuals might be helped to control their own aggressive reactions by being taught how to produce images involving one of the three factors. Cognitive behavior techniques such as those used by Meichenbaum (1985) have been successful in teaching people to cope with stressful situations by relaxing and employing other helpful imaging. Therefore, we might expect that aggressive responding could be diminished in a similar way. For example, a person with a history of angry outbursts in workplace situations could be taught to imagine pleasurable sexual activities during such situations in order to counteract the rage. He or she would practice imaging both the situations and the activities in the therapist's office until ready to apply the technique in the workplace.

SUMMARY

The social learning approach to understanding aggression emphasizes how the observation of aggression can lead to its acquisition, maintenance, and expression. This approach complements the respondent and operant mechanisms for the effects of experience in the occurrence of aggressive behaviors. Albert Bandura is responsible for much of the development of social learning theory. His early studies showed how small children will copy an adult model's aggression toward an inflatable doll. While he includes many principles from the area of operant learning, he stresses how a modeling process is responsible for learning behaviors, including aggression. Also, he emphasizes the role of cognition in affecting behaviors, as the person evaluates situational variables such as the intent of another person's acts, one's own capabilities for carrying out an aggressive act, and the probable outcome of the act.

Social learning principles have been applied in attempts to determine how aggressive behaviors can be controlled by authority figures, non-aggressive models, cognitive manipulations, and incompatible environments. There have been some successful demonstrations of control over aggression that may lead to successful treatment techniques.

Suggested Readings

The social psychology literature involving aggression is very extensive, and we discuss only a small sample of the major contributions to introduce the field to the reader and illustrate its approach in studying aggression. The next chapter explores more fully the work done primarily by social psychologists on the influences of the media on aggression. We will cite further contributions in later chapters as we discuss other topics.

Berkowitz, L. (1993). *Aggression: Its causes, consequences, and control.* New York: McGraw-Hill, Inc.

Geen, R. G. (1990). *Human aggression.* Pacific Grove, CA: Brooks/Cole Publishing.

CHAPTER 9

Media Influences

In the previous chapter, we described the basic elements of social learning and detailed the mechanics of imitative learning. We saw how aggressive behaviors may be taught via the presentation of a model or by reinforcement. The presence of appropriate stimuli served as a means of initiating the aggression. Maintenance of aggression was effected with direct reinforcement, by models, or by self-provided factors. In the last case especially, aggressive behavior may occur excessively in the absence of moderating influences from the environment. Now we will examine the possibilities for social learning effects on aggression via the media. Television, films, and the print media together provide an extensive source of possible models for aggression, and several studies have been carried out to determine their contributions to aggressive behaviors. We will review some representative ones here.

Most studies of the media have focused on television, since television viewing has become more and more extensive, and instances of aggression seem to be increasing concurrently. The largest number of studies have been done in the United States. However, concern for the effects of television on aggression and other behaviors extends beyond the United States. Although television sets are not as widely owned in many other countries as they are here, television is very popular, and its effects, especially on children's behaviors, are of great interest.

There have been three principal ways for assessing the influence of television on aggression. *Surveys* of television content have been carried out to determine the number of aggressive episodes portrayed and analyze the characteristics of aggressive encounters. *Correlational studies* have been done to compare the amount of violence viewed with the actual aggressive acts displayed by viewers. Finally, *experimental studies* have been executed, in which researchers manipulate the nature of the materials viewed to ascertain if subsequent aggressive acts are affected. Many studies have been interpreted to suggest that viewing televised aggression has a causal effect in increasing real-life violence. However, no complete agreement on a causal relationship exists. We will discuss the data from each of these approaches.

SURVEY STUDIES

Surveys of the aggressive content of television have involved measurement of such variables as how much occurs, who is involved, what are the means employed, what are the consequences, where and when it occurs, and how realistic it is. Thus, tabulators hope to discover what lessons are learned about aggression in terms of whether it is encouraged, to whom it is expected to be directed, and in what situations. Some workers are interested in more general factors such as how the viewers' understanding and attitudes toward aggression are affected and whether acceptance of it is increased.

Organizations such as the National Coalition on Television Violence (NCTV) have engaged groups of viewers to watch and rate television shows on the basis of the number of violent acts portrayed per hour. They then publicize their findings by ranking programs, as well as ranking the networks and sponsors by the degree of violence in the programs. In addition, they monitor the amount of apparent direct imitation of unusual violent acts displayed on television entertainment or news programs. With these methods, NCTV has become a zealous leader of a multifaceted campaign to reduce violence in the media. By the early 1990s, a large decrease in violence on television in the United States took place. Although incidences of television violence had been rising until the mid-1980s, they declined by more than 40 percent by 1990.

Survey studies have been taken to suggest that television, along with other media, teaches "lessons": for example, Life is violent; Violence often succeeds; Good guys can be violent **and** good; Victimization is common, especially against women, non-whites, and foreigners, who lack power; Non-whites and foreigners often are violent; and Aggression does not always hurt. Given such "lessons," it might be asked why such offerings are allowed to continue. The programs are, of course, often very popular and so are supported by both viewers and the television industry.

Support of violent programs by the television industry is, of course, linked to their popularity. Higher ratings are rewarding indications of success for actors, directors, and others producing these programs. High ratings are also critical for selling the programs to sponsors. The popularity of violent programs for viewers might be explained by the various reinforcers the programs presented. As indicated by Bandura's work (see p. 147), it may be reinforcing for a person to see someone being hurt. While this is primarily true if the hurt is a sign of a successful counterattack against the person's attacker, this reinforcing characteristic probably would generalize (extend) to seeing other non-attackers being hurt. In addition, it might be reinforcing in itself to see the heightened activity associated with violence. People do many things to seek increased stimulation (e.g., attend rock concerts) and watching violence may be another way to obtain such reinforcement. Also, of course, some of the "lessons" taught by television help make violence more reinforcing (e.g., good guys are violent and good) and thus make violent television more popular.

While the popularity of violent television programs has much support by viewers and the industry, these sources do not give much support to the idea that the violence may have negative effects. These effects are facilely dismissed by many people. For example, although violent acts in cartoons may approach one per minute, they are seen by many as being purely entertaining, with no effects on behavior in real life. Similarly, the commercial networks have typically denied that violent television can produce acts of aggression in viewers (although they have reduced program violence in response to pressure). Paradoxically, they seek advertisers on the basis that commercials **can** influence other behaviors of their viewers. The survey studies themselves, of course, do not demonstrate influences of television on actual violence, since they usually do not include measurement of viewers' aggression. Rather, they base their concern on the results of past studies of viewing-aggression relationships like those we review below.

CORRELATIONAL STUDIES

Correlational studies have involved measuring the amount of violence viewed on television as well as the amount of aggression displayed by viewers. Aggression has been measured in various ways, mostly indirect, such as by the viewer's self-rating, ratings done by peers or caretakers, written tests, and, at times, by observations done by the experimenters themselves. Although investigators supposedly realize that they are measuring two dependent variables and therefore are not demonstrating causation, significant positive correlations between the two variables often are then taken to support the argument that viewing violence results in increased violent acts by the viewers.

An example of the correlational approach is the work of McCarthy and colleagues. McCarthy, Langner, Gerstein, Eisenberg, and Orzeck (1975) performed extensive studies in several populations. They found a positive correlation between total television viewing by 700 elementary school children and their aggression as measured by incidences of fighting and delinquency, and by whether they lived in an aggressive situation, such as one involving parental conflict. In further studies with secondary school and nursery school children, they reported significant correlations between TV viewing and aggression for children of all ages, both sexes, from wide socioeconomic levels, and many ethnic groups as well, living in several different countries. The authors indicated that their findings were significant for total TV viewing measures and weighted (adjusted for total television time) violence viewing, not for just simple viewing of TV violence.

The McCarthy et al. study is one of several (e.g., see the work of Joy and colleagues discussed later in this chapter) that have found or discussed a relationship between overall television viewing and viewer aggression. At times, this measure of viewing may be done for simplicity, since it is easier to assess total viewing time than to define violent programs and measure their viewing. However, this measure may lead investigators to incorrectly conclude that violence is being viewed or that this is responsible for a significant correlation between this viewing and aggression. An individual who watches an especially great amount of television may do so because of a lack of many other activity opportunities. For example, a child who watches much television may not have much opportunity to interact with his parents or engage in activities where he will learn alternatives to being violent. Montenegro 1984 discusses other deleterious effects of extensive television viewing on children's development as outlined on p. 162. There are thus other possibilities besides watching violent programming **per se** that might explain a correlation between watching television and being violent.

Although a simple correlational study does not demonstrate causation, some investigators believe that a technique called cross-lagged correlation comes closer to doing so. With this technique, measures of a first variable taken at one point in time are compared to those of a second variable assessed at a later time. A commonly cited example of the cross-lagged approach is the work of Eron, Huesmann, Lefkowitz, and Walder (1972) who carried out a 10-year study, starting with assessments of viewing violence on television and the aggressive characteristics of 875 third-grade children (of about eight years of age) and taking similar measurements of both variables in 427 of them so that they were able to test when they were in the "thirteenth" grade (the year after they graduated high school, roughly at about age 19). The amount of violent television viewing was assessed by interviewing the children's parents, and their aggressive characteristics measured by self-ratings, ratings done by peers (e.g., acquaintances and classmates), and by scores on subsections of the Minnesota Multiphasic Personality Inventory (MMPI). The MMPI is a widely researched psychological test developed to assay various characteristics of a responder's personality by asking how he or she behaves or thinks in various situations.

Eron and Huesmann and their colleagues found their most consistent and strong results for boys. They reported a low but significant .21 correlation between TV violence watching and peer estimates of the eight-year-old viewers' aggression. This means that, in general, the more violence watched by the boys, the higher their peers' rating of the boys' aggression. These results correspond to those in other studies. However, an insignificant correlation was found between these two measures in the 19 year olds. More important to the relevance of this study were the correlations found between TV violence viewing by the young subjects and their aggression when older. While the correlations between TV violence seen and self-rated and MMPI-assessed aggression were positive, they were not significant. However, a significant .31 correlation was found between TV violence viewed and peer ratings of aggression. That is, the young boy who viewed more violent TV was more likely to be rated as an aggressive older child. Although there was a higher (.38) correlation between the aggressiveness at the two ages, the cross-lagged correlation between TV viewing habits and aggression was taken to support a causal relationship between the two variables: that viewing violence on television at a young age produces aggressive acts at an older age.

In further research by the Eron and Huesmann group, 12 years later, a canonical (combining several measures) correlation of .41 was found between watching violent television at age eight and several measures of aggression at age 30 (Eron & Huesmann, 1984). Eron (1987) suggests that this research supports the view that individuals learned attitudes and behavioral norms from their early viewing, and that this resulted in later increases in aggression. However, we should also note that significant correlations occurred between peer ratings of aggression of the eight year olds and the later measures of aggression at age 30. This might indicate that some other general aggressiveness factor was functioning over this period of time, and it affected both the choice of television viewing and aggression. We will examine this and other criticisms of the research more fully later in this chapter.

EXPERIMENTAL STUDIES

Experimental studies of the effects of media violence have been done both in the laboratory and more natural settings. In the laboratory, researchers have often used classical social learning techniques, in which subjects are shown the media violence and then their aggression is assessed while directed toward a Bobo doll or by pressing buttons to shock someone else in the teacher-learner setting. The studies done in more natural settings have involved measures of actual aggression in a population after viewing media violence. Both types of studies have provided support for a causal link between viewing symbolic aggression and aggressive acts.

An example of the laboratory study of aggression is the work reported by Geen (1981) who studied the effects of justifying viewed media violence. Some boys were first insulted and then shown clips from *The French Connection* that involved either exciting action scenes with or without violence. Then they saw one of three clips from *Rollerball* in which the violence was justified, unjustified, or given no explanation. Finally, Geen allowed the subjects to be aggressive by criticizing the person who originally insulted them.

More of what Geen categorized as aggressive criticism occurred after the viewing of the justified *Rollerball* sequences. For some reason, this increase was significant only for the boys who saw the exciting *French Connection* scenes. The author felt that possibly viewing the violent *French Connection* scenes desensitized them to the effects of the *Rollerball* viewing.

In work done in several countries, Goldstein, Rosnow, Raday, Silverman, and Gaskell (1975) studied the effects on punitiveness after viewing violence. They showed a violent film to males and then solicited their recommendations for criminal penalties. More severe penalties were recommended after viewing violence and this punitiveness was taken as a measure of aggression. However, perhaps the results could be seen as reflecting an increase in the perception of the need to control violence, in the same way that a person watching a film on the harmful effects of smoking might be more likely to favor restrictions on it. Again, it is evident how restrictions on the production of human aggression in the laboratory may limit our study of it. Fewer restrictions occur in the field experiments that we will consider next, although serious ethical questions arise as well as concerns about lack of appropriate control procedures. Nevertheless, they are of interest because they make an initial attempt to extend the laboratory work on media violence and aggression to natural settings.

One field study of the effects of viewing violence on aggression was done in the United States and Belgium with institutionalized delinquent boys by Berkowitz and Leyens and their colleagues (Parke, Berkowitz, Leyens, West, & Sebastian, 1977). In one part of the study, they showed the boys violent films for one or five nights and then studied their aggression in everyday encounters as well as in the laboratory. They found that the boys who viewed more of the violent films were more aggressive in daily activities as well as more easily provoked in the laboratory setting. This effect was especially strong in boys who previously rated low in aggression assessments. The implications for such effects of media violence on everyday aggression are important. These results suggest that not only does viewing violence increase aggression in already aggressive boys but that it can also make relatively non-aggressive boys into aggressive ones. The study also found that the nights' viewing effects can carry over to subsequent days.

A field observation by Joy, Kimball, and Zabrack (1986) yielded results that would seem to extend the effects noted by Berkowitz and his colleagues. Joy et al. took advantage of the isolation of a region in northern Canada to study the effects of introducing television to a population. They determined elementary school children's verbal and physical aggression rates in one (target) town before and after the arrival of television service and compared them to those for two other towns that already had television available, one including U.S. networks. Both verbal and physical aggression in the target town increased after the introduction of television, to a point where they were higher than those of the comparison towns. Actual television watching was not measured; however, the programming available in the target town was Canadian, which would make the effect even more remarkable, if true. A 1981 rating of violent acts by NCTV indicated that Canadian television contained one-fourth of the acts of violence found in U.S. networks, a level set as a goal by NCTV. We might therefore ask if the goal levels set by the watchdog organization are appropriate (since low-violence Canadian television apparently produced increased aggression) or if serious methodological problems are involved with assessing the effects of media violence on aggression (perhaps watching television violence did not produce increased aggression). Perceptive readers will correctly predict the second choice.

In the Canadian study, the introduction of relatively nonviolent television programming accompanied an increase in aggression exceeding that found in a town where more violent programming was available. Among several questions that these results suggest is whether some other factor besides the introduction of television might have produced the effect found. For example, perhaps there was a change in the number and types of activities shared by parents and children.

THE DEBATE OVER INTERPRETATION OF THE RESEARCH

The work reviewed in Chapter 8 on sociopsychological effects on aggression would seem to give good support to the proposition that viewing media violence can increase aggression. Social learning theory indicates that observations of behaviors can lead to the acquisition and repetition of them, so we might surmise that exposure to violent acts portrayed symbolically on television, in movies, or in print would result in increased levels of these acts by the witness. In fact, correlative studies show a positive relation between television viewing and aggression, and laboratory and field studies report a causative relationship between viewing violence and exhibiting aggression. However, some questions remain concerning the strength of this evidence. These questions involve how great any effects are, whether actual aggression will result from media viewing, and whether all significant variables were considered.

We may address the question of the size of the effects of viewing violence by remembering the magnitude of the correlations. For example, Eron et al. (1972) found a significant correlation of .31 between eight-year-old children's viewing of TV and the aggression of 19-year-old youths. If television had a powerful effect, we might expect to see correlations closer to unity. Therefore, while we could argue that any effect that seems to increase aggression is undesirable, the extent of the measured effect of television on aggression should be placed in its proper perspective. Even such a strong supporter of the social learning thesis as Chaffee (1972) indicates that not more than 10 percent of the violence that occurs can be attributed to television. Similarly, Huesmann and Miller (1994) summarize a series of correlative studies and indicate that they account for only between 1 and 23 percent of the occurrences of aggression measured in the children studied. However, they speculate that this small effect may accumulate over time to produce a socially significant one as the children mature.

The question of whether actual aggression is produced by the viewing of media violence recalls previous challenges to the common laboratory approaches to the study of human aggression. Freedman (1984), among others, indicates that while the laboratory studies report increases in "aggression," a question arises whether they involve an appropriate measure of it. He points out that striking a Bobo doll or pushing a shock button are only analogs of real-life aggression, and they may not correlate highly with actual aggression. Thus, he questions the generalizability of laboratory findings. Acts such as striking the Bobo doll are socially acceptable. They involve no retaliation and are not punished, and they are even encouraged by the experimenter. Further, the experimenter's implicd demands are strong. The subjects might feel that, since the experimenter obviously chose the film, he probably approves of it, as he probably approves of the subject's aggression. Indeed, in the teacher-learner paradigm, the experimenter instructs the subject-teacher to press the shock buttons of the apparatus that the experimenter provides. Freedman's criticisms are similar to those we discussed earlier.

Many concerns have been expressed about whether the appropriate variables have been manipulated in studies of the relationship between media violence and viewer aggression. For example, most studies select an unrepresentative sample of TV programming, usually those with the maximum amount of violence, while in real life a mix of violent and non-violent programs are watched. Social learning theorists such as Baron have reported that viewing a non-violent model can decrease aggression, so it might be expected that the effects of non-violent shows might offset those of violent shows. Further, the viewing settings employed in the laboratory studies are not representative of home settings, which often have co-viewers or, at the very least, the general presence of parents or others.

Field studies of media effects on aggression have been criticized for being poorly controlled, perhaps reflecting the difficulties of doing research outside the laboratory. For example, an experiment by Feshbach and Singer (1971) with institutionalized delinquent boys apparently produced a greater effect of **non**-violent shows on producing aggression. However, independent analysis of this study revealed that, because of the children's demands, *Batman* was included as one of the non-violent samples, and that the other non-violent shows were rather boring, possibly leading to a contribution of frustration to the levels of aggression measured.

Methodological flaws have been pointed out in the field studies of Leyens, Berkowitz, and their colleagues. For example, boys in different units of the institution were not equal in their original levels of aggression, an inappropriately small sample was used, and invalid statistical assumptions were made. Therefore, any effects could result from other uncontrolled and unmeasured variables. Further, inconsistent effects were obtained. Some effects were seen for only one day and on only one measure of aggression. Still other field studies have reported no effects of viewing violence, indicating that the influence of such viewing may be more limited than earlier reports suggest. Wood, Wong, and Chachere (1991) analyzed studies that involved exposing children to media violence and then observing their violence in unstructured situations immediately afterward. They found a significant small to medium effect on aggression. However, seven of 23 studies reported more aggression by control group children. This last finding supports the conclusion that the effects of viewing television violence are not terribly strong. The authors themselves indicate that they do not expect that such viewing effects will be found to be among the most important determinants of aggression, although they maintain that the effect is not trivial. It might be more profitable to look elsewhere for causes of aggression.

Perhaps an important factor determining whether viewing of aggression will have an effect is the delay between exposure to the violence and the measure of aggression. Work with the effects of pornography by Donnerstein and others indicates that viewing violent sexual material might increase aggression in non-angered subjects or that previously angered subjects might be more aggressive after viewing sexually arousing but non-violent material. However, subjects typically are tested immediately after viewing the material. Malamuth and Ceniti (1986) found that longer-term (four week) exposure to either violent or non-violent material had no effect three to 14 days later on male aggression against women in a teacher-learner situation. The authors indicated that the effects of exposure to violence might dissipate rapidly afterward. This suggests that the laboratory findings of effects on aggression of viewing violence might be limited in their application to real-life situations. A similar criticism has been directed at laboratory studies suggesting that viewing pornography increases aggression. For example, Smith and Hand (1987) found that coeds at a small college reported no increases in aggression by male dates following showing of a non-violent pornographic movie on campus. Amount of aggressive acts by males did not differ from that displayed in the weeks before and after showing of the film, and the aggression of males who had seen the film was no different from that of those who had not.

It has been suggested that the number of reports indicating a relationship between viewing violence and exhibiting aggression has been grossly exaggerated. Freedman

(1984) points out that some supporters of the relationship, in their enthusiasm to get legislators or others to censor television violence, have suggested that as many as 2500 studies have demonstrated the relationship. However, this number refers to all studies that have been done on television in general. Freedman found that as of 1984, only 500 published papers had dealt with television and violence. Even this number does not represent the number of **studies** done, for many papers simply reported on the work of others. Less than 100 actual studies had been carried out up to that time. Few of these had been done outside the laboratory, and very few were published in refereed journals. Such journals accept work only after it has been evaluated for scientific validity by professional reviewers. Other journals may publish anything, regardless of its scientific merit, if it is deemed of potential interest to readers or simply if the author pays to have it published. While the referee system does not guarantee impartial publication of only valid work, most scientists consider it a critical component in their evaluation of a study's seriousness.

A final point that has been raised about the relationship between media violence and aggressive acts involves correlation studies. While a consistent, although low, positive correlation has been found, and this may be the strongest evidence for a relationship, researchers point out (once more) that a correlative relationship, especially at a low level, does not tell us that watching media violence **causes** aggression. Moreover, it does not tell us anything about directionality. That is, from the results, it is just as possible to claim that being aggressive causes increased viewing of media violence.

Attempts to use correlation studies to prove that viewing media violence causes aggression have not been convincing to most analysts, although the cross-lagged correlation studies by Eron are considered to come the closest to doing so. However, following additional research, Eron and his colleagues (Huesmann, Lagerspetz, & Eron, 1984) concluded that there is a bidirectional causal effect relating watching violence on television and being aggressive. We should also note that these studies are limited in that the clear, consistent results involved only boys, not girls, and were significant for only one measure of aggression.

Critics such as Freedman have concluded that while it is possible that a causative relationship exists between viewing aggression and being aggressive, this has not yet been proven. It is just as possible that a third factor, such as a personality trait, or some biopsychological influence, is involved that affects both the selection of viewing violence and being aggressive.

The debate about the relationship between viewing violence and committing aggressive acts has spawned further discussions concerning the effects of television in general and its sociological implications. It is interesting to note how some participants select from the data the facts supporting their positions, while ignoring other dissonant information. Results from studies whose authors do not support an effect on aggression are taken by others to justify such an effect. Critics of Freedman's 1984 paper accuse him of ignoring supportive effects while they in turn ignore his later critiques. Another example of selective use of information is seen in the paper of Montenegro (1984), who made some legitimate points about the deleterious effects of extensive television viewing on general development processes. The child who is watching television excessively is foregoing learning experiences that derive from interactions in play with peers, from interchanges with parents, and from reading. General physical development and well-being may be affected if the child does not engage in exercise and does not obtain sufficient sleep. Television is seen as a passive, restricted way to obtain input, involving only the auditory and visual senses and lacking the tactile and olfactory sensations and motor activity ideally needed for best learning.

Montenegro cited a U.S: Surgeon General's report on television (Pearl, 1982) that indicated that measures of intelligence and school performance were inversely related to the amount of television watched. In an independent presentation given at the same conference, Huston (1984) referred to the Surgeon General's report and cited the data for the **beneficial** effects of television viewing for children of lower socioeconomic class and lower intelligence. It seems that their reading and school work improve as they are exposed to more television. The stimulation provided by TV counters the generally unstimulating environment in which they are being raised. On the other hand, Huston noted that the deleterious effects on school performance of extensive television viewing do occur for individuals from higher income families and with higher intelligence levels, apparently because they do not receive the beneficial effects of the stimulating environment that surrounds them. Further selective utilization of the data occurred when Montenegro, after indicating that poor learning results from watching television, again referred to the Surgeon General's report and indicated that the appropriate conclusion was that television does increase aggression in its viewers, assumedly due in great part to the social learning occurring during viewing.

Inconsistency in the interpretation of television's effects unfortunately is not unique. We noted earlier how other supporters of the aggression-producing effects of television watching typically ignore learning of non-violent behaviors from television. As Rubinstein pointed out (1976), many political axes are being ground by individuals and groups involved in the studies of TV and violence. The people who do not agree with the conclusions of the Surgeon General's review (the 1972 effort for which Rubinstein was vice-chair) accuse the committee that prepared it of being biased. The conclusions themselves are also distorted by others. Part of the actual statement indicated that there was evidence that televised violence **may** lead to increased aggressive behavior, but then this was restricted to "certain subgroups" of children, and the generalizability of the findings was not affirmed. This was a conservative statement, indicating the possibility that television affects violence but not acknowledging that this effect had been conclusively demonstrated. The statement has been interpreted by both sides of the debate as supporting their positions.

Freedman (1992) points out the even stronger conclusion for the 1982 review by U.S. government agencies, in which most evidence was taken to support a causal effect of television on violence. In light of what he characterizes as inconclusive evidence, he attributes that support in part to selective emphasis on positive results and discounting of negative ones. He also indicates that scientists' personal biases about the harmfulness of television violence and their professional investments in their earlier studies are responsible for the support.

A tempering analysis of the TV-violence dispute was presented by Kaplan and Singer (1976). These authors examined three basic hypotheses for the effects of TV on aggression: that it increased it; that it decreased it; and that it had no effect. On reviewing the available data, they concluded that the third hypothesis—no effect—was the most plausible to accept at that time. While they did not decide that viewing TV does not cause aggression, they indicated that the opposite also had not been demonstrated. They concluded that although the laboratory studies show the possibility for an effect, they have not proven its probability since the studies deal with only a limited aspect of the aggression equation. Further, they wrote that television might be serving as a scapegoat, an easy target, while other important contributions to aggression, such as poor economic development and social and cultural factors, are being ignored.

The political implications of the TV-violence debate, especially as it has developed in England, were examined from a sociological perspective by Murdock (1982). Because his approach presents an interesting argument and illustrates a very different way of analyzing the problem, we will attempt to summarize it here, with apologies for any misperceptions resulting from unfamiliarity with the subtleties of his thinking. Murdock criticizes the individualistic approach of the analysis of the effects of television on aggression and indicates that we should address institutional or more general aspects of aggression. From his apparently Marxist perspective, he sees the polemic concerning aggression as one directed toward the working-class delinquent youth by the ruling class. This argument, he says, is a means of preserving the status quo and is aided by the media's treatment of the TV-violence relationship. Further, he states that the argument diverts attention from the role of social forces involving deprivation and disadvantage that affect these youths.

Murdock dismisses the laboratory studies of aggression as being irrelevant because they involve either college students or inmates in artificial situations, not working-class youth in their real-life environments. After reviewing various improvements in approaches to addressing the problem of aggression, he suggests that a subcultural analysis is desirable, in which we examine the oppressed status of working-class youth and explain the role of youth violence as part of a class struggle.

Murdock believes television has two major potential influences. First is its role in affecting the youths, as it encourages consumerism and produces frustration in the un- or underemployed youths who cannot share in the fruits of society. In its portrayal of masculinity, television may legitimize violence between males (or provide a type of teaching in addition to simple observational learning). Television is also considered a means of publicizing and labeling delinquent violence and helping to legitimatize repressive countermeasures. Thus, Murdock indicates that television programming is not something that increases aggression by a social learning process but is a medium that alters social-class perceptions.

Given these questions about the relationship between the media and aggression, and the challenges to the very relevance of the questions, we might ask why the belief in the relationship is so pervasive. The answer may have more to do with propaganda effects than with the science of psychology. Bandura's original work with the Bobo dolls produced very striking and widely disseminated photographs. It also fit people's preconceptions concerning the effects of models on behavior. Consequently, many questions were not asked about long-term effects or the applicability of the results to real life. The correlative studies were misunderstood as demonstrating causation. Again, preconceptions are important. People were concerned with the increased violence in society, noted the amount of violence in the media, and were most ready to use the media as a scapegoat. However, even this argument may not be appropriate.

As we can see in Figure 9.1, there was no apparent consistent relationship between the rate of TV violence and contemporary rates of violent crime in the United States during the 1980s. While a parallel increase occurred from 1980 to 1981, in just about all subsequent years the direction of change in each measure is opposite. That is, when television violence increases, crime decreases, and vice versa. However, the changes were not necessarily proportional to each other. For example, the largest increase in TV violence, from 1983 to 1984, was accompanied by little change in violent crime. Any conclusions about the relationship between TV violence and societal aggression must be qualified. Nevertheless, the repeated exposure of the results of the relatively few studies and cases of real-life imitations of viewed violence, such as the Russian roulette scene in Viet Nam from *The Deerhunter* or of gang violence that followed films such as *New Jack City*, made relatively limited data look more important than the data justified.

The academic debate over whether television violence causes significant societal violence has continued, including responses to Freedman and his rebuttal, in the 1986 volume of the journal where his 1984 article was published. In basic agreement with Freedman, other reviewers, such as Gunter (1994), have analyzed the original as well as more recent experimental and correlative studies done in both laboratory and natural environments and have found much of the evidence inconclusive because of relatively small effects and inconsistent results. However, Gunter also acknowledges that the majority view of investigators indicates a causal effect. This majority continues to argue in support of their position.

Figure 9.1   Television violence measures and violent crime rates from 1980 to 1990. Data for TV violence were taken from reports of the National Coalition on Television Violence. Data for violent crimes are from the *FBI Uniform Crime Reports.*

A recent text contains chapters by both Freedman and his critics. Freedman (1992) again reviewed various areas of the research, including more recent studies done in the natural environment. He again found insufficient evidence for stating that watching violence on television causes violent behavior. While he acknowledged that some research areas have stronger support (e.g., more aggressive children watch more violent television; laboratory television experiments produce increases in aggression), he feels that there is not enough basis for a causal relationship. The reply to Freedman, by Huesmann, Eron, Berkowitz, and Chaffee (1992), criticized him for various aspects of his criticism, such as not giving sufficient weight to the possibilities of generalization to real life of the laboratory studies, and for selective and biased analysis of other types of studies. However, they in turn did not answer all of his criticisms. As is common in such academic debates, the participants seem to be talking "at" each other instead of communicating with each other, and neither side is a clear victor.

In a less confrontational situation, Huesmann and Miller (1994) discuss work with long-term effects that followed the early cross-lagged correlation studies done with Eron. They describe what they feel is a more convincing path analysis statistical approach and discuss support for Huesmann's ideas that exposure to violent television in early life can affect the cognitive development of children (forming cognitive "scripts" that guide later behaviors) and result in increased aggressiveness in later life. They also indicate how studies carried out in several countries support the generality of such effects. While critics probably would find fault with the lack of consistent effects across countries and genders, the authors find support in the consistencies as opposed to the exceptions. They do acknowledge limits to the research and the weakness of the observed effects. And they also recognize that aggression has a number of more important causes, including the biological, psychological, and social factors we discussed in earlier chapters. Some of these factors are also seen to prevent aggression-producing effects of watching violent television. However, they believe that watching violent television does have a significant socially important effect on aggression.

Although viewing violence might make a contribution to increased aggression, we must understand that the evidence for this view is not unquestionably convincing. On the basis of such suggestive but faulty evidence, many individuals and organizations have encouraged the government to censor the media. However, the implications of such censorship for civil liberties are important, as we pointed out earlier concerning the attempts to limit pornography. Instead of mounting yet another attack on the First Amendment, perhaps it would be wiser to explore and attempt to control the many other more certain contributions to aggression. Thus, instead of making people feel better by railing against a popular, though possibly insignificant target, more might be accomplished by addressing the biological and environmental factors in society that already have been shown to affect aggression.

EDUCATIONAL ATTEMPTS TO DECREASE VIOLENCE

If it is established that viewing violent media increases real-life aggression, perhaps we might ameliorate such effects by educational techniques. Linz, Wilson, and

Donnerstein (1992) describe how the harmful effects of viewing sexual violence can be reduced by several techniques, including pre-film messages and post-viewing debriefings that describe the possible harmful effects of viewing violence and help to dispel misconceptions about sexual violence. Roberts (1993) suggests a similar approach with adolescents. He indicates that while research does not support a case that massive effects result from exposure to media violence, there does seem to be evidence for an effect on aggression in small numbers of youths. He suggests that teachers and parents can help to counter these effects by discussing the meanings of media messages.

Friedlander (1993) offers the possibilities of employing television itself to help decrease violence, especially that directed against children. He also argues that the media makes a relatively small contribution to violence. The important causes of violence are found in social factors, such as poverty and lack of opportunity. These factors produce the violence that both affects and instructs violence in the young. While we cannot change these factors quickly or easily, Friedlander indicates that television can be employed to help counter violence. He points to a 1986 meta-analysis by Hearold indicating that prosocial effects of television (e.g., on self-control, altruism, various socially desirable behaviors) usually are higher than antisocial effects (e.g., on law breaking, use of aggression). Friedlander suggests that television could be used in a media campaign to decrease violence, especially as directed against children. The same sort of success from campaigns to buy commercial products or protect the forests might result if efforts are directed to counter violence and protect and value children. At present, Friedlander's suggestions are theoretical, but perhaps they will be followed as another attempt to use educational techniques for decreasing aggression.

SUMMARY

Social learning theory suggests that individuals can acquire complex behaviors, including aggression, by observing those behaviors. The extensive presentation of aggressive models in the media, especially television, has led to concerns that media exposure may increase real-life aggression. A number of studies, of several different types, have been carried out to investigate this possibility.

Survey studies involve measuring aggression shown on television, as well as analyzing the lessons taught by the medium. These studies have documented the relative amounts of violence shown on various programs, as well as yearly changes in overall violence, and have indicated how television portrays violence unrealistically and inappropriately.

Correlational studies involve measures of either total television viewing or viewing of violent programming and compare the viewing to various measures of aggression by the viewers. Researchers have reported significant positive correlations, indicating that a relation exists between viewing television and being aggressive. While these simultaneous measures do not show that one variable causes the other, longitudinal studies, spanning up to 22 years, have found significant relations between childhood viewing of violent television and the aggressiveness of the children as adults. Various shorter longitudinal studies carried out in several countries give general support to these findings.

Experimental studies of the effects of viewing violence on subsequent aggression have been carried out in both laboratory and less controlled settings. The laboratory work has found increases in various types of aggression, after different levels of provocation of subjects, along with the media viewing. Some of the other work has been carried out in institutions, where exposure to violent television has been reported to be followed by increased aggressive interactions by residents. In more natural settings, introduction of television to a community has been found to increase aggression in the children of that community.

The positive results of most of these studies have led many researchers in the area to conclude that viewing violence on television causes increased aggression. However, critics of this conclusion have suggested that the studies contain various methodological weaknesses. Further, inconsistencies in results and the modest size of correlations are interpreted to suggest that a causal effect of viewing violence on aggression has not been demonstrated. At least one critic dismisses the causal effect and is more concerned with the sociopolitical implications of television content on social relationships.

The response to an assumed effect of television violence on aggression might include censorship. Alternatively, educational techniques can be employed to reduce any harmful effects of viewing violence. In addition, the effects on behavior of viewing television could be utilized to promote prosocial behaviors that help reduce societal violence.

Suggested Reading

The Berkowitz and Geen texts suggested at the end of the previous chapter both include an elaboration of the current social psychological approach to understanding the effects of the media on aggression.

PART III

Problems with Aggression in Specific Populations

The first two parts elaborated on various factors that help produce aggressive behaviors. Biological variables, including genetic mechanisms, chemical influences (involving sexual and neuronal hormones), and neuroanatomic factors can all contribute to the expression of aggression. Influences of environmental stimuli, ranging from simple stimuli to complex social ones, and how they combine with learning mechanisms are also factors in the control of aggression. To illustrate their various contributions to aggression, we have used applications of these factors to various organisms, from lower animals to both normal and abnormal human populations, as examples. Now our focus will shift to particular groups of humans who are involved with problems of aggression as the various contributing factors operate in certain populations. Thus, we will address some of the major problem areas in contemporary U.S. society—delinquency of minors, the physical and sexual abuse of children, and the abuse of wives and rape of females. We will also examine the incidences and control of aggression in psychiatric populations.

As we describe the work in the various problem areas, it should be evident that in many cases the information comes from sources where the ideals of objective definition and reliable measurement are left aside. The experimental work with aggression we discussed in the first two parts is typically carried out under controlled conditions, where we can observe a particular type of well-defined aggression systematically. In the problem areas in this part, the definitions of aggression are not always clear, and the measurement is not consistently precise since investigators are working in uncontrolled, real-life settings. Consistent with the orientation of this text, we have tried to focus primarily on work that involves objective definitions and measurement. However, definitions in some of the cited work are at times rather broad in order to encompass the variety of behaviors. "Crime," which does not always involve aggressive acts, is used interchangeably with "aggression." "Violence" is used not only for intensive aggression but also for any type of harm done to an individual. Also, because most aggression is of a criminal nature, we must realize that measurement is usually indirect.

All problems of aggression are not included here. Many, involving adult delinquency, abuse of the elderly, and war may come to mind. However, the areas selected should provide readers with a better appreciation of the practical nature of problems in aggression and how the contributions discussed in the first two sections eventually affect incidences of aggression.

CHAPTER 10
Delinquency in Minors

Delinquency by minors has received increasing media attention because it involves escalating public levels of violence and results in death and serious injury to uninvolved bystanders. It is important for us to consider the amount and nature of this violence, its possible contributors, and how we might address the problems.

We will first briefly consider whether aggression by youths has indeed increased. We must discriminate between unjustified sensationalism, in which the media or others exaggerate the extent of a problem, and the existence of a substantial problem. Next, we will explore the specific nature of youth aggression, especially as it occurs in gangs. The chapter will include descriptions of some aggressive behaviors of delinquent youths as reported by trained observers. These observations can provide not only a description of the behaviors but can also include characterization of the events surrounding them. This suggests an analysis of the environmental influences over delinquent aggression and possibilities for modifying the behaviors. We will address problems in instituting treatment programs and will describe a promising social-behavioral program. In line with our broader orientation, we will discuss the development of theories of delinquency, including biological theories. Approaches that integrate biological, psychological, and social factors will be described. We hope that readers will come to better appreciate better the causes of individual aggression in everyday life as illustrated in this problem population.

RECENT CHANGES IN JUVENILE VIOLENT CRIME RATES

Although some success has been claimed in reducing increases in overall violent crime rates, incidents involving youths are increasing. These increases occurred especially in homicides, but more recently have included other violent crimes. For example, in the 1990 *Uniform Crime Reports* (FBI, 1990), the overall violent crime arrests for all youths under 18 had risen only about 30 percent over the previous 10 years, compared to an almost 50 percent increase for people over 18. However, homicide arrests for youth were up 60 percent, compared to a 5 percent rise for adults. Essentially, all the rise for youth took place in the previous five years. In the years since the 1990 report, homicide arrests of youth continue to escalate, reaching a level of about two and one-half times what they were in 1981. Arrests for other violent crimes, such as assault and robbery, rose more than three times more rapidly for youths than for adults in the five years prior to 1993. These figures support the idea that violence by youths in the United States not only is increasing but also is growing much faster than violence by adults.

TRENDS IN THE AGGRESSION OF JUVENILE GANGS

Galen (1982) characterized and described some of the aggressive behaviors of youth gangs in Brooklyn, New York, in the 1980s. As a police officer in the Gang Intelligence Unit, Galen noted how, in his experience, the basic causes of aggression by gangs have changed over the past several decades. In the 1950s, fights occurred over territory, over girls, and because of ethnic factors, perhaps similar to conditions portrayed in *West Side Story*. Little aggression was directed against the community. While definitive evidence is not available for a parallel, the first two types might well resemble the territorial and sexual aggression types Moyer (1968) postulated. Although Moyer later decided that territorial aggression was not biologically based, the presence of these types of aggression might warrant a closer examination of the animal data for better understanding of the human problems.

Galen noted that after a relative decrease in gang violence in Brooklyn in the 1960s, the post–Viet Nam era was characterized by increased unemployment and hence more survival-related crimes against property. By the 1980s, the violence committed by gang members had become a major problem, and gang membership had grown. New York City had about 130 gangs, for a total of over 10,000 members. About one-third of these gangs were based in the southern part of Brooklyn.

He described several of the violent episodes involving one of the gangs he studied. Some entailed deaths of the gang members, such as when one was shot while swimming in a pool located in another gang's territory, or when two were killed as part of an intra-group power struggle. In other cases, non-gang members—a priest and a business owner—were killed in connection with a robbery; the businessman's home was burglarized by gang members during his funeral. Some of the other gang violence was impressively cruel. In one case, a young man had his head half blown away with a shotgun, then was trussed up, burned, and defecated on. In another, after some girls who were being chased took refuge in a rival gang's club house, the other gang set it on fire and then shot at the rival gang as they tried to escape from the blaze. Galen's overall picture of gang aggression is one of a high level of violence.

Despite this high level of gang violence, Galen reported a low level of consequation for the aggression. Few gang members were successfully prosecuted (punished). Sometimes they were actually reinforced for threatening further violence. In the case of the murdered priest, his colleagues who had witnessed the killing would not testify, possibly because they were intimidated. Thus, from the point of view of the gang members, they avoided jail by threatening the survivors. Galen reported that attempts were being made to involve both gang members and community business leaders in a program to combat the problems by trying to increase employment opportunities and training. However, the success of the program was still uncertain by the end of his study.

In the latter part of the 1980s and continuing into the 1990s, the problems of youth gangs and their associated violence have been increasingly highlighted by the media. Oriented commonly on ethnic or immigrant bases and supported by drug sales, the size of these gangs ranges from small neighborhood groups of 20 to 30 to nationwide affiliations of thousands. Their drug profits allow them to supply themselves with the latest, most sophisticated communication devices and weapons. It is not uncommon to read or hear about planned murders, random shootings, and torture and assault. These occur most commonly in the larger cities, but have also been increasingly reported in less populated areas.

A BEHAVIORAL ANALYSIS OF AGGRESSION
BY YOUNG DELINQUENTS

While print media reports, television shows, and movies present startling indications of the problem, trained scientific observers can provide us with more objective reports and suggest causal factors. One such report was made by Stumphauzer, Veloz, and Aiken (1981), who studied gang activities in the East Los Angeles area. They offered what was called an ethnographic description of the factors affecting gang behaviors. This was derived from their studies in the area, in which 18 gangs were located in a space of about seven square miles. The basic approach of this study is similar to that used in the applied analysis of behavior: general problems were characterized in terms of specific component behaviors, and the forces maintaining those behaviors were analyzed. However, the group also broadened their analysis to include naturalistic, ecological variables and biological and social-cultural influences.

Stumphauzer, et al. found that they could characterize the problems of the gangs in terms of **behavioral excesses** and **deficits.** Excesses are behaviors that occur too often. Examples included here were the use of guns, assault, and robbery. Deficits—behaviors that took place too infrequently—included attending school, holding a job, and being involved in positive community activities. The authors also noted environmental and behavioral assets, such as family relations and competitive skills, which might be used to help reduce future problems. Stumphauzer et al. detailed several factors that maintained the problem behaviors. Negative reinforcement of aggressive behaviors was seen to support those behaviors (aggression gets them out of problem situations). For example, the gang members were reinforced for attacking or threatening others. They intimidated their victims enough to prevent reporting the gang members to the police, and they thus escaped prosecution. Positive reinforcement also helped maintain delinquent acts. The gangs derived prestige from such acts; they seemed to savor the media attention and enjoyed being filmed for news programs. Prison jackets, brought back from relatively rare times of incarceration, were prized and worn with pride, perhaps as evidence of how bad (in the original sense) the individuals were. Even the police sometimes seemed to reinforce delinquents' acts, because they made their duty hours more exciting. Apart from these maintaining factors, there seemed to be scant application of factors for discouraging delinquency. Punishment, in the form of successful prosecutions and prison time for gang members, seldom occurred. Further, except as we note below, little was done to strengthen prosocial behaviors to replace antisocial ones.

In addition to reinforcing consequences for delinquent behaviors, Stumphauzer et al. also noted some controlling antecedent social stimuli. For example, gang leaders were important models for other members. The older ones, or "los veteranos," were influential in the same three ways noted in Bandura's work reviewed earlier: they developed the origins of aggressive acts (or most of the other excesses and deficits), initiated them, and helped maintain them. Such **stimulus control,** however, can also effect a reduction in aggressive acts. Just as the "veteranos" increased the acts, they also helped to decrease them via modeling influences. Other stimulus control effects that decreased aggression were observed: attacks against or in the presence of older adults, especially women, would not usually occur. Also, mothers, small children, and old men usually would not be attacked.

Stumphauzer et al. also attempted to determine why an environment that so strongly supported aggressive acts did not affect all the young men who lived there, some of whom managed to avoid the trap of delinquency. They hypothesized that an examination of their behaviors might help to find a way to teach others how to succeed similarly. Apparently, however, such success was not too common, for Stumphauzer et al. described only two brothers who were able to resist problems. Apparently they were reinforced for special non-delinquent skills and also took special precautions to avoid problem situations. The older brother was good at restoring automobiles. For this he received not only money but also prizes, social praise, and self-reinforcement. The younger brother was adept at working on bicycles and earned the respect of his peers for this. Of further help to the brothers was that they did not wear clothing associated with any gang and did not use drugs. They were skilled at recognizing potential trouble situations, such as gatherings of groups of youths, wild parties, and police patrols, and would avoid them. They engaged in cognitive processing involving defining and evaluating potential problem settings. They even reported engaging in "self-talk" in such settings to help keep themselves out of trouble. Although receiving relatively modest social reinforcement from others for non-delinquent behaviors, they managed to maintain them in an essentially delinquent environment.

Stumphauzer et al. suggest that an effective treatment for the problem of delinquency would require changing the environmental conditions that support it. Ideally, the conditions of poverty and unemployment would be reduced, replaced by job training and increased employment opportunities. Galen reported plans to implement these ideas in his study of New York City gangs. Stumphauzer et al. also suggest measures consistent with behavior theory—that is, reinforcers that help maintain gang violence should be reduced. For example, the media attention given to individuals might be more carefully controlled. Certainly, profits from drug sales and their associated violence must be curtailed. Also, in a plan to eliminate delinquency, behaviors incompatible with aggression would be reinforced to supplant the aggression. Special programs or work to benefit the neighborhoods of the gangs would be instituted so as to direct behaviors in a more pro-social way. Further, increasing the reliability and effectiveness of punishment for aggression would also help suppress this behavior. This would necessitate a major improvement in the criminal justice system. While none of these suggestions may be easy to follow, they represent reasonable solutions based on sound behavioral principles.

In 1986, Stumphauzer (1986) did further work with the problems of delinquency. He compiled introductory descriptions of his and others' behavioral approaches to preventing and treating delinquency in several different settings. The programs include applications in correctional institutions and group homes, in the public schools, and in places of employment, as well as in private homes and the community. Personnel involved in these settings are taught the principles of social learning, including frequent use of behavior contracts, social skills training, and some cognitive behavioral approaches. Such a multiple setting effort that employs a number of approaches may be vital for enhancing the probability of success in reducing juvenile delinquency. The analyses of delinquent behaviors done by workers such as Stumphauzer are valuable because they pinpoint the problem areas and lead to concrete suggestions for solutions, as opposed to the approach of others who may decry the general problem of delinquency but have no systematic way of approaching it.

SOME PROBLEMS IN DEVELOPING PROGRAMS

The ethnographic approach of Stumphauzer to treating delinquency is an example of a promising strategy. It not only considers what influences increase delinquent behaviors but also provides suggestions for how those behaviors could be reduced and replaced with more acceptable ones. In his recent work, Stumphauzer indicates how the treatment of delinquency should involve multiple settings, including the home, schools, places of employment, and the community. This broad approach is soundly based and should be more successful than more limited past methods.

One obvious and common limitation to treating delinquency is an economic one. Programs for job training and generation of employment opportunities typically depend on availability of government funds or support from the private sector. Unfortunately, the public and its representatives are usually not as supportive of preventative measures as corrective/punitive ones. This was evident during the debate for the crime bill in Congress in 1994, during which there seemed to be more support for such measures as increased death penalties and more severe penalties for recidivists than for programs aimed at preventing crimes through education and counseling. People are more likely to rally behind stronger legal penalties for delinquency than to encourage programs of education and training that will help prevent delinquency, even if such programs are less costly in the long run. Behavioral principles can help us understand such orientations. The imprisonment of a gang member involves immediate removal (negatively reinforcing) of a danger to people, while the results of a remedial program, if it does indeed work, are extensively delayed. Meanwhile, delinquents are still free and are potential threats to the people. It is little wonder that the public usually chooses a sure, quick result over an uncertain, delayed outcome. On the other hand, the occurrence of riots has resulted in increased support for combatting delinquency, as people become convinced that simple imprisonment does not prevent wide-scale problems and that another approach must be tried.

The private sector might contribute to combatting delinquency if it can be shown that direct benefits will result. Here again, however, the controllers, in the form of board of director members or stockholders, may not support such a venture because benefits are not certain or quickly realized.

Another limitation in effectively treating delinquency involves authority. Typically, public institutions where innovative programs are likely to be proposed are governed by an unresponsive bureaucratic structure that resists change; they do not possess the flexibility needed to implement a program. Alternatively, professional and community support for a new program may falter because of fears that institutional security will be compromised or that harm to community residents will occur. The opposition to treatment or housing of special psychiatric populations in residential areas is one reflection of these fears.

A personal example might help illustrate this institutional fear of new programs. When considering a position as a prison psychologist, I was full of ideas (admittedly idealistic) for programs involving applications of behavioral principles to the problems of adult offenders and inquired about the possibilities for instituting new programs. I was told that this was possible—as long as no basic procedures were changed and no possible threat to security was perceived. In other words, there was little real hope that new programs would be supported. The warden obviously was primarily concerned with maintaining his good record of preventing escapes rather than allowing any trial programs that might help prisoners. Indeed, the one innovative program designed for that prison was so misshapen by the time monetary and security considerations were applied that it was essentially worthless. There is no point in initiating any program under such constraints since it is almost certain to fail and then would be a convenient example for those who would stymie future treatment innovations.

I have also witnessed how institutional support can facilitate a program. While a graduate student, I worked at the research facility headed by renowned behavioral psychologist Nathan Azrin. Apart from its studies of aggression and other projects, the facility was developing the first major token economy system, in which behavioral principles were being applied to psychotic patients (Ayllon & Azrin, 1968). Tokens, which could be exchanged for various backup reinforcers such as cosmetics or even a nicer room, were used in place of real money as effective immediate reinforcers for appropriate behaviors. This program, which served as a model for others and greatly advanced our knowledge of how behaviors can be managed in complex situations, would not have succeeded without the active support of the superintendent of the hospital, R. C. Steck. He facilitated the work in many ways, obtaining financial, logistic, and political aid wherever and whenever possible. In addition, he vigorously defended the program and its developers from attacks by detractors from within and without the hospital. Such administrative support is invaluable, albeit rather unusual.

Not only does a program need support for success, it must also be well planned. Basic behavioral procedures have occasionally been inverted by the formulation of plans that simply control inappropriate behaviors instead of supporting the development of appropriate ones. At times, plans have failed because they have been forced on the clients instead of being developed in a cooperative effort. An appropriate institutional behavioral program should include extensive training of employees in basic behavioral principles, require ongoing behavioral measures of clients' progress, and afford frequent supervision by a knowledgeable, responsible professional. Mistreatment of clients can be prevented by making the plans and procedures open to concerned individuals from outside the program. This is especially important in programs for institutionalized clients, because institutions are inherently a closed society. In these programs, individuals (e.g., relatives, government agency representatives, and those from the media) may be invited to examine the details of the program and its results. This openness can serve to foster support for the program as well as avoid misinterpretation of its procedures by the public.

A POSSIBLE MODEL FOR A PREVENTATIVE PROGRAM FOR JUVENILES

One promising behavioral approach for the preventative treatment of predelinquent youth has come out of the University of Kansas, known as the Achievement Place and/or Teaching-Family program. Actually, the original Achievement Place (Phillips, 1968) was a community-based home located in Lawrence, Kansas, and the Teaching-Family program was developed from experiences with this model as well as from the program located at Boys Town in Nebraska. The nationwide program now includes several regional training sites that set up and supervise Teaching-Family homes in many communities. In addition, Aggressive Youth workshops are held throughout the United States so that youth workers not affiliated with the Teaching-Family sites can learn how to prevent and control aggressive outbursts as well as address other behavioral problems.

The basic clientele of the Teaching-Family homes are adolescent boys or girls whom the courts have considered delinquent, pre-delinquent, or perhaps neglected; that is, those who have either exhibited delinquent behaviors or are judged to be in need of special treatment to prevent them from developing such behaviors. Six to eight children live with an adult couple in a family-style setting.

What differentiates the Teaching-Family settings from other residential programs is that the "parents" are extensively trained in the application of behavioral techniques to help control inappropriate behaviors, such as aggression, and know how to teach appropriate social interaction skills. The training is a process that begins prior to a placement and continues during the residency. Behaviors of both the children and the parents are measured, and supervision of the homes is done on a regular basis.

The procedures followed by the teacher-parent have been extensively elaborated in a thick guidebook (e.g., Phillips, Phillips, Fixsen, & Wolf, 1974), which includes specific information for managing behaviors, including aggressive outbursts. With the guidebook, the parent is prepared to handle an emergency without reverting to spontaneous and possibly inappropriate reactions. For other situations, explanations are given for how standard behavioral techniques—for example, shaping—can be used to develop a simple task such as following instructions, often a problem for the children. Token reinforcement systems are used in some cases, although the system is flexible enough so that the youths can help select a specific program they would be willing to follow. In addition, the whole family regularly meets to resolve any difficulties and make basic decisions on how home affairs are managed.

An interesting aspect of the Teaching-Family program is that residency can be either voluntary or established with a provision that appropriate behaviors will allow an individual to move out of the home. Voluntary residency serves as a **countercontrol**. Here, clients have some control over parents in that if they do not like the parenting they can leave. Because a number of losses reflect negatively on the parents, this encourages the parents to run the home as well as possible within the bounds of their charge; hence, the countercontrol. In the other option, the ultimate reinforcer of being able to return home (when feasible) serves to aid the progress of the client in learning socially acceptable behaviors.

The Boys Town program is separated from the surrounding community, but other Teaching-Family homes are community based. Thus, clients are able to learn their new behavior patterns in a more natural environment. They attend public schools, possibly live in their old neighborhood, and continue to interact with family and friends. Behavioral studies indicate that training in the natural environment is usually desirable because newly learned behaviors more easily transfer (e.g., see Martin & Pear, 1996). That is, the acceptable social behaviors taught in the Teaching-Family home located in a community are more likely to come under the control of the community environment than if those behaviors were taught in another environment such as an isolated institution.

Although it may sound encouraging that the Teaching-Family homes are run on established behavioral principles, we still need to determine if this can be done successfully. The effects of Teaching-Family homes on the behaviors of their clients have been compared with the effectiveness of more traditional institutional youth homes (Kirigin, Braukmann, Atwater, & Wolf, 1982). While the results are promising, they do not provide evidence of this program's overwhelming superiority. Criminal offenses committed by residents during treatment in the Teaching-Family programs were significantly reduced compared to those of residents in traditional youth homes. However, a measure of offenses taken one year after treatment was not different statistically from that for traditional homes, even though the measure did show a lower percentage of Teaching-Family youths committing offenses. Therefore, it must be concluded that the Teaching-Family program is a step in the right direction, but has not necessarily provided an ideal solution for reducing delinquent behaviors in youths. With attention to these attempts, we hope that the system will continue to be improved to provide an effective model and an actual reduction in delinquent behaviors by transferring the effective control obtained during residency to everyday neighborhood settings.

Kazdin (1985) reviewed the various approaches to dealing with antisocial behaviors that constitute so much of the problem in delinquents. He was concerned about the lack of long-term effectiveness of Teaching-Family homes, but found no alternative approaches that systematically demonstrated such effectiveness. He described two promising treatments: parent management training and behavioral family therapy. Both approaches emphasize the learning and application of behavioral principles, as in the Teaching-Family method. Here, however, the principles are applied in the real homes of the youths. Behaviors of parents and other family members are changed to improve communication and increase positive interaction, and children are taught more appropriate behaviors. By training in the natural environment, these programs should be effective in establishing more lasting control over delinquent behaviors.

Feindler and Ecton (1986), like Kazdin, acknowledge the limited effectiveness of traditional behavioral programs. They have developed a cognitive behavioral approach in which adolescents are taught to recognize situations and thoughts that lead to aggression. With this approach, adolescents learn to control their aggressive reactions and are also taught social skills for facilitating non-aggressive interactions. Again, as in the Teaching- Family program, the technique produces rather good results while being applied. However, long-term effectiveness was not demonstrated.

FURTHER VARIABLES AFFECTING JUVENILE AGGRESSION

Although behavioral approaches to treating problems of delinquency may improve with further refining of these programs, they may also reach some limit of success if they do not incorporate consideration of all the variables that help determine delinquent behaviors. We mentioned some of these variables involving sociological factors in relation to the ethnographic approach of Stumphauzer et al. and their suggestion to work with youths in a variety of settings (e.g., home, work, school). To some extent the Teaching-Family approach includes such variables in that it attempts to train acceptable behaviors within a community setting with the expectation that they will be maintained more readily. By teaching the youths how to control their aggressive reactions in the Teaching-Family home, it was expected that they will also be able to control them in the neighborhood environment. Adding the programs discussed by Kazdin and Feindler and Ecton might increase the effectiveness of the Teaching-Family program by facilitating transfer of gains made to additional social settings. However, a more complete approach might also consider the influences of other variables, including biological ones. Kazdin advocates a multifaceted approach that would address a number of the various influences on antisocial behaviors and recognizes the special role of drug treatments in appropriate cases, which affect behavior by changing biological activities.

TACTICAL IMPLICATIONS OF VARIOUS THEORIES OF DELINQUENCY

Various orientations to understanding delinquency have been popular at different times and each implies a way of treating delinquents. However, in their original forms, none were successful enough to obtain or maintain their popularity. Historically, biological contributions to delinquent behavior were some of the first considered. Early theories of criminality, such as that of Lombroso (1876), viewed criminal traits as being inherited. Criminality was thought to reflect an inherited degenerate biological process that could not be reversed, although it may operate in conjunction with the individual's experience. In such instances, rehabilitation may help reverse the experiential influences. In other cases, tactics to combat criminality included devising ways of identifying such individuals, perhaps by accompanying physical traits, and incarcerating them to control their behaviors. Of course, no rehabilitation was attempted or expected.

With the increased popularity of Freud's theory at the turn of the century, criminality was seen as being a more flexible characteristic, occurring from dynamic interactions of the id, ego, and superego. The past experiences of an individual, along with possible stress at a very early age, sometimes were thought to produce the situation responsible for the criminal behaviors of adolescence or adulthood. Therefore, such effects possibly could be reversed by appropriate individual treatment.

Social theories of delinquency later became popular. The delinquent person was depicted as a product of socioeconomic forces. It was felt that many criminal behaviors occurred because a deprived individual was blocked from sharing in society's affluence. One solution for this problem, of course, would be to change the basic nature of such a society. Therefore, this understanding of delinquency has many political implications. Indeed, sociology in general is very highly politicized, because its various theories have important implications for how societies should be better organized.

The most recent major influence on the understanding and treatment of delinquency probably has been the behavioral approach, like that applied in the Teaching-Family program. This approach puts great emphasis on the individual's learning experiences as a contributor to the development of delinquent behaviors and suggests how learning principles can also be utilized to eliminate these behaviors. Although this approach has shown good promise, it has also not yet provided a satisfactory solution to the problem.

CONTEMPORARY BIOLOGICAL APPROACHES TO DELINQUENCY

Great strides have recently been made in our understanding of aggression by using the biological approach. Therefore, we may find it helpful to reconsider this approach, with its rapidly developing information base, for more extensive use in the future.

Workers such as Lewis (1981) have suggested that biological treatments may be useful for controlling delinquent aggression by juveniles. Some possibilities include the use of shock treatment with insulin or electroconvulsive stimuli as a short-term means of controlling persistent violent episodes. (It is assumed that if these rather radical treatments are used, it would only be after careful review and other less drastic treatments had been attempted.) Phenytoin (Dilantin) has also been effective in some cases, even when no abnormalities in the EEG are evident. Mood disorders involving aggression have also been treated with monoamine oxidase inhibitors, tricyclic antidepressants, and lithium, and methylphenidate (Ritalin) has been successfully employed to control the aggression associated with ADHD cases.

Biological factors have come to be appreciated in studies linking antisocial behaviors with such genetically influenced disorders as schizophrenia, hyperactivity, and depression. Further possible genetic contributions to criminality are discussed by Wilson and Herrnstein (1985). They review evidence similar to that discussed in Chapter 2 for the inheritance of increased aggression and how gender as well as its associated hormones are related to aggression. They also give supporting evidence that genetically determined constitutional factors such as body type, in addition to intelligence and personality (including the psychopathic), are related to criminality. Although they also consider how environmental factors influence criminality, they recognize that their inclusion of evidence for a strong genetic contribution to criminality would be controversial. Indeed, many find it disturbing that biologically derived influences might work to increase criminality. (Wilson and Herrnstein generated even more controversy when they considered possible inherited differences in intelligence between races, with their implications for higher levels of delinquency in African Americans. While they did not find definitive evidence for an inherited basis for lower intelligence at that time, work published by Murray and Herrnstein in 1994 has generated even more controversy with its apparent findings that lower intelligence in African Americans has a genetic base independent of environmental factors.)

TOWARD AN INTEGRATIVE APPROACH

Despite the impressive advances in biological treatments and the arguments for biological factors in aggression, the more common contemporary approach includes a greater appreciation of the multiplicity of influences over aggression. Biologically oriented workers more readily recognize experiential contributions to critical genetic, biochemical, and neural influences. On the other hand, the environmentally oriented understand the possibility that, while overwhelming social or environmental factors do affect aggression, we should not overlook potentially important biological contributions.

The orientation of this book supports the common contemporary approach by considering multiple interacting contributions to the causes and control of aggression. This orientation is somewhat similar to that of Lewis (1981), who also encourages a **biopsychosocial** approach to the problem, although she emphasizes the biological contributions even more strongly than we have here.

Lewis makes an important case for including consideration of biological contributions to aggression early in the treatment of a case. Thus, strong biological factors may be more successfully treated than if they were ignored until delinquent behaviors were fully established. Lewis indicates that single-faceted approaches, whether biological or environmental, are doomed to fail. Behavior therapy or psychotherapy by itself will not always succeed, nor will a psychopharmacological approach that does not acknowledge individual differences and environmental influences. According to Lewis, a combination of psychotherapeutic, educational, and medical assessment of the juvenile offender should be completed before prescribing a specific program. The need for drugs must be determined, provisions for the treatment and monitoring of the aggressive behaviors must be made, and residential intervention, at the natural home, if possible, must be provided. In addition, just as with normal individuals, the care system should be long term. The therapist-parent-teacher-physician support system that should be started at an early age must be maintained into the client's twenties.

Goldstein (1991), while not stressing biological contributions as much as Lewis, notes that biology does have an effect that we should recognize. He, like Lewis, stresses that a comprehensive strategy is needed to address youth violence. His strategy considers biological factors, individual differences, social and economic influences, as well as learning, all affecting delinquency. An approach that integrates work with individuals, gangs, and the community is recommended as having the best chance of success. Goldstein's approach corresponds to that of this text—that the best expectation of success in treating delinquents lies in a multifaceted effort. Such an effort would include controlling violent behaviors, increasing pro-social behaviors, and providing positive outcomes for such behaviors.

Lamentably, as with suggestions made earlier, Lewis', Goldstein's, or others' prescriptions for controlling delinquency may be ideally correct, but they certainly would be difficult to put into practice. However, we must realize that in the absence of such ideal measures, the problems of juvenile aggression will persist.

SUMMARY

Aggressive behavior by juveniles has received increased attention in recent years since it has involved public acts of violence that at time result in injury or death to bystanders. Arrest statistics indicate that youth involvement in homicides as well as other violent crimes has been increasing dramatically and at a rate much greater than that for adults. The aggressive acts of gang members are especially violent and brutal. Careful observation and analysis of the aggressive behaviors help indicate how social and environmental factors serve to produce and support these acts. These analyses also can be employed in attempts to modify the factors to help control the aggression. However, implementation is difficult to achieve in the absence of both philosophical and financial support. Societies seem to prefer quick, retributive punishment over more long-term education and training programs. Even when training programs are authorized, various impediments hinder their progress.

Some programs based on behavioral principles show promise for preventing and reducing juvenile aggression. These have been applied in both group as well as regular homes. They have helped increase appropriate communication and positive social interactions while controlling aggressive outbursts. However, their long-term effectiveness has not been demonstrated.

Consideration of biological contributions to juvenile aggression may help develop effective ways of controlling that aggression. However, there is resistance to recognizing the biological influences and applying biological treatments. This resistance is increased by fears that racial bias has motivated some investigators and that their work will be used to justify inappropriate discriminatory practices.

An effective approach to controlling juvenile delinquency will involve an appreciation of the various factors that contribute to it. A multifactorial approach that addresses biological, psychological, and social contributions to aggression is more likely to succeed compared to more narrow approaches.

Suggested Reading

Goldstein, A. P. (1991). *Delinquent gangs: A psychological perspective.* Champaign, IL: Research Press.

CHAPTER 11

Physical and Sexual Abuse of Children

Aggressive acts directed toward children constitute a serious problem, which evokes strong emotional reactions in those who become aware of it. It is difficult for people to accept that a parent could inflict severe damage on a powerless child or how a relative or other adult could force sexual behavior on a young person. In fact, until relatively recently, most abusive acts directed against children were often ignored or hidden. The extent of the problem was not appreciated. Lately, the existence of such abuse has been recognized, and a number of studies have led to a better understanding of its causes and to development of attempts to control abuses.

This chapter will consider situations in which children are the objects of two basic types of aggression. We will deal mainly with physical aggression directed against children in the home—child abuse. We will also investigate physical and sexual aggression involved in sexual abuse. The settings for the sexual abuse we describe are either within the family (in which case it would be a type of child abuse), or extrafamilial.

We will discuss the problems involved in defining and measuring physical abuse, along with attempts to measure the abuse. The outcomes of surveys and direct observations have been useful for identifying perpetrators as well as the correlates and causes of abuse. We will briefly describe some theories of the causes of abuse and summarize a treatment program for parents.

The understanding of sexual abuse of children includes problems with identifying the nature of the offenders and the stimuli that arouse them. We include a description of an objective method to help accomplish this. Also, we examine the bases and various procedural components of effective behavioral and conditioning treatments.

Several sources provide information for the area of child abuse, including the disciplines of criminal justice, sociology, and social work, in addition to psychology. We hope that readers will better understand the complexity of factors contributing to aggression directed toward children and derive some ideas for its prevention and treatment.

PHYSICAL AGGRESSION IN THE HOME

Defining and Measuring the Problem

The media have provided numerous shocking examples of the existence and severity of the physical abuse of children. Although there is no doubt that such terrible events occur, the extent to which aggression is directed toward children is not clear. Graphic depictions of abused children are difficult to forget, and the effect of showing a relatively small number of such examples probably is to magnify the public's estimate of the severity of the problem. Similarly, the effects of zealous child welfare advocates to increase public awareness of this problem probably leads to an exaggeration of the extent to which it does occur.

Mash and Wolfe (1991) point out how the great variety of definitions, methods of measurement, and research designs have resulted in contradictory findings or inadequately supported "facts" about child abuse. Various investigators utilize different definitions of it. For example, some include physical punishment, such as spanking, as an instance of aggression. Others add witnessing of parents' fighting or arguing as instances of abusive treatment of children. Indeed, child abuse has been defined to include a wide range of behaviors, from physical beatings to negligence, such as failure to send children to school or get medical inoculations. Some investigators are more restrictive in their definitions, listing only physical harm with fists or weapons. Similarly, the measurements of instances of aggression directed toward children have been quite variable, as they have been taken from varied sources: police reports, general surveys, or systematic statistically valid samplings of the population. Therefore, we should not find it surprising that estimates of child abuse in the United States have ranged from 30,000 to over four million per year, or over 2 percent of the total population (see Straus & Gelles, 1990a).

The great variety of definitions and types of measurement makes it difficult to analyze the problem of child abuse. In Chapter 1, we stressed the primary importance of objective definition and measurement of aggression. In the area of child abuse, many definitions are subjective and arbitrary, and measures are not reliable. Readers of reports should carefully attend to just how the abuse is defined and measured prior to evaluating the extent of the problem. For example, while parental responsibility for education and preventative medical care is of concern, it probably should not be grouped with the direct production of physical injury. The studies we discuss here will primarily be those employing objective definitions of aggression similar to that given on page 6. The studies selected also employ reliable measurement techniques.

One systematic national survey by Straus and Gelles (1990a) defined very severe child abuse to include violent acts such as kicking, biting, punching, hitting or trying to hit with an object (excluding objects commonly used to punish, such as belts), beating, and threatening or using a gun or knife. The authors interviewed members of 6000 families in 1985 and found an annual abuse incidence rate of 2.3 percent.

Similarly, a U.S. government-sponsored survey conducted in 1985 found severe abuse (physical damage or threat of it) to occur at a rate of 1.9 percent. Both surveys determined that abuse rates were almost twice as high in 1975. Although the approximately 2 percent of the children severely abused might not feel better about the overall reduction, the apparent progress is encouraging. Possible reasons for the improvement may be related to better economic conditions and lowered birth rates, according to the surveyors. As we will see, these variables are correlated with child abuse rates. It is also possible that self-disclosure of the abuse has decreased as stricter penalties are enforced—that is, the apparent decrease may reflect a decrease in detection, not in actual rates.

In contrast to the survey statistics from 1975–1985, officially enumerated child abuse cases increased. There were reports of 10 percent annual increases in child abuse in the years since the mid-1970s. It has been suggested that increased awareness of child abuse, as well as compulsory reporting laws, have contributed to the rise in reported cases (Straus & Gelles, 1990b). It has also been found that this increase is an artifact of changes in referral and reporting practices (Bagley, 1990) and inappropriate calculations. For example, possibly two-thirds of the cases included are later dismissed as being erroneous, and about one-fifth of other cases are repeat offenses. Thus, the true number of new cases of abuse may be only about 15 percent of the reported number. However, this is no reason to relax efforts to control abuse; any act of abuse is horrible and any incidence level above zero should be of concern.

Development of Concern about Abuse

The change in society's attention to child abuse is the latest in a series of changes that have occurred over the last several decades. Prior to the 1960s, there was a general legal and societal tolerance of family violence toward children. Instances of spontaneous aggression or planned aggressive punishment were seen as normal. If a serious injury of a child was brought to the attention of police, physicians, or even neighbors, it may have been easily dismissed as an accident. Possibly, if the incident involved someone of a lower social class or a minority, it may have been seen as deliberate abuse. Basically, however, the existence of any significant problem of child abuse was ignored. A major change occurred when Kempe, Silverman, Steele, Droegemueller, and Silver (1962) published their first comprehensive study of the extensive physical injuries suffered by some children, named the **Battered Child Syndrome**. The graphic descriptions and pictures of these beaten children were very effective in bringing attention to the problem and initiating measures to deal with it.

By 1973, the concern with aggression toward children was broadened and referred to as **child abuse** in the federal act of that name. The abuse now included not only physical injury but also psychological, mental, and sexual harm, as well as educational, nutritional, and medical negligence. Thus, the legal definition of abuse goes beyond the definition of aggression we use here. Under the federal law, in addition to state legislation, child welfare agencies and protective services could now attempt to deal with the problems. This is in contrast to the situation for most of the last century, where a child neglect case would have to be referred to the Society for the Prevention of Cruelty to Animals (SPCA), an animal welfare organization. A society for the prevention of cruelty to **children** was not established until the 1870s.

Identification of the Agent of Abuse

Once attention was concentrated on the problem of child abuse, people turned their focus to identifying the perpetrators of the abuse (or, of greater concern here, those who physically aggressed against the children). Surveys and delimited studies sometimes included measures not only of all instances of aggression involving children, but also of the abusing agents. Thus, in a survey by Straus, Gelles, and Steinmetz (1980), for example, sibling aggression was measured and found to occur at about an 80 percent level, with males engaging in more aggression than females. This is perhaps not surprising to the casual observer of some families. Similarly, it is not surprising to find that 18 percent of the children were reported to have struck their parents (although it may be disconcerting to discover that this measure included the relatively ineffective blows of three to four year olds, the rate for 15 to 17 year olds was still 10 percent). Of even more interest was the finding that mothers were equally or more likely than fathers to have abused their children (i.e., committed acts directed to hurt them).

The reliability of this finding from indirect assessments (that mothers are more abusive than fathers) is supported by direct behavioral observations made in homes by Reid, Taplin, and Lorber (1981). We will discuss the details of their technique later; even with a different measurement methodology, they also found that mothers were more likely than fathers to aggress physically against their children. Possibly this reflects a greater amount of time spent with children, with increased responsibility for child-rearing and more possibilities for frustrating interactions. Or perhaps the fathers were more effective punishers (the behavior they punished stopped) and therefore had fewer reasons to engage in aggressive behaviors. Nevertheless, if aggressiveness is judged simply by frequency of abusive acts, the results apparently are an exception to previous observations that males usually are more aggressive than females. We will examine other variables correlated with abuse by parents, as well as some of the reasons why mothers as well as fathers may engage in abusive behaviors.

Correlational approaches to understanding child abuse have been examined by Gelles (1982). Socioeconomic family status has been negatively correlated with abuse and general domestic violence, although of course the correlation is not perfect; upper-class families also engage in abuse. Race also has been examined, but here, not surprisingly (there is no broadly substantiated evidence that race is related to aggression), no consistent relationship has been found. For example, African American families have been found to commit more, engage in less, or have comparable amounts of child abuse in comparison to other races. Relatively long-term stress, in the form of un- or underemployment, financial problems, and single parent families, as we might expect, correlates positively with abuse, as has social isolation. Such isolation, in which someone either has no neighbors or does not interact with them, might contribute because appropriate models of care are not provided and no checking-restraining influence is present. Other factors that have been positively correlated are low birth weight, prematurity, handicaps, and larger families. Sons of fathers who abuse their wives are more likely to become child abusers than sons of those who did not. Further, being abused as a child is positively correlated with being an abusing adult. We must remember that these findings are correlational, not causal. Again, because two variables are correlated or occur together does not mean that one causes the other. However, many people assume that this is the case. For some correlations, such as between family size and abuse, it usually is obvious that increase in family size does not necessarily cause an increase in abuse levels. However, for other correlations, such as that between being a victim of abuse and a later perpetrator, the correlation is misinterpreted as a causal relationship. This may happen because the correlations are high and the relation fits our idea of the influences of modeling on acquiring aggressive behaviors. If an individual experiences abuse and perhaps also sees it applied to siblings by a parent, he or she might learn via the modeling process that this is the way to treat children. Therefore, as an adult, the person may treat his or her own children in this way. However, being abused as a child does not necessarily make a person an abuser as an adult. In fact, many abused children do not become abusers. Being abused and being an abuser are each affected by their own causal (independent) variables. Finding that they occur in the same person does not show that the first is the independent variable for the second (dependent) variable.

The case for a cycle of abuse from parent to child to child-as-parent seems to be supported by data such as those collected by Straus, Gelles, and Steinmetz (1980), who asked abusive and non-abusive parents to recall instances of being abused by each parent when they were 13 year olds. They found that 18.5 percent of individuals who were abused twice or more by their mothers were abusers as adults, while only 11.8 percent of individuals abused less than twice, also by their mothers, became abusers. A similar relationship characterized abuse by their fathers (16.7 percent versus 13.2 percent). Thus, while the rates of abused children becoming abusers were not high in themselves, the difference in historical abuse rates between present abusers and non-abusers might be taken as evidence that abuse of a child increases the chances that the child will become an abuser. It also, of course, should be noted that the data used are not necessarily reliable. Asking many years after the fact for recollections of childhood abuse would not seem to be a highly reliable way to collect data. Other factors may also have affected the results. For example, perhaps people who abuse their children are more likely to recall their own experiences as victims than those not abusing their children.

Researchers have questioned the Straus et al. study. Of particular concern is why the data were so categorized and what the results would be if, for example, recollections of four or more abuse instances at 10 years old were analyzed. The authors gave no rationale for their particular subdivision of the data in their analysis. Another subdivision might have produced a different outcome.

Potts and Herzberger (1979) analyzed much of the literature linking being abused with later abuse perpetration and noted that, in general, the studies suffer from a poor database. At times, claims for a link have been made without supporting data. In other studies, very small sample sizes have been used, often with no controls. Even when the appropriate sample sizes and controls were employed, the correlations have been relatively small.

We must remember (once again!) that a correlation between two dependent variables not only fails to demonstrate causation, but also does not show any direction of causality. This admonition parallels the discussion of the correlational data relating media violence and aggression, where most data do not show directionality. In the present situation, for example, a substantial correlation has been found between parents striking their children and these children striking their parents. Although we might assume that the parents struck first and evoked counterstrikes by the children, the correlational data do not demonstrate this. Possibly the children were originally highly aggressive and elicited this abuse. Another correlation is between being abused as a child and being an adult abuser, with the assumption that the former causes the latter. However, another interpretation is that the aggressive children elicited abuse, then later, as adults, continued to be aggressive against their own children. Thus, a case could be made that some other variable, such as an aggressive personality characteristic, affects both whether children are abused and whether they become abusers. Correlative data do not allow us to determine whether one causal factor or another is functioning.

A conservative interpretation of the research would be that being abused as a child may be a contributing risk factor for that child to become an abuser as a parent, but that this relation has not been demonstrated to be strong; certainly the relationship has not been shown to be a causal one. As in any positive correlation, the fact of the correlation may reflect common relevant independent variables and may be a good basis for further study for determining those variables. Further, the establishment of risk factors, including previously being a victim or being unemployed, may help predict whether an individual will abuse a child. These data are useful, but we must take care to avoid misrepresenting their implications.

Theoretical Approaches to Understanding Child Abuse

In trying to understand child abuse, many investigators have attempted to integrate it with various theories associated with the social sciences, sometimes incorporating one or more of the risk factors we have mentioned. It is not within the scope of this text to consider these theories in depth, yet a brief summary of some of them, as described by Gelles (1982) would be useful for giving readers some idea of their variety.

Theoretical approaches are of several general types. Psychological-psychiatric theories emphasize the individual as an abuser and often describe the psychopathological processes involved. Social psychological theories stress the individual's interactions with the social environment. They often discuss the role of stress from intrafamilial and external socioenvironmental factors as influencing abusive behaviors. Sociological theories tend to analyze large-scale influences, such as social structures and cultural attitudes. These theories may not be as familiar to readers and we will briefly examine several of those especially developed to describe familial violence.

Goode's Resource Theory, presented in 1971, has as its basic premise that all social systems depend to some extent on force or the threat of its use as one of several basic resources. The use of force occurs when an individual lacks other resources. For example, a normal father has many resources and does not need force. This is unlike the abusive father, who may lack resources such as an education, job prestige, income, or interpersonal skills, and who therefore may resort to force. Goode's theory also incorporates the un- or underemployment factors others have found that correlate with abuse. Un- or underemployment also produces frustration, which we earlier saw as a contributor to aggression. Another sociological theory, formulated by Straus in 1973, is the General Systems Theory. Straus sees the family as a purposive, goal-seeking adaptive system. Violence may result from the way the system is set up. If the system functions on negative feedback that uses unconstructive criticism for any problems, then violence is likely to occur. In comparison, a system based on constructive positive feedback will not result in violence. A parent who teaches a child how to clean his room more efficiently, rather than only criticizing when it is not done, is employing constructive positive feedback.

Another interesting formulation that goes beyond individual and social psychological theories is Burgess' Evolutionary Theory, presented in 1979. Burgess looked at the development of violence over time and across cultures and found parental investment factors that determined the probability of abuse. This approach appears to be derived from economic theory; according to Burgess, the parent is more likely to damage, via abuse, a child who has a lower potential value or in whom less has been invested. Therefore, the child with whom less bonding has occurred, who is of a lower social class, from a large family, not biologically related or perhaps not biologically or psychologically perfect (i.e., handicapped), is more likely to be abused.

Some Criticisms of Methodology and Analysis

Gelles (1982) makes some good criticisms of the quality of attempts to study and understand family violence, including child abuse. As in several other areas, Gelles finds that the definitions of abusive behaviors are poor or inconsistent. For example, in a study he coauthored (Straus, Gelles, & Steinmetz, 1980), a three-year-old child's kicking of a parent is grouped with much more serious assaults by teenagers. Further, the measures of violence are typically indirect and hence unreliable. They are not taken from actual observation but from interviews or questionnaires. In addition, they tend to be derived from small, biased samples, often cases reported to the police or those handled by social workers. There certainly is a degree of selectivity in such sources, as they usually involve only the worst cases or a delimited segment of society.

Gelles indicates that distortion of child abuse data can occur in two basic ways. One has been called the Woozle Effect (after one of Milne's whimsical Winnie-the-Pooh stories) in which a particular study might find some effect on abuse rates under specific circumstances. Perhaps a special definition of abusive behavior or observation of the behavior in a delimited group was employed to determine rates. Those results are then reported elsewhere as a generally applicable explanation of abuse, with no regard to the original qualifying circumstances. A second distortion occurs when a very small but consistent effect, perhaps found over several studies, is translated to represent a very large effect. The effect is magnified in the reporting, but actually is still very small. The measure of childhood abuse victims (actually recipients of punishment) who become adult perpetrators might fall into this category. The 3 to 7 percent higher abuse levels reported by Straus et al. (1980), if reliable, may represent an increase over the abuse levels committed by adults not punished as children, but these levels of increase do not justify the tremendous emphasis put on such data, not to mention the unjustified attribution of causation to a correlational finding.

Unfortunately, in the search for simple solutions for emotionally distressing problems such as child abuse, there is a tendency to dichotomize. It is much easier to classify someone as having been either abused or not and then determine whether he or she probably is an abuser, instead of facing the fact that the decision of guilt is not such an easy one. Overlooked are the 71.5 percent of the people in the Straus study who were punished by their mothers and **not** presently thought to be child abusers and the 11.8 percent of non-punished individuals who **were** child abusers. Widom (1989) makes a similar point in her study of the relation between childhood abuse and later delinquency. Although she found a significant relationship, the effects were relatively modest. For example, abused or neglected children were more likely than control children to be arrested later as an adult for a violent offense, but the relative percentages were modestly different: 11 percent of abused children were later arrested as adults, but so were 8 percent of the non-abused. She saw that variables such as sex, race, and age were stronger predictors of violence. She also underscores that while 11 percent of the abused and neglected children were arrested for violence when they were adults, 89 percent were not. Abuse and neglect may contribute to later violence, but they certainly do not guarantee it.

Direct Measurement and Analysis of Abuse

In an attempt to obtain a detailed analysis of the contributions to and controls over aggression directed toward children, some behaviorally oriented professionals have made observations in actual home settings. Although such observations may still be faulted because they do not include a representative sample of society, as Gelles would require, they do excel in their employment of objective and consistent definitions and provision for a direct measure of abuse as it occurs in the natural environment. Thus, these observations may provide information for understanding the causes of the aggression as well as suggestions for its prevention and treatment.

Reid, Taplin, and Lorber (1981), made home observations of interactions between children and their parents in order to obtain information that might help differentiate between interaction patterns in homes where abuse occurs and where it does not. They studied 88 families classified as distressed because a child conduct problem had been registered. Of this total, 27 families were designated abusive, because child abuse had also occurred there. Finally, by advertising, they found and observed 27 other control families, where no distress or abuse had been noted.

Before proceeding with a description of this study, we should note a methodological problem inherent in such work. The control families may have represented a biased sample because some special unrecorded factors may have led them to volunteer, just as students from an introductory psychology class who volunteer for a psychology experiment may not be typical undergraduates. Such individuals might be highly motivated academically, for example, in that they are especially intellectually interested or, perhaps at the other end of the scale, in dire need of extra credit to improve their grades. Just as it is risky for us to consider student volunteers as typical "normal" students (or humans), it is risky to assume that the control family volunteers here represented normal families. Similar comments might be made about representativeness of the families in the other two groups, of course. Nevertheless, investigators had to work within such constraints and collected demographic data on the families to allow comparison of the characteristics of each group.

Reid et al. obtained information on a target child for each family as well as for some family characteristics, and averaged the data for each group. They calculated the average age of the child, sex, and birth order for each group. The families' intactness (whether both parents were living at home) and socioeconomic level were also measured. No statistical analyses were reported, but most of the data seemed comparable. Just about all the target children were boys eight or nine years old who were approximately the third born in their families. About two-thirds to three-quarters of the families were intact. Possibly the distressed and abusive families were larger, in that the reported range of birth order reached seven or eight; it reached only five in the control families. Also, the reported socioeconomic level may have been lower in abusive families than in control families. These data are of interest in light of the factors correlated with abuse that we discussed earlier and included in the parental investment factors of Burgess' Evolutionary Theory. However, in the absence of further analysis by Reid et al., we will assume that they did not note any differences between the groups and accept their tacit assumption that none existed.

Reid et al. carried out systematic observations of the families. During every home visit, each family member was observed for two five-minute sessions to obtain a representative sample of their behaviors. Each six seconds during these times, behaviors from a selection of 29 categories were recorded if they occurred. Also recorded were the positive or negative reactions by other family members to those behaviors. Of especial interest were 14 behaviors in a category called Total Aversive Behavior, which included acts usually aversive to parents and children, such as crying, whining, demands, noncompliance, destructiveness, and hitting or grabbing. After their observations, the rates and outcomes of these aversive behaviors were calculated and classified according to which family members were involved.

The measures of aversive behaviors showed that mothers of the abused children exhibited almost twice as many abusive behaviors than mothers from either of the other two groups. Fathers of abused children also had a slightly higher rate than fathers in the other groups, but this was not found to differ statistically. The rates of aversive behavior of the fathers of abused children were only about half the rates of the mothers of these children and close to those of the mothers of the non-abused children. Also, the abused children had significantly higher rates of aversive behaviors than children in the control families. Their rates also were higher, but not significantly so, than those for the other distressed family children. Although we might expect the increased rate of aversive behaviors by a parent (the families were classified as abusive because of past problems), the finding that the mothers primarily exhibited these behaviors was not necessarily predicted. As we have already noted, the father is commonly assumed to be the perpetrator of abusive behaviors in the family.

Analysis of the directionality of aversive behaviors found by Reid et al. showed that children of both distressed and abusive families directed more of these behaviors toward their mothers than children of the control families, with an insignificantly larger amount directed by the children of distressed families. To a lesser, but still significant extent, both groups also directed more aversive behaviors toward their fathers than the control group children. Here, the differences in amounts for the abusive versus the distressed family children were negligible. The parents of both distressed and abusive families directed more aversive behavior toward their children than the parents of the control families. Higher rates occurred for the mothers than for the fathers (as noted above), with an insignificantly greater amount of aversive behavior directed by the abusive mothers toward their children than by distressed mothers toward theirs.

Reid and his colleagues analyzed the rates of the most extreme aversive behaviors, such as physically negative (painful contact) and command negative (threats). The highest rates were for those directed by abusive mothers toward their children. Comparing the slight difference in overall aversive behaviors exhibited by mothers of abused children versus mothers from distressed families, with the differences between aversive behaviors directed toward mothers by the children in the two distressed groups, it is tempting to speculate that the aversive behaviors occur because they control other behaviors or are attempts to control other behaviors. That is, children in distressed families might be preventing (controlling) abuse by being more aggressive, while mothers in the abusive families are trying to achieve control by their abusive behaviors. In light of a lack of significant differences in this study, this possibility will have to await further exploration.

Reid et al. measured the number of aversive behaviors directed between the parents in the abusive, distressed, and control families. Rates for the abusive groups (in both directions between the spouses) were significantly higher than for each of the other two groups, which differed only slightly. Thus, abused children are part of a family in which the overall level of aversive behaviors is elevated, not just the behavior directed at them.

In addition to these different levels of aversive behaviors, Reid et al. measured the behavioral management skills and efficiency of the parents. In all three groups, more than two-thirds of the children's aversive behaviors were reinforced. That is, when the children acted badly in some way, they received some payoff, such as getting what they were demanding or receiving something to placate them. Such consequences would be expected to maintain or increase the aversive behaviors. Punishment of these behaviors was also attempted, but with differing results, especially for abusive mothers. Punishment was effective (the behavior did not continue) only slightly less than half of the time for them. Thus, their aversive behaviors, when used as punishers, had a relatively poor controlling function. In comparison, abusive family fathers effectively punished about 75 percent of the time. Normal family fathers were much more effective punishers, stopping their children's aversive behavior at a rate of about 87 percent.

Training Parents

From the studies done by their group, Reid et al. view child abuse as resulting from situations where children act aggressively and parents react with their own aggressive behaviors, in part as a desperate attempt to assert control. As we can see from the above data, the parents, especially abusive mothers, are not very effective in achieving this control. One suggested solution is to train the parents to be more effective controllers. Patterson, a colleague of Reid, has developed parent training techniques for various problem situations that occur in families (Patterson, 1976). They include an introduction to behavioral principles and methods, such as reinforcement and punishment, as well as instruction and practice in how to apply them most effectively. In the abusive family situation, presumably the parents were taught not only how positive reinforcement increases behaviors, but also how they had been reinforcing aversive behaviors in their children. Although reinforcement techniques are favored, parents would also be instructed in how to employ punishment most effectively when necessary for suppressing a dangerous aversive behavior. While it must be kept in mind that aversive control can increase aggressive behavior, punishment can also be used as a relatively rapid means of stopping an aversive behavior so that a more acceptable behavior can be substituted.

Once the parents were trained, preliminary results indicated reductions in total aversive behavior scores between the abusive mothers and their children. Presumably, as the children's aversive behaviors were no longer reinforced and the mothers became more effective controllers, the previous environmental support for aversive behaviors was reduced. The appropriateness of the use of Patterson's technique is supported by its initial success. This technique is also recommended because it applies established principles of learning. Kazdin (1985) has indicated that such a technique can be successful in solving a wide range of behavior problems.

The behavioral work of investigators such as Reid et al. helps increase our understanding of how physical abuse toward children occurs within the family environment. Such work has contributed some promising ways of treating abuse. Again, as we saw in our discussion about delinquency, consideration of other factors from the biological and sociological areas might help us to better comprehend the causes of child abuse and make treatment even more effective. Thus, it might be beneficial to examine biological factors that play a part in producing both parental and child aversive behaviors and also to question how sociocultural influences operate in the family setting. It is critical that effective treatment and prevention programs be developed and applied as quickly as possible to help protect youth from physical abuse by their elders.

SEXUAL AGGRESSION

Forced sexual contact between adults and children may often include acts that physically injure the child and thus fall easily within our definition of aggressive behavior. Indeed, Abel, Becker, Murphy, and Flanagan (1981) note that in one measure of the rape of children by unrelated men, 58 percent were carried out with excessive force, resulting in injury to 42 percent of the victims. This class of sexual activity outside the family is referred to as **pedophilia**, while such contact inside the family is called **incest**. Although some of the acts are perpetrated by women, and some of the activity is between members of the same sex, heterosexual contact between men and young girls (under 13) is more common and will be our primary focus.

Identifying the Offender

Some problems associated with sexual aggression against children include identifying individuals who engage in such behavior, analyzing the factors that contribute to it, and assessing the outcome of treatment. Related to this assessment is the determination of whether it is safe to release an individual once treatment has been completed. Although the individual may be asked about his sexual feelings toward young girls, his answers will not necessarily be truthful, considering that his survival in a prison setting or his release from prison depend on these replies.

Abel et al. have employed a method that promises to be a sensitive, discriminating way to measure male sexual arousal to children. Basically, it involves using an automatic physical measure of penile erection while sexual stimuli are presented by video or audiotape. The basic apparatus had been developed for a similar study of men who raped women, and was used to measure the relative arousing effects of sexual stimuli involving either mutual consent, violent rape, or physical assault. Several studies by Abel and others with similar devices have found that the arousal patterns differ for normal men as compared to rapists and even help discriminate among rapists with different histories. A related question for men who sexually abuse children is whether pedophiles and incestual abusers have essentially the same patterns of arousal or whether they differ. Some professionals feel the incestuous man is responding to an opportunity for sex that is available within a family situation, and that his deviancy is produced by factors different from those that operate on a pedophile, who is especially attracted to young girls unrelated to him. Therefore, it might be expected that the two classes of offenders would respond differently to potentially arousing sexual stimuli.

To test arousal to sexual stimuli, six audiotapes were prepared portraying sexual encounters with girls, ranging from a scene in which the girl initiated the activity, through scenes of various levels of coercion, up to forced physical assault. Also prepared was a tape describing mutual adult sexual behavior. Although the subjects were listening to fantasy scenes, these scenes were perhaps the closest reasonable approximation to reality that could be used. The men were asked to listen to each scene while their physical (penile) arousal was measured. They were also asked to try either to suppress or not suppress their erection. In addition, they were asked to give a verbal report of their arousal to each scene. The subjects were incarcerated volunteers who were pedophiles, incestual offenders, and other sexual deviates.

The study's results were presented in terms of the physical arousal as well as the self-reported arousal for each scene. Of special interest was the pattern of the incestual offenders. They showed relatively high levels of physical arousal for the scenes involving initiation of sexual activity by the child and for mutually initiated activity. The more coercive scenes still produced some arousal, comparable to that for the mutual adult sex scene. Since the child described in the tapes was not related to the men, it would seem that young girls in general were sexually exciting to them. This suggests that the incestuous male is not just responding to the opportunity for sex in his home but may be attracted to other girls as well. However, the self-reported arousal scores were especially discrepant from the physical response for the more coercive scenes and the adult episode; the men reported lower arousal levels while becoming increasingly physically aroused to increasingly coercive scenes and reported much higher scores than the actual physical response for the adult scene.

The pedophiles' response patterns were roughly similar in that they were aroused by all the scenes, with perhaps a decreasing trend as the scenes became more coercive. An exception was that a scene of physical coercion without violence produced greater arousal. They also tended to underreport their arousal to less acceptable scenes, including that of physical coercion, and to overreport their arousal to the mutual adult scene. An exception was that they overreported their arousal to the scene where the girl initiated the encounter.

The other sexual deviates, who had not been reported to have abused children, showed great variability in their physical arousal responses to the taped scenes. On average, they displayed greater responding to all stimuli, compared to the two groups of child molesters. However, they showed by far the highest arousal to the mutual adult sex scene, implying that they were relatively more excited by adult sexual stimuli than by stimuli associated with children.

A detailed breakdown of the results allowed comparison of arousal levels for non-aggressive sexual encounters with children versus those with adults and for aggressive versus non-aggressive sexual encounters with children. For the first measure, the incestuous fathers had higher relative arousal than pedophiles. This gives further support to the idea that the fathers are unusually aroused by any young girls, related or not. In the other measure, the pedophiles were more highly aroused by the aggressive sexual encounter scenes. This result correlates with the higher rates of aggression reported for these men and helps differentiate them from the incestual fathers.

The Abel et al. technique might prove helpful in the future, if validated, for providing an objective index of sexual interest in children by men who are accused of child molestation. However, this use would incur many of the same problems found currently with a polygraph test for deception. A significant error rate, leading to false assumptions of innocence or guilt, could not be eliminated, and the machine could be used in violation of the rights of the accused. A more probable use would be in checking on the progress of therapy and improving the way in which self-reports are gathered and interpreted.

We might recognize the effects of the tapes of Abel et al. on sexual arousal in terms of a classical conditioning mechanism. If sexual arousal had occurred with children in the past, then a description of sexual activity with children would be expected to function as a conditioned stimulus for such arousal. For the pedophiles, the higher level of arousal related to aggressive interactions might reflect a higher amount of aggression in their past sexual encounters with young girls. The conditioning mechanism may also have produced a misinterpretation of the results. Incestuous men may not have had so great a sexual attraction to unrelated girls as was interpreted. Instead, they might have been demonstrating another phenomenon of classical conditioning—generalization. It is possible that they were aroused by tapes of the unrelated girls because of their similarity to their own daughters.

To prevent misinterpretations of Abel et al.'s data and avoid other related difficulties, researchers could have employed a few controls. One would be to include a taped episode of an incestual encounter, in order to yield comparative data for sexual activities with related and unrelated children. The results of such a comparison would be of interest not only for understanding incestuous fathers but also for pedophiles, to determine if pedophiles would also be aroused in both cases. Another control would be to test a group of normal men to supplement the control group used here, of deviates who did not molest children. Another laboratory study has shown that normal men are also physically aroused to erotic stimuli associated with children (Langevin, Hucker, Ben-Aron, Purins, & Hook, 1985). Such arousal could occur as a result of generalization from their other adult sexual experiences. This measure would help provide a baseline from which to measure any deviance of the sexual responses of the child molesters.

Treatment of the Abuser

In addition to his work with the measurement of sexual arousal, Abel has also been active in the area of treatment of the sexual offender or deviate (Barlow & Abel, 1981). Some of the methods developed to help individuals with inappropriate sexual arousal could be employed in treating the child molester. One treatment used historically is aversion therapy. Its aim is to reduce the reinforcing properties of undesirable reinforcers via a classical conditioning technique. In the present case, the undesirable reinforcer is a young girl. Aversion therapy would involve showing pictures of a girl while administering an aversive stimulus, such as painful electric shock. Thus, the individual conditioned by this method is more likely to avoid such a stimulus and theoretically would not be sexually aroused by it. Barlow and Abel indicate that the procedure is very successful, more than twice as successful in comparison to traditional therapy. On the other hand, Rosen and Beck (1988) report that the results of aversion therapy are enhanced if the treatment is carried out cognitively; that is, by simply imagining the stimulus of the girl and associating it mentally with something painful. A further variation in such treatment would be to employ aversion relief. The subject imagines leaving the undesirable stimulus, perhaps to approach a more acceptable one, such as an adult female, and associates this with the withdrawal of the painful stimulus.

Rosen and Beck discuss several other methods that have helped decrease arousal to deviant sexual stimuli. These include masturbatory satiation, during hour-long association of masturbation with verbalized deviancies. Also effective has been the use of biofeedback for arousal along with shock punishment for erections produced by the deviant stimuli.

Barlow and Abel indicate that an important advance in treating sexual deviancy was to realize that it was more than just a problem of inappropriate arousal. Various other factors contribute to the control of the deviant behaviors involved. Therefore, for example, the role of antecedent stimuli in controlling deviant activities should be assessed. Researchers should try to identify the various stimuli during which the deviancy occurs so that they might be controlled. For example, the pedophile might be more likely to initiate his behavior while watching children running around during school recess. He can be instructed to avoid this setting. Sexual deviancy also involves various behavioral excesses. That is, the pedophile obviously engages in an excess of approaching and engaging young girls in sexual activity of various types. These activities may be decreased, via the effects of aversion therapy, if they are no longer reinforced. Continued reinforcement, of course, remains to impede therapeutic progress. Any residual deviant behavior, along with its aggression, is powerfully reinforced by sexual stimulation. A complete behavioral understanding involves consideration of both antecedent and subsequent stimuli (outcomes) that accompany a behavior.

Very critical to achieving control of deviancy is the identification and treatment of behavioral deficiencies in the pedophile. He may have deficits in approaching and engaging adult females in sociosexual activity. These behavior deficits may include prosaic ones such as asking someone for a date and engaging in appropriate conversation with a woman. To the extent that such deficiencies exist, they can be treated by various behavioral techniques. For example, behaviors associated with approaching women, such as making eye contact, engaging in conversation, and demonstrating appropriate affect, can be taught by modeling, roleplaying, and rehearsal.

A problem related to the pedophile's behavioral deficiencies may be that he is not sexually aroused by the appropriate stimuli associated with a woman. Such deficits in sexual arousal can be decreased by conditioning methods that function in the opposite direction as aversion therapy. Images of a woman can be associated with sexual arousal (e.g., presented during masturbation) to condition such images to be more reinforcing. Such techniques have been successful in the past, especially that of Laws, when blocks of sessions are alternated between associations with deviant and non-deviant sexual fantasies until the non-deviant fantasies produce greater arousal (Rosen & Beck, 1988). The success rate promises to increase as the development of the techniques continues. Similar behavioral techniques have been used successfully in the treatment of rapists, as we will see in the next chapter. More controversial somatic therapies, involving psychosurgery or hormonal therapy, have been reported to work for pedophiles as well as rapists. We will also discuss these as we deal with aggression directed against adult women. A more extensive discussion can be found in the suggested readings.

SUMMARY

The abuse of children involves aggressive physical acts directed toward them in their homes (child abuse) or aggressive physical and sexual acts that occur both within and outside the home (sexual abuse). Both types of abuse have only recently received serious attention in the United States.

Child abuse has been defined in a number of ways. This has made it difficult to measure the extent to which it occurs. Straus and his colleagues have used a consistent definition involving physical harm and have carried out several surveys on the incidences of abuse as well as the variables correlated with it. One finding, supported by a similar finding from a direct observation study, is that mothers are more likely than fathers to strike their children. Various social and environmental factors, such as unemployment, other long-term stresses, and single parent status, are correlated with abuse. Being abused as a child is also correlated with being an abuser. However, no causal relationship between being abused and becoming an abuser has been established. A number of theories have been proposed to explain child abuse, but methodological problems and misinterpretation of data have hindered the development of adequate theories.

Direct observation of abuse in the home has been employed to help determine contributing factors. It was found that much abusive behavior occurs in ineffective attempts to control children's aversive behaviors. Training parents to utilize effective behavioral control techniques helps reduce their abusive behaviors.

Sexual abuse of children often involves physical injury. Abuse that occurs within the family, or incest, has been thought to have a different basis than non-familial pedophilia. However, measurement of the sexual arousal of incestuous and pedophilic abusers suggests overlapping factors in the two sexual deviancies. Such measures can help analyze the causes of the abuse and also serve to assess the effectiveness of treatment. Treatments include reduction of sexual arousal to stimuli involving children, enhancing sexual arousal to stimuli involving adults, and training behaviors to support appropriate sexual activities.

Suggested Readings

Maletzky, B. M. (1991). *Treating the sexual offender*. Newbury Park, CA: Sage.
Widom, C. S. (1989). The cycle of violence. *Science, 244*, 160–166.

CHAPTER 12
Wife Abuse and Rape of Women

In the previous chapter, which dealt with aggression directed against children, the topic was divided into sections on physical attack and attack involving heterosexual activities. The same approach seems appropriate here. This chapter will discuss women as the targets of primarily physical assaults in their homes as well as women as victims of rape. There will be more lengthy treatment of the material on sexual aggression since the literature is more extensive and controversial. Sexual aggression directed toward women might involve a wide variety of activities—for example, sexual harassment. However, we will limit our discussion to those behaviors directed toward physical damage, consistent with our definition of aggression given in Chapter 1.

In examining physical assaults in the home, we will see that a parallel exists with the area of child abuse in that the problem was not widely recognized until relatively recently. In fact, the attention paid to child abuse was probably instrumental in bringing subsequent attention to wife abuse. As with child abuse, Straus and his colleagues have made an important contribution to its measurement.

Since feminists have added much to the literature on the causes of wife abuse, we will summarize an illustrative feminist perspective, along with other possibilities for the causes of this abuse. In addition, we will discuss possible treatments based on principles and approaches discussed earlier.

We will address sexual aggression in the form of rape in this chapter because of the physical damage commonly involved. Special problems with societal attitudes toward both rapist and victims will also be discussed. There are many theories about its causes, ranging from those that consider it deriving from natural or biological factors, psychopathological bases, or psychosociological sources. Psychopathological theories suggest several categories of rapists with different motivations, and so we will assess the possibilities for stopping a rapist with respect to these categories. We also will describe some preventative strategies and treatment of rapists.

PHYSICAL AGGRESSION

Definition and Measurement

Physical aggression directed against women in their homes is included in what others refer to as spouse abuse, battered wives, or, more broadly, family violence. The last category, of course, includes violence directed at any family member. Aggression between siblings and that against older family members, such as grandparents, is of concern but essentially is not part of our focus. The previous chapter described aggression directed by parents against their children. As we saw, the understanding and treatment of child abuse have been affected by societal attitudes and law and were not attended to until relatively recently. A similar pattern has occurred concerning spouse abuse. As Gelles (1982) pointed out, our attitude toward spouse abuse historically was to accept it either as an aberration or part of a legitimate punishment process directed by a husband against his wife. Only if the abuse resulted in very serious injury was it considered assault and therefore prosecuted. Such an attitude was exemplified by the 1824 ruling of the Mississippi Supreme Court that husbands were immune from assault and battery charges for "moderate" chastisement of their wives. Of course, one might wonder how "moderate" was defined and how it could be confused with assault in the case under question. The decision reflected norms established by English common law, such as the "rule of thumb." A wife could be beaten with a stick as long as its thickness did not exceed that of the thumb. Even as late as 1974, California law decreed that in order to be prosecuted for injuring his wife, a husband must cause more injury than that involved for a charge of battery.

In the early 1970s, when Pizzey described women who had been beaten by their husbands, the seriousness of spousal assault was brought to the public's attention (Martin, 1981). Since then, laws have been passed to help protect spouses, class action suits have brought more uniform protection from the police, and spouse abuse shelters have been established to house those who need to escape from their homes. However, problems remain concerning persistent societal attitudes about the abuse. People still label spouse-caused damage as accidental when they see individuals who are injured, and they tend to deny the existence of a more general problem. For example, a police captain in a town where a spouse abuse shelter recently had been established, with much publicity, declared in an interview that no serious problem existed in his community. Individuals in authority to recommend prosecution for suspected abuse may continue to follow the "stitch rule": if not many stitches are required to repair the damage, it is not serious enough to pursue.

Although legal protection from spouse abuse generally is available, it is not always utilized. The problem is with the willingness of battered spouses to file or follow through with official complaints. At times the spouses are intimidated from pursuing the matter, or conflicting emotions of love and fear may make it difficult to decide to proceed. Sometimes, once authorities are involved, the couple unites against them. However, an increased awareness of the abuse problem has resulted in policy changes in some areas. For example, in one Michigan city, police are required to make an arrest, regardless of any second thoughts on the part of the abused spouse, if they are called to a home where spousal violence has occurred in the past and they find evidence of further abuse. Some police forces now include training in handling domestic violence situations. With such increased awareness, one hopes other such measures will result in more effective treatment of spouse abuse cases.

The incidence of reported intra-spousal violence in the United States is high. Although estimates vary, such aggression may account for perhaps one-eighth of American violent crimes. Further, the violence occurring in the family affects others, particularly the police who are called in to respond to it. A significant number of deaths and injuries to policeofficers on duty occur while they are answering domestic complaints (Dutton, 1981). Straus and his colleagues, (Straus & Gelles, 1990a) attempted to obtain a definitive estimate of familial violence by interviewing a representative national sample of over 6,000 families. Violence, defined as any act directed to hurt someone, was found to have occurred between 16 percent of spouses during the previous year. The relative incidence of serious spouse beating (kicking, biting, hitting with fist or weapon, beating up, use or threat with weapon) was at about 6 percent.

A controversial aspect of the survey findings of Straus and Gelles was that the amount of serious spouse beating directed at husbands by wives was comparable, if not higher, to that directed at wives by husbands (4.8 percent versus 3.6 percent). In contrast to a significant decrease found in child abuse between surveys of 1975 and 1985, the rate of spousal abuse decreased only modestly. Most of the decline was in husband-to-wife abuse. Steinmetz's (1978) report on the rate of husband abuse in the earlier survey received great criticism from feminists, who either rejected her analysis of the data or dismissed the seriousness of aggression directed by wives toward their husbands, citing differences in consequences of such acts for men and women. Indeed, Straus and his colleagues acknowledged these differences in their analyses of the earlier survey. The analysis of the later survey includes indications of the greater amount of physical injuries that occur to women (Straus & Gelles, 1990a). However, the authors also point out that wives commit about the same number of spousal murders as husbands. Even if female violence is seen as retaliatory or defensive, it obviously can be very severe and should not be dismissed. The political ramifications of accepting the Straus and Gelles data might be that attention would be directed away from female victims, and efforts to pass legislation to protect them might be more easily thwarted. Perhaps a better approach would be to say that any wife-protection laws might be drafted to include protection measures for both spouses. However, regardless of these findings, most of the literature on spouse abuse assumes that the victim is the woman.

Causal Factors

An example of a feminist interpretation of the bases of wife abuse is presented by Walker (1981). From a feminist-political perspective, violence is seen to derive from the unequal power relationships existing between men and women. In Walker's view, the sexism perpetrated by society is the root of all violence toward women because it supports power inequalities. This sexism has its origins in patriarchal religions and cultural training. Men are seen to act violently toward women either to maintain their power or try to regain it, and they are supported in this by society and its legal system. The expected role of man is that of the strong, aggressive individual, while that of woman is as the passive one who is even expected to support her husband in his aggressive activities, or at least accept them.

Walker indicates that in cases of severe abuse, the woman may suffer from "learned helplessness," a concept taken from original work by Seligman, Maier, and Geer (1968). Their experiment showed that if strong shocks were administered to dogs without giving them a chance to escape, they subsequently would not learn a simple escape response when made available. Instead, they stayed in the shock area and took the shocks. The interpretation of these results was that the animals learned in the first part of the study that nothing that they could do would help them and that this learned helplessness prevented the subsequent adaptive learning. We should note that there have been challenges to the interpretation of these data, yet the concept of helplessness has been applied to various situations in attempts to explain why people do not make an effort to get out of bad situations. Thus, women who continue to live in or return to a home where they have been beaten regularly are seen to have given up trying to help themselves. Other factors, of course, affect such decisions, such as the lack of an alternative shelter and survival support, as well as the passivity previously mentioned, in addition to conflicting emotional feelings toward the husband or about separation from other family members.

Apart from the factors Walker discusses, it might be expected that many causes contributing to child abuse would also be important in spouse abuse. For example, un- or underemployment would produce a frustrating situation in which aggression is more likely. This may be made even more probable if the couple is in contact for greater amounts of time when both are unemployed and at home together. Other stresses, such as financial problems, illness, or pregnancy, might also be correlated with spouse abuse. Social isolation, lack of religion, low socioeconomic status, and abuse of alcohol and other drugs are other factors important from a sociological perspective and may help understand the general problem of abuse.

Various other causal factors can produce spouse abuse by an individual. Independent variables such as brain dysfunctions, abnormal neurochemical activities, and reinforcement history can result in a general increase in aggression that may be directed toward a spouse. Also, modeling influences might directly affect spouse abuse; for example, a man who witnessed abuse of his mother by his father and imitates it. Modeling also might be expected to affect the form of a wife's response to beating by her husband, in imitation of how she saw her mother react to beating by her father.

Possibilities for Treatment

Just as the factors that cause or correlate with child abuse may be similar to those related to spouse abuse, treatments similar to those mentioned for child abuse should be effective in reducing spouse abuse. If the abuse is seen as a last desperate attempt to exert control, then teaching alternate, non-violent techniques should lead to a re-

duction in the abuse. Assertiveness training, in which individuals are taught to recognize and stand up for their own rights, would seem to be helpful for reducing the
passivity of women. To the extent that this training may also include instructions in
how to appropriately express both positive and negative thoughts and feelings while
respecting the rights and feelings of others, it should also prove helpful to men. Anger
control techniques, such as those developed by Novaco (1978), may be helpful in
treating spouse abuse. He proposes a combination of tactics, such as learning to relax instead of becoming angry in a situation, learning to recognize and counter dysfunctional cognitive reactions to a situation, and then providing reinforcement for using these tactics and reducing aggressive responding. These tactics appear to work.
Neidig, Friedman, and Collins (1985) have reported success in a similar approach,
which includes similar techniques. Their couples were taught in 10 weekly sessions.
Four months after training, 87 of the 100 couples were violence free.

   The problem of spouse abuse is one that can be controlled. What is needed is the
recognition that it has distinct causes and that these causes can be modified. Also
needed, of course, are sufficient resources to support the psychological, social, and
educational efforts for dealing with the problem.

SEXUAL AGGRESSION

Definition and Societal Attitudes

   Rape, involving forced sexual intercourse, is of concern here because of the physical damage often inflicted on the victim. We will focus on the factors that result in
such damage when rape is committed against women. The term "rape" is used as a
general term to label sexual behavior perceived by the victim as being forced on her.
We will not address legal and ethical distinctions between seduction and rape of partners, whether married ("marital rape") or not ("date rape"), nor will we consider the
rape of children and men. However, we should note that the rape of adult males occurs often enough so that at least some rape laws have been rewritten to make them
gender free. Further, although most rape of males is committed by other males, heterosexual rape of males also occurs (Struckman-Johnson, 1988).

   Because the legal definition of rape is unclear and its reporting is inconsistent, incidence levels are not easy to determine. In 1990, the reported rate, including forcible
rape, assaults, and attempts, was 80 per 100,000 women in the United States, up 24
percent from 10 years earlier (FBI, 1990). The actual rate may have been much higher
than that reported. This imprecision is related to the legal definition in that acts such
as marital rape might not be recognized. The report rate is also affected by reluctance
on the part of the victims to go to the police because of feelings of shame or embar-
rassment. Insensitive practices by police have contributed to the problem, although
progress is being made in making the report of rape less stressful for the victim.

   Historically, the legal system has been biased against the rape victim because it
has been difficult to convict the rapist, in comparison to other criminals (Robin, 1977).
The victim had to demonstrate that she resisted, with maximal force, throughout, and
that she risked or sustained injury defending herself against an attack that threatened
her with death or serious bodily harm. While a robbery victim may without prejudice

submit instead of resisting or running away, the rape victim was expected to endanger herself so that the sexual activity would not be considered consensual. Fortunately, state laws are being changed to be more sensitive to the complexities of rape situations. However, biased laws or at least biased judges and jury members still exist, and it is not uncommon to hear of injustices in the legal treatment of rape cases. (Although we should also acknowledge that in some cases where there is increased sensitivity to bias, the injustice occurs against the accused rapists.)

Attempts have been made to assess attitudes concerning rape in social psychological studies such as that done by Malamuth, Haber, and Feshbach (1980). They asked male and female college students to read one of two sexual passages, then one on a rape, and then gave them a questionnaire that included items on their conceptions concerning the rapist and the victim and asked for their predictions of how others and themselves might behave in the situation.

Malamuth et al. found that in comparison to the male students, females tended to perceive the rapist as being more dangerous and saw his activity as less justified. The females also perceived the victim as feeling more pain and exhibiting more resistance. These male-female differences were as we would predict, yet the results for questions concerning predictions were surprisingly more similar. Answers were given on a five- point Likert scale, ranging from 5 (very much or 100 percent), to 3 (don't know), to 1 (none or 0 percent). Both sexes predicted that a substantial number of men would rape if they were able to do so without being caught. The Likert scores for both sexes on this question were about 2.7. Also, a relatively high number of both sexes indicated that about 25 percent of women would derive some pleasure from the rape experience. It is surprising that not only some men but also some women seemed to view forced sex as possibly pleasurable. The average ratings of the females were only slightly lower than those of the males, at about 2.2, (although the females also indicated, with a 1.1 rating, that they themselves would not enjoy being raped). Further, the 2.2 is an average and assumedly includes a number of answers from the high end of the scale. Some females probably estimated that 50 or 75 percent of women would experience some pleasure from a rape. The authors indicated that when the subjects predicted their own behaviors, 17 percent of the males indicated that they would rape if in the situation of the story, with 50 percent indicating that they would rape if they would not be caught.

The results of this study have been viewed with alarm for what they seem to show concerning societal attitudes about rape—that women may well enjoy it and that many men would commit it if given the opportunity. Although these results are disturbing, they should be qualified. For example, in deriving the 50 percent figure for potential rapists, the authors included all responses greater than 1 on the Likert scale. Thus, they included answers of 2 (unlikely) or 3 (uncertain) in the calculation. A more clear statement of the results might have been that 50 percent of the respondents would not absolutely rule out raping a woman if assured that they would not be caught.

Given the possibilities of different interpretations by respondents to the language of the question and of some unmeasured effect of specific materials presented, perhaps the result of Malamuth et al.'s study does not reflect a significant threat concerning rape. In addition, the measure taken was an indirect one. The answers given on a questionnaire distributed during a laboratory experiment do not necessarily reflect how individuals would act in reality. Therefore, while it should be disturbing that all the male college students in this sample would not assure that they would not rape, we should not expect that a high proportion of them actually are ready to do so. Nevertheless, there may be justification for perceiving what seems to be a rather cavalier male attitude concerning rape as well as some lack of sensitivity in females concerning its effects.

Possible Causes and Representative Theories

The search, by many professionals, for the causes of rape has resulted in a large number of proposals, with no one cause gaining consensus. Professionals have employed a wide range of approaches so that the behaviors of any one rapist might be explained in a number of ways, because these professionals also impose their own conceptions on his acts, emphasize difference aspects of his behaviors, and employ different types of data (observations and interviews with the rapist or his victim, questionnaires, penile measures, projective tests). Consequently, the resulting theories of rape differ in terms of the relative roles of sex and aggression, the rapist's basic motivations, and the number of types of rapist.

Apart from different emphases on the basic causes of rape, there are differences in whether rape involves separate psychopathological states or is an extreme of normal behaviors. Some biological theories, as well as some social theories, treat rape as an extreme behavior. For example, socially based feminist theories of rape, which are popular, portray rape not as a sexual act but as a political one, used to help control and dominate women (e.g., see Marolla & Scully, 1986). These feminist theories maintain that society fosters hostile attitudes toward women and deviant attitudes about their sexuality. Rape is thus seen as a logical outgrowth of such attitudes. In support of this view, Marolla and Scully found that both rapists and other felons share attitudes about the appropriate roles of women in society, the acceptability of violence against women, and beliefs in stereotypes about rape (e.g., that accused men are often innocent; that women invite rape). These attitudes are considered to be generated by society and acquired by individuals by social learning processes, such as those we discussed in Chapters 8 and 9.

Biological Theories

The possibility of biological mechanisms for rape are suggested by the existence of common biological influences over sexual and aggressive behaviors. Controls governing consensually based sexual behavior might dysfunction to produce the forced sexual aggressive behavior of rape. Earlier, especially in Chapter 2, we saw that aggressive and sexual behaviors sometimes occurred together and how particular brain structures and sexual hormones are involved in both behaviors. These observations were made in both lower animals and humans. Biological mechanisms for rape also are suggested by its occurrence in other animals. There is some evidence that rape happens in such species as ducks and orangutans and even in relatively primitive forms such as insects and worms (Lessem, 1980). This sexual behavior involves coercion instead of consent and is described as a sudden attack involving forced copulation. Ellis (1989), in partial support for an evolutionary theory of rape, cites over 50 published reports of forced copulations, in a wide range of species, from invertebrates to monkeys and apes. As Lessem suggests, rape may have a selective advantage because, when it leads to procreation, the rapist's genes are propagated. Since behaviors, including rape, of the lower animals are thought to be extensively under the control of biological influences, these reports of rape indicate that a biological mechanism may be present. Therefore, it would be profitable for us to examine the possibilities that such mechanisms operate in humans as well, and contribute to the possibility of rape.

Thornhill and Thornhill (1992) have proposed a controversial model of rape from the sociobiological perspective. They consider rape to have a basis in evolution; they believe it occurs under genetically transmitted biological controls because it was a behavior that helped early man adapt and survive, by aiding reproductive success. They cite numerous studies to support their position that coercive sexuality is an evolved characteristic. For example, they note work by Malamuth and others who found that normal men are sexually aroused by media that portray rapes about as much as when consensual sex is portrayed.

The Thornhills' 1992 paper was published in a journal that invites other professionals to publish comments on its articles, thus providing a sample of reactions to the work. The Thornhills were criticized on many grounds, primarily for overemphasizing biological factors to the relative exclusion of those emphasized by feminist and other social theories. Some critics did not reject the sociobiological orientation but suggested that other adaptive mechanisms besides rape (e.g., advantages of women's selection of mates) might be considered. Some proposed that the sociobiological orientation had some good factual support but was too narrowly focused and should include more analysis of other contributions to rape.

Ellis (1991) proposed a theory that purports to combine elements of sociobiological, feminist, and social learning theories. However, it seems primarily focused on evolutionary bases for rape, with relatively modest roles for learning mechanisms. Ellis argues that unlearned drives for sex and for possessing and controlling things combine to produce forced sexual behavior. He indicates that rape is primarily a sex-oriented behavior and discusses, among other facets, the behaviors of date rapists to support his position. The date rapist is seen to obtain sex with physical force only after other, non-violent means are exhausted (such as using alcohol and pressuring the victim for sex). An interesting part of Ellis' theory is how the presence of testosterone during the prenatal development of the nervous system produces an increased sex drive as well as a lowered sensitivity to events associated with rape. Brain mechanisms are developed that are more sensitive to testosterone after puberty. This results in an increase in sexual activity and a decrease in sensitivity to threats of punishment for rape and to the suffering of the victims.

Ellis includes a learning factor in his theory, as the rapist attempts various tactics, including increased use of force, and is successful (reinforced). The concerns of feminists and social learning theorists are included by assigning a minor role to pornography. Pornography is seen to support the acquisition, by the social-learning mechanism of modeling, of the sexist attitudes and male domination activities that feminists feel are the major causes of rape. Nevertheless, Ellis' theory focuses mainly on how biological factors contribute to rape.

He supports his theory in part by reference to research on the effects of testosterone on neural development and function and on sexual motivation. However, no one has demonstrated that these factors do produce acts of rape. As we indicated in Chapter 2, the results of attempts to determine the relation between testosterone and various types of human aggression have not been consistent. Similarly, inconsistent results have occurred in efforts to find a relationship between testosterone and human sexual aggression. For example, Rada, Laws, Kellner, Stivastava, and Peake (1983) found that testosterone levels were not significantly higher for violent sex offenders compared to non-violent offenders or normal controls. Finally, the studies cited in Chapter 2 indicating that sexual aggression can be decreased by anti-androgens do not demonstrate a specific role of hormones in rape. This chemical castration treatment can produce decreases in all sexual behavior, not just rape-related ones. For example, anti-androgens have been used to treat non-violent sexual deviancies, such as voyeurism and exhibitionism (Fedoroff, Wisner-Carlson, Dean, & Berlin, 1992).

Any biological mechanisms for rape probably will be found to result as a failure of normal control mechanisms. It is important to understand how such failure might occur and contribute to rape. Because of the increased emphasis on the discovery of biological contributions to behavior, more of these elements will most likely be recognized in theories of the bases of rape.

Groth's Psychopathological Theory

One of the most widely cited theories on the causes of rape is that developed by Groth and his colleagues (see Groth & Birnbaum, 1979). In an early study, Groth and Burgess (1977) considered rape a sexual deviation, but also saw it as the expression or satisfaction of needs that were not primarily sexual. That is, although the male's sexual pleasure or mutual enjoyment of he and the victim may be involved, it is secondary to the use of force. In their study of rapists and their victims, done in the early 1970s in the Boston area, they found that in no case was rape the only means of sexual contact with women. One-third of the rapists were married, and the rest either had girlfriends or went to prostitutes. No seduction attempts were made toward their victims and no great amount of sexual satisfaction, in terms of ejaculation, seemed to be involved, given that one-third of the men were sexually dysfunctional during the rape, and over half of the victims were negative for sperm after the attack. In contrast, force was a common element during the rapes, with 62 percent of the victims suffering injury.

From their interviews, Groth and Burgess felt that rapes could be categorized in one of two classes by the basic motivation involved. **Anger rape,** which constituted about one-third of the cases, was characteristic of men who sought revenge or retaliation against women. It involved use of excessive force, insults, profanity, and degradation of the victim. It was often unpremeditated. **Power rape,** representing about two-thirds of the cases, was committed by men who derive pleasure from the helplessness of females. The act was premeditated and mentally rehearsed, accompanied by fantasies that the woman would enjoy it and that he would perform well sexually. The act might not include physical harm, although harm might occur over time. The two types of rape were distinguished, yet each might include elements of the other. Rape was seen to result either from a reaction to extraordinary life stress (perhaps, for example, long-term unemployment) that overwhelmed the man's usual psychological resources or from his poor self-image (e.g., he thinks he is worthless) and insufficient development of life- coping skills (such as those that would result in normal relations with women). In later work, Groth and Birnbaum differentiated a third type, **sadistic rape.** This has elements of the anger rape, in that force and abuse are involved, and of power rape, because premeditation occurs and the attack is more long-lasting. Here, the rapists are sexually excited by the involvement of excessive physical force, and at times include ritualized acts, including torture and bizarre, symbolic destruction, and sometimes even elimination of his victim.

Groth continues to employ these three classifications of rape in his studies. He has found them appropriate not only for the disadvantaged population for which he originally formulated them but also for more highly educated groups. In addition, he has started to explore, in conjunction with workers at Johns Hopkins University, biological factors that might contribute to rape. Besides the brain dysfunction suggested above, they have investigated genetic, biochemical, and sex hormone (testosterone) factors (Groth, personal communication, 1990). Berlin (1988) discusses some of the issues involved in this work assessing, with his colleagues, various biological mechanisms that contribute to rape. One fascinating approach used a PET scan to measure brain activity during sexual arousal and search for differences between a class of rapist and sexually normal men. Although they have not yet identified any differences, they apparently were successful in determining that the activity of opiate receptors in the thalamus changes during sexual arousal.

Other Representative Theories

The work on the causes of rape done by other professionals has somewhat overlapped the studies of Groth, although different labels and sometimes different numbers of types are proposed, as each addresses different factors and possibly uses different populations. Unfortunately, these various orientations have made it difficult to develop a widely accepted theory of rape. We will review several attempts to understand rape from different points of view (as summarized by Rada, 1978) to help readers appreciate the multiplicity of approaches and see how they vary according to the original biases and interests of their authors.

A sociological interpretation of rape was developed by Amir (1971), who divided types of rape according to the social roles they fulfill. **Role-expressive rapes** occur for participation in a group, as in gang rapes; they do not take place for sexual satisfaction. **Role-supportive rapes** occur to maintain membership in a group or for sheer sexual gratification. Other rapes have no social role significance. They are idiosyncratic or a symptom of psychopathology or special circumstances. The first two types of rape are not considered the result of deviant sexuality but instead occur because of participation in a group that condones force in obtaining goals.

Guttmacher and Weihofen (1952) classified rapes according to one of three motivational patterns. One type occurs as an explosive relief of pent-up sexual impulses and thus would seem to be primarily **sexually** motivated. A second type has a **sadistic** motivation. This is committed by men who hate women; they are thought to manifest their aggression via a sexual attack. The last type is the **anti-social**, wherein rape is one of many acts against society. These categories of rape seem to parallel three of the six sociobehavioral classes of rape proposed by Gebhard, Gagnon, Pomeroy, and Christenson (1965). The other three classes described by Gebhard et al. are those committed by inebriated men, by men employing a double standard (attacking "bad" women is OK), and by men miscellaneously categorized as mentally dysfunctional.

Cohen, Garofalo, Boucher, and Seghorn (1971) talked of the three aims of rape and placed them within a psychodynamic context. **Aggressive rape** involves sex as an aggressive instrument. The perpetrator attempts to humiliate and defile a woman, who may be a complete stranger. This occurs to compensate for a castration phobia. **Sexual rape** involves aggression as an instrument for sex. Relatively little violence is involved, unless necessary to subdue the victim. The man might fantasize that he will perform well. The rape is said to be a defense against homosexual wishes that bother the man. **Sex-aggression diffusion rape** has a strong sadistic component. The man needs some degree of violence to become sexually excited. All three types closely parallel those of Groth regarding the behaviors involved, with additional postulation of psychic motivations.

A behavioral interpretation of rape was presented by Abel, Blanchard, and Becker (1978), who also delineated three basic causes of rape. As one cause, a man has a deficit in being sexually aroused by non-rape sexual stimuli. He achieves the arousal only with forced, aggressive cues. This would seem to describe the sadistic rapist. A second cause occurs when a man is excessively aroused by forced sexual contact. This would seem to describe someone further up on the continuum shared by the first type. The third cause of rape occurs when a man has inadequate heterosexual skills. He cannot establish social relations in a normal way and therefore turns to rape. This may involve the same individuals who are the power rapists of Groth.

Rada (1978), in addition to reviewing these theories, listed his own five clinical categories of rapists. These include some of those detailed above, such as the sadistic and the sociopathic, as well as some whose characteristics are included in descriptions of other theorists. Rada lists **psychotic** as a separate category that is constituted by insane individuals such as schizophrenics and those having organic brain syndrome. These would be part of the larger miscellaneous group in the categorization of Gebhard and his colleagues that we already discussed. Rada labels another group as **situational stress,** where a man may, for example, lose his job, become agitated and depressed, and commit rape impulsively; the rape usually is not excessively violent. Groth cites such stress as one of the two principal causes of rape. The combination of impulsiveness and lack of violence are not found in Groth's categories of rapes; his **anger** rapist sometimes acts impulsively but also uses excessive force. Rada's last category includes men with a **masculine identity conflict.** These men have an actual or perceived deficiency in their male roles. This group may include timid or shy men and hypermasculine body builders. The rapes are more planned and violent, and may include gang rapes. These would be included in some of the antisocial categories previously described, in Abel et al.'s group with inadequate social skills, and perhaps in Cohen et al.'s aggressive group of rapists.

The variety of theories would seem to reflect a lack of agreement among professionals regarding the causes of rape. Because each has focused on the variables most relevant to his specialty, each has developed concepts of types of rapists that do not seem to correspond to those of other professionals, apart from some apparent overlaps (e.g., for the sadistic rapist). However, even this more obvious category is not universally included. Even the oft-cited Groth missed it in his first classification attempt. Nevertheless, we can draw several generalities from these approaches. There seem to be four basic types of rapists: **the sadistic woman hater, the sociopath, the sexual deviate, and the socially inadequate**. The rapes committed by these individuals may be differentiated in terms of whether they are planned or impulsive, how much violence is involved, and the primacy of sex or violence. Regretfully, none of the theories addresses all these variables in a way that provides a consistent, attractive model for other workers to follow, so the field is left with no common base. The approach that eventually leads to the best prediction, treatment, and control of rape will become, assumedly, the most popular and so will facilitate future progress. One promising attempt at integration was made by Hall and Hirschman (1991), who developed a model of rapists that incorporates different levels of a few of the basic motivating factors found in other studies. This integration postulates four basic subtypes of rapists; each is based on the prevalence of physiological, cognitive, affective, or personality dysfunctions. Validation of the model is yet to be accomplished.

Strategies for Dealing with Rapists

One area of concern in rape is how a woman might prevent it from occurring. Aside from obvious strategies, such as avoiding isolated dark areas and dangerous interactions and keeping one's home secure, resistance strategies might also be employed once an actual confrontation occurs. Physical self-defense, screams, verbal aggression, flattery, humor, and faking fainting or illness are all possible tactics. The first three, because they involve some type of aggression and noxiousness, might be expected to elicit counteraggression if they are not sufficiently intense to overcome the attacker. The last three are calculated to distract the attacker and decrease his emotional arousal. However, they would not be expected to work in all cases, especially with the sadistic rapist. Indeed, given the multiple causes of rape we have summarized, it would be surprising if any one resistance tactic were consistently effective.

Marques (1981) has studied the effectiveness of several types of rape resistance strategies. She noted that there seemed to be no consensus as to which strategies were most effective, and little actual research has been done on the effects of victim responses to the rapist. She attempted to incorporate an objective technique in a study designed to assess the effects of three commonly recommended responses. The first response, **assertive refusal**, combined an angry tone of refusing to be intimidated or even touched, followed by a declaration that the victim was leaving. The second, a **plea for sympathy**, included a tearful begging to be released unharmed and an indication either that she had been hospitalized or that her fiancé would leave her if she were raped. The third response, **establishing a relationship**, involved calmly talking to the rapist and trying to get him to talk about himself and believe that his victim was concerned that he was troubled. Each of these strategies or a nonverbal control interval were presented as part of an audiotape, following introductory passages used to set the scene and describe initiation of the attack. The tapes were played one at a time to volunteers who were convicted rapists to determine how they thought they would respond and how sexually aroused they became. Sexual arousal was measured by self- report as well as a physical measure of changes in penile circumference similar to that used for child molesters.

The physical measure of arousal (erection) yielded results that varied greatly with each individual. Also, the individual arousal responses to each condition were not always in the same direction across individuals. These inconsistent results made it more difficult to interpret the effects of the strategies. However, researchers could discern some general effects. The data for each resistance strategy, when compared, showed a principal effect of the sympathy plea. While the other two strategies and the control typically produced little effect or even a reduction in the erection produced by the preparatory scene, the sympathy plea consistently produced the highest physical arousal. These data alone would suggest that, for this group of rapists, a sympathy plea would be counterproductive for inhibiting rape based on sexual motivation. The rapists' self-reports also supported this finding in that they indicated a slightly higher (but non-significant) tendency to complete a rape if a woman pleaded for sympathy. Alternatively, this weak correlation between the physical arousal levels and self-report of the probability of rape completion might reflect a more important role of aggression in the determination of rape. Indeed, in Marques' study, self-reported feelings of anger were most highly correlated with the subjects' predictions that they would rape. Further, the assertive refusal strategy produced greater amounts of reported anger and a greater tendency of the rapist to claim he would hurt the victim. However, the correlation between self- reports of a tendency to complete the rape and other factors was highest (.57) when both anger and sexual arousal were combined. Thus, both factors operating together were important in determining whether the rape would be completed.

The technique and procedures used by Marques have other limitations; they involved a limited number of the total population of rapists, and used an audiotape of only a few of many possible settings, victims, and resistance strategies. However, this method has the potential to be a very useful tool in determining strategies most likely to avert rape. The physical erection measure can provide an objective indication that would corroborate or deny any self-report of arousal. Since the arousal component seems to be very important in determining if a rape will be completed, an objective measure of this is most desirable.

Marques' study suggests that none of the strategies tested would be especially successful in preventing rape. Also, no strategy had particularly good effect when the rapists were divided into "dominant" and "tentative" categories on the basis of their own categorizations of their approaches. It appears that the assertive refusal might very well be more dangerous because the victim is more likely to be harmed. These results suggest that no one strategy is preferable, and that a flexible combination of approaches might be best.

Marques' finding that no particular rape resistance strategy would be successful is characteristic of many studies in this area. Prentky, Burgess, and Carter (1986) noted this inconsistency and attempted to formulate resistance strategies that would be appropriate for each of four types of rapists (essentially the three categories Groth described plus a sociopathic type). They were especially interested in the relation of physically aggressive resistance, compared to non-resistance, with injury to the victim.

Prentky et al. obtained most of their information from the case files of over 100 rapists who were committed to a treatment center for sexual offenders on the basis of being especially and repeatedly violent. Although the amount of violence differed for rapist types, they found that, within each type, the worst violence before or during the rape occurred when the victim aggressively resisted. Less brutal violence or the absence of physical aggression was associated with a lack of physical resistance. The authors recognized that they studied a select group of more violent rapists and that they had correlative, not causative, evidence on the relation between rapist and victim aggression. That is, they did not show whether the victim or the rapist initiated the violence. However, they felt it important to consider alternatives to aggressive resistance. They did not test the strategies, but made suggestions based on others' studies and their own clinical experience.

Prentky et al. suggested that the optimum response to a rapist is escape, if it can be employed successfully. A next alternative is verbal resistance, trying to make the rapist aware of the victim as an individual. Strategies involving appeals to sympathy or feigning sickness are considered not consistently effective. Aggressive resistance is recommended only in cases where it can be utilized quickly and effectively, such as by someone well trained in the martial arts. As suggested above (in line with a general thesis of this text), an aggressive response by the victim might precipitate aggression by the rapist. Finally, acquiescence or the absence of any resistance is recommended only if all other strategies fail and the victim feels that it will reduce physical injury.

Prentky et al. discuss the effectiveness of the various strategies based on characteristics and motivations of the types of rapists. They suggest how the potential victim might adjust her strategies according to the type of rapist she encounters. Unfortunately, as the authors recognize, this presents an enormous task of analysis to a terrified woman who is suddenly confronted by a rapist. Although some victims have successfully used various strategies, it is not likely that a significant impact on rape incidence could result from attempts to train women to utilize such a complex approach.

Prevention of Rape

Although any reduction in the amount of rapes is desirable, it would seem that victim strategy studies have not resulted in the development of effective tactics. It is important to consider other approaches to limiting rape incidence. Rehabilitative treatments, discussed in the following section, may help prevent repetition of rapes. However, these treatments occur after someone has been victimized. It would be preferable, although certainly not easier, to apply preventative measures, including education. Feminist and social learning theorists emphasize the role of experiences in the production of rape behaviors, and even a more biologically oriented theorist such as Ellis includes an important role of learning. Students of courtship rape (including date and marital rape), such as Shotland (1992), discuss the effect on rape probability of expectations concerning sex, perceptions about the sexual responses of others, and attitudes about rape and women. These influences are all acquired by learning. It would seem important to develop educational plans, starting with young children, that could help prevent rape by countering the various learning processes that contribute to rape. Swift (1985) discusses some preliminary approaches in this area, including teaching alternatives to violence, modifying sex role stereotypes, and using television to model prosocial behaviors.

Treatment of Rapists

Apart from preventative and resistance strategies for controlling rape, the treatment of rapists themselves has also been attempted. To the extent that biological factors, such as brain or biochemical dysfunctions are prevalent in rapists, they may be addressed directly. In the case of psychoses, drug therapy may be very critical. The anti-androgenic hormonal therapy approach discussed in Chapter 2 may aid in decreasing a man's overall sexual activity, including not only rape but also other sexually deviant behaviors that may be directed against women. This, of course, is a radical approach, since it would decrease appropriate as well as deviant activity and would control only as long as the administration of the anti-androgenic drug was continued. Fedoroff et al. demonstrated how the combination of weekly anti-androgen injections and group therapy resulted in reduced relapse rates if maintained over a five-year period. Another radical approach involves psychosurgery. Dieckman, Horn, and Schneider (1979) made lesions in one side of the ventromedial hypothalamus and just in front of the hypothalamus (areas that had been shown to be involved in both sexual and aggressive behaviors, as well as in eating) in 11 male sexual offenders. They reported effective decreases in sexual drive with no negative side effects except some increase in eating.

A less radical, more accepted alternative approach to treating rapists is to try to change an individual's behavior with environmental manipulations. Behavioral change methods such as those described in Goldstein and Keller (1987) or in Novaco (1978), which have worked in reducing other types of aggressive behaviors, may also be applied successfully to the rapist's aggression. At times they are used in conjunction with hormonal therapy.

The question of whether the individual rapist has primarily sexual or aggressive goals may require some alteration of methods, but the behavior therapist should be capable of helping the rapist change his behavioral patterns. That is, the rapist can be taught methods to control his anger, decrease his negative cognitions concerning women, and increase more positive thoughts about them. He can be taught more adequate social skills for interacting with women. Precipitating stress factors, such as financial problems and unemployment, can be reduced by general approaches such as financial counseling and guidance in job-search strategies. The key to success in such therapy is to recognize the particular causes of an aggressive behavior and treat them directly.

The sexual behavior of the rapist may be defined as one controlled by the wrong stimuli. That is, he may be considered excessively reinforced when he commits forced sexual acts or deficiently reinforced by normal sexual activity. Therefore, some treatments attempt to change the stimuli that affect the rapist. Abel, Blanchard, and Becker (1978) have used cognitive behavioral techniques to make rape stimuli aversive, while enhancing the reinforcing strength of normal sexual stimuli. In an aversion therapy procedure, they tell the rapist to produce a graphic image of himself committing rape and then imagine experiencing some horrible event, such as his own wife being raped.

This is calculated to condition the original rape activity to be very aversive by associating it with the second activity. Further, an aversion relief component may be included, in which the rapist imagines behaving more acceptably and then receiving something desirable, such as being released from prison.

Abel, et al. also have worked to enhance sexual arousal to non-deviant stimuli using fading and masturbatory conditioning. In fading, a man might be exposed to slides of deviant stimuli that produce arousal, followed by slides that more closely approximate non-deviant stimuli, which are slowly substituted while maintaining the arousal. In masturbatory conditioning, a man would be asked to view or imagine the non-deviant stimuli while masturbating. For example, he might view slides of his wife or imagine engaging in foreplay and having sex with a willing partner. Such a procedure is designed to condition sexual arousal to the non-deviant stimuli. In addition to such conditioning, Abel et al. trained their clients to enhance their social skills. They employed modeling, role playing, and rehearsal of social skills: making eye contact, conversing appropriately with a woman, and expressing affection in an acceptable way. In later work, Abel and his colleagues (Abel, Becker, & Skinner, 1987) suggest that, in addition to these procedures, a total treatment program might include sex education as well as treatment of cognitive distortions concerning women, and of any sexual dysfunctions that impede normal sexual relationships.

SUMMARY

Two forms of aggression directed against women are wife abuse and rape. Although wife abuse was not commonly recognized as a serious problem until the early 1970s in the United States, it has been found to constitute a significant part of violent crimes committed. Straus and his colleagues found, as they had with child abuse, that women account for a great amount of aggressive behaviors. At the extreme end of the violence continuum, women commit as many spousal murders as men. However, within the area of more common marital aggression, that directed by husbands against their wives usually has more severe consequences.

The causes of wife abuse are seen by feminists to result from inequalities of power, as society supports a dominant role for men and a passive one for women. Alternatively, various possible biological, psychological, and social causes contribute to the abuse. Recognition of the causes suggests possible treatment tactics for the control of abuse.

Sexual aggression, in the form of rape, has been increasing in the United States. Despite changes in legal statutes that place less burden on the victim to prove involuntary participation, concerns still exist about societal attitudes regarding the innocence of the victim.

There has been a wide variety of theories of rape behavior. Biological theories see rape as the remainder of a sexual behavior that had an adaptive role during human evolution. Thus, it would be an extreme of a natural behavior. Feminist and some social learning theorists treat rape as a learned behavior, encouraged by sociopolitical structures that denigrate women and support beliefs that make rape more acceptable.

Psychopathological theorists believe that rape is a deviant behavior produced by various motivations or learned via various experiences.

A number of strategies for stopping a rapist have been proposed, but no one technique is consistently successful. This differential success may be due in part to the differences between rapists. It would be preferable to prevent rapes from starting, and educational approaches offer good possibilities for this. These approaches would help develop appropriate attitudes about sex roles as well as foster prosocial behaviors. The treatment of rapists is also important. It may involve biological factors, such as hormone levels, that support the behavior or, more often, behavioral treatments for controlling aggression and decreasing the power of deviant sexual stimuli in favor of normal sexual stimuli.

Suggested Readings

The text by Maletzky recommended at the end of the previous chapter contains material also pertinent here.

Martin, D. (1981) *Battered wives*. San Francisco, CA: Volcano Press

CHAPTER 13

Violence in Psychiatric Populations

Although aggression is not a problem in the majority of psychiatric patients, it is common. Aggression is an important component of the behaviors characteristic of at least eight psychiatric classifications in the DSM-IV (see p. 40). This chapter will discuss some of these classifications. As previously, we include some background information to inform readers unfamiliar with this subject.

We will describe both behavioral and drug-based approaches to treating aggression. Some of the behavioral treatments should be recognized from principles and applications described earlier.

Although the present chapter is organized around specific psychiatric classifications involving aggression, readers should be aware that such aggression may occur in relation to a variety of environmental situations, including those discussed in the previous three chapters. That is not to say that all the aggression in these chapters is the result of some psychiatric disturbance. However, some of it certainly is related.

RECOGNITION OF THE EXISTENCE OF A PROBLEM

The realization that some psychiatric disorders may include problems with aggressive behaviors is important for ensuring the safety of both professionals and laypeople who interact with psychiatric patients. Recognition of the possibility for aggressive behaviors will help them take appropriate precautions. On the other hand, to a great extent the general public is far too ready to assume that psychiatric patients will be aggressive. Opposition to halfway houses or residential treatment centers often includes alarmist predictions of the general mayhem that would be inflicted on neighborhood children and defenseless adults if such a program were located there. With this in mind, we should emphasize that many psychiatric classifications do not include aggression as a component and that appropriate screening and maintenance processes typically are set up to ensure that patients who are candidates for residential placement will not present serious problems of aggressiveness. Unfortunately, some advocates for the psychiatric population err in the opposite direction of the neighborhood alarmists and blithely assert that no threat whatsoever exists.

Monahan (1992) takes a moderating position on aggression in psychiatric populations. In his earlier work, he denied any association between mental disorders and violence. His more recent analysis of data on both the incidence of violence in those diagnosed with mental disorders as well as the incidence of mental disorders in those committing violent crimes convinced him that violence has a modest yet consistent link with mental disorders. The author's position is that while almost 90 percent of those with mental disorders are not violent, the violence in the remaining 10 percent should be recognized.

Some psychiatric workers find that aggression is more than a modest problem. For example, the June 1987 issue of *Psychiatric Annals* was devoted to aggression in psychiatric patients, acknowledging the seriousness of the problem. Liberman, Marshall, and Burke (1981) suggest that the probability of incidences of aggression in psychiatric populations is seriously underestimated. Since the worst cases are kept hospitalized longer and if released are more likely to be reinstitutionalized more quickly, the relatively few incidences of aggression that occur outside institutions do not adequately represent the general problem of aggression in psychiatric cases. Systematic measures of incidences in institutions have yielded rather high rates of aggression. For example, in a study of 1400 patients in a California mental hospital, a rate of about 2000 violent acts per month was estimated, approaching a level of two per patient. In an Illinois institution, a study of incidences in two wards found a rate of one aggressive episode for each 30 minutes of waking time. This rate occurred even though patients were receiving intensive, positively oriented milieu and social learning therapy. Such studies give sound support to the idea that aggression in psychiatric patients is an important problem.

Once this problem is recognized, the appropriate treatment must be determined. Behaviorally oriented therapists may observe that both biological and environmental influences are at work; however, often they de-emphasize the former in favor of the latter. They may acknowledge that biological factors define the individual's basic capacities, but also point out that these interact with environmental factors, stressors, drugs, and past history to determine if aggression will occur. Workers such as Liberman and his colleagues emphasize the limits of biological factors. They indicate that the temporal lobe's role in producing uncontrolled episodes of aggression has been sensationalized. Also, while admitting that therapeutic drugs may be useful in controlling aggression in particular, well-defined psychiatric disorders, they also cite paradoxical effects, when drugs have exacerbated rather than alleviated a problem. They are concerned with abuses in administering drugs, maintaining that physicians tend to turn to them as an easy means of controlling difficult cases or that ward personnel object to elimination or reductions in doses for the same reason.

In an approach opposite that of many behaviorally oriented therapists, some psychiatrists, such as Itil (1981) and Tupin (1988), recognize that aggression is a product of a multitude of factors, including social, environmental, genetic, and psychopathological processes, yet emphasize the benefits of using drugs to control the problem and employing physiological measures to guide their administration and evaluate their effectiveness.

SOME PSYCHIATRIC DISORDERS WITH AGGRESSIVE COMPONENTS

Schizophrenia

Schizophrenia is the most commonly diagnosed psychosis (incapacitating mental disorder involving impaired contact with reality); it occurs in approximately 1 percent of the population. Almost one-half of the patients in mental hospitals are schizophrenic. The schizophrenic is commonly characterized by **positive symptoms** of disordered thoughts, lack of contact with reality, delusions, and hallucinations. **Negative symptoms** include a lack of affect (emotion), low motivational levels, little speech, and social withdrawal. In addition to these symptoms, aggression may occur, either in a chronic form or in more isolated outbursts.

Various types of strong evidence point to a genetic component in schizophrenia, including findings of increased incidences within families living together or separated by adoption. Twin studies show that the concordance rate is perhaps five times greater in genetically identical monozygotic twins compared to dizygotic twins (Farmer, McGuffin, & Gottesman, 1987). Given a genetic component, this implies biological causes of schizophrenia. The most common finding is that an excess in activity of dopamine is important. This **dopamine hypothesis** is supported by the success in use of drugs that block dopamine receptor sites.

The most common drugs for treating schizophrenia are the **major tranquilizers** (also known as neuroleptics or antipsychotic drugs). Prior to the discovery of these drugs in the 1950s, little effective treatment was available for psychotics. Common reports depict veritable bedlams, involving great chaos, including excessive, dangerous aggression by some patients. Those who were violent would be restrained in straitjackets, perhaps even shackles and chains, or might be confined to cells. Potential weapons had to be kept from them. Once antipsychotic drugs were introduced, an impressive reduction usually occurred in the patients' level of agitation, which allowed for decreased use of physical restraints.

Chlorpromazine and thioridazine are two major tranquilizers frequently used to control aggressive schizophrenic patients. They are both very effective in blocking dopaminergic receptors, thus reducing the schizophrenic symptoms that produce aggression. According to Itil, dosage may be varied according to the individual's sex, age, and health, and the drug used may vary for individuals with different subtypes of schizophrenia or different patterns of aggression. An especially effective antiaggressive major tranquilizer for schizophrenics is a phenothiazine derivative called periciazine or propericiazine. Although not employed widely in the United States, it has been used extensively in Europe with good results in terms of controlling aggression associated with schizophrenia. It is not, however, as effective as other neuroleptics for controlling other schizophrenic problems such as the positive symptoms (e.g., hallucinations) described earlier. It also has a strong analgesic effect and has been used to control pain; part of its effectiveness on aggression may be related to this effect.

In cases of extremely dangerous aggressive outbursts by schizophrenics, drugs with short-term quieting effects are used. These may include sedatives or anxiolytics. These anxiolytics, including those commonly known as Valium and Librium, are called **minor tranquilizers**. As noted in Chapter 5, Tupin (1988) has suggested that tranquilizers be employed as a first step in treating the aggressive schizophrenic in an emergency situation.

Affective Disorders

A second common group of psychoses that includes aggression as a component is the **Mood Disorders** (earlier called **Major Affective Disorders**). Between 25 to 50 percent of institutionalized psychiatric patients are classified as having a mood disorder. As the name implies, the major component of this disorder is a disturbance of emotional mechanisms in an individual.

One type of affective disorder is called **Major Depressive Disorder**, also referred to as **unipolar depression**. It is characterized by excessive crying, pacing, low energy levels, poor sleep, and deficits in motivational systems such as those involved with sex and eating. Aggression also may occur; the depressed individuals may attempt suicide or the murder of people close to them, possibly in an attempt to spare them the suffering perceived by the depressed individual. Also, in a condition of agitated depression, individuals may become aggressive against others.

Bipolar Disorder involves both depression and mania. The individual usually is depressed for a relatively long period, possibly several months, and then shifts into a shorter manic phase. This phase is distinguished by abnormally increased energy in activity and thoughts and little sleep. The person may be euphoric or irritable and aggressive, with the latter occurring especially when unrealistic projects are blocked or ideas not accepted by others.

The affective disorders, like schizophrenia, seem to have a genetic basis; incidences are higher among blood relatives, and twin studies also have supported the idea of a genetic factor. There also is a possibility that major depressive disorder is linked to sex chromosomes, because women are much more likely to have this disorder. Incidences of bipolar disorder are approximately the same in men and women. In 1987, a marker for bipolar disorder was reported on chromosome 11 in an Amish population (Egeland, Gerhard, Pauls, Sussex, Kidd, Allen, Hostetter, & Housman, 1987) but this finding was later reported by many of the same investigators to be wrong or incomplete (Kelsoe, Ginns, Egeland, Gerhard, Goldstein, Bale, Pauls, Long, Kidd, Conte, Housman, & Paul 1989).

The physiological perturbations involved in affective disorders are not well established, or at least investigators have not arrived at a consensus as to what they are. Much evidence points to the involvement of the monoamines, especially serotonin and norepinephrine. For example, correlational studies have found links between suicide and low serotonergic activity, and between manic episodes and high noradrenergic levels. In the first studies, researchers measured the levels of a metabolite or breakdown product of serotonin in the cerebrospinal fluid taken from individuals who had attempted suicide (Träskman, Åsberg, Bertilsson, & Sjöstrand, 1981). Those individuals had much lower levels of this product in comparison to control subjects. People with levels of serotonin lower than normal are more likely to actually kill themselves (Roy, DeJong, & Linnoila, 1989).

As cited earlier, a relationship between norepinephrine levels and mania was found in the work of Bunney, Goodwin, and Murphy (1972), who studied men institutionalized with bipolar disorder. They conducted behavioral observations for depression or mania every eight hours, and took urine samples each day to be analyzed for neurotransmitter metabolites. The investigators found elevations in the levels of norepinephrine metabolites 24 hours prior to the onset of manic episodes. Thus, noradrenergic activity related to mania preceded behavioral manifestations, suggesting the possibility of either a causal role of noradrenalin or at least that it was correlated with some causal variable. In other words, the possibility of some undetected primary precipitating events operating to produce both the noradrenalin increase and mania could not be ruled out.

Although evidence shows that the noradrenergic or serotonergic levels are altered in affective disorders, the exact way in which the systems are involved is being debated. In one approach, investigators examined the effects of successful drug treatment attempts on various neuronal receptor sites and neurotransmitter systems. The drugs most commonly used for treating depression are the **tricyclic antidepressants**. The first part of their name derives from their basic molecular structure, which has three linked rings of carbon atoms. Their relevant biochemical effects are to increase either serotonergic or noradrenergic levels, which eventually result in alterations in the sensitivity of the neurotransmitter systems. (The exact nature of the change or changes is disputed.) Agitated patients may have their aggression controlled when given the serotonergic type (as occurs with the popular antidepressant Prozac that is not a tricyclic), which is more sedating, while others may receive the noradrenergic type in order to increase their activity levels and remove the depressed state that might lead to suicide and other aggressive behaviors.

Monoamine oxidase inhibitors (MAOI) are also used for depressed patients. By inhibiting the inhibitors (MAO) of monoamines, their amounts, including serotonin and noradrenalin, are increased. However, although MAOIs do give relief from depression and its associated aggression, they also can cause unwanted side effects. They may produce increases in blood pressure and can interact with certain foods and other drugs to produce extreme increases in monamine levels.

A third popular treatment for depressed patients is **electroconvulsive therapy** (ECT) or other shock therapies. Tricyclics take a few weeks to begin working; shock treatment produces a more rapidly acting effect if, for example, it is necessary to bring a patient more quickly out of a suicidal state. The use and exact nature of shock therapy's effects have been greatly debated, but it still is extensively relied on.

For bipolar disorder, a common treatment is **lithium carbonate.** Investigators have not determined the exact nature of the neurochemical effects of lithium, which may increase serotonergic levels and decrease levels of noradrenalin, dopamine, and acetylcholine. It has been very effective in treating the manic state, without pushing individuals back into depression. As we mentioned in Chapter 5, it has also been used to control the aggression of non-psychotics.

Brain Dysfunctions

The phrase **Mental Disorder Due to a General Medical Condition** (previously **Organic Mental Syndrome** or **Disorder**, or **Organic Brain Disorder**) is used to label individuals who present psychiatric problems that can be linked to identifiable impaired brain function. This impairment may be caused by various means, including trauma, illness, and sometimes drugs. If only drugs or toxins are involved, it is labeled a Substance-Induced Disorder. If the impairment involves damage of centers for the inhibition of aggression or excitation of centers for its production, aggression may increase. Depending on the source of the problem, some treatment is possible.

In cases where aggression is produced by the effects of continued drug use or ongoing disease, direct treatment of the source may help if the brain has not been extensively damaged or the problem is a functional one, such as a metabolic disorder that is affecting brain activities. Thus, direct treatment may include restrictions in access to drugs, supplementation with dietary components such as critical vitamins, or medical control of an infection.

In cases of permanent brain damage, neurosurgeons might remove a tumor or cyst that is producing pressure on neural structures or threatening to damage them if allowed to grow. Neurosurgery also may be necessary to remove irritating structures, such as scar tissue, that produce seizures. Vascular surgery may help restore the blood supply to areas affected by a stroke. Drug therapy may also be of help in controlling aggression associated with the brain dysfunction.

Drug-induced aggression is sometimes treated by administering minor tranquilizers. Neuroleptics have been used for cases of dementia. The drugs used vary according to the age, health, and accompanying signs of the problem. For example, older patients may be treated with a neuroleptic such as thioridazine, because it has few harmful side effects on their fragile cardiovascular systems. On the other hand, the use of neuroleptics in epileptic patients would be contraindicated, because they facilitate neuronal discharges. Instead, physicians use barbiturates and anxiolytics, in addition to antiepileptic drugs.

In cases of permanent brain damage, drug treatment may not completely control aggression. The drugs can also have undesirable side effects on basic body functions or other brain mechanisms affecting cognitive activities or motivational systems. One successful but rather rare alternative treatment has involved direct electrical stimulation of the brain, as we described in Chapter 4. For example, Heath, Llewellyn, and Rouchell (1979) reported moderate or significant long-term improvement in five organic brain syndrome patients during a procedure of intermittent stimulation in the medial cerebellum. The authors also reported success in patients with schizophrenia, depression, and seizure disorders.

Various combinations of therapies have been attempted to treat brain dysfunctions that produce aggression. The relatively new area of behavioral neuropsychology integrates information on the neural areas damaged and considers this in designing a successful behavioral treatment for a particular case. The work of Krawchik, also discussed in Chapter 4, is an example of this approach. She treated an aggressive young man who had brain damage from encephalitis. While his organically based aggression was controlled by psychosurgery and a neuroleptic, his environmentally maintained aggression was treated with behavioral techniques, including extinction and shaping.

Without using drugs, Liberman, Marshall, and Burke (1981) have rather successfully applied behavioral treatments to brain-damaged aggressive patients. They have obtained from 50 to 75 percent overall improvement by analyzing individuals' behavioral problems and developing effective strategies for decreasing inappropriate behaviors and increasing appropriate ones. One patient of Liberman et al., Fred, had frontal and parietal lobe damage (essentially a prefrontal lobotomy) that had been caused by an automobile accident. (Although prefrontal lobotomies usually produce a quieting effect, some involve structures that disinhibit aggression.) He was very abusive verbally and also hit and spit on people. His spitting behavior sometimes exceeded 1000 times per day in the psychiatric ward where he lived. His fights with others had left him with damaged teeth and broken bones. He also engaged in wall banging, door slamming, and theft. Researchers decided to punish his aggression with timeouts. When the typical 15-minute time out proved ineffective, it was extended to 24 hours. The reinforcers removed were tokens used on the ward, as well as all social interactions with the staff. After this measure was effective, the timeout durations were gradually reduced to the original 15 minutes. Once aggressive behaviors were under control, Fred was reinforced for increased positive behaviors. For example, his normal speech was strengthened to create a substitute for his previous lewd and aggressive talk.

A second patient of Liberman et al. was Joe, who had suffered a brain hemorrhage related to a congenital vascular malformation at the base of his brain. Joe had some motor problems that necessitated the use of a cane and at times a wheelchair. All this made him extremely dependent on others and apparently frustrated him. He had violent outbursts during which he attacked or shot at relatives and broke windows and damaged objects in his home. While he was living in a nursing home, he attacked an elderly roommate with his cane and killed him. To control his assaultive behavior, Joe was asked to sign a behavioral contract specifying that if no attacks occurred for seven days, he would be able to go home for a visit. He was given positive reinforcement for improved verbal and social behaviors. He was trained to assert himself verbally, rather than physically, in an appropriate manner. Role playing was used to teach Joe how to control his anger in an ascending hierarchy of situations that had previously provoked his outbursts. Thus, his outbursts were controlled by reinforcing their absence and teaching him appropriate substitute behaviors.

While Liberman and his colleagues had good success with their behavioral treatment, the results might have been even more promising if drug therapy had also been used. As with other problems of aggression, a broad treatment approach that attends to the biological, psychological, and social aspects of the individual situation and thus addresses several variables affecting aggression probably would be more effective than a more delimited approach.

Disorders Originating in Childhood

Attention-Deficit/Hyperactivity Disorder or **ADHD** sometimes is accompanied by aggressive behavior problems. While ADHD is typically associated with children, it sometimes also persists into adulthood. As we mentioned earlier, a common drug treatment for the problem involves psychostimulants. The basic problem with the attention of the ADHD patient seems to be the opposite of the schizophrenic, whose difficulties include extensive attention. While psychostimulants, such as the amphetamines, may put a normal person into a psychotic state—probably by excessively activating normal attentional mechanisms—these drugs seem to have a beneficial effect for the relatively inactive attentional mechanisms of the ADHD patient. Long-term use, however, also has deleterious effects on such body functions as growth, kidney activities, and appetite and possibly affects cognitive functions. Therefore, non- pharmaceutical treatments such as behavior therapy have increasingly been used.

A combination of environmental and biological approaches may be most helpful in treating ADHD. Hinshaw, Buhrmester, and Heller (1989) studied ADHD boys who had been trained to control their anger by cognitive behavior modification. After they were trained, the boys were given Ritalin or a placebo. Those who received the drug showed better self-control and less retaliation when taunted by their peers. Alternatively, the drugs might be used to help bring the hyperactivity under control initially, while the behavioral treatment could be used to achieve long-term control. Tupin (1988) cites success in adult hyperactives with the anticonvulsant carbamazepine, which is also used for affective disorders.

Mental Retardation, a type of developmental disorder, may be accompanied by uncontrolled aggressive behavior, although it is not necessarily a predominant characteristic of the retarded. Since the causes of retardation are numerous, it should not be surprising that a wide number of drugs have been used to treat the aggression associated with it. Thus, both major and minor tranquilizers, antiepileptics, and lithium have been successfully utilized in different cases. Behavioral treatments have also been used extensively to control aggression in the retarded, often in the absence of any drug treatment.

Two examples of the behavioral treatment of aggression associated with retardation are found in the work by Liberman, Marshall, and Burke cited above. The case of Barney involved a 40-year-old man who demonstrated a number of disturbing behaviors, including aggressive hugging of other people. His hugs were so strong that they injured others and therefore needed effective treatment. The basic procedure involved a combination of mild punishment and reinforcement for acceptable social behaviors. The punishment was a slap on his hand, accompanied by withdrawal of all other social attention—a type of timeout. In addition, Barney was reinforced with candy and praise or positive attention when he interacted with others without grabbing them. His grabbing behaviors directed against ward staff members decreased substantially during the first two weeks of treatment. Later, the treatment was extended successfully to control his grabbing of people outside the ward.

Liberman et al. also treated Sally, a moderately retarded 20 year old. Sally had exhibited numerous destructive behaviors directed at both ward property and people. In addition, she stalked other people, following them around and standing closely in front of them in a provoking way. She was treated with a combination of a 15-minute timeout for any hitting and shoving, along with positive reinforcement for appropriate social behaviors. In the latter procedure, she was reinforced with one minute of undivided staff attention for approaching a staff member and interacting appropriately, maintaining an appropriate distance and posture, and speaking clearly enough to be understood. Again the treatment was successful in reducing her aggressive behaviors, while increasing desirable ones. Carr, Newsom, and Binkoff (1980) worked with a boy who aggressed to escape demands made on him, such as following an order. They successfully extinguished the aggressive behaviors and trained a substitute behavior.

Conduct Disorder occurs primarily in male children, more commonly in those whose parents have Antisocial Personality Disorder (see p. 225) or other psychiatric problems. The DSM-IV (see p. 40) characterizes conduct disorder as involving persistent violations of the rights of others or social norms. More than half the behavioral criteria for this diagnosis include persistent aggression against other people, animals, or property. Behaviors range from threats and fighting to rape and assault (even, rarely, homicide). There may be little concern for the feelings of others and few indications of remorse for the acts committed. Conduct disorder children are often also ADHD individuals. Initiation of conduct disorder problems in childhood, prior to the age of 10 (as opposed to after) is more likely to involve aggression followed by problems with aggression as adults.

The studies of juvenile delinquency discussed in Chapter 10 probably included many individuals with conduct disorders. Itil (1981) indicates that some neuroleptics, especially pericyazine, have been successfully used in conduct disorder cases, both for acute outbursts as well as treatment of longer-term aggressive problems. In cases where EEGs are abnormal, antiepileptics have also been found helpful in controlling aggression. Behavioral training in social skills could also be very effective in such cases and Chapter 10 discussed some of these approaches. Stumphauzer (1981) has made a start at developing an ethnobehavioral analysis and treatment of East Los Angeles gang members. Also, the teaching-family approach of Phillips and his colleagues shows good promise. Although it has primarily been developed to treat the pre-delinquent, we would not be surprised if they have dealt with some conduct disorder cases as well.

Severe Aggressive Disorders Found in Adults

Antisocial Personality Disorder is a diagnosis limited to individuals over 18 years of age. It may include individuals who are commonly called sociopaths or, more archaically, psychopaths. It involves long-term patterns of undesirable behavior that started with conduct disorder before the individual was 15. At times it follows in individuals who have been labeled as having ADHD at a younger age. Basically, it involves continuous antisocial behavior that violates the rights of others, and often includes being aggressive against them. Sociopathic individuals react in abnormally reduced ways to noxious stimuli (e.g., see Hare, Frazelle, & Cox, 1978). Again, as we noted for the conduct disorders, individuals with the antisocial personality classification constitute a number of the cases of aggression problems discussed earlier. For example, some classifications of rapists include a sociopathic individual.

Several drug treatments have been successful in treating antisocial personality disorder, according to Itil, including his favored neuroleptic, pericyazine. In cases of residual hyperactivity that persists into adulthood, psychostimulants are reported to be helpful. In addition, anti-androgens seem to work in cases where sexual aggression has been involved. Further, lithium has been used with success by such investigators as Sheard, who worked with violent prisoners. Behavioral treatment of adults with antisocial personality has not been notably successful in general, in contrast to more promising results with younger delinquents.

Intermittent Explosive Disorder may be differentiated in part from the antisocial personality diagnosis because it involves several discrete episodes of assaultive behavior directed against others or against property, rather than being part of a consistent pattern of aggressive behavior. The episodes occur with rapid onset, out of proportion to their antecedents, and are followed by a rapid offset. For this reason, they sometimes have been referred to as "spells." Indeed, they may appear to resemble epileptic seizures in that they may be preceded by an affective change and include autonomic nervous system activities. The episodes may also be accompanied by subtle sensory changes. Afterwards, the patient may have amnesia for what occurred during the episode. If the patient is aware or is told of some violence that occurred, he or she usually expresses remorse.

Despite the similarities of explosive disorder episodes to an epileptic crisis, confirmation of brain tumors or seizure disorders in the patients historically has not been high. In fact, the DSM IV, while indicating that some neurological abnormalities (e.g., in reflexes), EEG slowing, and serotonin alterations may be present, differentiates the individuals with this disorder from those with specific medical causes of aggression, such as identified brain damage. Thus, general sources of neurological disturbances, such as infantile seizures, head trauma, and encephalitis can be antecedents in people classified as having the disorder, but any disturbance that produces damage to a brain structure that inhibits aggression, for example, would result in the General Medical Condition classification described above.

Drug treatment of the explosive disorder patient has varied with individual cases. For rapid control of acute episodes of violence, barbiturates and minor tranquilizers are helpful. The use of tricyclic antidepressants has been tried but found to exacerbate the problem in certain cases (Monroe, 1970). In individuals where an EEG indicates a seizure disorder (and who therefore would not be classified as having explosive disorder under DSM IV), antiepileptics have helped control the aggression. In situations where a temporal lobe focus is found, special anticonvulsants, such as carbamazepine, are especially beneficial in controlling the psychomotor seizure disorder. In special cases, psychosurgery has been used to control the temporal lobe seizure disorder and its accompanying aggressive behaviors. Finally, in cases where an EEG indicates no seizure disorder, psychostimulants offer relief at times.

Itil has developed procedures based on pretreatment EEGs for selecting drugs for the explosive disorder patient as well as patients in other classifications. He has found some patients who have abnormally slow EEGs, others with abnormally fast EEGs, and still others who have epileptiform (resembling epilepsy) EEG activities. Drugs are selected to normalize the patterns. Patients who have very slow (delta) waves are given stimulants, those who have moderately slow (theta) waves receive certain anxiolytics, those with fast waves get specific neuroleptics, and, of course, epileptic patients are given anticonvulsant drugs. Perhaps with the more sophisticated EEG analysis and brain function imaging techniques that are becoming available, this method will be found useful.

An example of a behavioral approach for controlling explosive behavior is found in the work of Frederiksen and Rainwater (1981) with institutionalized young male psychiatric patients. The 18 patients had histories of several episodes of sudden, uncontrolled violence and were distressed and remorseful concerning their acts. Thus, they essentially fit the definition of intermittent explosive disorder.

A behavioral analysis of their problems showed that they had a number of difficulties, including social skills deficits—they were either too aggressive or too passive. They also had atypical cognitive behaviors, including mislabeling of others' behaviors as aggressive, and inappropriate expectations that others would act negatively instead of positively toward them. They reported elevated physiological arousal during their episodes (e.g., cardiovascular functions, respiration, and muscle tension increased), which were sometimes triggered by alcohol consumption. The aggressive behaviors seemed to be supported by their consequences. These men had often been reinforced (they gained what they wanted via aggression) and were rarely punished, at least not immediately.

Frederiksen and Rainwater developed a multiple approach for treating their clients' various problems. They trained them in social skills, teaching them alternative responses to situations that previously had caused their outbursts. They employed instruction, modeling, and role playing, showing them how to recognize trouble-causing interactions and how to handle these interactions more appropriately. They employed cognitive behavior modification to help the men restructure their inappropriate cognitive behaviors. They trained them in deep-muscle relaxation to aid in controlling any excessive physiological arousal, and used self-management techniques to help monitor any drinking problems. These techniques included training them to recognize situations where drinking might take place and develop strategies to prevent it from occurring.

The results of treatment were promising, although not universally successful. Generally, social skills were improved in the nine patients who completed treatment. For example, the rate of making appropriate, non-threatening requests of others went from 0 to nearly 100 percent. Also, cognitive behaviors were reported to be less negative, and some improvement of physiological arousal to problem situations was evident. All five patients who completed the program and were available for a follow-up assessment were reported to have a decrease in the severity and frequency of their outbursts.

Frederiksen and Rainwater's approach involved a very extensive treatment that might not be feasible in many cases. Also, they had a small number of clients, half of whom dropped out of the program. Thus, the generality of the results remains to be determined and some way must be found to reduce the rate of attrition. However, these results are promising and may provide a good starting point for future efforts. As in the other psychiatric problem areas in this chapter, these populations are difficult to treat. For the most part, progress has been made in understanding both biological and environmental contributions to their problems and in applying this understanding to help control the aggression involved. Significant progress in this area should occur in the near future as new methodological advances are made and broader approaches are utilized incorporating biological and environmental factors.

SUMMARY

Aggression is a component of the behaviors in part of the psychiatric population. Although there is disagreement over the number of cases that involve aggression, the problem should be considered serious. Major treatment approaches have included the use of drugs and behavioral techniques.

The two major psychoses—schizophrenia and mood disorders—can both involve increased aggression. The principal biological problem in schizophrenia is believed to be an excess of the neurotransmitter dopamine. Antipsychotic drugs effectively block dopamine and help control aggressive and other problem behaviors. The bases of the mood disorders are not as clear as that for schizophrenia, although much evidence supports involvement of norepinephrine and serotonin. Drugs are selected to elevate one or both of these for depressed patients, and lithium is commonly used for manic patients.

Brain dysfunctions can be treated by several medical techniques, including neurosurgery, drugs, and even brain stimulation. Behavioral treatments have also been successful by rewarding nonaggressive behaviors.

Problems originating in childhood, such as hyperactivity and retardation, may include excessive aggressive behaviors. Successful treatment has resulted from both drug and behavioral approaches.

The adult with antisocial personality disorder (the sociopath) primarily has been treated with drugs, since behavioral treatments have yielded relatively little success. It is evident from the large prison populations that no treatment approach has been consistently successful.

Intermittent explosive disorder, which includes outbursts of assaultive behaviors, has many characteristics resembling those of seizures associated with aggression. However, brain dysfunction is usually not found, and the DSM IV excludes brain-damaged individuals from this category. Some in the past who have had brain damage have been helped with brain surgery or antiseizure drugs. A treatment dealing with behavioral as well as physiological components of the problem may be a productive approach.

Suggested Reading

Roth, L. H. (Ed.) (1987). *Clinical treatment of the violent person.* New York: Guilford

Postscript

In the work you have just read, I have attempted to inform you about some of the principal causes of aggressive behavior. I have addressed the contributions that derive from the biology of individuals, their learning experiences, and the people who surround them. The biopsychosocial approach taken here recognizes that multiple interacting variables contribute to the determination of aggression.

In the area of biology, I have discussed how genetic mechanisms operate to increase aggression and how sexual and hormonal factors may increase or decrease it. I have also presented evidence about how various areas of the brain contribute to the control of aggression. Further, we examined the role of brain chemicals in controlling aggression, which led to describing how various drugs can affect aggressive behaviors.

The effects of learning experiences on aggression were treated in terms of two major approaches. We saw how some stimuli can elicit aggression without training and how these effects can be extended to new sets of stimuli via classical conditioning. Then I discussed how the consequences of aggressive behaviors can increase or decrease future occurrences of the behaviors via operant conditioning.

I described the effects of other people on aggression in the context of social learning. Here, I discussed how the aggressive acts of others, observed either directly or symbolically, may influence the aggression of the observer.

In the last part of the book, I gave illustrations of how the various causes of aggression operate in four major areas of contemporary concern. I talked of how aggression is produced in the young delinquent. I discussed the causes of both physical and sexual aggression directed at children and at women, both in the home and outside it. Finally, I depicted the incidence and control of aggression associated with various psychiatric classifications.

I hope that you have finished this book with a greater knowledge of the many causes of aggression, an appreciation of the possibilities for controlling it, as well as an understanding of some of the reasons why we have failed to effectively control it. One reason for this lack of success is in the investigative approaches of popular attempts to determine the causes of aggression. I devoted a significant amount of the book to basic methodological questions, such as the importance of both an adequate definition of the behavior and a reliable measurement technique as a prerequisite to determining the causes of aggression. I indicated that many who have studied aggression have failed to define and measure it appropriately. Further, I reviewed somewhat controversial challenges to commonly accepted "truths" about contributions to aggression in such areas as the media, child abuse, sexual assault, and psychiatric populations. My purpose was to help you to view the work on the causes of aggression more critically and encourage you to carefully analyze the various attempts to understand aggression. Thus, I expect that you will understand better why we have not yet controlled it.

In my opinion, adequate control of aggression is not an unrealistic goal for a society. It certainly is a reality in innumerable discrete settings. Although, practically, we probably cannot eliminate problematic aggression, we certainly can do much to diminish its incidence. We do know a great deal about the causes of aggression; what we need is a comprehensive approach, with an appreciation for the various contributions of the biology, learning mechanisms, and social experiences of individuals. There is no one factor that overwhelmingly produces aggression. Therefore, individuals who focus on "*the* cause" of aggression will do little except to produce an unwarranted sense of accomplishment for themselves. The attempts to control media violence and pornography may come to mind as examples. Further, any successful approach to controlling aggression must be based on the type of objectively supported information we have discussed, not on unfounded opinions of persuasive "experts" or self-serving demagogues.

Continued research on the causes of aggression should benefit from the dramatic advances being made in the biological area. I expect that developments in genetic sequencing, neuroanatomical imaging, and neurochemical analysis will facilitate further discovery and possibly control of the important variables related to these areas. Applications of neuroanatomical work to the area of neuropsychological testing should help us analyze more accurately brain dysfunctions related to aggression. Advances in the biochemical area should result in more efficient pharmaceutical means of controlling aggression. Meanwhile, unaccompanied by the "whistles and bells" of the instrumentation used in biological approaches, further research on the environmental contributions to aggression will result in sure advances in this area. More effective behavioral approaches will be developed and applied, increasingly integrated with biological approaches.

Education has the potential to provide a major contribution to the control of aggression. Such education would be a preventative measure that informs individuals and caregivers about the causes of aggression. Starting with pre- and postnatal health care, an awareness of the causes of aggression would progress through the raising and formal education of children, and continue into adult social settings. Unfortunately and realistically, however, I do not see modern society willing to invest adequate resources in such extensive efforts, because they are—mistakenly—perceived to have only uncertain, delayed benefits. We are much more likely to resort to threats or punishment to control aggression. I would hope, however, that the materials presented in this book will serve to contribute to this educational process and thus facilitate progress in the understanding and control of aggression.

References

Abel, E. L. (1977). The relationship between cannabis and violence: A review. *Psychological Bulletin, 84*(2), 193–209.

Abel, G. G., Becker, J. V., Murphy, W. D., & Flanagan, B. (1981). Identifying dangerous child molesters. In R. B. Stuart (Ed.), *Violent behavior: Social learning approaches to prediction, management and treatment* (pp. 116–137). New York: Brunner/Mazel Publishers.

Abel, G. G., Becker, J. V., & Skinner, L. J. (1987). Behavioral approaches to treatment of the violent sex offender. In L. H. Roth (Ed.), *Clinical treatment of the violent person* (pp. 95–118). New York: Guilford.

Abel, G. G., Blanchard, E. B., & Becker, J. V. (1978). An integrated treatment program for rapists. In R. T. Rada (Ed.), *Clinical aspects of the rapist*. New York: Grune and Stratton.

Adamec, R. (1976). Hypothalamic and extrahypothalamic substrates of predatory attack suppression and the influence of hunger. *Brain Research, 106*, 57–69.

Adams, D. B. (1971). Defence and territorial behaviour dissociated by hypothalamic lesions in the rat. *Nature, 232*, 573–574.

Ajmone-Marsan, C., & Ziven, L. S. (1970). Factors related to the occurrence of typical paroxysmal abnormalities in the EEG records of epileptic patients. *Epilepsia, 11*, 361–381.

Alpert, J. E., Cohen, D. J., Shaywitz, B. A., & Piccirillo, M. (1981). Neurochemical and behavioral organization: Disorders of attention, activity, and aggression. In D. O. Lewis (Ed.), *Vulnerabilities to delinquency* (pp. 109–171). New York: SP Medical and Scientific Books.

Alves, C. N., Goyos, A. C., & Carlini, E. A. (1973). Aggressiveness induced by marihuana and other psychotropic drugs in REM sleep deprived rats. *Pharmacology, Biochemistry, and Behavior, 1*, 183–189.

American Psychiatric Association (1987). *Diagnostic and statistical manual of mental disorders* (Third, Revised ed.). Washington, DC: American Psychiatric Association.

American Psychiatric Association (1994). *Diagnostic and statistical manual of mental disorders* (Fourth ed.). Washington, DC: American Psychiatric Association.

American Psychological Society. (1992). Human capital initiative: report of the national behavioral science research agenda committee. *American Psychological Society Observer, 5*(February–Special Issue), 1–33.

Amir, M. (1971). *Patterns of forcible rape.* Chicago: University of Chicago Press.

Amsel, A., & Roussel, J. (1952). Motivational properties of frustration: I. Effect on a running response of the addition of frustration to the motivational complex. *Journal of Experimental Psychology, 43*, 363–368.

Anderson, C. A. (1989). Temperature and aggression: The ubiquitous effects of heat on the occurrence of human violence. *Psychological Bulletin, 106*, 74–96.

Andy, O. J., & Jurko, M. F. (1972). Thalamotomy for hyperresponsive syndrome: Lesions in the centermedianum and intralaminar nuclei. In E. Hitchcock, L. Laitinen, & K. Vaernet (Ed.), *Psychosurgery* (pp. 127–135). Springfield, IL: Charles C Thomas.

Antelman, S. M., Rowland, N. E., & Fisher, A. E. (1976). Stress related recovery from lateral hypothalamic hyperphagia. *Brain Research, 102*, 346–350.

Åsberg, M., Bertilsson, L., & Mårtensson, B. (1984). CSF monoamine metabolites, depression, and suicide. In E. Usdin, M. Åsberg, L. Bertilsson, & F. Sjöqvist (Ed.), *Frontiers in biochemical and pharmacological research in depression* (vol. 39, pp. 87–97). New York: Raven Press.

Ayllon, T., & Azrin, N. H. (1968). *The token economy: A motivational system for therapy and rehabilitation.* New York: Appleton-Century-Crofts.

Azrin, N. H., & Hutchinson, R. R. (1967). Conditioning of the aggressive behavior of pigeons by a fixed-interval schedule of reinforcement. *Journal of the Experimental Analysis of Behavior, 10*, 395–402.

Azrin, N. H., Hutchinson, R. R., & Hake, D. F. (1966). Extinction-induced aggression. *Journal of the Experimental Analysis of Behavior, 9*, 191–204.

Azrin, N. H., Hutchinson, R. R., & Hake, D. F. (1967). Attack avoidance and escape reactions to aversive shock. *Journal of the Experimental Analysis of Behavior, 10*, 131–148.

Azrin, N. H., Hutchinson, R. R., & McLaughlin, R. (1965). The opportunity for aggression as an operant reinforcer during aversive stimulation. *Journal of the Experimental Analysis of Behavior, 8*, 171–180.

Azrin, N. H., Hutchinson, R. R., & Sallery, R. D. (1964). Pain-aggression toward inanimate objects. *Journal of the Experimental Analysis of Behavior, 7*, 223–228.

Badawy, A. A.-B. (1986). Alcohol as a psychopharmacological agent. In P. F. Brain (Ed.), *Alcohol and aggression* (pp. 55–83). Dover, NH: Croom Helm.

Bagley, C. (1990). Is the prevalence of child sexual abuse declining? Evidence from a random sample of 750 young adult women. *Psychological Reports, 66*, 1037–1038.

Bancroft, J. (1993). The premenstrual syndrome—a reappraisal of the concept and the evidence. *Psychological medicine, Monograph supplement 24*, 1–52.

Bancroft, J., Williamson, L., Warner, P., Rennie, D., & Smith, S. K. (1993). Perimenstrual complaints in women complaining of PMS, menorrhagia, and dysmenorrhea: Toward a dismantling of the premenstrual syndrome. *Psychosomatic medicine, 55*, 133–145.

Bandler, R. A. (1971a). Direct chemical stimulation of the thalamus: Effects on aggressive behavior in the rat. *Brain Research, 26*, 81–93.

Bandler, R. A. (1971b). Chemical stimulation of the rat midbrain and aggressive behaviour. *Nature, 229*, 222–223.

Bandler, R. J. (1975). Predatory aggression: Midbrain-pontine junction rather than hypothalamus as the critical structure? *Aggressive Behavior, 1*, 261–266.

Bandler, R. J., & Abeyewardene, S. (1981). Visual aspects of centrally elicited attack behavior in the cat: "Patterned reflexes" associated with selection of and approach to a rat. *Aggressive Behavior, 7*, 19–39.

Bandler, R. J., & Flynn, J. P. (1972). Control of somatosensory fields for striking during hypothalamically elicited attack. *Brain Research, 38*, 197–201.

Bandura, A. (1969). *Principles of behavior modification*. New York: Holt, Rinehart and Winston.

Bandura, A. (1973). *Aggression: A social learning analysis*. Englewood Cliffs, NJ: Prentice-Hall, Inc.

Bandura, A. (1994). Social cognitive theory of mass communication. In J. Bryant, & D. Zillman (Ed.), *Media effects: Advances in theory and research* (pp. 61–90). Hillsdale, NJ: Lawrence Erlbaum Associates.

Bandura, A., Ross, D., & Ross, S. A. (1961). Transmission of aggression through imitation of aggressive models. *Journal of Abnormal and Social Psychology, 63*, 575–582.

Bard, P. (1928). A diencephalic mechanism for the expression of rage with special reference to the sympathetic nervous system. *The American Journal of Physiology, 84*, 490–515.

Bard, P., & Mountcastle, V. B. (1948). Some forebrain mechanisms involved in expression of rage with special reference to suppression of angry behavior. *Research Publication of the Association for Research in Nervous and Mental Disease, 25*, 362–404.

Bard, P., & Rioch, D. M. (1937). A study of 4 cats deprived of neocortex and additional portions of the forebrain. *Johns Hopkins Hospital Bulletin, 60*, 73–147.

Barfield, R. J. (1984). Reproductive hormones and aggressive behavior. In K. J. Flannelly, R. J. Blanchard, & D. C. Blanchard (Ed.), *Biological perspectives on aggression* (vol. 169, pp. 105–134). New York: Alan R. Liss, Inc.

Barfield, R. J., & Sachs, B. D. (1970). Effect of shock on copulatory behavior in castrate male rats. *Hormones and Behavior, 1*, 247–253.

Barinaga, M. (1995). Researchers broaden the attack on Parkinson's disease. *Science*, pp. 455–456.

Barlow, D. H., & Abel, G. G. (1981). Recent developments in assessment and treatment of paraphilias and gender-identity disorders. In W. E. Craighead, A. E. Kazdin, & M. J. Mahoney (Ed.), *Behavior modification: Principles, issues, and applications* (pp. 337–356). Boston: Houghton Mifflin Co.

Baron, R. A. (1972). Aggression as a function of ambient temperature and prior anger arousal. *Journal of Personality and Social Psychology, 21*, 183–189.

Baron, R. A. (1974). Sexual arousal and physical aggression: The inhibiting influence of "cheesecake" and nudes. *Bulletin of the Psychonomic Society, 29*, 217–219.

Baron, R. A. (1976). The reduction of human aggression: A field study of the influence of incompatible reactions. *Journal of Applied Social Psychology, 6*, 260–274.

Baron, R. A. (1977). *Human aggression*. New York: Plenum Press.

Baron, R. A. (1978a). The influence of hostile and nonhostile humor upon physical aggression. *Bulletin of Personality and Social Psychology, 4*, 77–80.

Baron, R. A. (1978b). Aggression-inhibiting influence of sexual humor. *Journal of Personality and Social Psychology, 36*, 189–197.

Baron, R. A. (1979). Aggression, empathy, and race: Effects of victim's pain cues, victim's race, and level of instigation on physical aggression. *Journal of Applied Social Psychology, 9*, 103–114.

Baron, R. A. (1983). The control of human aggression: A strategy based on incompatible responses. In R. G. Geen, & E. I. Donnerstein (Ed.), *Aggression: Theoretical and empirical reviews* (vol. 2. Issues in Research, pp. 173–190). New York: Academic Press.

Baron, R. A., & Ball, R. L. (1974). The aggression-inhibiting influence of nonhostile humor. *Journal of Experimental Social Psychology, 10*, 23–33.

Baron, R. A., & Bell, P. A. (1975). Aggression and heat: Mediating effects of prior provocation and exposure to an aggressive model. *Journal of Personality and Social Psychology, 31*, 825–832.

Baron, R. A., & Bell, P. A. (1977). Sexual arousal and aggression by males: Effects of type of erotic stimuli and prior provocation. *Journal of Personality and Social Psychology, 35*, 79–87.

Baron, R. A., & Kepner, C. R. (1970). Model's behavior and attraction toward the model as determinants of adult aggressive behavior. *Journal of Personality and Social Psychology, 14*, 335–344.

Baron, R. A., & Ransberger, V. M. (1978). Ambient temperature and the occurrence of collective violence: The "long hot summer" revisited. *Journal of Personality and Social Psychology, 36*(351–360).

Beach, F. A. (1948). *Hormones and behavior.* New York: Hoefer.

Beeman, E. A. (1947). The effect of male hormones on aggressive behavior in mice. *Physiological Zoology, 20*, 373–405.

Beleslin, D. B., & Stefanović-Denić, K. (1986). A dose response study of aggressive behavioral effects of intracerebroventricular injections of carbachol in cats. *Physiology and Behavior , 36*, 75–78.

Bell, P. A., & Baron, R. A. (1981). Ambient temperature and human violence. In P. F. Brain, & D. Benton (Ed.), *Multidisciplinary approaches to aggression research* (pp. 421–430). New York: Elsevier/North-Holland Biomedical Press.

Benjamin, R., Mazzarins, H., & Kupfersmid, J. (1983). The effect of time-out (TO) duration on assaultiveness in psychiatrically hospitalized children. *Aggressive Behavior, 9*, 21–27.

Benton, D. (1981a). The measurement of aggression in the laboratory. In P. F. Brain, & D. Benton (Ed.), *The biology of aggression* (pp. 487–502). Alphen aan den Rijn, The Netherlands: Sijthoff & Noordhoff.

Benton, D. (1981b). The extrapolation from animals to man: The example of testosterone and aggression. In P. F. Brain, & D. Benton (Ed.), *Multidisciplinary approaches to aggression research* (pp. 401–418). New York: Elsevier/North Holland Biomedical Press.

Berkow, R. (Ed.). (1987). *The Merck Manual* (Fifteenth). Rahway, NJ: Merck Sharp and Dohme Research Laboratories.

Berkowitz, L. (1983). Aversively stimulated aggression. Some parallels and differences in research with animals and humans. *American Psychologist, 38*, 1135–1144.

Berkowitz, L. (1993). *Aggression: Its causes, consequences, and control.* New York: McGraw-Hill, Inc.

Berkowitz, L., & Geen, R. G. (1966). Film violence and the cue properties of available targets. *Journal of Personality and Social Psychology, 3*, 525–530.

Berkowitz, L., & LePage, A. (1967). Weapons as aggression-eliciting stimuli. *Journal of Personality and Social Psychology, 7*, 202–207.

Berlin, F. S. (1988). Issues in the exploration of biological factors contributing to the etiology of the "sex offender," plus some ethical considerations. *Annals of the New York Academy of Sciences, 528*, 183–192.

Bernard, B. K., & Paolino, R. M. (1974). Time-dependent changes in brain biogenic amine dynamics following castration in male rats. *Journal of Neurochemistry, 22*, 951–956.

Berry, M. S., & Brain, P. F. (1986). Neurophysiological and endocrinological consequences of alcohol. In P. F. Brain (Ed.), *Alcohol and aggression* (pp. 19–54). Dover, NH: Croom Helm.

Berry, M. S., & Smoothy, R. (1986). A critical evaluation of claimed relationships between alcohol intake and aggression in infra-human animals. In P. F. Brain (Ed.), *Alcohol and aggression* (pp. 84–137). Dover, NH: Croom Helm.

Berry, R. M., & Jack, E. C. (1971). The effect of temperature upon shock-elicited aggression in rats. *Psychonomic Science, 23*, 341–343.

Bioulac, B., Benezech, M., Renaud, B., & Noel., B. (1978). Biogenic amines in 47,XYY syndrome. *Neuropsychobiology, 4*, 366–370.

Björkvist, K., & Niemelä, P. (Eds.). (1992). *Of mice and women: Aspects of female aggression.* New York: Academic Press.

Blanchard, R. J., Takahashi, L. K., & Blanchard, D. C. (1977). The development of intruder attack in colonies of laboratory rats. *Animal Learning and Behavior, 5*, 365–368.

Blumer, D., & Migeon, C. (1973). Treatment of impulsive behavior disorders in males with medroxy-progesterone acetate. *American Psychiatric Association meetings*

Boshka, S. C., Weisman, M. H., & Thor, D. H. (1966). A technique for inducing aggression in rats utilizing morphine withdrawal. *Psychological Record, 16*, 541–543.

Bostow, D. E., & Bailey, J. B. (1969). Modification of severe disruptive and aggressive behavior using brief timeout and reinforcement procedures. *Journal of Applied Behavior Analysis, 2*, 31–37.

Brady, J. V., & Nauta, W. J. H. (1953). Subcortical mechanisms in emotional behavior: Affective changes following septal forebrain lesions in the albino rat. *Journal of Comparative and Physiological Psychology, 46*, 339–346.

Brain, P. F. (1983). Pituitary-gonadal influences on social aggression. In B. B. Svare (Ed.), *Hormones and aggressive behavior* (pp. 3–25). New York: Plenum.

Brain, P. F. (1986). Alcohol and aggression—the nature of a presumed relationship. In P. F. Brain (Ed.), *Alcohol and aggression* (pp. 212–223). Dover, NH: Croom Helm.

Brain, P. F., & Benton, D. (Eds.). (1981a). *The biology of aggression.* Alphen aan de Rijn, The Netherlands: Sijthoff & Noordhoff.

Brain, P. F., & Benton, D. (Eds.). (1981b). *Multidisciplinary approaches to aggression research.* Amsterdam: Elsevier/North-Holland Biomedical Press.

Brain, P. F., Simon, V., Hasan, S., Martinez, M., & Castano, D. (1988). The potential of anti-estrogens as centrally-acting antihostility agents: Recent animal data. *International Journal of Neuroscience, 41*, 169–177.

Bremer, F. (1936). Nouvelles recherches sur le mechanisme du sommeil. *Comptes Rendus de la Societe de Biologie, Paris, 122*, 339–346.

Bremer, J. (1959). *Asexualization: A follow-up study of 244 cases.* New York: Macmillan.

Bronson, F. H., & Desjardins, C. (1968). Aggression in adult mice: Modification by neonatal injections of gonadal hormones. *Science, 161*, 705–706.

Brower, K. J., Blow, F. C., Eliopulos, G. A., & Beresford, T. P. (1989). Anabolic androgenic steroids and suicide. *The American Journal of Psychiatry, 146*, 1075.

Brown, G. L., Ballanger, J. C., Minichiello, M. D., & Goodwin, F. K. (1979). Human aggression and its relationship to cerebrospinal fluid 5–hydroxyindoleacetic acid, 3–methoxy-4–hydroxylphenylglycol, and homovanillic acid. In M. Sandler (Ed.), *Psychopharmacology of aggression* (pp. 131–148). New York: Raven Press.

Brown, G. L., Goodwin, F. K., & Bunney, W. E., Jr. (1982). Human aggression and suicide: Their relationship to neuropsychiatric diagnoses and serotonin metabolism. In B. T. Ho, J. C. Schoolar, & E. Usdin (Eds.), *Serotonin in biological psychiatry* (vol. 34, pp. 287–307). New York: Raven Press.

Brunner, H. G., Nelen. M., Breakefield, X. O., Ropers, H. H., & van Oost, B.A. (1993). Abnormal behavior associated with a point mutation in the structural gene for monamine oxidase A. *Science, 262*, 578–580.

Bunney, W. E., Goodwin, F. K., & Murphy, D. L. (1972). The "switch process" in manic-depressive illness. III. Theoretical implications. *Archives of General Psychiatry, 27*, 312–317.

Bushman, B. J., & Cooper, H. M. (1990). Effects of alcohol on human aggression: An integrative research review. *Psychological Bulletin, 107*, 341–354.

Buss, A. H., Booker, A., & Buss, E. (1972). Firing a weapon and aggression. *Journal of Personality and Social Psychology, 22*, 296–302.

Caggiula, A. R. (1972). Shock-elicited copulation and aggression in male rats. *Journal of Comparative and Physiological Psychology, 80*, 393–397.

Candland, D. K., Bryan, D. C., Nazar, K. J., Kopf, K. J., & Sendor, M. (1970). Squirrel monkey heart rate during formation of status orders. *Journal of Comparative and Physiological Psychology, 70*, 417–423.

Cannon, W. B., & Britton, S. W. (1925). Studies on the conditions of activity in endocrine glands: XV, Pseudoaffective medulliadrenal secretion. *The American Journal of Physiology, 72*, 283–294.

Cantwell, D. P. (1981). Hyperactivity and antisocial behavior revisited: A critical review of the literature. In D. O. Lewis (Ed.), *Vulnerabilities to delinquency* (pp. 21–38). New York: SP Medical and Scientific Books.

Caplan, P. J., McCurdy-Myers, J., & Gans, M. (1992). Should 'premenstrual syndrome' be called a psychiatric abnormality? *Feminism and psychology, 2*(1), 27–44.

Caprara, G. V., Renzi, P., D'Augello, D., D'Imperio, G., Rielli, I., & Travaglia, G. (1986). Interpolating physical exercise between instigation to aggress and aggression: The role of irritability and emotional susceptibility. *Aggressive Behavior, 12*, 83–91.

Carder, B., & Olson, J. (1972). Marihuana and shock induced aggression in rats. *Physiology and Behavior, 8*, 599–602.

Carlini, E. A. (1978). Effects of cannabinoid compounds on aggressive behavior. *Modern Problems in Pharmacopsychiatry, 13*, 82–102.

Carlini, E. A., & Mazur, J. (1970). Development of fighting behavior in starved rats by chronic administration of (—)delta-9-tetra cannabinol and cannabis extracts. *Communications in Behavioral Biology, 5*, 57–61.

Carlsmith, J. M., & Anderson, C. A. (1979). Ambient temperature and the occurrence of collective violence: A new analysis. *Journal of Personality and Social Psychology, 37*, 337–344.

Carr, E., Newsom, C. D., & Binkoff, J. A. (1980). Escape as a factor in the aggressive behavior of two retarded children. *Journal of Applied Behavior Analysis, 13*, 101–117.

Carroll, B. J., & Steiner, M. (1978). The psychobiology of premenstrual dysphoria: The role of prolactin. *Psychoneuroendocrinology, 3*, 171–180.

Carroll, D., & O'Callaghan, M. A. J. (1981). Psychosurgery and the control of aggression. In P. F. Brain, & D. Benton (Ed.), *The biology of aggression* (pp. 457–471). Rockville, MD: Sijthoff and Noordhoff.

Chaffee, S. H. (1972). Television and adolescent aggression. In G. A. Comstock, & E. A. Rubinstein (Eds.), *Television and social behavior* (vol. 3). Washington, DC: U. S. Government Printing Office.

Cherek, D. R. (1984). Effects of cigarette smoking on human aggressive behavior. In K. J. Flannelly, R. J. Blanchard, & D. C. Blanchard (Eds.), *Biological perspectives on aggression* (vol. 169, pp. 333–344). New York: Alan R. Liss, Inc.

Chi, C. C., & Flynn, J. P. (1971). Neural pathways associated with hypothalamically elicited attack behavior in cats. *Science, 171*, 703–705.

Christiansen, K., & Knussmann, R. (1987). Androgen levels and components of aggressive behavior in men. *Hormones and Behavior, 21*, 170–180.

Coffey, B. J. (1988). Child psychiatry problems. In J. P. Tupin, R. I. Shader, & D. S. Harnett, & (Eds.), *Handbook of clinical psychopharmacology* (pp. 211–244). Northvale, NJ: Jason Aronson Inc.

Cohen, M. L., Garofalo, R., Boucher, R., & Seghorn, T. (1971). The psychology of rapists. *Seminars in Psychiatry, 3*, 307–327.

Conner, R. L., & Levine, S. (1969). Hormonal influences on aggressive behavior. In S. Garattini, & E. B. Sigg (Eds.), *Aggressive behaviour* (pp. 150–163). Amsterdam: Excerpta Medica.

Conners, C., Kramer, R., Rothschild, G., Schwartz, L., & Stone, A. (1971). Treatment of young delinquent boys with diphenylhydantoin sodium and methylphenidate. *Archives of General Psychiatry, 24*, 156–159.

Cowan, P. A., & Walters, R. H. (1963). Studies of reinforcement of aggression: I. Effects of scheduling. *Child Development, 34*, 543–551.

Craft, M., Ismail, I. A., Krishnamurti, D., Mathews, J., Regan, A., Seth, R. V., & North, P. M. (1987). Lithium in the treatment of aggression in mentally handicapped patients: A double-blind trial. *British Journal of Psychiatry, 150*, 685–689.

Crowe, R. R. (1975). An adoptive study of psychopathy: Preliminary results from arrest records and psychiatric hospital records. In R. R. Fieve, D. Rosenthal, & H. Brill (Eds.), *Genetic research in psychiatry*. Baltimore, MD: The John Hopkins University Press.

Dalton, K. (1964). *The premenstrual syndrome*. Springfield, IL: Charles C Thomas.

Darwin, C. (1859). *The origin of species by means of natural selection or the preservation of favored races in the struggle for life* (First [reprint] ed.). Garden City, NY: Dolphin Books.

Datla, K. P., Sen, A. P., & Bhattacharya, S. K. (1992). Dopaminergic modulation of footshock induced aggression in paired rats. *Indian Journal of Experimental Biology, 30*, 587–591.

Delgado, J. M. R. (1955). Cerebral structures involved in transmission and elaboration of noxious stimulation. *Journal of Neurophysiology, 18*, 261–275.

DeSisto, M. J., & Huston, J. P. (1971). Aggression and reward from stimulating common sites in the posterior lateral hypothalamus of rats. *Communications in Behavioral Biology, Part A, 6*, 295–306.

Devane, W. A., Hanus, L., Breuer, A., Pertwee, R. G., Stevenson, L. A., Griffin, G., Gibson, D., Mandelbaum, A., Etinger, A., & Mechoulam, R. (1992). Isolation and structure of a brain constituent that binds to the cannabinoid receptor. *Science, 258*, 1946–1949.

Devinsky, O., & Bear, D. (1984). Varieties of aggressive behavior in temporal lobe epilepsy. *American Journal of Psychiatry, 141*, 651–656.

Dieckmann, G., Horn, H.-J., & Schneider, H. (1979). Long-term results of anterior hypothalamotomy in sexual offences. In E. R. Hitchcock, H. T. J. Ballantine, & B. A. Meyerson (Eds.), *Modern concepts in psychiatric surgery* (pp. 187–195). New York: Elsevier/North-Holland Biomedical Press.

Dollard, J., Doob, L. W., Miller, N. E., Mowrer, O. H., & Sears, R. R. (1939). *Frustration and aggression*. New Haven, CT: Yale University Press.

Donnerstein, E. (1980). Aggressive erotica and violence against women. *Journal of Personality and Social Psychology, 39*, 269–277.

Donnerstein, E., & Barrett, G. (1978). The effects of erotic stimuli on male aggression towards females. *Journal of Personality and Social Psychology, 36*, 180–188.

Donnerstein, E., Linz, D., & Penrod, S. (1987). *The question of pornography: Research findings and policy implications*. New York: The Free Press.

Donnerstein, E., & Wilson, D. W. (1976). Effects of noise and perceived control on ongoing and subsequent aggressive behavior. *Journal of Personality and Social Psychology, 34*, 774–781.

Drtil, J. (1969). The disturbances of higher nervous activity preceding aggression of prisoners. *Acta Nervosa Superior (Praha), 11*, 297.

Dugdale, R. L. (1877). *The Jukes: A study in crime, pauperism, disease, and heredity*. New York: Putman.

Dutton, D. G. (1981). Training police officers to intervene in domestic violence. In R. B. Stuart (Ed.), *Violent behavior: Social learning approaches to prediction, management and treatment* (pp. 173–202). New York: Brunner/Mazel Publishers.

Ebel, A., Mack, G., Stefanovic, V., & Mandel, P. (1973). Activity of choline acetyltransferase and acetylcholinesterase in the amygdala of spontaneous mouse-killer rats and in rats after olfactory bulb removal. *Brain Research, 57*, 248–251.

Egeland, J. A., Gerhard, D. S., Pauls, D. L., Sussex, J. N., Kidd, K. K., Allen, C. R., Hostetter, A. M., & Housman, D. E. (1987). Bipolar affective disorders linked to DNA markers on chromosome 11. *Nature, 325*, 783–787.

Egger, M. O., & Flynn, J. P. (1963). Effect of electrical stimulation of the amygdala on hypothalamically elicited attack behavior in cats. *Journal of Neurophysiology, 26*, 705–720.

Ehrenkranz, J., Bliss, G., & Sheard, M. H. (1974). Plasma testosterone: Correlation with aggressive behavior and social dominance in man. *Psychosomatic Medicine, 36*, 469–475.

Eibl-Eibesfeldt, I., Schiefenhövel, W., & Heeschen, V. (1989). *Kommunikation bei den Eipo: eine humanethologische Bestandsaufnahme.* Berlin: Dietrich Reimer.

Eichelman, B. (1977). Neurochemical studies of aggression in animals. *Psychopharmacology Bulletin, 13*, 17–19.

Eichelman, B., & Barchas, J. D. (1975). Facilitated shock-induced aggression following antidepressive medication in the rat. *Pharmacology, Biochemistry, and Behavior, 3*, 601–604.

Eisenberg, G. J. (1980). Children and aggression after observed film aggression with sanctioning adults. *Annals of the New York Academy of Science, 347*, 304–318.

Ellis, L. (1989). *Theories of rape: Inquiries into the causes of sexual aggression.* New York: Hemisphere Publishing.

Ellis, L. (1991). A synthesized (biosocial) theory of rape. *Journal of Consulting and Clinical Psychology, 59*(5), 631–642.

Ellison, G. D., & Flynn, J. P. (1968). Organized aggressive behavior in cats after surgical isolation of the hypothalamus. *Archives Italiennes de Biologie, 106*, 1–20.

Emley, G. S., & Hutchinson, R. R. (1983). Unique influences of ten drugs upon post-shock biting attack and pre-shock manual responding. *Pharmacology, Biochemistry, and Behavior, 19*, 5–12.

Eriksson, E., Sundblad, C., Lisjö, P., Modigh, K., & Andersch, B. (1992). Serum levels of androgens are higher in women with premenstrual irritability and dysphoria than in controls. *Psychoneuroendocrinology, 17*(2/3), 195–204.

Eron, L. D. (1987). The development of aggressive behavior from the perspective of a developing behaviorism. *American Psychologist, 42*, 435–442.

Eron, L. D., & Huesmann, L. R. (1984). The control of aggressive behavior by changes in attitudes, values, and the conditions of learning. In R. J. Blanchard, & D. C. Blanchard (Eds.), *Advances in the study of aggression* (vol. I, pp. 139–171). Orlando, FL: Academic Press.

Eron, L. D., Huesmann, L. R., Lefkowitz, M. M., & Walder, L. O. (1972). Does television violence cause aggression? *American Psychologist, 27*, 253–263.

Erpino, M. J., & Chappelle, T. C. (1971). Interactions between androgens and progesterone in mediation of aggression in the mouse. *Hormones and Behavior, 2*, 265–272.

Everett, G. M. (1977). The pharmacology of aggressive behavior in animals and man. *Psychopharmacology Bulletin, 13*, 15–17.

Fagot, B. I. (1984). The consequents of problem behavior in toddler children. *Journal of Abnormal Child Psychology, 12*, 385–396.

Falconer, M. A., Hill, D., Meyer, A., & Wilson, J. L. (1958). Clinical, radiological, and EEG correlations with pathological changes in temporal lobe epilepsy and their significance in surgical treatment. In M. Baldwin, & P. Bailey (Eds.), *Temporal lobe epilepsy* (pp. 396–410). Springfield, IL: Charles C Thomas.

Falk, J. L. (1966). The motivational properties of schedule-induced polydipsia. *Journal of the Experimental Analysis of Behavior, 9*, 19–28.

Farmer, A., McGuffin, P., & Gottesman, I. (1987). Twin concordance for DSM-III schizophrenia. *Archives of General Psychiatry, 44*, 634–641.

Fausto-Sterling, A. (1986). *Myths of gender: Biological theories about women and men.* New York: Basic Books, Inc.

Favazza, A. R. (1987). *Bodies under siege.* Baltimore, MD: Johns Hopkins University Press.

Federal Bureau of Investigation (FBI). (1990). *Uniform crime reports for the United States.* Washington, DC: U. S. Government Printing Office, 1991–282-076/45217.

Fedoroff, J. P., Wisner-Carlson, R., Dean, S., & Berlin, F. S. (1992). Medroxy-progesterone acetate in the treatment of paraphilic sexual disorders. *Clinical processes: Pharmacotherapy and group therapy, 18*(3/4), 109–123.

Feindler, E. L., & Ecton, R. B. (1986). *Adolescent anger control: Cognitive-behavioral techniques.* New York: Pergamon Press.

Fenwick, P. (1989). The nature and management of aggression in epilepsy. *Journal of Neuropsychiatry, 1*, 418–425.

Fernández, Y., Falzon, M., Cambon-Gros, C., & Mitjavila, S. (1982). Carbaryl tricompartmental toxicokinetics and anticholinesterstase activity. *Toxicology Letters, 13*, 253–258.

Fernández de Molina, A., & Hunsperger, R. W. (1959). Central representation of affective reactions in forebrain and brain stem: Electrical stimulation of amygdala, stria terminalis, and adjacent structures. *Journal of Physiology (London), 145*, 251–265.

Feshbach, S., & Singer, R. D. (1971). *Television and aggression: An experimental field study.* San Francisco, CA: Jossey-Bass.

Floody, O. R. (1983). Hormones and aggression in female mammals. In B. B. Svare (Ed.), *Hormones and aggressive behavior* (pp. 39–89). New York: Plenum Press.

Floody, O. R., & Pfaff, D. W. (1977). Aggressive behavior in female hamsters: The hormonal basis for fluctuations in female aggressiveness correlated with estrous state. *Journal of comparative and physiological psychology, 91*, 443–464.

Flory, R. (1969). Attack behavior as a function of minimum inter-food interval. *Journal of the Experimental Analysis of Behavior, 12*, 825–828.

Frederiksen, L. W., & Rainwater, N. (1981). Explosive behavior: A skill development approach to treatment. In R. B. Stuart (Ed.), *Violent behavior: Social learning approaches to prediction, management and treatment* (pp. 265–288). New York: Brunner/Mazel Publishers.

Freedman, J. L. (1984). Effect of television violence on aggressiveness. *Psychological Bulletin, 96*, 227–246.

Freedman, J. L. (1992). Television violence and aggression: What psychologists should tell the public. In P. Suedfeld, & P. E. Tetlock (Eds.), *Psychology and social policy* (pp. 179–189). New York: Hemisphere Publishing.

Freedman, J. L., Levy, A. S., Buchanan, R. W., & Price, J. (1972). Crowding and human aggressiveness. *Journal of Experimental Social Psychology, 8*, 528–548.

Friedlander, B. Z. (1993). Community violence, children's development, and mass media: In pursuit of new insights, new goals, and new strategies. *Psychiatry, 56*(February), 66–81.

Frodi, A., Macaulay, J., & Thome, P. R. (1977). Are women always less aggressive than men? A review of the experimental literature. *Psychological Bulletin, 84*, 634–660.

Galen, J. (1982). In P. Marsh, & A. Campbell (Eds.), *Aggression and violence* (pp. 242). New York: St. Martin's Press.

Gandelman, R., vom Saal, F. S., & Reinisch, J. M. (1977). Contiguity to male foetuses affects morphology and behavior of female mice. *Nature, 266*, 722–724.

Gebhard, P. H., Gagnon, J. H., Pomeroy, W. B., & Christenson, C. V. (1965). *Sex offenders.* New York: Harper & Row.

Gedye, A. (1990). Dietary increase in serotonin reduces self-injurious behaviour in a Down's syndrome adult. *Journal of Mental Deficiency Research, 34*, 195–203.

Geen, R. G. (1978). Effects of attack and uncontrollable noise on aggression. *Journal of Research in Personality, 12*, 15–29.

Geen, R. G. (1981). Behavioral and physiological reactions to observed violence: Effects of prior exposure to aggressive stimuli. *Journal of Personality and Social Psychology, 40,* 868–875.

Geen, R. G. (1983). Aggression and television violence. In R. G. Geen, & E. I. Donnerstein (Eds.), *Aggression: Theoretical and empirical issues* (vol. 2. Issues in research, pp. 103–125). New York: Academic Press.

Geen, R. G. (1990). *Human aggression.* Pacific Grove, CA: Brooks/Cole.

Geen, R. G., & O'Neal, E. C. (1969). Activation of cue-elicited aggression by general arousal. *Journal of Personality and Social Psychology, 11,* 289–292.

Geen, R. G., & Stonner, D. (1971). Effects of aggressiveness habit strength on behavior in the presence of aggression-related stimuli. *Journal of Personality and Social Psychology, 17,* 149–153.

Gelles, R. J. (1982). Domestic criminal violence. In M. E. Wolfgang, & N. A. Weiner (Eds.), *Criminal violence* (pp. 210–235). Beverly Hills, CA: Sage Publications.

Gershon, S., & Shaw, F. H. (1961). Psychiatric sequelae of chronic exposure to organophosphorus insecticides. *Lancet, 1,* 1371–1374.

Gianutsos, G., & Lal, H. (1976). Blockade of apomorphine-induced aggression by morphine or neuroleptics: Differential alteration by antimuscarinics and naloxone. *Pharmacology, Biochemistry and Behavior, 4,* 639–642.

Gianutsos, G., & Lal, H. (1978). Narcotic analgesics and aggression. *Modern Problems in Pharmacopsychiatry, 13,* 114–138.

Goddard, H. H. (1912). *The Kallikak family: A study in the heredity of feeble- mindedness.* New York: Macmillan.

Goldstein, A. P. (1991). *Delinquent gangs: A psychological perspective.* Champaign, IL: Research Press.

Goldstein, A. P., & Keller, H. (1987). *Aggressive behavior: Assessment and intervention.* New York: Pergamon Press.

Goldstein, J. H. (1989). Violence in sports. In J. H. Goldstein (Ed.), *Sports, games, and play: Social and psychological viewpoints* (pp. 279–297). Hillsdale, NJ: Lawrence Erlbaum Associates.

Goldstein, J. H., Rosnow, R. L., Raday, T., Silverman, I., & Gaskell, G. D. (1975). Punitiveness in response to films varying in content: A cross-national field study of aggression. *European Journal of Social Psychology, 5,* 149–165.

Goltz, F. (1892). Der Hund ohne Grosshirn. *Pflugers Archiv für die gesamte Physiologie des Menschen und der Tiere, 51,* 570–614.

Goodman, J., & Loftus, E. F. (1992). Judgment and memory: The role of expert psychological testimony on eyewitness accuracy. In P. Suedfeld, & P. E. Tetlock (Eds.), *Psychology and social policy* (pp. 267–282). New York: Hemisphere Publishing.

Gottesman, I. I., & Shields, J. (1972). *Schizophrenia and genetics—A twin study vantage point.* New York: Academic Press.

Gottschalk, L. A., Buchsbaum, M. S., Gillin, J. C., Wu, J., Reynolds, C. A., & Herrera, D. B. (1991). Positron-emission tomographic studies of the relationship of cerebral glucose metabolism and the magnitude of anxiety and hostility experienced during dreaming and waking. *Journal of Neuropsychiatry, 3,* 131–142.

Goy, R. W. (1968). Organizing effects of androgen on the behaviour of rhesus monkeys. In R. P. Michael (Ed.), *Endocrinology and human behaviour* (pp. 12–31). London: Oxford University Press.

Greenberg, G. (1972). The effects of ambient temperature and population density on aggression in two inbred strains of mice, Mus Musculus. *Behaviour, 42,* 119–130.

Grossman, S. P. (1963). Chemically-induced epileptiform seizures in the cat. *Science, 142,* 409–411.

Groth, A. N., & Birnbaum, H. J. (1979). *Men who rape: The psychology of the offender.* New York: Plenum Press.

Groth, A. N., & Burgess, A. W. (1977). Rape: A sexual deviation. *American Journal of Orthopsychiatry, 47,* 400–406.

Guhl, A. M. (1956). The social order of chickens. *Scientific American, 194,* 42–46.

Gunter, B. (1994). The question of media violence. In J. Bryant, & D. Zillman (Eds.), *Media effects: Advances in theory and research* (pp. 163–211). Hillsdale, NJ: Lawrence Erlbaum Associates.

Gur, R. C., Mozley, L. H., Mozley, P. D., Resnick, S. M., Karp, J. S., Alavi, A., Arnold, S. E., & Gur, R. E. (1995). Sex differences in regional cerebral glucose metabolism during a resting state. *Science, 267,* 528–531.

Guttmacher, M. S., & Weihofen, H. (1952). *Psychiatry and the law.* New York: Norton.

Halbreich, U., & Tworek, H. (1993). Altered serotonergic activity in women with dysphoric premenstrual syndromes. *International journal of psychiatry in medicine, 23,* 1–27.

Hall, C. S., & Klein, S. J. (1942). Individual differences in aggressiveness in rats. *Journal of Comparative Psychology, 33,* 371–383.

Hall, G. C. N., & Hirschman, R. (1991). Toward a theory of sexual aggression: A quadripartite model. *Journal of Consulting and Clinical Psychology, 59,* 662–669.

Hare, R. D., Frazelle, J., & Cox, D. N. (1978). Psychopathy and physiological responses to threat of an aversive stimulus. *Psychophysiology, 15,* 165–172.

Harlow, H. F., & Harlow, M. K. (1962). Social deprivation in monkeys. *Scientific American, 207,* 137–146.

Harris, M., & Huang, L. (1974). Aggression and the attribution process. *Journal of Social Psychology, 92,* 209–216.

Hartmann, D. P. (1969). Influence of symbolically modeled instrumental aggression and pain cues on aggressive behavior. *Journal of Personality and Social Psychology, 11,* 280–288.

Heath, R. G. (1955). Correlations between levels of psychological awareness and physiological activity in the central nervous system. *Psychosomatic Medicine, 17,* 383–395.

Heath, R. G. (1963). Electrical self-stimulation of the brain in man. *American Journal of Psychiatry, 120,* 571–577.

Heath, R. G., Llewellyn, R. C., & Rouchell, A. M. (1979). Brain mechanisms in psychiatric illness: Rationale for and results of treatment with cerebellar stimulation. In E. R. Hitchcock, H. T. J. Ballantine, & B. A. Meyerson (Eds.), *Modern concepts in psychiatric surgery* (pp. 77–84). Amsterdam, The Netherlands: Elsevier/North-Holland Biomedical Press.

Heath, R. G., & Mickle, W. A. (1960). Evaluation of seven years experience with depth electrode studies in human patients. In E. R. Ramey, & P. S. O'Doherty (Eds.), *Electrical studies on the unanesthetized brain* (pp. 214–247). New York: Harper and Row.

Heimburger, R. F., Small, I. F., Small, J. G., Milstein, V., & Moore, D. (1978). Stereotaxic amygdalotomy for convulsive and behavioral disorders. *Applied Neurophysiology, 41,* 43–51.

Heimburger, R. F., Whitlock, C. C., & Kalsbeck, J. E. (1966). Stereotaxic amygdalotomy for epilepsy with aggressive behavior. *Journal of the American Medical Association, 198,* 165–169.

Herrmann, W. M., & Beach, R. C. (1978). The psychotropic properties of estrogens. *Psychopharmacologia, 11,* 164–176.

Hess, W. R. (1957). *The functional organization of the diencephalon.* New York: Grune and Stratton.

Hess, W. R., & Brügger, M. (1943). Das subkorticale Zentrum der affektiven Abwehrreaktion. *Helvetica Physiologica et Pharmacologica Acta, 1,* 33–53.

Hicks, D. J. (1968). Effects of co-observer's sanctions and adult presence on imitative aggression. *Child Development, 39,* 303–309.

Hilton, S. M., & Źbrozyna, A. W. (1963). Amygdaloid region for defence reactions and its efferent pathway to the brain stem. *Journal of Physiology (London), 165*, 160–173.

Hinshaw, S. P., Buhrmester, D., & Heller, T. (1989). Anger control in response to verbal provocation: Effects of stimulant medication for boys with ADHD. *Journal of Abnormal Child Psychology, 17*, 393–407.

Hirose, S. (1977). Psychiatric evaluation of psychosurgery. In W. H. Sweet, S. Obrador, & J. G. Martin-Rodríguez (Eds.), *Neurosurgical treatment in psychiatry, pain, and epilepsy* (pp. 203–209). Baltimore, MD: University Park Press.

Hitchcock, E. (1979). Amygdalotomy for aggression. In M. Sandler (Ed.), *Psychopharmacology of Aggression* (pp. 205–215). New York: Raven Press.

Hokanson, J. E. (1970). Psychophysiological evaluation of the catharsis hypothesis. In E. I. Megargee, & J. E. Hokanson (Eds.), *The dynamics of aggression* (pp. 74–86). New York: Harper and Row.

Hollister, L. E., & Csernansky, J. G. (1990). *Clinical pharmacology of psychotherapeutic drugs.* New York: Churchill Livingston.

Hood, K. E., & Cairns, R. B. (1988). A developmental-genetic analysis of aggressive behavior in mice. II. Cross-sex inheritance. *Behavior Genetics, 18*, 605–619.

Horsley, V., & Clarke, R. H. (1908). The structure and function of the cerebellum examined by a new method. *Brain, 31*, 45–124.

Huesmann, L. R., Eron, L. D., Berkowitz, L., & Chaffee, S. (1992). The effects of television violence on aggression: A reply to a critic. In P. Suedfeld & P. E. Tetlock (Eds.), *Psychology and social policy* (pp. 191–200). New York: Hemisphere Publishing.

Huesmann, L. R., Lagerspetz, K., & Eron, L. D. (1984). Intervening variables in the television violence-aggression relation: Evidence from two countries. *Developmental Psychology, 20*, 746–775.

Huesmann, L. R., & Miller, L. S. (1994). Long-term effects of repeated exposure to media violence in childhood. In L. R. Huesmann (Ed.), *Aggressive behavior: Current perspectives* (pp. 153–186). New York: Plenum Press.

Hunsperger, R. W. (1956). Affektreaktionen auf elektrische Reizung im Hirnstamm der Katze. *Helvetica Physiologica et Pharmacologia acta, 14*, 70–92.

Huston, A. (1984). Mass media and education. *XVI Pan American Child Conference.* Washington, DC: Organization of American States.

Hutchings, B., & Mednick, S. A. (1974). Registered criminology in the adoptive and biological parents of registered male criminal adoptees. In S. A. Mednick, F. Schulsinger, J. Higgins, & B. Bell (Eds.), *Genetics, environment and psychopathology.* Amsterdam: North Holland/Elsevier.

Hutchinson, R. R. (1973). The environmental causes of aggression. In J. K. Cole, & D. D. Jensen (Eds.), *Nebraska symposium on motivation* (vol. XX, pp. 155–181). Lincoln: University of Nebraska Press.

Hutchinson, R. R., Azrin, N. H., & Hunt, G. M. (1968). Attack produced by intermittent reinforcement of a concurrent operant response. *Journal of the Experimental Analysis of Behavior, 11*, 489–495.

Hutchinson, R. R., Emley, G. S., & Krasnegor, N. A. (1977). The effects of cocaine on the aggressive behavior of mice, pigeons and squirrel monkeys. In E. H. Ellinwood, & M. M. Kilbey (Eds.), *Cocaine and other stimulants* (vol. 21, pp. 457–480). New York: Plenum Press.

Hutchinson, R. R., Pierce, G. E., Emley, G. S., Proni, T. J., & Sauer, R. A. (1977). The laboratory measurement of human anger. *Biobehavioral Reviews, 1*, 241–259.

Hutchinson, R. R., & Renfrew, J. W. (1966). Stalking attack and eating behaviors elicited from the same sites in the hypothalamus. *Journal of Comparative and Physiological Psychology, 61*, 360–367.

Hutchinson, R. R., Renfrew, J. W., & Young, G. A. (1971). Effects of long-term shock and associated stimuli on aggressive and manual responses. *Journal of the Experimental Analysis of Behavior, 15*, 141–166.

Hutchinson, R. R., & Renfrew, J. W. (1978). Functional parallels between the neural and environmental antecedents of aggression. *Neuroscience and Biobehavioral Reviews, 2*, 33–58.

Hutchinson, R. R., Ulrich, R. E., & Azrin, N. H. (1965). Effects of age and related factors on the pain-aggression reaction. *Journal of Comparative and Physiological Psychology, 57*, 365–369.

Hyde, J. S., & Sawyer, T. F. (1977). Estrous cycle fluctuations in aggressiveness of house mice. *Hormones and Behavior, 9*, 290–295.

Inselman, B. R., & Flynn, J. P. (1972). Modulatory effects of preoptic stimulation on hypothalamically-elicited attack in cats. *Brain Research, 42*, 73–87.

Itil, T. M. (1981). Drug therapy in the management of aggression. In P. F. Brain, & D. Benton (Eds.), *Multidisciplinary approaches to aggression research* (pp. 489–502). New York: Elsevier/North-Holland Biomedical Press.

Jacobs, P. A., Brunton, M., Melville, M. M., Brittain, R. P., & McClemont, W. F. (1965). Aggressive behaviour, mental subnormality and the XYY male. *Nature, 208*, 1351–1352.

Johansson, G. G. (1981). Neural stimulation as a means of generating standardized threat under laboratory conditions. In P. F. Brain, & D. Benton (Eds.), *Multidisciplinary approaches to aggression research* (pp. 93–100). New York: Elsevier/North-Holland Biomedical Press.

Johnson, J. M. (1984). Psychiatric uses of antiadrenergic and adrenergic blocking drugs. *Journal of Nervous and Mental Disease, 172*(3), 123–132.

Johnson, R. N. (1972). *Aggression in man and animals*. Philadelphia: W. B. Saunders.

Joy, L. A., Kimball, M. M., & Zabrack, M. L. (1986). Television and aggressive behavior. In T. M. Williams (Ed.), *The impact of television: A natural experiment involving three towns*. New York: Academic Press.

Julien, R. M. (1995). *A primer of drug action* (7th ed.). New York: W. H. Freeman.

Kaada, B. R. (1951). Somato-motor, autonomic, and electrocorticographic responses to electrical stimulation of "rhinencephalic" and other structures in primates, cat, and dog. *Acta Physiologica Scandinavica, 24*(Supplement 83), 1–285.

Kahn, M. W. (1966). The physiology of catharsis. *Journal of Personality and Social Psychology, 3*, 278–286.

Kalinowsky, L. B., Hippius, H., & Klein, H. E. (1982). *Biological treatments in psychiatry*. New York: Grune & Stratton.

Kanki, J. P., & Adams, D. B. (1978). Ventrobasal thalamus necessary for visually- released defensive boxing of rat. *Physiology and Behavior, 21*, 7–12.

Kantak, K. M., Hegstrand, L. R., Whitman, J., & Eichelman, B. (1980). Effects of dietary supplements and tryptophan-free diet on aggressive behavior in rats. *Pharmacology, Biochemistry, and Behavior, 12* 173–179.

Kaplan, R. M. (1984). The measurement of human aggression. In R. M. Kaplan, V. J. Konečni, & R. W. Novaco (Eds.), *Aggression in children and youth* (pp. 44–72). The Hague, Netherlands: Martinus Nijhoff.

Kaplan, R. M., & Singer, R. D. (1976). Television violence and viewer aggression: A reexamination of the evidence. *The Journal of Social Issues, 32*(4), 35–70.

Karli, P., & Vergnes, M. (1964). Dissociation experimentale du comportement d'agression interspecifique Rat-Souris et du comportement alimentaire. *Comptes Rendus des Seances de la Societe de Biologie (Paris), 158*, 650–653.

Kazdin, A. E. (1985). *Treatment of antisocial behavior in children and adolescents*. Homewood, IL: The Dorsey Press.

Keehn, J. D. (1976). Schedule-dependent aggression. In E. Ribes-Iñesta, & A. Bandura (Eds.),

Analysis of delinquency and aggression (pp. 9–33). New York: Lawrence Erlbaum Associates.

Kelsoe, J. R., Ginns, E. I., Egeland, J. A., Gerhard, D. S., Goldstein, A. M., Bale, S. J., Pauls, D. L., Long, R. T., Kidd, K. K., Conte, G., Housman, D. E., & Paul, S. M. (1989). Re-evaluation of the linkage relationship between chromosome 11p loci and the gene for bipolar affective disorder in the Old Order Amish. *Nature, 342,* 238–243.

Kempe, C. H., Silverman, F. N., Steele, B. F., Droegemueller, W., & Silver, H. K. (1962). The battered child syndrome. *Journal of the American Medical Association, 181,* 107–112.

King, D. J., Turkson, S. N. A., Liddle, J., & Kinney, C. D. (1980). Some clinical and metabolic aspects of propranolol in chronic schizophrenia. *British Journal of Psychiatry, 137,* 458–468.

King, H. E. (1961). Psychological effects of excitation in the limbic system. In D. E. Sheer (Ed.), *Electrical stimulation of the brain* (pp. 477–486). Austin: University of Texas Press.

King, M. B., & Hoebel, B. G. (1968). Killing elicited by brain stimulation in rats. *Communications in Behavioral Biology, Part A, 2,* 173–177.

Kirigin, K. A., Braukmann, C. J., Atwater, J. D., & Wolf, M. M. (1982). An evaluation of teaching-family (Achievement Place) group homes for juvenile offenders. *Journal of Applied Behavior Analysis, 15,* 1–16.

Kleinig, J. (1985). *Ethical issues in psychosurgery.* London: George Allen and Unwin.

Kling, A. (1972). Effects of amygdalectomy on social-affective behavior in nonhuman primates. In B. E. Eleftheriou (Ed.), *The neurobiology of the amygdala* (pp. 511–536). New York: Plenum Press.

Klüver, H., & Bucy, P. C. (1939). Preliminary analysis of functions of the temporal lobes in monkeys. *Archives of Neurology and Psychiatry, 42,* 979–1000.

Konečni, V. (1975). The mediation of aggressive behavior: Arousal level vs. anger and cognitive labeling. *Journal of Personality and Social Psychology, 32,* 706–712.

Krawchik, R. (1986). Pavlov: Neuropsicología del comportamiento. *V Congreso, Asociación Latinoamericano de Análisis y Modificación del Comportamiento,* Caracas, Venezuela.

Kreutz, L. E., & Rose, R. M. (1972). Assessment of aggressive behavior and plasma testosterone in a young criminal population. *Psychosomatic Medicine, 34,* 321–332.

Kruk, M. R., Van der Poel, A. M., & De Vos-Frerichs, T. P. (1980). The induction of aggressive behaviours by electrical stimulation in the hypothalamus of male rats. *Behaviour, 70,* 292–322.

Kulkarni, A. S. (1968). Muricidal block produced by 5-hydroxytryptophan and various drugs. *Life Sciences,* 125–128.

Lagerspetz, K. M. J. (1979). Modification of aggressiveness in mice. In S. Feshbach, & Λ. Fraczek (Eds.), *Aggression and behaviour change* (pp. 66–82). New York: Praeger.

Lagerspetz, K. M. J. (1981). Combining aggression studies in infra-humans and man. In P. F. Brain, & D. Benton (Eds.), *Multidisciplinary approaches to aggression research.* New York: Elsevier/North Holland Biomedical Press.

Lagerspetz, K. M. J., Björkqvist, K., & Peltonen, T. (1988). Is indirect aggression typical of females? Gender differences in aggressiveness in 11- to 12-year-old children. *Aggressive Behavior, 14,* 403–414.

Lagerspetz, K. M. J., & Lagerspetz, K. Y. H. (1983). Genes and aggression. In E. C. Simmel (Ed.), *Aggressive behavior: Genetic and neural approaches* (pp. 89–101). Hillsdale, NJ: Lawrence Erlbaum Associates.

Lagerspetz, K. Y. H., Tirri, R., & Lagerspetz, K. M. J. (1968). Neurochemical and endocrinological studies of mice selectively bred for aggressiveness. *Scandinavian Journal of Psychology, 9,* 157–160.

Lamprecht, F., Eichelman, B., Thoa, N. B., Williams, R. B., & Kopin, I. J. (1972). Rat fighting behavior: Serum dopamine-beta-hydroxylase and hypothalamic tyrosine hydroxylase. *Science, 177*, 1214–1215.

Lang, A. R., Goeckner, D. J., Adesso, V. J., & Marlett, G. A. (1975). Effects of alcohol on aggression in male social drinkers. *Journal of Abnormal Psychology, 84*, 508–518.

Langevin, R., Hucker, S. J., Ben-Aron, M. H., Purins, J. E., & Hook, H. J. (1985). Why are pedophiles attracted to children? Further studies of erotic preference in heterosexual pedophilia. In R. Langevin (Ed.), *Erotic preference, gender identity, and aggression in men: New research studies* (pp. 181–209). Hillsdale, NJ: Lawrence Erlbaum Associates.

Leaf, R. C., Wnek, D. J., Gay, P. E., Corcia, R. M., & Lamon, S. (1975). Chlordiazepoxide and diazepam induced mouse-killing by rats. *Psychopharmacologia, 44*, 23–28.

Lessum, D. (1980). Animal outlaws. *Science Digest*, Special Edition, pp. 62–63.

Levine, L. J. (1972). *Forensic odontology today—A "new" forensic science*. Reprint. Washington, DC: U.S. Department of Justice, 7.

Levy, I. V., & King, I. A. (1953). The effects of testosterone propionate on fighting behavior in young C57BL/10 mice. *Anatomical Record, 117*, 562–563.

Lewis, D. O. (Ed.). (1981). *Vulnerabilities to delinquency*. New York: SP Medical and Scientific Books.

Lewis, D. O., Shanak, S. S., Pincus, J. H., & Glaser, G. H. (1981). Delinquency and seizure disorders: Psychomotor epileptic symptomatology and violence. In D. O. Lewis (Ed.), *Vulnerabilities to Delinquency* (pp. 39–55). New York: SP Medical and Scientific Books.

Leyhausen, P. (1956). *Verhaltensstudien an Katzen*. Berlin: P. Varey Verlag.

Libby, J. D., Polloway, E. A., & Smith, J. D. (1983). Lesch-Nyhan syndrome: A review. *Education and training of the mentally retarded, 18*, 226–231.

Liberman, R. P., Marshall, B. D. J., & Burke, K. L. (1981). Drug and environmental interventions for aggressive psychiatric patients. In R. B. Stuart (Ed.), *Violent behavior: Social learning approaches to prediction, management and treatment* (pp. 227–264). New York: Brunner/Mazel Publishers.

Lindvall, O., Brundin, P., Widner, H., Rehncrona, S., Gustavii, B., Frackowiak, R., Leenders, K. L., Sawle, G., Rothwell, J. C., Marsden, C. D., & Björklund, A. (1990). Grafts of fetal dopamine neurons survive and improve motor function in Parkinson's disease. *Science, 247*, 574–577.

Linscheid, T. R., Iwata, B. A., Ricketts, R. W., Williams, D. E., & Griffin, J. C. (1990). Clinical evaluation of the Self-Injurious Behavior Inhibiting System (SIBIS). *Journal of Applied Behavior Analysis, 23*, 53–78.

Linz, D., Wilson, B. J., & Donnerstein, E. (1992). Sexual violence in the mass media: Legal solutions, warnings, and mitigation through education. *Journal of social issues, 48*(1), 145–171.

Livingston, S. (1964). Epilepsy and murder. *Journal of the American Medical Association, 188*, 172.

Lloyd, C. W. (1964). Treatment and prevention of certain sexual behavioral problems. In C. W. Lloyd (Ed.), *Human reproduction and sexual behavior* (pp. 498–510). Philadelphia: Lea and Febiger.

Lombroso, C. (1876). *L'Uomo delinquente*. Milan, Italy: Hoepli.

Lorimer, F. M. (1972). Violent behavior and the electroencephalogram. *Clinical Electroencephalography, 3*, 193.

Lovass, O. I., & Simmons, J. Q. (1969). Manipulation of self-destruction in three retarded children. *Journal of the Experimental Analysis of Behavior, 2*, 143–157.

Luchins, D. I. (1984). Carbamazepine in psychiatric syndromes: clinical and neuropharmacological properties. *Psychopharmacology Bulletin, 20*, 569–571.

Maccoby, E. E., & Jacklin, C. N. (1974). *The psychology of sex differences*. Stanford, CA: Stanford University Press.

MacDonnell, M. F., & Flynn, J. P. (1966). Control of sensory fields by stimulation of hypothalamus. *Science, 152*, 1406–1408.

MacDonnell, M. F., & Flynn, J. P. (1968). Attack elicited by stimulation of the thalamus and adjacent structures of cats. *Behaviour, 31*, 185–202.

MacDonnell, M. F., & Ehmer, J. (1969). Some effects of ethanol on aggressive behaviour in cats. *Quarterly Journal of Studies in Alcohol, 30*, 312–319.

MacDonnell, M. F., Fessock, L., & Brown, S. H. (1971). Aggression and associated neural events in cats: Effects of p-chlorophenylalanine compared with alcohol. *Quarterly Journal of Studies on Alcohol, 32*, 748–763.

Mace, F. C., Page, T. J., Ivancic, M. T., & O'Brien, S. (1986). Effectiveness of brief time-out with and without contingent delay: A comparative analysis. *Journal of applied behavior analysis, 19*, 79–86.

MacLean, P. D., & Delgado, J. M. R. (1953). Electrical and chemical stimulation of frontotemporal portion of limbic system in the waking animal. *Electroencephalography and Clinical Neurophysiology, 5*, 91–100.

MacLean, P. D., & Ploog, D. W. (1962). Cerebral representation of penile erection. *Journal of Neurophysiology, 25*, 29–55.

Malamuth, N. M., & Ceniti, J. (1986). Repeated exposure to violent and nonviolent pornography: Likelihood of raping ratings and laboratory aggression against women. *Aggressive Behavior, 12*, 129–137.

Malamuth, N. M., Haber, S., & Feshbach, S. (1980). Testing hypotheses regarding rape: Exposure to sexual violence, sex differences, and the "normality" of rapists. *Journal of Research in Personality, 14*, 121–137.

Maletzky, B. M. (1991). *Treating the sexual offender*. Newbury Park, CA: Sage Publications.

Malsbury, C. W. (1971). Facilitation of male copulatory behavior by electrical stimulation of the medial preoptic area. *Physiology and Behavior, 7*, 797–805.

Mark, V. H., & Ervin, F. R. (1970). *Violence and the brain*. New York: Harper and Row.

Marolla, J., & Scully, D. (1986). Attitudes toward women, violence, and rape: A comparison of convicted rapists and other felons. *Deviant behavior, 7*, 337–355.

Marques, J. K. (1981). Effects of victim resistance strategies on the sexual arousal and attitudes of violent rapists. In R. B. Stuart (Ed.), *Violent behavior: Social learning approaches to prediction, management and treatment* (pp. 138–172). New York: Brunner/Mazel Publishers.

Martin, D. (1981). *Battered Wives* (Revised, Updated ed.). San Francisco, CA: Volcano Press.

Martin, G., & Pear, J. (1996). *Behavior modification: What it is and how to do it* (Fifth ed.). Englewood Cliffs, NJ: Prentice-Hall, Inc.

Martindale, D. A. (1971). Territorial dominance behavior in dyadic verbal interactions. *79th Annual Convention of the American Psychological Association*, Washington, DC.

Mash, E. J., & Wolfe, D. A. (1991). Methodological issues in research on physical child abuse. *Criminal Justice and Behavior, 18*, 8–29.

Masserman, J. H. (1942). The hypothalamus in psychiatry. *American Journal of Psychiatry, 98*, 633–637.

Matthews, R., Paulus, P., & Baron, R. A. (1979). Physical aggression after being crowded. *Journal of Nonverbal Behavior, 4*, 5–17.

Mawson, A. R. (1987). *Transient criminality: a model of stress-induced crime*. New York: Praeger.

Mazur, A. (1983). Hormones, aggression, and dominance in humans. In B. B. Svare (Ed.), *Hormones and aggressive behavior* (pp. 563–576). New York: Plenum Press.

McCarthy, E. D., Langner, T. S., Gerstein, J. C., Eisenberg, J. G., & Orzeck, L. (1975). Violence and behavior disorders. *Journal of Communication, 25*(4), 71–85.

McDonough, J. H. J., Manning, F. J., & Elsmore, T. F. (1972). Reduction of predatory aggression of rats following administration of delta-9–tetrahydrocannabinol. *Life Sciences, 11, Part I,* 103–111.

Mednick, S. A. (1981). The learning of morality: Biosocial bases. In D. O. Lewis (Ed.), *Vulnerabilities to delinquency* (pp. 187–204). New York: SP Medical and Scientific Books.

Meichenbaum, D. H. (1985). *Stress inoculation training.* New York: Pergamon Press.

Melo, L. L., Cardoso, S. H., & Brandão, M. L. (1992). Antiaversive action of benzodiazepines on escape behavior induced by electrical stimulation of the inferior colliculus. *Physiology and Behavior, 51,* 557–562.

Menkes, D. B., Taghavi, E., Mason, P. A., & Howard, R. C. (1993). Fluoxetine's spectrum of action in premenstrual syndrome. *International clinical psychopharmacology, 8,* 95–102.

Meyer-Bahlburg, H. F. L. (1981). Sex chromosomes and aggression in humans. In P. F. Brain, & D. Benton (Eds.), *The biology of aggression* (pp. 109–123). Rockville, MD: Sijthoff and Noordhoff.

Meyer-Bahlburg, H. F. L., & Ehrhardt, A. A. (1982). Prenatal sex hormones and human aggression: A review, and new data on progestogen effects. *Aggressive Behavior, 8,* 39–62.

Miczek, K. A. (1978). Delta-9–tetrahydrocannabinol: Antiaggressive effects in mice, rats, and squirrel monkeys. *Science, 199,* 1459–1461.

Milgram, S. (1963). Behavioral study of obedience. *Journal of Abnormal and Social Psychology, 67,* 371–378.

Miller, N. E. (1948). Theory and experiment relating psychoanalytic displacement to stimulus-response generalization. *Journal of Abnormal and Social Psychology, 43,* 155–178.

Monahan, J. (1992). Mental disorder and violent behavior. *American Psychologist, 47,* 511–521.

Money, J., & Ehrhardt, A. A. (1968). Prenatal hormone exposure: Possible effects on behaviour in man. In R. P. Michael (Ed.), *Endocrinology and human behaviour* (pp. 32–48). London: Oxford University Press.

Money, J. (1970). Use of an androgen-depleting hormone in the treatment of male sex offenders. *The Journal of Sex Research, 6,* 165–172.

Monroe, R. R. (1970). *Episodic behavioral disorders: A psychodynamic and neurophysiologic analysis.* Cambridge, MA: Harvard University Press.

Monroe, R. R., & Lion, J. R. (1978). Review of current research. In R. R. Monroe (Ed.), *Brain dysfunction in aggressive criminals* (pp. 15–59). Lexington, MA: D. C. Heath.

Monroe, R. R., Balis, G. U., & McCulloch, D. (1978). Criterion of brain instability: EEG activation. In R. R. Monroe (Ed.), *Brain dysfunction in aggressive criminals* (pp. 105–120). Lexington, MA: D. C. Heath.

Montenegro, H. (1984). Children and television. *XVI Pan American Child Conference,* Washington, DC: Organization of American States.

Moyer, K. E. (1968). Kinds of aggression and their physiological basis. *Communications in Behavioral Biology, 2,* 65–87.

Moyer, K. E. (1976). *The psychobiology of aggression.* New York: Harper & Row.

Mueller, C. W. (1983). Environmental stressors and aggressive behavior. In R. G. Geen, & E. I. Donnerstein (Eds.), *Aggression: Theoretical and empirical reviews* (vol. 2. Issues in research, pp. 51–76). New York: Academic Press.

Murdock, G. (1982). Mass communication and social violence. In P. Marsh, & A. Campbell (Eds.), *Aggression and violence* (pp. 242). New York: St. Martin's Press.

Narabayashi, H. (1972). Stereotaxic amygdalotomy. In B. Eleftheriou (Ed.), *The neurobiology of the amygdala* (pp. 459–483). New York: Plenum Press.

Narabayashi, H., Nagao, R., Saito, Y., Yoshida, M., & Nagahata, M. (1963). Stereotaxic amygdalotomy for behavioral disorders. *Archives of Neurology, 9,* 1–16.

Neidig, P. H., Friedman, D. H., & Collins, B. S. (1985). Domestic conflict containment: A spouse abuse treatment program. *Social Casework, 66,* 195–204.

Nelson, G. K. (1974). Neuropsychological research approaches in the epilepsies. *South African Medical Journal, 48*, 657.

Netter, F. H. (1983). *Nervous System* (Second ed.). West Caldwell, NJ: CIBA Pharmaceutical Co.

Nikulina, E. M., Avgustinovich, D. F., & Popova, N. K. (1992). Selection for reduced aggressiveness towards man and dopaminergic activity in Norway rats. *Aggressive Behavior, 18*, 65–72.

Novaco, R. W. (1978). Anger and coping with stress. In J. Foreyt, & D. Rathjen (Eds.), *Cognitive behavior therapy: Therapy, research and practice*. New York: Plenum Press.

O'Callaghan, M. A. J., & Carroll, D. (1982). *Psychosurgery: A scientific analysis*. Ridgewood, NJ: George A. Bogden and Son, Inc.

Olds, J., & Milner, P. (1954). Positive reinforcement produced by electrical stimulation of septal area and other regions of rat brains. *Journal of Comparative and Physiological Psychology, 47*, 419–427.

Olweus, D. (1983). Testosterone in the development of aggressive antisocial behavior in adolescents. In K. T. Van Dusen, & S. A. Mednick (Eds.), *Prospective studies of crime and delinquency* (pp. 237–247). Boston: Kluwer-Nijhoff.

Olweus, D., Mattsson, A., Schalling, D., & Low, H. (1988). Circulating testosterone levels and aggression in adolescent males: A causal analysis. *Psychosomatic medicine, 50*, 261–272.

Panksepp, J. (1971). Aggression elicited by electrical stimulation of the hypothalamus in albino rats. *Physiology and Behavior, 6*, 321–329.

Papez, J. W. (1937). A proposed mechanism of emotion. *Archives of Neurology and Psychiatry, 38*, 725–743.

Parke, R. D., Berkowitz, L., Leyens, J. P., West, S. G., & Sebastian, R. J. (1977). Some effects of violent and nonviolent movies on the behavior of juvenile delinquents. In L. Berkowitz (Ed.), *Advances in experimental social psychology* (vol. 10, pp. 135–172). New York: Academic Press.

Parke, R. D., Ewall, W., & Slaby, R. G. (1972). Hostile and helpful verbalizations as regulators of nonverbal aggression. *Journal of Personality and Social Psychology, 23*, 243–248.

Parlee, M. B. (1973). The premenstrual syndrome. *Psychological Bulletin, 80*, 454–465.

Patterson, G. R. (1976). *Living with children: New methods for parents and teachers*. Champaign, IL: Research Press.

Patterson, G. R., Dishion, T. J., & Bank, L. (1984). Family interaction: A process model of deviancy training. *Aggressive Behavior, 3*, 253–267.

Patterson, G. R., Littman, R. A., & Bricker, W. (1967). Assertive behavior in children: A step toward a theory of aggression. *Monographs of the Society for Research in Child Development, 32*(No. 5, Serial No. 113).

Pavlov, I. P. (1927). *Conditioned reflexes*. Translated by Anrep, G. V. New York: Dover Publications Inc.

Pearl, D. (Ed.). (1982). *Television and behavior: Ten years of scientific progress and implications for the eighties*. Washington, DC: U. S. Government Printing Office.

Persky, H., Smith, K. D., & Basu, G. K. (1971). Relation of psychologic measures of aggression and hostility to testosterone production in man. *Psychosomatic Medicine, 33*, 265–277.

Persky, H., Zuckerman, M., & Curtis, G. C. . (1978). Endocrine function in emotionally disturbed and normal men. *Journal of Nervous and Mental Disease, 146*, 488–497.

Pertovaara, A., Huopaniemi, T., Virtanen, A., & Johansson, G. (1984). The influence of exercise on dental pain thresholds and the release of stress hormones. *Physiology and Behavior, 33*, 923–926.

Peters, J. M. (1967). Caffeine-induced hemorrhagic automutilation. *Archives of Internal Pharmacodynamic Therapeutics, 169*, 139–146.

Phillips, E. L. (1968). Achievement Place: Token reinforcement procedures in a home- style rehabilitation setting for "pre-delinquent" boys. *Journal of Applied Behavior Analysis, 1*, 213–223.

Phillips, E. L., Phillips, E. A., Fixsen, D. L., & Wolf, M. M. (1974). *The teaching-family handbook*. Lawrence: University of Kansas Printing Service.

Pontius, A. A. (1984). Specific stimulus-evoked violent action in psychotic trigger reaction: A seizure-like imbalance between frontal lobe and limbic systems? *Perceptual and Motor Skills, 59*, 299–333.

Pope, H. G., & Katz, D. L. (1990). Homicide and near-homicide by anabolic steroid users. *Journal of Clinical Psychiatry, 51*, 28–31.

Post, R. M. (1989). Anticonvulsants in the treatment of aggression and dyscontrol. In R. M. Post, M. R. Trimble, & C. E. Pippenger (Eds.), *Clinical use of anticonvulsants in psychiatric disorders* (p. 184). New York: Demos.

Potegal, M., Blau, A., & Glusman, M. (1981). Inhibition of intraspecific aggression in male hamsters by septal stimulation. *Physiological Psychology, 9*, 213–218.

Potts, D., & Herzberger, S. (1979). Child abuse: A cross generational pattern of child rearing? *Annual meetings of the Midwestern Psychological Association*, Chicago.

Prentky, R. A., Burgess, A. W., & Carter, D. L. (1986). Victim responses by rapist type: An empirical and clinical analysis. *Journal of Interpersonal Violence, 1*(1), 73–98.

Rada, R. T. (1978). Classification of the rapist. In R. T. Rada (Ed.), *Clinical aspects of the rapist* (pp. 117–132). New York: Grune and Stratton.

Rada, R. T., Laws, D. R., Kellner, R., Stivastava, L., & Peake, G. (1983). Plasma androgens in violent and nonviolent sex offenders. *Bulletin of the AAPL, 11*(2), 149–158.

Rambling, D. (1978). Aggression: A paradoxical response to tricyclic antidepressants. *American Journal of Psychiatry, 135*, 117–118.

Randrup, A., & Munkvad, I. (1969). Relation of brain catecholamines to aggressiveness and other forms of behavioural excitation. In S. Garattini, & E. B. Sigg (Eds.), *Aggressive behaviour* (pp. 228–235). Amsterdam: Excerpta Medica.

Rapoport, J. L., Bushbaum, M. S., Zahn, T. P., Weingartner, H., Ludlow, C., & Mikkelsen, E. J. (1978). Dextroamphetamine: Cognitive and behavioral effects in normal prepubertal boys. *Science, 199*, 560–563.

Redmon, W. K. (1987). Reduction of physical attacks through differential reinforcement of other behavior. *Journal of Child and Adolescent Psychotherapy, 4*, 107–111.

Reeves, A. G., & Plum, F. (1969). Hyperphagia, rage and dementia accompanying a ventro-medial hypothalamic neoplasm. *Archives of Neurology, 20*, 616–624.

Reid, J. B., Taplin, P. S., & Lorber, R. (1981). A social interactional approach to the treatment of abusive families. In R. B. Stuart (Ed.), *Violent behavior: Social learning approaches to prediction, management and treatment* (pp. 83–101). New York: Brunner/Mazel Publishers.

Reid, R. R., & Yen, S. S. C. (1981). Premenstrual syndrome. *American Journal of Obstetrics and Gynecology, 139*, 85–104.

Reis, D. J., & Gunne, L.-M. (1965). Brain catecholamines: Relation to the defense reaction evoked by amygdaloid stimulation in the cat. *Science, 144*, 450–451.

Reis, D. J. (1972). The relationship between brain norepinephrine and aggressive behavior. *Research Publications of the Association for Research in Nervous and Mental Diseases, 50*, 266–297.

Reis, D. J., Doba, N., & Nathan, M. A. (1973). Predatory attack, grooming, and consummatory behaviors evoked by electrical stimulation of cat cerebellar nuclei. *Science, 182*, 845–847.

Renfrew, J. W. (1966). *The relation of hypothalamic electrode locus and interstimulation interval to self-stimulation by the rat*. M. A., Southern Illinois University at Carbondale.

Renfrew, J. W. (1969). The intensity function and reinforcing properties of brain stimulation that elicits attack. *Physiology and Behavior, 4*, 509–515.

Renfrew, J. W. (1979). *Las bases de la agresión y su análisis científico.* Montevideo: Interamerican Children's Institute/Organization of American States.

Renfrew, J. W. (1981). Analysis of aggression produced by electrical brain stimulation. In Brain, P. F. and Benton, D. (Eds.), *Multidisciplinary approaches to aggression research.* Amsterdam: Elsevier/North-Holland Biomedical Press, pp. 295–307.

Renfrew, J. W., & Hutchinson, R. R. (1983a). Discriminated instrumental learning by an acute encéphale isolé preparation. *Physiology and Behavior, 30*, 703–709.

Renfrew, J. W., & Hutchinson, R. R. (1983b). The motivation of aggression. In E. Satinoff, & P. Teitelbaum (Eds.), *Motivation* (vol. 6, pp. 511–541). New York: Plenum Press.

Renfrew, J. W., & LeRoy, J. A. (1983). Suppression of shock elicited target biting by analgesic midbrain stimulation. *Physiology and Behavior, 30*, 169–172.

Reynolds, B. A., & Weiss, S. (1992). Generation of neurons and astrocytes from isolated cells of the adult mammalian central nervous system. *Science, 255*, 1707–1710.

Reynolds, G. S., Catania, A. C., & Skinner, B. F. (1963). Conditioned and unconditioned aggression in pigeons. *Journal of the Experimental Analysis of Behavior, 6*, 73–74.

Richards, R. W., & Rilling, M. (1972). Aversive aspects of a fixed-interval schedule of food reinforcement. *Journal of the Experimental Analysis of Behavior, 17*, 405–411.

Roberts, D. F. (1993). Adolescents and the mass media: From "Leave it to Beaver" to "Beverly Hills 90210." *Teachers College Record, 94*(3), 629–644.

Roberts, H. J. (1988). Reactions attributed to aspartame-containing products: 551 cases. *Journal of Applied Nutrition, 40*, 85–94.

Roberts, W. W., & Keiss, H. O. (1964). Motivational properties of hypothalamic aggression in cats. *Journal of Comparative and Physiological Psychology, 58*, 187–193.

Robin, G. D. (1977). Forcible rape: Institutionalized sexism in the criminal justice system. *Crime and Delinquency, 23*, 136–153.

Rohles, F. H. (1967). Environmental psychology: A bucket of worms. *Psychology Today, 1*, 54–63.

Rosen, R. C., & Beck, J. G. (1988). *Patterns of sexual arousal: Psychophysiological processes and clinical applications.* New York: Guilford.

Rosenzweig, N., & Gardner, L. M. (1966). The role of input relevance in sensory isolation. *American Journal of Psychiatry, 122*, 920–928.

Rossi, C., Marino, R., Jr., & Yazigi, L. (1979). Personality studies in surgery for epilepsy. In E. R. Hitchcock, H. T. Ballantine Jr., & B. A. Meyerson (Eds.), *Modern concepts in psychiatric surgery* (pp. 131–144). Amsterdam: Elsevier/North Holland Biomedical Press.

Rosvold, H. E., Mirsky, A. F., & Pribram, K. H. (1954). Influence of amygdalectomy on social behavior in monkeys. *Journal of Comparative and Physiological Psychology, 47*, 173–178.

Roy, A., DeJong, J., & Linnoila, M. (1989). Cerebrospinal fluid monoamine metabolites and suicidal behavior in depressed patients. *Archives of General Psychiatry, 46*, 609–612.

Rubinstein, E. A. (1976). Warning: The Surgeon General's research program may be dangerous to preconceived notions. *The Journal of Social Issues, 32*(4), 18–34.

Rubio, E., Arjona, V., & Rodríguez-Burgos, F. (1977). Stereotaxic cryohypothalamotomy in aggressive behavior. In W. H. Sweet, S. Obrador, & J. G. Martin-Rodríguez (Eds.), *Neurosurgical treatment in psychiatry, pain, and epilepsy* (pp. 439–444). Baltimore, MD: University Park Press.

Russell, G. W., & Pigat, L. (1991). Effects of modelled censure/support of media violence and need for approval on aggression. *Current psychology: Research and reviews, 10*(1 and 2), 121–128.

Salzman, C., Kochansky, G. E., Shader, R. I., Porrino, L. J., Hormatz, J. S., & Sweet, C. P. J. (1974). Chlordiazepoxide-induced hostility in a small group setting. *Archives of General Psychiatry, 31*, 401–405.

Sano, K., & Mayanagi, Y. (1988). Posteromedial hypothalamotomy in the treatment of violent, aggressive behaviour. *Acta Neurochirurgica* (Suppl. 44), 145–151.

Santos, M., Sampaio, M. R. P., Fernández, N. S., & Carlini, E. A. (1966). Effects of Cannabis sativa (marihuana) on the fighting behavior of mice. *Psychopharmacologia, 8*, 437–444.

Sassenrath, E. N., Rowell, T. E., & Hendrickx, A. G. (1973). Perimenstrual aggression in groups of female rhesus monkeys. *Journal of Reproduction and Fertility, 34*, 509–511.

Schachter, S., & Singer, J. E. (1962). Cognitive, social and physiological determinants of emotional state. *Psychological Review, 69*, 379–399.

Schiefenhövel, W. (1980). Aggression and aggression-control among the Eipo, Highlands of West-New Guinea. *NATO Advanced Study Institute on The Biology of Aggression*, Chateau de Bonas, France.

Schlinger, B. A., & Callard, G. V. (1989). Aromatase activity in quail brain: Correlation with aggressiveness. *Endocrinology, 124*, 437–443.

Schreiner, L., & Kling, A. (1953). Behavioral changes following rhinencephalic injury in cats. *Journal of Neurophysiology, 16*, 643–659.

Schvarcz, J. R. (1977). Results of stimulation and destruction of the posterior hypothalamus: A long-term evaluation. In W. H. Sweet, S. Obrador, & J. G. Martin-Rodríguez (Ed.), *Neurosurgical treatment in psychiatry, pain, and epilepsy* (pp. 429–438). Baltimore, MD: University Park Press.

Schwartz, D. C. (1968). On the ecology of political violence: "The long hot summer" as a hypothesis. *American Behavioral Scientist* (July-August), 24–28.

Scott, J. P., & Marston, M. V. (1953). Nonadaptive behavior resulting from a series of defeats in fighting mice. *Journal of Abnormal and Social Psychology, 48*, 417–428.

Searle, L. V. (1949). The organization of hereditary maze-brightness and maze-dullness. *Genetic Psychology Monographs, 39*, 279–325.

Seligman, M. E. P., Maier, S. F., & Geer, J. (1968). The alleviation of learned helplessness in the dog. *Journal of Abnormal Psychology, 78*, 256–262.

Sem-Jacobsen, C. W., & Torkildsen, A. (1960). Depth recording and electrical stimulation in the human brain. In E. R. Ramey, & D. S. O'Doherty (Eds.), *Electrical studies on the unanesthetized brain* (pp. 275–290). New York: Harper & Row.

Senault, B. (1970). Comportement d'agressivite intraspecifique induit par l'apomorphine chez le rat. *Psychopharmacologia, 20*, 389–394.

Serafetinides, E. A. (1970). Psychiatric aspects of temporal lobe epilepsy. In E. Niedermeyer (Ed.), *Epilepsy, modern problems of pharmacopsychiatry* (vol. 4, pp. 155–169). New York: Karger.

Sheard, M. H. (1969). The effect of p-chlorophenylalanine on behavior in rats: relation to brain serotonin and 5–hydroxyindoleacetic acid. *Brain Research, 15*, 524–528.

Sheard, M. H. (1971). Effect of lithium on human aggression. *Nature, 230*, 113–114.

Sheard, M. H. (1974). Hypothalamically elicited attack behavior in cats: Effects of raphe stimulation. *Journal of Psychiatric Research, 10*, 151.

Sheard, M. H., Astrachan, D. I., & Davis, M. (1977). The effects of d-lysergic acid diethylamide (LSD) upon shock elicited fighting in rats. *Life Sciences 20* (3):427–430.

Sheard, M. H., & Davis, M. (1976). p-Chloroamphetamine: Short and long term effects upon shock-elicited aggression. *European Journal of Pharmacology, 40*, 295–302.

Sheard, M. H., & Flynn, J. P. (1967a). Facilitation of attack behavior by stimulation of the midbrain of cats. *Brain Research, 4*, 324–333.

Sheard, M. H., & Flynn, J. P. (1967b). The effects of amphetamine on attack behavior in the cat. *Brain Research, 5*, 330–338.

Sheard, M. H., Marini, J. L., Bridges, C. I., & Wagner, E. (1976). The effect of lithium on impulsive aggressive behavior in man. *American Journal of Psychiatry, 133,* 1409–1413.

Shotland, R. L. (1992). A theory of the causes of courtship rape: Part 2. *Journal of Social Issues, 48*(1), 127–143.

Siann, G. (1985). *Accounting for aggression: Perspectives on aggression and violence.* Boston: Allen & Unwin.

Siegel, A., & Chabora, J. (1971). Effects of electrical stimulation of the cingulate gyrus upon attack behavior elicited from the hypothalamus in the cat. *Brain Research, 32,* 169–177.

Siegel, A., & Flynn, J. P. (1968). Differential effects of electrical stimulation and lesions of the hippocampus and adjacent regions upon attack behavior in cats. *Brain Research, 7,* 252–267.

Siegel, A., & Skog, D. (1970). Effects of electrical stimulation of the septum upon attack behavior elicited from the hypothalamus in the cat. *Brain Research, 23,* 371–380.

Silver, J. M., & Yudofsky, S. C. (1987). Aggressive behavior in patients with neuropsychiatric disorders. *Psychiatric annals, 17*(6), 367–370.

Simon, N. G., & Cologer-Clifford, A. (1991). In utero contiguity to males does not influence morphology, behavioral sensitivity to testosterone, or hypothalamic androgen binding in CF-1 female mice. *Hormones and Behavior, 25,* 518–530.

Skinner, B. F. (1938). *The behavior of organisms.* New York: Appleton-Century-Crofts.

Smith, D. E., King, M. B., & Hoebel, B., G. (1970). Lateral hypothalamic control of killing: Evidence for a cholinoceptive mechanism. *Science, 167,* 900–901.

Smith, M. D., & Hand, C. (1987). The pornography/aggression linkage: Results from a field study. *Deviant Behavior, 8,* 389–399.

Sperber, N. D. (1990). Lingual markings of anterior teeth as seen in human bite marks. *Journal of Forensic Sciences, 35,* 838–844.

Spiegel, E. A., Wycis, H. T., Freed, H., & Orchnik, C. (1953). Thalamotomy and hypothalamotomy for the treatment of psychoses. *Research Publications of the Association of Nervous and Mental Disorders, 31,* 379–391.

Spitz, R. A. (1945). Hospitalism: An inquiry into the genesis of psychiatric conditions in early childhood. *Psychoanalytic Study of the Child, 1,* 53–74.

Sprague, J. M., Chambers, W. W., & Stellar, E. (1961). Attentive, affective, and adaptive behaviors in the cat. *Science, 133,* 165–173.

Stachnik, T. J., Ulrich, R. E., & Mabry, J. H. (1966). Reinforcement of aggression through intracranial stimulation. *Psychonomic Science, 5,* 101–102.

Steinmetz, S. K. (1978). The battered husband syndrome. *Victimology, 2,* 499–509.

Stolk, J. M., Conner, R. L., Levine, S., & Barchas, J. D. (1974). Brain norepinephrine metabolism and shock-induced fighting in rats: Differential effects of shock and fighting on the neurochemical response to a common foot-shock stimulus. *Journal of Pharmacology and Experimental Therapy, 190,* 193–209.

Straus, M. A., & Gelles, R. J. (1990a). How violent are American families? Estimates from the national family violence resurvey and other studies. In M. A. Straus, & R. J. Gelles (Eds.), *Physical violence in American families: Risk factors and adaptations to violence in 8,145 families* (pp. 95–112). New Brunswick, NJ: Transaction Publishers.

Straus, M. A., & Gelles, R. J. (1990b). Societal change and change in family violence from 1975 to 1985 as revealed by two national surveys. In M. A. Straus, & R. J. Gelles (Eds.), *Physical violence in American families: Risk factors and adaptations to violence in 8,145 families* (pp. 113–131). New Brunswick, NJ: Transaction Publishers.

Straus, M. A., Gelles, R. J., & Steinmetz, S. K. (1980). *Behind closed doors: Violence in the American family.* New York: Doubleday/Anchor.

Struckman-Johnson, C. (1988). Forced sex on dates: It happens to men, too. *Journal of Sex Research, 24,* 234–241.

Stumphauzer, J. S. (1986). *Helping delinquents change: A treatment manual of social learning approaches*. New York: Haorthe Press.

Stumphauzer, J. S., Veloz, E. V., & Aiken, T. W. (1981). Violence by street gangs: East side story? In R. B. Stuart (Ed.), *Violent behavior: Social learning approaches to prediction, management and treatment* (pp. 68–82). New York: Brunner/Mazel.

Svare, B. (1980). Testosterone propionate inhibits maternal aggression in mice. *Physiology and Behavior, 24*, 435–439.

Svare, B., & Gandelman, R. (1973). Postpartum aggression in mice: Experiential and environmental factors. *Hormones and Behavior, 4*, 323–334.

Svare, B. B., & Mann, M. A. (1983). Hormonal influences on maternal aggression. In B. B. Svare (Ed.), *Hormones and aggressive behavior* (pp. 91–104). New York: Plenum Press.

Swift, C. (1985). The prevention of rape. In A. W. Burgess (Ed.), *Rape and sexual assault: A research handbook* (pp. 413–426). New York: Garland Publishing.

Tardiff, K. (1989). *Assessment and management of violent patients*. Washington, DC: American Psychiatric Press.

Taylor, S. P., & Gammon, C. B. (1975). Effects of type and dose of alcohol on human physical aggression. *Journal of Personality and Social Psychology, 32*, 169–175.

Taylor, S. P., & Leonard, K. E. (1983). Alcohol and human physical aggression. In R. G. Geen, & E. I. Donnerstein (Eds.), *Aggression: Theoretical and empirical reviews* (vol. II, pp. 77–101). New York: Academic Press.

Taylor, W. N. (1991). *Macho medicine: A history of the anabolic steroid epidemic*. Jefferson, NC: McFarland & Co.

Thiessen, D. D. (1976). *The evolution and chemistry of aggression*. Springfield, IL: Charles C Thomas.

Thompson, T., & Sturm, T. (1965). Classical conditioning of aggressive display in Siamese fighting fish. *Journal of the Experimental Analysis of Behavior, 8*, 397–403.

Thornhill, R., & Thornhill, N. W. (1992). The evolutionary psychology of men's coercive sexuality. *Behavioral and Brain Sciences, 15*(2), 363–421.

Toch, H. (1969). *Violent men*. Chicago: Aldine Press.

Todd, J. T., Morris, E. K., & Fenza, K. M. (1989). Temporal organization of extinction-induced responding in preschool children. *The Psychological Record, 39*, 117–130.

Toner, B. S., Woodfill, G. L., & Renfrew, J. W. (1990). The effects of an appetite suppressant and a phenylalanine-based dietary sweetener on aggression in rats. *Eastern Psychological Association Convention*, Philadelphia, PA.

Träskman, L., Åsberg, M., Bertilsson, L., & Sjöstrand, L. (1981). Monoamine metabolites in CSF and suicidal behavior. *Archives of General Psychiatry, 38*, 631–636.

Tryon, R. C. (1930). Studies in individual differences in maze ability. *Journal of Comparative Psychology, 11*, 145–170.

Tupin, J. P. (1977). Letter to the editor: Usefulness of lithium for aggressiveness. *American Journal of Psychiatry, 135*, 1181.

Tupin, J. P. (1988). Violence. In J. P. Tupin, R. I. Shader, & D. S. Harnett (Eds.), *Handbook of clinical psychopharmacology* (pp. 111–120). Northvale, NJ: Jason Aronson, Inc.

Turner, C. W., Fenn, M. R., & Cole, A. M. (1981). A social psychological analysis of violent behavior. In R. B. Stuart (Ed.), *Violent behavior: Social learning approaches to prediction, management and treatment* (pp. 31–67). New York: Brunner/Mazel Publishers.

Turner, C. W., & Leyens, J.-P. (1992). The weapons effect revisited: The effects of firearms on aggressive behavior. In P. Suedfeld, & P. E. Tetlock (Eds.), *Psychology and social policy* (pp. 201–221). New York: Hemisphere Publishing.

Ulrich, R. E., & Azrin, N. H. (1962). Reflexive fighting in response to aversive stimulation. *Journal of the Experimental Analysis of Behavior, 5*, 511–520.

Ulrich, R. E., & Craine, W. H. (1964). Behavior: Persistence of shock-induced aggression. *Science, 143*, 971–973.

Ulrich, R. E., Wolfe, M., & Dulaney, S. (1969). Punishment of shock-induced aggression. *Journal of the Experimental Analysis of Behavior, 12*, 1009–1015.

Valenstein, E. S. (1973). *Brain control*. New York: John Wiley and Sons.

Valenstein, E. S. (Ed.). (1980). *The psychosurgery debate*. San Francisco: W. H. Freeman and Co.

Valenstein, E. S. (1986). *Great and desperate cures: The rise and decline of psychosurgery and other radical treatments for mental illness*. New York: Basic Books.

Valenstein, E. S., Cox, V. C., & Kakolewski, J. W. (1970). Re-examination of the role of the hypothalamus in motivation. *Psychological Review, 77*, 16–31.

Valzelli, L. (1973). The "isolation syndrome" in mice. *Psychopharmacologia, 31*, 305–320.

Valzelli, L. (1981). *Psychobiology of aggression and violence*. New York: Raven Press.

Valzelli, L., & Bernasconi, S. (1973). Behavioral and neurochemical aspects of caffeine in normal and aggressive mice. *Pharmacology, Biochemistry, and Behavior, 1*, 251–254.

Vergnes, M., & Karli, P. (1963). Declenchement du comportement d'agression interspecifique Rat-Souris par ablation bilaterale des bulbes olfactifs. Action de l'hydroxyzine sur cette agresivite provoquee. *Comptes Rendus de la Societe de Biologie, Paris, 157*, 1061–1063.

Vergnes, M., Penot, C., Kempf, E., & Mack, G. (1977). Lesion selective des neurones serotoninergiques du raphe par la 5,7–dihydroxytryptamine: Effets sur le comportement d'agression interspecifique du rat. *Brain Research, 133*, 167–171.

Vernon, W., & Ulrich, R. E. (1966). Classical conditioning of pain-elicited aggression. *Science, 152*, 668–669.

Viken, R. J., & Knutson, J. F. (1992). Relationship between shock-induced aggression and other laboratory tests of agonistic behavior in rats. *Aggressive Behavior, 18*, 53–63.

Vollmer, T. R., Iwata, B. A., Zarcone, J. R., Smith, R. G., & Mazaleski, J. L. (1993). The role of attention in the treatment of attention-maintained self-injurious behavior: Noncontingent reinforcement and differential reinforcement of other behavior. *Journal of Applied Behavior Analysis, 26*, 9–21.

Wahler, R. G., & Fox, J. J. (1980). Solitary toy play and time out: A family treatment package for children with aggressive and oppositional behavior. *Journal of Applied Behavior Analysis, 13*, 23–39.

Waldbillig, R. J. (1980). Suppressive effects of intraperitoneal and intraventricular injections of nicotine on muricide and shock-induced attack on conspecifics. *Pharmacology, Biochemistry, and Behavior, 12*, 619–623.

Waldeck, B. (1973). Sensitization by caffeine of central catecholamine receptors. *Journal of Neural Transmitters, 34*, 61–72.

Walker, L. E. (1981). A feminist perspective on domestic violence. In R. B. Stuart (Ed.), *Violent behavior: Social learning approaches to prediction, management and treatment* (pp. 102–115). New York: Brunner/Mazel Publishers.

Walters, R. H., & Brown, M. (1963). Studies of reinforcement of aggression: III. Transfer of responses to an interpersonal situation. *Child Development, 34*, 563–571.

Walters, R. H., Thomas, E. L., & Acker, C. W. (1962). Enhancement of punitive behavior by audiovisual displays. *Science, 136*, 872–873.

Wasman, M., & Flynn, J. P. (1962). Directed attack elicited from hypothalamus. *Archives of Neurology, 6*, 220–227.

Wender, P. H. (1988). Attention deficit disorder, residual type (ADD,RT) or adult hyperactivity. In J. P. Tupin, R. I. Shader, & D. S. Harnett (Eds.), *Handbook of clinical psychopharmacology* (pp. 357–374). Northvale, NJ: Jason Aronson Inc.

Wender, P. H., Rosenthal, D., & Katz, S. S. (1968). A psychiatric assessment of the adoptive parents of schizophrenics. In D. Rosenthal, & S. S. Katz (Eds.), *The transmission of schizophrenia*. London: Pergamon Press.

Wheatley, M. D. (1944). The hypothalamus and affective behavior in cats: A study of the effects of experimental lesions, with anatomic correlations. *Archives of Neurology and Psychiatry, 52*, 296–317.

White, J. W. (1983). Sex and gender issues in aggression research. In R. G. Geen, & E. I. Donnerstein (Eds.), *Aggression: Theoretical and empirical reviews* (vol. 2, pp. 1–26). New York: Academic Press.

White, L. S. (1979). Erotica and aggression: The influence of sexual arousal, positive affect, and negative affect on aggressive behavior. *Journal of Personality and Social Psychology, 37*, 591–601.

Widom, C. S. (1989). The cycle of violence. *Science, 244*, 160–166.

Williams, D. (1969). Neural factors related to habitual aggression: Consideration of differences between those habitual aggressives and others who have committed crimes of violence. *Brain, 92*, 503–520.

Wilson, J. Q., & Herrnstein, R. J. (1985). *Crime and human nature*. New York: Simon and Schuster.

Witkin, H. A., Mednick, S. A., Schulsinger, F., Bakkestrom, E., Christiansen, K. O., Goodenough, D. R., Hirschorn, K., Lundsteen, C., Owen, D. R., Philip, J., Rubin, D. B., & Stocking, M. (1976). Criminality in XYY and XXY men. *Science, 193*, 547–554.

Wolpe, J. (1958). *Psychotherapy by reciprocal inhibition*. Stanford, CA: Stanford University Press.

Wood, W., Wong, F. Y., & Chachere, J. G. (1991). Effects of media violence on viewers' aggression in unconstrained social interaction. *Psychological Bulletin, 109*, 371–383.

Woodman, D., & Hinton, J. (1978). Catecholamine balance during stress anticipation: An abnormality in maximum security hospital patients. *Journal of Psychosomatic Medicine, 22*, 477–483.

Woodworth, C. H. (1971). Attack elicited in rats by electrical stimulation of the lateral hypothalamus. *Physiology and Behavior, 6*, 345–353.

Yalom, I. D., Green, R., & Fisk, N. (1973). Prenatal exposure to female hormones. *Archives of General Psychiatry, 28*, 554–561.

Zanchetti, A., & Zoccolini, A. (1954). Autonomic hypothalamic outbursts elicited by cerebellar stimulation. *Journal of Neurophysiology, 17*, 475–483.

Zeman, W., & King, F. A. (1958). Tumors of the septum pellucidum and adjacent structures with abnormal affective behaviors: An anterior midline structure syndrome. *Journal of Nervous and Mental Disease, 127*, 490–502.

Zillmann, D., & Cantor, J. R. (1976). Effect of timing of information about mitigating circumstances on emotional responses to provocation and retaliatory behavior. *Journal of Experimental Social Psychology, 12*, 38–55.

Zillmann, D., Johnson, R. C., & Day, K. D. (1974). Attribution of apparent arousal and proficiency of recovery from sympathetic activation affecting excitation transfer to aggressive behavior. *Journal of Experimental Social Psychology, 10*, 503–515.

Author Index

Abel, E. L., 96
Abel, G. G., 194–97, 210, 214, 215
Abeyewardene, S., 57
Acker, C. W., 135
Adamec, R., 60
Adams, D. B., 62
Aiken, T. W., 173
Ajmone-Marsan, C., 69
Alavi, A., 80
Allen, C. R., 220
Alpert, J. E., 71, 89
Alves, C. N., 96
Amir, M., 209
Amsel, A., 116
Andersch, B., 40
Anderson, C. A., 112
Andy, O. J., 75
Antelman, S. M., 34
Arjona, V., 75
Arnold, S. E., 75
Åsberg, M., 90
Astrachan, D. J., 97
Atwater, J. D., 178
Avgustinovich, D. F., 89
Ayllon, T., 176
Azrin, N. H., 34, 35, 55, 105–7, 109, 111, 114,
    117, 118, 124, 128, 129, 131, 132, 134, 176

Badawy, A. A.-B., 94
Bagley, C.. 186
Bailey, J. B., 138
Bakkestrom, E., 30
Bale, S. J., 220
Balis, G. U., 69
Ball, R. L., 150
Ballanger, J. C., 90
Bancroft, J., 41
Bandler, R. A., 56, 59, 86–88
Bandura, A., 119, 135, 141–48, 150, 152, 163,
    174
Bank, L., 130
Barchas, J. D., 87, 88
Bard, P., 60, 61
Barfield, R. J., 34, 36
Barinaga, M., 73
Barlow, D. H., 197
Baron, R. A., 33, 106, 109, 111–14, 135,
    148–51, 154, 159
Barrett, G., 113
Basu, G. K., 35
Beach, F. A., 35
Beach, R. C., 39
Bear, D., 68
Beck, J. G., 151, 197, 198

Subject Index